G000149983

Mastering Enterprise SOA with SAP NetWeaver® and mySAP™ ERP

Scott Campbell
Vamsi Mohun

1807
WILEY
2007

Wiley Publishing, Inc.

Mastering Enterprise SOA with SAP NetWeaver® and mySAP™ ERP

Published by
Wiley Publishing, Inc.
10475 Crosspoint Boulevard
Indianapolis, IN 46256
www.wiley.com

Copyright © 2007 by Wiley Publishing, Inc., Indianapolis, Indiana

Published simultaneously in Canada

ISBN-13: 978-0-471-92015-1
ISBN-10: 0-471-92015-0

Manufactured in the United States of America

10 9 8 7 6 5 4 3 2 1

1MA/QV/RQ/QW/IN

No part of this publication may be reproduced, stored in a retrieval system or transmitted in any form or by any means, electronic, mechanical, photocopying, recording, scanning or otherwise, except as permitted under Sections 107 or 108 of the 1976 United States Copyright Act, without either the prior written permission of the Publisher, or authorization through payment of the appropriate per-copy fee to the Copyright Clearance Center, 222 Rosewood Drive, Danvers, MA 01923, (978) 750-8400, fax (978) 646-8600. Requests to the Publisher for permission should be addressed to the Legal Department, Wiley Publishing, Inc., 10475 Crosspoint Blvd., Indianapolis, IN 46256, (317) 572-3447, fax (317) 572-4355, or online at http://www.wiley.com/go/permissions.

LIMIT OF LIABILITY/DISCLAIMER OF WARRANTY: THE PUBLISHER AND THE AUTHOR MAKE NO REPRESENTATIONS OR WARRANTIES WITH RESPECT TO THE ACCURACY OR COMPLETENESS OF THE CONTENTS OF THIS WORK AND SPECIFICALLY DISCLAIM ALL WARRANTIES, INCLUDING WITHOUT LIMITATION WARRANTIES OF FITNESS FOR A PARTICULAR PURPOSE. NO WARRANTY MAY BE CREATED OR EXTENDED BY SALES OR PROMOTIONAL MATERIALS. THE ADVICE AND STRATEGIES CONTAINED HEREIN MAY NOT BE SUITABLE FOR EVERY SITUATION. THIS WORK IS SOLD WITH THE UNDERSTANDING THAT THE PUBLISHER IS NOT ENGAGED IN RENDERING LEGAL, ACCOUNTING, OR OTHER PROFESSIONAL SERVICES. IF PROFESSIONAL ASSISTANCE IS REQUIRED, THE SERVICES OF A COMPETENT PROFESSIONAL PERSON SHOULD BE SOUGHT. NEITHER THE PUBLISHER NOR THE AUTHOR SHALL BE LIABLE FOR DAMAGES ARISING HEREFROM. THE FACT THAT AN ORGANIZATION OR WEBSITE IS REFERRED TO IN THIS WORK AS A CITATION AND/OR A POTENTIAL SOURCE OF FURTHER INFORMATION DOES NOT MEAN THAT THE AUTHOR OR THE PUBLISHER ENDORSES THE INFORMATION THE ORGANIZATION OR WEBSITE MAY PROVIDE OR RECOMMENDATIONS IT MAY MAKE. FURTHER, READERS SHOULD BE AWARE THAT INTERNET WEBSITES LISTED IN THIS WORK MAY HAVE CHANGED OR DISAPPEARED BETWEEN WHEN THIS WORK WAS WRITTEN AND WHEN IT IS READ.

For general information on our other products and services or to obtain technical support, please contact our Customer Care Department within the U.S. at (800) 762-2974, outside the U.S. at (317) 572-3993 or fax (317) 572-4002.

Library of Congress Cataloging-in-Publication Data

Campbell, Scott, 1968–
  Mastering enterprise SOA with SAP NetWeaver and mySAP ERP/ Scott Campbell, Vamsi Mohun.
    p. cm.
  ISBN-13: 978-0-471-92015-1 (cloth/website)
  ISBN-10: 0-471-92015-0 (cloth/website)
  1. Information technology—Management. 2. Computer network architectures. 3. Web servers—Management. 4. Business enterprises—Computer networks—Management. I. Mohun, Vamsi, 1971– II. Title.
  HD30.2.C356 2006
  658.4'038028553—dc22

                          2006023390

Trademarks: Wiley, the Wiley logo, and related trade dress are trademarks or registered trademarks of John Wiley & Sons, Inc. and/or its affiliates, in the United States and other countries, and may not be used without written permission. SAP, SAP NetWeaver, and mySAP are trademarks or registered trademarks of SAP AG in Germany and in several other countries. All other trademarks are the property of their respective owners. Wiley Publishing, Inc., is not associated with any product or vendor mentioned in this book.

Wiley also publishes its books in a variety of electronic formats. Some content that appears in print may not be available in electronic books.

About the Authors

Scott Campbell has more than 15 years' experience in the IT industry. He is currently a Partner with MomentumSI Inc., where he leads the firm's SAP NetWeaver practice, which helps organizations develop their ESA road maps and leverage NetWeaver tools to build process-driven composite applications, and delivers training and mentoring for developers, architects, and managers in working in SOA and Web Services environments. Prior to MomentumSI, he worked for a leading customer relationship management (CRM) consultancy, and spent five years as a developer, analyst, and division IT manager at 3M Company. He holds an undergraduate degree in business and a master's degree in Information Technology from the University of Texas at Austin.

Vamsi Mohun is a Principal Consultant in the SAP NetWeaver Practice at MomentumSI, Inc. He works with clients to propose and execute solutions related to enterprise architecture, service enablement, and systems integration. He has been consulting for more than 10 years and has successfully delivered projects to several Global 1000 organizations. He holds a master's degree in Computer Engineering from Michigan Technological University.

Credits

Executive Editor
Robert Elliott

Development Editor
Kevin Shafer

Technical Editor
Kaj van de Loo

Copy Editor
Nancy Rapoport

Editorial Manager
Mary Beth Wakefield

Production Manager
Tim Tate

Vice President and Executive Group Publisher
Richard Swadley

Vice President and Executive Publisher
Joseph B. Wikert

Project Coordinator
Ryan Steffen

Graphics and Production Specialists
Lauren Goddard
Joyce Haughey
Jennifer Mayberry
Barbara Moore
Lynsey Osborn
Alicia B. South

Quality Control Technicians
John Greenough
Brian H. Walls

Proofreading and Indexing
Techbooks

Anniversary Logo Design
Richard Pacifico

Contents

Foreword

Service-Oriented Architecture (SOA) in general, and Enterprise SOA or Enterprise Services Architecture (ESA) in particular, may very well be the most important evolution in enterprise architecture and enterprise systems since the advent of client/server architecture in the early nineties and before . . . well, who knows what. Client/server in itself is just a way to build applications, but a few things came together to make a "perfect storm" that paved the way for its success. The availability of UNIX and associated smaller and cheaper servers in the datacenter, together with the spread of PCs to every desktop, provided the necessary technical infrastructure. Perhaps more important, the wave of decentralization that went through large enterprises created a demand for ERP and other systems for smaller-sized companies or divisions. In large enterprises, central IT decision-making and central deployment on mainframes was succeeded by decentralized decision-making and decentralized deployment on client/server hardware.

Similarly, many factors are contributing to the success of ESA, and I personally (as well as SAP as a company) have been intimately involved in this evolution. After having led the first R/3 implementation in Sweden, I joined SAP in 1995 in application development. Working intimately with customers, I got really interested in how to use technology to support business. After the rapid deployment of R/3 and other ERP systems in the late 1990s (in part fueled by the Y2K concerns), our customers had standardized and streamlined processes. They now came to us saying, "We now have deployed SAP and standardized our processes and are happy with that, but our competitors have done the same — how can you help us differentiate from the competition?"

For a company like SAP that had built its success on standardization and best practices, the question of differentiation was somewhat awkward. Nevertheless, we started looking into this. By working with customers, we learned a lot about business differentiation and how IT supports it. Many innovative business ideas were supported by "weekend projects" executed by some local IT guys. While these solutions often met the immediate need of the business, integration into the major back-end applications (and the processes supported by them) remained a problem. We realized that the problem was about integrating differentiating processes with standardized processes.

Around the same time, Web Services standards started to emerge. Simple Object Access Protocol (SOAP) had been around since 1998 but started to gain broader acceptance in 2001. Web Services Definition Language (WSDL) added a machine-readable interface description, and the all-important idea of being able to access functionality and data of a system without knowing its implementation. These two standards were enough to at least make it plausible that we would achieve platform interoperability relatively soon. This was really interesting to us at SAP because we had realized that much of the differentiating work was done on platforms other than ours (such as Microsoft Windows, Office, and later, .NET, Java, or some of the other tools that existed back then). The integration to the standardized processes supported by SAP software, of course, required platform interoperability, which we now saw was within reach.

Another business driver besides the quite generic need to differentiate from the competition was the increased focus on creating shareholder value by restructuring an enterprise. Mergers and acquisitions needed to be integrated quickly. Partners were integrated into business processes tighter than ever before. If a support function that had been in-house "forever" was world-class, it could be spun off as a separate entity; if it was not, it could be outsourced. Employees could suddenly become individual contractors and later employees of service providers. Traditional company boundaries were becoming blurred. We saw all of this happening in our customer base, and SAP software was right in the middle of it.

When we officially launched Enterprise Services Architecture, along with SAP NetWeaver, in January 2003, the factors that would make it successful were all there:

- The business need for more, faster, and cheaper integration between different kinds of software

- The existing software assets in the form of SAP and other large client/server applications

- The tools to build new, differentiating applications

- The Web Services standards to tie it all together

In hindsight, it is no wonder that Enterprise Services Architecture has had such a fundamental impact on the way we think about enterprise software and how to use it to address business problems.

The last few years at SAP with our customers and partners have certainly been exciting. The realization that the openness that comes with ESA opens up new business opportunities led us to the formulation of a platform strategy, which, in turn, requires an ecosystem innovating around it. SAP has transformed itself from an application provider to a solutions company with a platform strategy. Looking forward, it seems likely that SOA and ESA really will lead to better-run businesses supported by an open IT platform, tightly integrated for control and visibility, and, at the same time, loosely coupled for agility and flexibility.

What can we do today to get there? It should be clear that adopting ESA in an enterprise is a process of several, if not many, years. However, each IT project can be a step in the right direction. There is a whole lot we can do today, and that is where this book has an important role to play. The authors are using their understanding of the principles of ESA, along with their practical experience working with ESA and SAP NetWeaver, to demonstrate what can be done today. This book not only is an important tool for anyone who wants to apply ESA, it also carries an important message: *This is the time to start and get serious.* The original mix of business drivers and available tools and technologies creates both demand and supply for ESA-based solutions.

All the factors discussed here must be taken into account when defining and planning an ESA project. First and foremost, the business problem you want to address must be important and relevant, and lend itself to a solution based on ESA. A typical sign is that you must support a unique or rapidly changing process that requires data and functionality from existing enterprise systems. A strong platform in the form of solid underlying business applications certainly helps. Then you must have the right tools and technologies in place, and last but not least, you must have the methodology and skills to create the desired solution.

This book is a practical guide on how to use SAP NetWeaver and ESA to address business problems. Having a strong conceptual foundation and architecture is more important than using any particular tool or technology. What I like about the book is that it helps you put that foundation in place. This allows you to best plan for and plug into the ongoing, future innovation coming from SAP and our ecosystem.

SAP is today delivering business solutions based on a platform strategy. A key part of ESA and the platform strategy is openness for innovation in the ecosystem. SAP's own solutions are being designed and delivered around the concept of end-to-end processes with users in control of their work, with access to rich information, and connected to solid, optimized business processes implemented in a business process platform. These are complemented by innovative partner products. The potential for innovation all around the platform is enormous. Look for a lot to come in the future. At SAP, we seriously believe in ESA and use it on a daily basis, as we work with customers, partners, and internally. You can (and should) do the same, and this book will help you.

Kaj van de Loo
SAP Labs

Acknowledgments

As with the creation of every book, many people are involved in the project. The authors would like to recognize Bob Elliot, our acquisitions editor, who helped shape the vision with his suggestions for handling things that popped up along the way. Special thanks also to our development editor, Kevin Shafer, who made life a lot easier by managing and coordinating all our efforts, and without whose coaching we never would have made it to the finish.

There are many people at SAP who contributed ideas, insights, and assistance, both formally and informally, including Elvira Wallis, Jose Velasco, Anders Ranum, Jerome Delune, and their Product Definition colleagues as well as the SAP MDE team, and especially Jaideep Adhvaryu for his thoughts on ESA and the SAP ecosystem. Thanks also to Aaron Williams, who provided an in-depth understanding of the ES-Community, and Mario Herger, who helped make sure the ideas and content on analytics and Visual Composer were as current as possible.

We especially appreciate the work of the SAP Product Management team, which gives many great presentations at SAP conferences to keep customers and partners current on the technology changes associated with ESA. The team answered many of our questions, and helped simplify some complex ideas. This team included Michael Eacrett, Matt Kangas, Paul Medaille, Ginger Gatling, and especially Franklin Herbas, who offered many great ESA examples and ideas.

Thanks to the team at Pavilion Technologies, including Don Hart, Matt Tormollen, and especially Dave Cooper, who shared their vision for how ISVs can work together with SAP to create valuable xApps, and Kelly Babbit and Sam Zayed at Perfect Commerce who shared their insights on the SAP Supplier Network and working with SAP NetWeaver to integrate customers and partners.

Our friends Paul Kurchina and James Chang helped with content and made invaluable introductions along the way. They also gave plenty of feedback from their own authoring experiences. We also appreciate the support from Jeff Schneider, Yujian Yan, Alex Rosen, Hjalmer Danielson, and our MomentumSI colleagues who shared ideas and helped out during the time-consuming work.

Most of all, we'd like to recognize Kaj van de Loo at SAP, who served as our technical editor and primary SAP contact/mentor throughout this project. He has such a unique and practical understanding of ESA from both a business and technology perspective, as well as an understanding of how customers really drive how SAP is applying SOA and BPM technologies in the real world. His ideas, clarifications, and support on the project were tremendous, especially given his very busy schedule.

Finally, Scott would like to thank Barbara, Lauren, and Tyler for their love and understanding during the many hours that went into this project, and for putting up with all the disruptions that came along with it, and especially give his thanks to God, who makes all things possible.

Introduction

Welcome to *Mastering Enterprise SOA with SAP NetWeaver® and mySAP ERP™*. This book takes you through the ins and outs of SAP's Enterprise Service-Oriented Architecture (SOA) / Enterprise Services Architecture (ESA) strategic road map. ESA affects SAP's entire product strategy and technical architecture, which means many things to SAP customers and partners. As you probably know, it was a very big deal in the IT industry when SAP moved from a mainframe-based architecture to client/server computing with the launch of R/3. The transition to ESA is even bigger.

SAP is applying the last decade of IT advances to the next generation of business applications. This includes areas such as the following:

- Service-Oriented Architecture (SOA)
- Business process management (BPM)
- Model-driven development
- User-centric computing
- Event-driven architectures (EDA)
- Infrastructure virtualization
- Modern approaches to enterprise architecture

All of these and more come together to support a new breed of SAP business solutions. As one enterprise architect put it, "We are moving from highly structured SAP systems to an unstructured SAP-world, and we're not sure we know internally what that means or how to best deal with the change."

Indeed, the new SAP architecture is based on the latest thinking in distributed computing. It offers many new options for how to define your landscape and tie together both SAP and non-SAP solutions. This book serves as a comprehensive guide to understanding SAP's ESA-based strategy. It can help you and your organization understand what ESA *really* is and how to make the transition. With it, you will see the goals and benefits of ESA, appreciate the technical foundations, understand the elements of successful adoption, and preview the SAP products and road map that make ESA a reality.

Why This Book Was Written

Many SAP professionals think they know what ESA is. More often than not, they are wrong. Or, perhaps more accurately, they see only part of the puzzle. And, as a result, they get only a portion of the benefits.

You have probably heard the classic poem "The Blind Men and the Elephant." Each man touched the elephant to determine what it was. One grabbed its leg and thought it was "like a tree." Another brushed against the trunk and believed it was "like a snake." The one who touched the tail was sure it was "a rope," and so on. The moral of the story is that people who see (or feel) only part of something can end up with an understanding that is incomplete. This in turn often leads to endless debates around something no one fully understands.

After spending lots of time with CIOs, CTOs, architects, and other IT leaders at the locations of SAP customers and partners, it became clear that very few knew what to do with ESA. They were looking for the easy answers and formulaic approaches to success that were part of every other technology adoption strategy. They were also unclear how to justify ESA. Many felt ill equipped to translate the capabilities into business benefits. And, inside their organizations, the debates between BASIS teams, SAP developers, non-SAP technologists, business people, and enterprise architects about ESA made you wonder why no one could see the elephant running through the room.

ESA is far more than "SAP's approach to SOA and Web Services." It is far more than the technologies inside SAP NetWeaver. It is far more than xApps and Web interfaces. And, it is about far more than simply implementing mySAP ERP or other Business Suite applications.

This book was written to help you address the ESA adoption opportunity that customers and partners have before them. It offers a comprehensive definition of ESA and its relationship to SAP NetWeaver and mySAP ERP as a foundation for getting started. It will also walk you through the many trade-offs, choices, and things to learn when it comes to ESA. There are many products and capabilities inside the SAP NetWeaver platform that enable ESA. This book will help you understand those, too.

At the same time, this book is also intended to support SAP partners. Those systems integrators and independent software vendors (ISVs) who offer complementary solutions to SAP have a whole new set of opportunities available to them as well. ESA and SAP NetWeaver encourage third parties to extend SAP's offerings in very meaningful ways. This notion of a partner ecosystem is vital to SAP customers, and will change the way they think about buying and implementing solutions from both SAP and non-SAP organizations.

To the extent that this book helps you take more informed steps toward ESA and get more value from it, then it will have served its purpose.

Who Should Read This Book

The primary audience for this book usually performs one of the following roles:

- Enterprise architects
- Application architects
- Software designers, developers and technical team leads
- Product managers and VPs of development for ISVs
- IT leaders and managers responsible for technology strategy or their company's SAP landscape
- SAP IT professionals in organizations planning for ESA or strategic SAP NetWeaver adoption
- Consultants and practice leads who specialize in delivering SAP solutions

A secondary audience who can benefit particularly from Parts I and II of this book includes the following:

- Business analysts responsible for aligning requirements with technology capabilities
- Business process owners interested in understanding how SAP will support more agile business process management and activity monitoring
- Business process subject matter experts involved in innovating and designing process improvements
- Executive sponsors for IT initiatives interested in the value proposition of ESA
- Executive management looking for ways to innovate or manage strategic business processes

It bears repeating that the primary goal of the authors is to equip SAP customers interested in understanding and successfully adopting ESA as a way to align their IT environments with business goals and processes. In addition, SAP partners can see how to leverage ESA and SAP NetWeaver to add meaningful value to their products and services by extending what SAP has to offer and becoming active players in the ESA ecosystem.

Ultimately, this book is for anyone who wants to become familiar with ESA. It offers practical advice and much "food for thought" on important considerations associated with moving forward with adoption. It explains the business benefits and objectives, as well as how ESA is realized through SAP NetWeaver and mySAP ERP. Anyone interested in understanding SAP's strategy and seeing how all these pieces fit together to support next-generation business solutions will benefit from reading this book.

Readers should expect the following as takeaways:

- A thorough understanding of ESA's strategic motivations and implications for SAP customers
- A look inside the features of SAP NetWeaver and how it is the enabling platform for ESA
- An appreciation for all the underlying business and IT alignment trends that drive ESA (including SOA, BPM, and model-driven development)
- Background in enterprise architecture and its impact on ESA adoption
- The impact ESA has on the delivery of business solutions such as mySAP ERP and other SAP or third-party composite applications
- A wealth of examples spanning the SAP tools that show how NetWeaver features come together to create composite applications
- Valuable considerations for adoption planning and execution of pilots and programs

What This Book Covers

SAP's ESA approach essentially offers a whole new set of enterprise services models that serve as abstractions to the company's business applications. In addition to this content, SAP also provides entirely new ways of working with those enterprise services to create more compelling business applications and solutions.

This book describes how the IT industry is evolving, and why it led SAP to make these changes. It will also cover the step-by-step way in which SAP has been transforming its product lines, along with the background information needed to plan into the future as technology and products continue to evolve.

This book also helps you understand how all the parts of SAP NetWeaver fit together so that you can create a bigger picture for your organization. While your data warehousing team might be focused only on BI, the integration team with XI, and business process owners with the new features of mySAP ERP and xApps, ESA is really about how all the pieces fit together into something even more powerful. For example, a salad, soup, an entrée, a bottle of wine, and dessert are all good by themselves, but they tend to be much better when put together into a meal. In the same way, having the big picture for ESA and how all the parts of NetWeaver complement each other will allow you to take maximum advantage of SAP's new architecture, throughout your business processes and IT landscape.

From an ESA adoption perspective, this book guides you through what SOA and BPM are all about, and how the way SAP supports these capabilities changes your solutions architectures. Enterprise architecture (EA) also plays a key role in successfully adopting ESA. Information about where EA fits in along with the key process and ingredients to run a successful transition to ESA are included. Finally, the book covers the different ways in which SAP customers and partners are using ESA to design their solutions architectures.

From an SAP NetWeaver perspective, this book walks you through a number of key tools and technologies in the platform. This includes XI, the SAP NetWeaver Portal, the Composite Application Framework (CAF), Guided Procedures, Web Dynpro, Visual Composer, SAP Analytics, and more to show how the SAP platform enables you to create ESA-based solutions.

How This Book Is Structured

This book is organized into three parts. The goal is to move you from theory to practice, and from IT capabilities to specific product sets and examples of the features in action.

Part I: Understanding SAP's ESA Strategy

Part I of this book is all about understanding what ESA is, the industry motivations behind SAP's strategy, and how this affects the products and solutions customers build internally, acquire from SAP, or get from third-party ISVs and systems integrators.

You will see how ESA, SAP NetWeaver, and mySAP applications fit together. You will also see how this will influence SAP's road map into the future. Finally, you will understand how SAP is going about creating a partner ecosystem, and what this means in terms of new packaged composite applications to solve high-ROI business problems.

Part I is organized as follows:

- *Chapter 1* — Understanding why ESA is coming and what the considerations are for different areas within your organization

- *Chapter 2* — The evolution of the IT industry and how SAP is combining SOA, BPM, EDA, model-driven development, and infrastructure virtualization into a unified "applistructure," along with the advantages this provides

- *Chapter 3* — A look inside the new architecture for the SAP NetWeaver platform, mySAP Business Suite applications, and future business solutions delivered by SAP and its partners

- *Chapter 4* — Coverage of the SAP ESA ecosystem and the many ways customers and partners influence SAP's enterprise service models and products, as well as how this leads to pre-integrated, complementary solutions from partners

Part II: Evaluating ESA Capabilities and Planning Your Adoption Road Map

Part II walks you through the technology and architectural foundations of ESA, along with the many capabilities SAP NetWeaver and mySAP ERP enable. This includes covering the SOA technology blueprints and BPM capabilities that serve as the foundation of SAP NetWeaver.

Part II also covers the impact of ESA on enterprise architecture and governance, along with how to plan and run an effective adoption program. Finally, Part II provides an overview of solutions architectures used by SAP customers and partners to provide examples of how the rich capability that ESA offers can be applied to business scenarios.

This section helps customers and partners alike begin to think about how to apply ESA to their own environments, and lays the foundation for building their own unique adoption plan, architecture, road map, and pilots for moving toward ESA and NetWeaver adoption.

Part II is organized as follows:

- *Chapter 5* — Understanding the structure and evolution of SOA technology and how SAP NetWeaver supports SOA

- *Chapter 6* — Understanding all the capabilities required to deliver end-to-end BPM solutions successfully, and how SAP enables this through current products and the content in its Enterprise Services Repository (ESR)

- *Chapter 7* — A background on EA and its important role in successfully adopting ESA

- *Chapter 8* — A look inside the processes used for adopting ESA, along with some of the risks, considerations, and ideal practices organizations can use to improve their chances for success

- *Chapter 9* — Coverage of various challenges faced by SAP customers and the ESA-based solutions architectures developed by these customers and ecosystem partners to get better results

Part III: Realizing ESA Through SAP NetWeaver

Part III is where the rubber meets the road. Because much of ESA is realized through the SAP NetWeaver platform, and NetWeaver itself is the foundation for all mySAP ERP and other Business Suite applications, it only makes sense to use the products to illustrate what's unique about ESA.

Here you will take a deeper dive into the many ESA-centric features such as user productivity, embedded analytics, business process management, and composite application development that come together in SAP NetWeaver.

As a result, you will see the tangible aspects of SAP NetWeaver for purposes of clearly illustrating how the components and capabilities work together to realize ESA. Examples are provided in the context of a business scenario from Part II to make it even more relevant.

Part III is organized as follows:

- *Chapter 10* — An introduction to the SAP NetWeaver platform architecture and some of the key ESA-enabling tools and technologies

- *Chapter 11* — An understanding of different approaches for creating enterprise services either from scratch, or based upon existing assets in your IT landscape

- *Chapter 12* — A demonstration of the process orchestration features in SAP NetWeaver that are a key enabler for achieving end-to-end BPM

- *Chapter 13* — A look at how to develop composite applications using CAF and Guided Procedures, as well as coverage on the more general topic of handling supporting user workflow management to achieve end-to-end BPM

- *Chapter 14* — Examples on how to use other technologies—such as the SAP NetWeaver Portal, Web Dynpro, and Visual Composer—to create additional user interfaces and Portal Business Packages

- *Chapter 15* — An explanation of the importance of embedded analytics and how they transform traditional BI processes to active ingredients in the creation of solutions architectures, along with examples of using Visual Composer

■ *Chapter 16* — A final summary of the impact ESA is having for SAP customers and partners, along with a future outlook, set of recommendations, and additional resources you can use to get started

What You Need to Use This Book

Beyond a general background with SAP business solutions and technologies, little else is needed to benefit from Parts I and II. To perform some of the exercises in Part III, access to an SAP NetWeaver landscape is required. Except where otherwise noted, the samples in this book were based upon the NW2004S edition. However, if you are using the previous NW2004 version of the platform, you will likely be able to perform many of the exercises with slight modifications because NW2004S represented a minor update for SAP NetWeaver.

Even without all the tools in place for performing the Part III exercises, you can still benefit by reading these chapters and seeing how SAP currently supports the realization of many ESA concepts. As technology matures and SAP's own road map evolves, the tools themselves may change, but the ESA design and implementation concepts and focus on modeling will remain the same.

Reader Guidelines and Final Considerations

This book is meant to be a beginning, rather than your final source for all things ESA. Think of it as a launching point for your ESA and SAP NetWeaver adoption initiatives. By understanding the end-to-end ESA road map with all its implications, you can make every implementation decision better. And, once you have identified the areas most relevant to your organization, this book can help guide you to valuable information resources where you can go deeper.

While this book will show you a lot about ESA-based development with SAP NetWeaver, it's not meant to be a complete reference for programming with the entire platform. Each aspect of SAP NetWeaver is a text unto itself, and there are many great authors who have published books, articles, tutorials, and online "how-to" guides to help you get started with the products. The book is also not a comprehensive business guide to all the features and functions within mySAP ERP. Again, this topic could span several texts, and there are plenty of other places to find this information.

Some of these references are provided in the text, as well as on the book's companion Web site. We recommend you check this Web site for updates and additional demos and other information.

Perhaps the most important guideline is that you must begin to see ESA and SAP NetWeaver as being about more than just SAP applications. ESA is about business processes that span across your entire IT landscape, and include many other purchased and custom-built solutions. We've spoken with hundreds of customers since the strategy was unveiled, and it is obvious that this shift in mindset is a big challenge. But once that hurdle is cleared, the opportunities become very apparent.

When you get through Chapter 1, you will be well on your way to realizing these key points. And, if you decide to act on that information, your overall IT road map will be much improved, regardless of the level of ESA and SAP NetWeaver adoption that your organization chooses. The authors leave you with this final point to ponder:

> *Know what's weird? Day by day, nothing seems to change, but pretty soon . . . everything's different.* — Calvin from the "Calvin and Hobbes" comic strip

What a perfect sentiment for the road to ESA. Something similar happened in the early days of client/server, Web computing, and every other major IT theme. Slowly but surely, they became a way of life to the point that no one gives them a second thought in how solutions are delivered today. ESA will eventually be the same way. So welcome to the future of SAP solutions.

Now, let's get started.

Understanding SAP's ESA Strategy

ESA Is Coming

Service-Oriented Architecture (SOA) is coming to your SAP landscape. SAP itself has been saying this for several years, ever since the company launched its Enterprise SOA / Enterprise Services Architecture (ESA) strategic road map. Yet even today, many customers and SAP partners are still just getting started in terms of having a real strategy for effective adoption. One reason is that the change to ESA represents such a large undertaking for SAP itself. It simply took a while to get the first major ESA-based products to market. Now that the company has completed much of the initial delivery plan, there are plenty of ways for both customers and partners to get started.

If your organization is just beginning to plan for ESA, you may find there is a lack of a shared understanding internally about the major architectural change that your SAP landscape is about to undergo. Hence, there is often no sense of urgency on the part of management to address ESA other than possibly dealing with upgrades to mySAP ERP or adopting certain SAP NetWeaver components. Many tactical benefits are associated with tackling these projects, but if that is the extent of your ESA adoption efforts, it is sort of like buying a fancy new sports car to drive around school zones at 20 mph.

SAP's ESA strategy is a large undertaking that encompasses many different business, technology, architecture, and product perspectives. The most important thing for every enterprise to recognize is that its path to ESA adoption will be unique because every organization has its own existing IT landscape, legacy systems, technology standards, IT processes, organizational structure, and culture as a starting point. Success with ESA requires a proactive approach to managing each of these elements.

If your organization is still viewing ESA tactically, believing it is more of a marketing message from SAP or a feature set that is part of your next upgrade, then your first step is to get clear on what ESA was meant to accomplish. The strategy was actually driven by leading customers and partners who had a new vision for how packaged business applications should be delivered. The goal was to extend beyond the client/server "ERP-in-a-box" model offered by products such as R/3.

This chapter provides the 50,000-foot overview that will help you:

- See the scope of Enterprise SOA and what it represents to SAP's customers and partner community

- Understand why SAP is reinventing itself around ESA and how important the approach is to the company

- Communicate across your organization the importance of starting to plan today for the changes that ESA will bring about

- Evaluate some myths and misconceptions you or others in your organization may have about ESA

- See some of the different perspectives for approaching ESA based on organizational roles and how this book may help you address them

- Establish filters by which you should evaluate ESA, SAP NetWeaver, and mySAP ERP in terms of your overall IT landscape

A New Blueprint for SAP Solutions

ESA is a completely new architectural blueprint for SAP. It contains both a technology aspect based on industry-driven SOA and related IT trends, as well as an enterprise business dimension built from SAP's Solution Maps and the company's deep horizontal and vertical process knowledge. In fact, the company itself has had a difficult time helping customers and partners fully understand the ESA road map, and how it is fundamentally different from just adopting SOA technologies. Even the terminology itself has evolved from "Enterprise Services Architecture" to "Enterprise SOA" to help alleviate some of the market confusion (see the sidebar "From Enterprise Services Architecture to Enterprise SOA").

What is confusing is that ESA truly is a blueprint. It is not something you can touch, buy, or install. Rather, ESA is SAP's overarching model for business-driven enterprise services and how they can be woven together to create applications that support business processes.

FROM ENTERPRISE SERVICES ARCHITECTURE TO ENTERPRISE SOA

Some customers and partners have had a difficult time understanding that SAP's ESA-based solutions are entirely based on standard SOA technologies, but at the same time are fundamentally unique from just adopting SOA technology itself.

SAP is combining the technology with its deep business process and industry knowledge to create a well-defined set of enterprise services models and SOA-enabled business applications. In other words, SAP really offers *applied SOA* in terms of using the technology to deliver business solutions in better ways. The company's SOA-based business process content, enterprise services models, and new applications really do add up to a unique value proposition.

SAP tried to explain the distinction by adopting the term "Enterprise Services Architecture" (ESA) to suggest a business solutions blueprint based on SOA. Unfortunately, some customers either equated ESA with SOA (seeing no distinction) or felt that ESA meant an SOA-like capability that was proprietary or tied only to SAP landscapes.

Eventually, SAP evolved to using "Enterprise SOA" terminology as a way for customers to be clear that its new software architecture really is based on standard SOA technologies. While this may not help everyone see the benefits of what happens when you apply SOA to create business solutions such as mySAP ERP, or deliver an inventory of rich enterprise service and process models as SAP is doing, it does better convey that SOA is at the heart of the blueprint.

This book uses the term "ESA" to refer to both "Enterprise Services Architecture" and "Enterprise SOA" as ways to describe the new SAP solutions architecture blueprint. You can read more on the specifics of the evolution of the terminology surrounding ESA from an SAP press release available at www.sap.com/company/press/factsheets/esa.epx.

ESA becomes reality through a combination of the SAP NetWeaver platform, along with changes in and around the mySAP Business Suite applications. NetWeaver offers a full set of enabling technologies needed for ESA. And, because NetWeaver serves as the foundation for mySAP ERP, other Business Suite applications, and new types of composite applications, the business solutions themselves enable the ESA blueprint in ways that make them far more flexible than ever before. From a technical perspective, SAP must deliver the following to make ESA real:

▪ Core services that are provided by the underlying business applications

▪ An integration platform to turn these application services into a set of meaningful enterprise service and process models

■ A composition, process management, and service consumption platform to transform these enterprise services and process models into solutions that are meaningful to end users or other applications

■ Support for IT industry standards and trends throughout

This obviously took some time to evolve from the proprietary client/server architecture supporting R/3.

Chapter 3 covers these relationships and the ESA-related product road map in greater detail. For now, Figure 1-1 should give you a basic idea of what the ESA blueprints are all about and how they relate to mySAP ERP and NetWeaver. Again, ESA offers a way to define the conceptual architectural models of your business and its technology solutions. SAP NetWeaver, mySAP ERP, and other products bring those models to life. They serve as the foundation for many types of business process–driven applications.

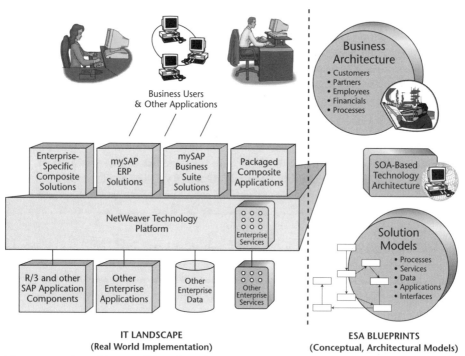

Figure 1-1: The architectural blueprints of ESA are realized through NetWeaver implementation, the inventory of enterprise services, and new applications composed on the platform.

Why ESA Is Critical to SAP

SAP spends a lot of time explaining why ESA is important to you. Whether you are a customer, an independent software vendor (ISV) offering complementary solutions to SAP applications, or a systems integrator specializing in SAP, there are definite ESA value propositions for you to consider. But what about from the SAP side? The authors believe that seeing the factors that motivated SAP to pursue ESA is one of the best ways to grasp the significance of the strategy and the opportunity it represents to your organization.

That is not to say that everything SAP has to recommend and offer is the right answer for your environment. If anything, ESA will force some interesting architectural choices within your IT landscape that traditionally were not required when implementing packaged business applications such as enterprise resource planning (ERP), customer relationship management (CRM), or supply chain management (SCM) products.

In fact, that is probably the main reason many customers and partners are underestimating the potential significance of ESA to their organization. They simply have so much experience with their current SAP environments, while ESA represents a whole new evolution around the original technical characteristics of R/3. Under ESA, SAP's business applications:

- Are much easier to integrate with both logically and technically
- Support the latest industry standard technologies
- Are designed for easy change to support your unique business processes
- Help you consolidate your IT environment from a business process perspective to lower total cost of ownership (TCO) where it makes sense
- Embrace much richer, user-friendly interfaces, whether based on the desktop, through a browser, or on mobile devices, or embedded within other applications
- Strongly encourage ISVs and systems integrators to contribute value to the business applications in a manner that is more seamless and cost-effective to SAP customers than traditional integration methods

Much of this book will help describe what these changes mean to you from both a business and technical perspective. You will also see many of the details associated with the architectural change and how the enabling tools and technologies work. For now, it makes sense to start from the perspective of how important success with ESA is to SAP itself in light of many industry forces. This may give you a leg up in understanding the major goals of the strategy, and the degree to which SAP is focused on successful execution. More important, it can help your organization get on the same page as far as the importance of ESA to your SAP landscape is concerned. It may also give you better insight into evaluating ESA's potential against other options for adopting SOA to manage business processes within your IT portfolio.

ESA Is a "Bet the Company" Strategy

SAP is obviously a "for profit" company so why would it be spending so much capital on all the R&D and marketing associated with ESA? After all, SAP is the world leader in enterprise business applications, and all this investment has to be a big drain on short-term profitability. The answer is simple. ESA is, without a doubt, a long-term competitive necessity for SAP.

By recognizing how vital ESA is to SAP's success, you can rest assured that SAP will continue to deliver many meaningful products that transform the entire SAP architecture. In fact, SAP itself has referred to ESA as a "bet the company" strategy.

It should go without saying that if something is this important to SAP, it ought to be very closely evaluated by any customer, ISV partner, or SAP systems integrator. Although SAP launched ESA in 2003, the more strategic adoption cycles are only just beginning *en masse*. As mentioned, part of the reason is because SAP itself has only recently reached the point in the implementation road map where customers and partners can begin to experience product implementations that support the strategic aspects of ESA. Until you could touch the tangible elements of ESA, it was hard to get serious about adoption beyond basic education and planning.

Another factor is that the realization of ESA requires a lot of cooperation across the IT organization (or the product development team within an ISV), as well as with their business counterparts. In many organizations, each stakeholder tends to see only the piece of the ESA puzzle that applies to him or her, so it can take a while to get to that shared understanding.

And, like any big change, discussions around ESA typically uncover many differences of opinion and some healthy skepticism as to how important the changes it brings about are, and, more important, what you should do about them. This is because the scope of SAP solutions now expands beyond the boundaries of a traditional SAP application landscapes.

Knowing that ESA is so vital to SAP's future should help you build consensus to actively evaluate where it fits in your organization. Having your own strategy and position is critical for the enterprise. The authors of this book have seen many companies that wish they could undo some recent architectural decisions and product investments because they misunderstood what ESA offered, or took only a short-term snapshot view of SAP's progress against the road map. By arming your organization with the overall story, you can help your team weigh the pros and cons of ESA, and begin to formulate your unique adoption story.

"BETTING THE COMPANY" ON ESA

ESA is a big deal not only for SAP, but also major industry technology partners who are working with the company to support the strategy. In fact, the company has been working for almost a decade on ways to break up its tightly coupled, monolithic applications into more adaptable pieces. The advent of Web Services and related technology standards enabled the strategy to gel into the ESA story.

Following are some selected quotations and announcements regarding ESA. They illustrate how big of a shift ESA represents and why your organization should be closely tracking and evolving your road map:

◆ "We made a big bet on the future . . . We used our cash flow, our ERP system, and made it the frontrunner to test and to show the market that this is indeed the next generation of enterprise applications." — Henning Kagermann, SAP CEO and Executive Board Member in Sapphire 2005 keynote.

◆ "We believe in this so much that we have bet the company."[1] — Shai Agassi, SAP Executive Board member

◆ "As platform success is determined in large part by the ecosystem, SAP has made major investments in attempts to advance in development and standards setting."[2] — Gartner

◆ "[ESA is] not just about making their applications work under a new architecture. SAP needs to address the entire work flow about how tasks get done."[3] — Henry Morris at IDC

◆ SAP licenses ESA middleware to tech heavyweights, including Microsoft, Adobe, Cisco Systems, Computer Associates, EMC, Intel, Mercury Interactive, Symantec, and Veritas for creating certified solutions. — Sapphire 2005 announcements

Because ESA is so comprehensive in scope, it is easy to get lost in the details of different products, components, or technologies. Just remember that all of the details roll up to support an overall vision, and that is where the real power of the new architecture can be realized.

ESA Was Triggered by Major Technology Changes

SAP is first and foremost a business solutions company. Believe it or not, you could argue that the traditional SAP R/3 ERP technology architecture was way ahead of its time from a pure computer science perspective when it was first created in the early 1990s. SAP moved what was essentially a mainframe business solutions package and created an entire enterprise class technology platform for developing and running business applications in a trustworthy and scalable client/server architecture. This was an incredibly sophisticated, technical approach for a business applications company, and reflected many ideas found in modern-day application platform architectures.

Of course, all this was done before the problems with managing client/server applications were well known and before any standard technologies existed for distributed computing or creating rich user interfaces at the business application level. The world has certainly gone through some major technology innovations since then. Now a monolithic business application such as R/3 is essentially a legacy architecture.

And, by supporting primarily Advanced Business Application Programming (ABAP) and BASIS technologies in tightly coupled and proprietary ways there were barriers to easily changing business processes implemented in a traditional SAP landscape. As you probably know, even if you created standards-based solutions outside of R/3 to augment processes, it was still relatively difficult to integrate them with the proprietary environment. So, a lot of what ESA does helps address what became inherent weaknesses in a traditional R/3 landscape from a technology and architecture perspective.

Obviously, the emergence of the Internet triggered a transformation in the IT industry. Web-based applications and distributed computing technologies have become the de facto way to create most new business solutions. And now SOA, model-driven development, event-driven architectures (EDA), business process management (BPM), and virtualization techniques are leading to unprecedented industry-wide standardization. Over time, this evolution has spread across four significant areas, as shown in Figure 1-2:

- *Standardization of how applications are integrated* — Web Services technology, Extensible Markup Language (XML), and SOA design patterns make it cheaper and easier for systems to talk with one another than ever before. This has breathed life into many older technology environments. Meanwhile, advanced integration capabilities such as transformation, routing, and messaging are becoming standardized and commoditized inside of common technology platforms such as Java, .NET, and open source LAMP (Linux, Apache, MySQL, Perl/PHP/Python). These capabilities are being delivered as both software solutions and as embedded hardware-based integration devices on a network.

- *Standardization for managing business processes separate from applications* — Business process management has become the latest focus of technology standardization. Once you have a common model for exposing services and integrating applications, business process logic can then be extracted from traditional systems. New composite applications that coordinate the process and intelligently respond to events can be assembled from models on top of the underlying applications.

- *Standardization of networking infrastructure to better support applications* — Once the network itself becomes aware of the business content passing through it, all sorts of new management, monitoring, and governance capabilities emerge to support business processes in real time.

- *User-centric approach for composing applications* — The advent of standards for exposing and integrating the business logic in applications has enabled a proliferation of technologies designed to make users more productive. The use of digital forms, office productivity applications, mobile devices, intelligent and interactive Web pages, and other event-driven UIs enables the creation of a better user experience. In addition, business intelligence analytics can be seamlessly embedded in the user's experience in new ways.

All major IT vendors have been working aggressively to create these standards, as well as to deliver products based upon them. As you can imagine, this posed both a great threat and terrific opportunity for a company like SAP that has always been a provider of business solutions. SAP just happened to deliver them by embedding the processes within proprietary, monolithic client/server applications such as R/3.

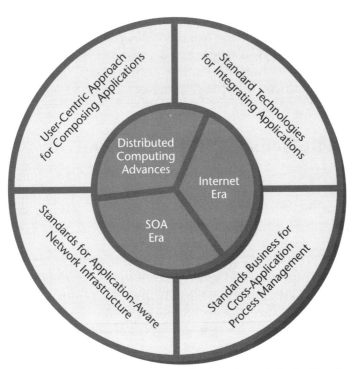

Figure 1-2: The effect of new standards and trends in the IT industry

Obviously, it was the support for business solutions, not the technology architectures that made packaged business applications such as ERP, CRM, SCM, and so forth popular in the first place. They essentially provided out-of-the box automation for key processes. So, if all these new standards mentioned enable you to pull out your most important business process logic from the underlying applications to overcome the problems associated with their inflexible technology architecture, then a good deal of value will flow into whatever solution becomes your new process management and composition infrastructure. From a business perspective, this means the underlying packaged business applications themselves begin to look more like legacy transaction processing systems.

NOTE IT trends such as the Internet, SOA, BPM, EDA, and model-driven development are driving standards that reshape applications you buy and extend from companies such as SAP or choose to build internally. This forces architecture and landscape choices you did not to have to make in the past.

Chapter 2 covers these trends in the technology industry and how they motivated the SAP strategy in greater detail. For now, simply recognize that these technology changes, fueled by the principles of SOA, have become a huge driver and enabling factor behind ESA. Because the entire IT and business applications marketplace is heading in this direction, you will be affected one way or another. The question is whether you will take SAP's ESA-centric approach, or look to adopt other alternatives for achieving a service-oriented and process-driven IT environment. Many organizations will choose a hybrid model, embracing a combination of the two.

ESA Is Focused on Delivering Business Solutions

SOA is clearly the latest major technology innovation for the IT industry. Interestingly, its significance has much more to do with how it can strategically affect a business. SOA has the potential to really transform IT beyond its roots of efficient transaction processing for standardized processes, which has been the focus of the last several decades.

Done right SOA is about making IT more agile, effective, and responsive. Not that these goals haven't been around forever, but the excitement around SOA has more to do with the new delivery of the industry-wide standards that make achieving these goals a real possibility in most organizations. And if, instead of being a bottleneck, IT can truly deliver process-driven applications faster, better, and cheaper, then the businesses can likewise innovate their processes faster, better, and cheaper than ever before. Part II of this book looks at many of the non-technical aspects associated with implementing SOA the "right way."

It was actually the inability to create strategic differentiation that became one of the main weaknesses of packaged business applications such as R/3, CRM, SCM, and so forth. They essentially put all customers on the same playing field in terms of "out-of-the-box" process automation that was difficult to augment or change.

R/3 moved SAP's business solutions from the R/2 mainframe architecture to client/server technology because it was the best way to deliver business applications at the time. Likewise, ESA represents a migration of business solutions to an architecture based on SOA, BPM, EDA, and model-driven development. To accomplish this, SAP is creating an SOA-based technology platform in NetWeaver. At the same time, the new mySAP ERP and other Business Suite applications are being redesigned to take advantage of the features SAP NetWeaver enables. Likewise, other vendors can use these same features to offer more compelling and better integrated commercial solutions.

The key for your organization is to avoid the trap of thinking SAP is suddenly shifting to compete purely as a technology component vendor such as IBM, BEA, or Sun. In fact, you will see in Chapter 3 that NetWeaver is intentionally not being positioned to compete on a feature/function basis against "best of breed" technology products. The company remains focused on delivering business solutions. In fact, the analyst firm Gartner has coined the term "Service-Oriented Business Applications" (SOBA) for business solutions created based on SOA. (See the sidebar "SOBA: Recognizing the Problem Was the Packaging.") Hence, NetWeaver is SAP's platform for how the company, customers, and partners can all use the same foundation and techniques to deliver service-oriented business solutions.

The real power of ESA comes from fully integrating the SAP business applications such as ERP with an SOA technology platform such as NetWeaver, and then complementing everything with a vibrant ISV and systems integrator ecosystem that fill in gaps in the SAP solution maps. Think of it as a business strategy and process-driven approach to enterprise and applications architecture. The combination means you can take the "out-of-the-box" processes and more easily adapt them to meet your enterprise's needs. You essentially get the best of both worlds from a process automation point of view. The concept is so powerful that its advantages will be covered from both a business and technology perspective throughout the rest of Part I of this book.

Essentially, SAP is betting that the winning value proposition is the delivery of extensive packaged application functionality that exposes and consumes vast amounts of industry-specific content and services, composed on top of a unified, SOA-based technology platform. Your organization's challenge will be to evaluate this approach against all the other SOA-based options, and then decide the degree to which ESA can help manage your application portfolio from a business-driven perspective.

> **SOBA: RECOGNIZING THE PROBLEM WAS THE PACKAGING**
>
> Ultimately, companies such as SAP are in the business of enabling a full set of end-to-end business processes. The traditional way to sell these process solutions was as discrete, standalone, monolithic applications such as R/3. The functionality was great, but flexibility was almost nonexistent.
>
> Custom-developed in-house applications experienced similar problems. Over time, they also became difficult to change to meet new business needs. The technology industry has evolved a concept known as Service-Oriented Architecture (SOA) into a new approach to building applications with better integration and flexibility in mind. Fueled by new standards and vendor cooperation, SOA has gained significant industry momentum as a new way of delivering business applications.
>
> The analyst firm Gartner coined the term "Service-Oriented Business Applications" (SOBA) to describe the re-packaging of these business applications in an SOA world.
>
> Hence, those same processes offered by SAP can now be delivered as part of a modern technology architecture, enabling you to overcome many of the existing limitations that made them difficult to integrate with and even harder to change. More important, they provide a number of additional benefits for aligning both the business and technical aspects of managing a process.
>
> SAP refers to its process and domain models as "business content." Today, the content is embedded inside actual applications such as R/3 in a tightly coupled manner. Under ESA, this same content will be delivered as a set of Lego-like building blocks that can be quickly assembled into applications that support your specific process needs. In effect, ESA helps repackage the SAP applications into SOBAs.

Some Misconceptions About ESA

SAP has done a good job of promoting the ESA vision and road map. But, as mentioned earlier, the change is so comprehensive and takes so long to realize that it is often difficult for customers and partners to fully digest it. The authors have encountered a number of SAP customer and partner comments around ESA that represent quick conclusions or misunderstandings based on information they have read, seen in a presentation, or picked up through discussions on the topic. These are worth evaluating because they may be areas where you or others in your organization have formed strong opinions regarding your road map.

Myth: ESA Is More Marketing Than Real Change

Without question, there has been a lot of marketing hype from SAP, analysts, consultants, and others about SOA and ESA. As you will see, an even greater amount of product engineering and enhancement of business content, applications, and services through ISV and systems-integrator partnerships is taking place. As mentioned, ESA really is a "bet the company" strategy for SAP. It just takes time to be fully enabled across the product line, which is why the original road map was four years long.

ESA represents a much greater architectural change than the migration from R/2 to R/3. If you have an SAP landscape, it will eventually be affected at some level by ESA. Likewise, the business impact has the potential to be far more significant as it does with any business-driven shift to SOA. This will take careful planning and leadership inside of your organization to enable the change to happen meaningfully and successfully. The key is in how you best prepare to tackle the challenge.

Myth: NetWeaver Is Just Repackaging of Old Ideas and Products

This is very similar to the first myth. It is true that the NetWeaver platform includes many SAP components and technologies that have been around for quite some time, which you are probably familiar with (such as the Business Information Warehouse, Enterprise Portal, and the ABAP Application Server). Naturally, SAP didn't just toss out all of its existing technical infrastructure and start from scratch in creating an integrated application platform.

SAP is, however, radically re-engineering these components to support standards, and is adding and maturing newer components and tools such as Exchange Infrastructure, Master Data Management, the Enterprise Services Repository, Visual Composer, and the Composite Application Framework. Most important, SAP is weaving the whole stack together into a unified set of technology services that support the realization of ESA. You will see more on this in Chapter 3.

Myth: ESA Is Just an SAP "Thing"

While it is true the ESA is SAP's future architecture, it is based on industry-standard SOA technologies. As mentioned earlier, SAP is following a technology trend that is being implemented by every major IT vendor in the industry.

In addition, ESA goes well beyond just SAP because the success of the strategy requires integrating business content and supporting new process-driven applications and business services developed by customers, third-party ISVs, and systems integrators. Finally, ESA means SAP products can now work better with the existing elements of your landscape, including legacy and custom applications, products purchased from other vendors, and platforms and infrastructure products that support your SOA and application development standards.

In fact, it is because ESA is about more than just the traditional SAP technologies and architecture that makes understanding and adopting it so difficult for existing customers. You have years of training, organizational design, and culture that put SAP into a specific box that no longer exists under ESA.

Myth: ESA Is Just SAP's Nickname for SOA

To some extent this is true. In fact, the company even repositioned the nickname from "Enterprise Services Architecture" to "Enterprise SOA." However, that is only half the story and the distinction SAP is making is very important. It's like making the distinction between client/server architecture and the functional design of R/3.

SOA is the technology blueprint upon which ESA is based. What distinguishes SAP's approach to ESA from "plain old" SOA is the business solutions architecture that comes along with it. SAP has created models for service-oriented applications, processes, and a library of functional enterprise services. In effect, it is the marriage of SOA technology with industry-driven business service models that combine to represent ESA.

What you should take away is that SAP's approach to SOA is first and foremost business process–driven, as opposed to tool, technology, and infrastructure focused. Organizations that try and evaluate ESA or similar approaches in terms of "best of breed" SOA technology stacks often miss this key point. It's comparing apples to oranges, which is why SAP made the distinction in the first place.

Myth: The SAP NetWeaver Platform Is Not as Good as Other Application and Integration Products You Have Seen

Actually, the authors tend to agree with this one in many cases. In fact, this may always be true in terms of a pure technology-based features and functions analysis. There will be "best of breed" products that offer better and easier-to-use technology capabilities than any one feature or capability in a major IT vendor's suite of solutions.

The focus of SAP NetWeaver is to deliver a fully integrated platform loaded with business process content from which you can run SOA-based applications from SAP and other ISVs, or use to compose the business differentiating ones that you need to create internally. The value of the platform is that the whole is greater than the sum of the parts.

In terms of the features and functions of individual NetWeaver capabilities, the best advice is that you should always pick the solution that meets your unique needs with the lowest total cost of ownership (TCO). That does not necessarily mean the "best" product from the technology feature and function perspective as many organizations are starting to figure out. Which ones are "best" is always a moving target.

You can best realize ESA by mixing and matching NetWeaver with other IT application and integration products and platforms that meet your needs. The hard part is doing the *objective* analysis to figure out which to use when.

Myth: You Have to Wait Until ESA Is "Finished"

By definition, SAP has not fully ESA-enabled all of its business and technology solutions because the initial road map is still underway. However, ESA itself is really only a set of architectural blueprints for delivering business solutions based on SOA technology. SAP has already released a number of services, processes, products, and technology capabilities that allow you to start implementing solutions based on the ESA blueprints today.

In fact, ESA will never be "finished" in the sense that SAP will continue innovating products and capabilities on this model well into the future. SAP will always be releasing new services, models, and applications based on ESA. And the company will continue to improve the underlying NetWeaver tools and technologies as standards themselves mature.

The point is that there is a strong foundation in place. ESA now enables SAP to release solutions faster than previous architectures allowed. And, because the new architecture is designed for more incremental updates of service content and application solutions, it makes it easier for customers to choose their adoption timelines of new features.

Similarly, Ecosystem ISV partners are already leveraging NetWeaver to power their own product solutions as well as developing ESA-based packaged composite applications in conjunction with SAP. They will continue to add services and solutions incrementally as well.

It was mentioned earlier that the shift to ESA is so significant in terms of just your SAP landscape, let alone the impact it can have on your overall enterprise architecture and application portfolio. It is likely that far more is available today for you to start planning, piloting, and delivering solutions than a typical organization can digest. As the ESA road map evolves, you will be better equipped to adopt new products and solutions from SAP and its partners.

Myth: You Have to Upgrade Your ERP or Business Suite Applications to Begin with ESA

While a fully ESA-enabled set of mySAP ERP and Business Suite scenarios will not be available until you upgrade, realizing elements of ESA can begin with whatever SAP application versions you have in place today. In fact, piloting solutions with SAP NetWeaver prior to upgrading is one of the ideal ways to prepare your longer-term ESA strategy.

As an example, an environment running Web AS 6.2 offers native support for XML, SOAP, and WSDL. That means you can work in conjunction with

SAP's Web Services infrastructure and other application-development capabilities to integrate applications using elements of the new architecture. And, of course, are many other ways to expose R/3 interfaces as Web Services, with or without SAP NetWeaver. More important, many of the ESA-based integration and composition scenarios can be realized by combining SAP NetWeaver with an R/3 landscape. This includes acquiring and running third-party packaged composite applications built for the platform.

If you have upgraded to mySAP ERP 2005, your SAP applications are already running natively on the NetWeaver platform and you can use the new SOA-based Enterprise Services Repository content and composition tools to build sophisticated ESA-based process-driven applications. The next generation of NetWeaver is labeled the Business Process Platform (BPP). It will deliver fully ESA-enabled industry versions of SAP business applications along with richer service-oriented models designed from the ground up with SOA in mind. This is covered in more detail later in this book.

Figure 1-3 provides a brief glimpse into the various landscape options for getting started with ESA today. More details around what can be done with regards to the versions of business applications and NetWeaver that you have are covered throughout the book. The key is seeing that you can begin with ESA regardless of the version of ERP you are using, and no business application upgrading is required to get started with certain scenarios if you so choose.

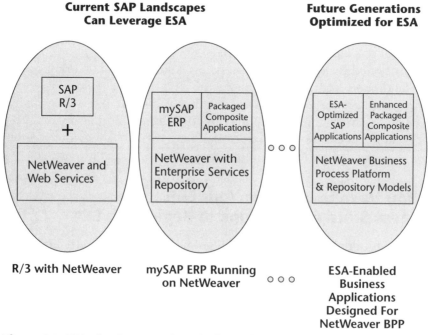

Figure 1-3: ESA adoption scenarios exist for multiple SAP application landscapes.

The following list provides a summary for this section by addressing the various myths in terms of what your organization should realize regarding ESA:

- ESA is a major architectural change for SAP solutions.

- SAP NetWeaver combines existing SAP components with new technologies into a unified platform.

- ESA is based upon industry-standard technologies.

- ESA extends SOA technology with an extensive library of enterprise service, process models, and composite application blueprints.

- SAP NetWeaver can integrate with other standards-based application platforms and products.

- You can get started with ESA today, regardless of the version of SAP business applications you are using.

Some Key Consideration Regarding ESA Adoption

The previous section should have dispelled some initial misconceptions you or others in your organization may have around ESA and SAP NetWeaver. One key point worth mentioning regarding the last myth is that its converse is also not true. Just because you upgrade to NetWeaver, mySAP ERP, or even the fully ESA-enabled versions of the mySAP Business Suite does not mean your organization has suddenly become a master of ESA. There is no free lunch when it comes to SOA adoption, with or without SAP's approach.

As mentioned, every enterprise's path to ESA is unique, and getting the benefits of an SOA approach to managing business processes in your IT portfolio will require careful planning, leadership, and skills development. The following sections cover some things you might want to be thinking about that can influence when, where, and how you might pursue ESA adoption within your organization.

Characteristics of Your Organization

A number of variables are related to your enterprise that will dictate a lot of when and how you tackle ESA. These will be covered in more detail in Part II where ESA adoption methodologies and enterprise architecture are discussed. For now, simply recognize that what is relevant to your situation may not be as important to another enterprise facing an entirely different scenario. Following are some of the most important considerations:

- The size and organizational structure of your enterprise.

- How enterprise architecture decisions are made (centralized, federated, distributed).

- Strategic value placed on business process innovation.
- Strategic value placed on IT.
- How IT is structured relative to its business counterparts.
- The amount of your application portfolio that SAP solutions represent.
- Proliferation of non-SAP application and integration technologies and standards.
- Versions of SAP you are running, and the upgrade and consolidation plans you have relative to SAP ERP or other Business Suite applications. As a reminder, you can get started in some capacity no matter what your landscape looks like today.

Of course, there are many other factors, but this should give you a good idea of the types of things you need to consider in scoping and developing your plans. For ISVs and systems integrators, Chapter 4 describes the SAP ecosystem and the factors related to your organization that may dictate how you choose to participate.

Roles Within Your Organization

As the previous section suggests, ESA requires that you build bridges across many areas of the organization. From a strategy perspective, building bridges between business and IT executives for aligning economics of IT portfolio management with business process portfolio management is vital to the success of your ESA adoption efforts. From an individual business process perspective, the most important bridge is the link between business process owners and the IT architecture and implementation teams that support them.

From a technical perspective, the most important bridge is between SAP application technology teams and their counterparts responsible for non-SAP applications and platforms, as well as with the enterprise architecture and infrastructure groups. Now that SOA permeates all the way to the network level, the traditional IT organizational structure and software development lifecycle roles have blurred. This gets even more interesting where parts of IT operations have been outsourced and cuts across company boundaries.

Naturally, ISVs and systems integrators who develop products around ESA will also need to align internally. Figure 1-4 highlights some of the many bridges that must be built to effectively plan for and adopt ESA.

The following sections offer some more specific goals to think about relative to ESA, depending on the roles you play in your organization. They should help provide a guide to how you and your team can apply the information you gather about ESA.

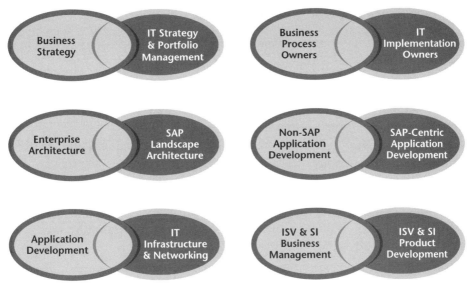

Figure 1-4: Effective planning and adoption of ESA requires better collaboration and alignment in multiple areas.

Business and IT Leadership

The primary goal at the leadership level is to see ESA as an enabler of better IT investment management from a business-process and value perspective. Successful adoption of an ESA strategy requires that you shift your focus to the following:

- Aligning processes with strategy
- Speeding up the time it takes for IT to enable changing of business processes
- Gaining more value from processes through better usability and more analytics and business intelligence capabilities
- Continually evaluating every part of your IT landscape relative to the strategic business value and level of differentiation it supports
- Lowering IT TCO, particularly in areas of maintenance, integration, and support for activities that add little differentiation value

Business Process Owners and Analysts

As the day-in and day-out beneficiaries of ESA, business process owners and analysts can help plan for ESA by doing the following:

- Managing your process portfolios
- Systematically identifying areas of opportunity where process changes offer real ROI for your organization
- Identifying processes and activities that have higher costs to execute than your competitors
- Understanding the key capabilities, analytics, and user experience characteristics of process-based composite applications
- Developing skills on your team for speeding up application change with model-driven development tools

Enterprise Architects

Enterprise architects play a vital role in ensuring the successful evaluation and adoption of ESA. They perform key bridging roles within IT, as well as between IT and the business by doing the following:

- Understanding the vision and possibilities of SOA and ESA from a business perspective, as well as a technical one
- Ensuring the rest of the organization follows a business approach to SOA, as opposed to a purely technical one
- Defining and managing the IT portfolio in alignment with the business process portfolio
- Working with colleagues in the SAP landscape to understand and evaluate the new SAP technologies, and helping to determine which options to adopt and where to augment them
- Identifying strategic application and infrastructure consolidation opportunities for lowering TCO
- Making architecture and governance policies truly actionable, supportable and enforceable in an efficient way

SAP IT Owners, Architects, Developers, and Administrators

For those in your organization who have primarily been focused on the SAP landscape, there are obviously many roles and opportunities associated with ESA adoption.

In addition to opportunities already described for the business process owners and the enterprise architects, those working mainly in the SAP landscape should focus on the following:

- Understanding the vision for ESA and the major capabilities needed for its realization

- Understanding SOA principles and industry evolution of standards

- Learning the landscape and architecture changes that come with the realization of ESA

- Building bridges with non-SAP architects and developers to help explain the new SAP environment and jointly plan its role in your landscape. SAP-centric professionals must be able to work across the organization on the future for processes that are executed both inside and outside of SAP.

- Focusing on the new service based options for integration and composition

- Learning about the architecture and delivery of composite applications

- Training on new skills associated with development and administration with SAP NetWeaver

Non-SAP IT Application Architects and Developers

Non-SAP IT professionals who recognize the major changes coming from SAP should begin to rethink how they work with their counterparts and integrate with their SAP landscape to deliver business solutions. This implies learning more about the application development and composition capabilities that are part of the NetWeaver platform and determining which to standardize on.

Areas of focus would include the following:

- ESA and SOA principles, standards, and a business process–driven approach to IT solution delivery

- Changes in SAP architecture and service-based approaches for integration of non-SAP applications

- Composite application development architectures and techniques

- Understanding the goals of improving user productivity and providing embedded analytics within the context of processes, along with the related NetWeaver capabilities for delivering non-SAP applications, data, and services in that context.

- Training on Java, .NET, and Web Service–based SAP development tools and technologies as appropriate for platform consolidation goals

- Working with SAP counterparts and enterprise architects to effectively implement and support new architectural standards and capabilities

Product Management and Technology Leadership Within ISVs

As mentioned, SAP is making it much easier for third-party ISVs to integrate complementary applications into an SAP landscape. This includes capabilities for running solutions on the SAP NetWeaver infrastructure, as well as using Web Services and composite application development techniques as replacements to traditional integration coding. More important, SAP is actively seeking ISVs that offer strategic complementary functionality either at the technical platform level, or in terms of horizontal or industry vertical business solutions. These features and functions can be packaged and sold in new ways in conjunction with SAP.

Those ISVs offering solutions with this type of potential should consider the following:

- Actively identifying those areas where your solutions complement SAP functionality, and the level of interest from SAP and customers in delivering them on NetWeaver or as sellable packaged composite applications

- Understanding the various certifications and new product delivery options SAP offers around the NetWeaver technical infrastructure

- Determining the value to your organization of actively participating within the SAP customer and partner ecosystem, and building your own execution road map

- Understanding the technical requirements and product engineering options associated with the certifications and delivering solutions as appropriate

- Understanding the details of composite applications for enabling faster time-to-market, lower overall costs to customers, and better user experiences from integrating with the service repository and delivering solutions using functions such as SAP Analytics and Guided Procedures

- Participating in SAP's Enterprise Services Community as appropriate to help define the overarching standards and interfaces associated with a certain industry or technology domain

Systems Integrators and Consulting Partners

Systems integrators who specialize in implementing mySAP ERP or other Business Suite applications, or delivering horizontal and vertical business solutions, should certainly understand the impact ESA will have on their offerings. They also have an opportunity very similar to ISVs in terms of turning their specific domain expertise and solutions into productized composite applications.

These organizations should focus on the following:

- Understanding the new business capabilities, architecture technologies, and products associated with ESA
- Developing skills in facilitating customer road map creation and ESA adoption
- Building capabilities in applicable NetWeaver features to ensure that you can effectively deliver solutions on the new platform
- Analyzing your own horizontal and vertical process solutions and expertise to identify areas that can be productized as packaged composite applications, and the perceived value from customers and SAP
- Evaluating cases where you have frequently modified R/3 or other Business Suite applications in the past to identify areas that can now be productized with composite solutions
- Understanding the technical and business requirements for delivering packaged composites and creating an execution road map where appropriate
- Participating in the Enterprise Services Community as appropriate

Goals for Making ESA Applicable to Your Enterprise

By now, you should realize that tackling the new SAP architecture means figuring out which capabilities are most important to your organization and how to apply them to your unique needs. This is very different from the old style of implementing SAP business applications where you looked for "out-of-the-box" solutions and then often tailored your process to what the application itself could do.

Of course, you can use the new capabilities offered by ESA to deliver business solutions in essentially the same manner as before. However, the real benefits will come from keeping a few guidelines in mind as you build your strategy. Following are some specific areas of focus you should be thinking about as you dive into the details of ESA, NetWeaver, and mySAP ERP. These will be covered in more detail in Part II of this book, and should remain an important focus for you throughout your ESA planning.

Making ESA Business Advantages Relevant

It is easy to get caught up with all the technology change associated with ESA because there are a lot of differences in moving to an SOA model of computing. The main objective is to enable you to deliver business solutions faster and support more frequent change in business processes, all while lowering the TCO within the IT landscape.

These important goals can never be realized unless you can identify specific scenarios that will benefit your organization. In other words, an "adopt it and they will come" approach rarely works with ESA. Instead of talking about agility, and flexibility in the abstract, IT and its business counterparts must actively work together to identify specific opportunities for improving business processes. For example:

■ Where would more timely, accurate, or integrated delivery of information make a difference in effective and efficient process execution?

■ Where would re-sequencing, automating, or eliminating process steps have a major ROI impact?

■ What changes in distribution or pricing would you make if they were easy to accomplish?

■ What processes offer the greatest potential for strategic differentiation, yet remain untapped by your organization?

■ How would improved customer, manager, supplier, or employee self-service affect the business?

These are just a very few basic examples of the kinds of questions you should be asking to find the unique impact points ESA may have for your organization. Every industry and business has its own value chain. The key is keeping this focus in mind, and applying it as you learn about the different features and capabilities ESA offers. SAP has published an Enterprise Services Design Guide, which can help you expand your thinking further[4]. You can find a link to this document on the book's companion web site.

If you are an ISV or systems integrator, it is likely you already have identified a number of the business process gaps and opportunities that exist in the industries you serve. This would give you a leg up in explaining to customers how ESA makes acquiring and managing solutions easier and more manageable than ever before.

Aligning the SAP Group with Enterprise Architecture Considerations

SOA and the other standards-based technology supported by ESA are not unique to SAP. More important, ESA has the potential to extend the SAP landscape beyond traditional SAP ERP and Business Suite applications to support end-to-end business processes.

This will raise a number of questions, and could lead to multiple approaches for tackling SOA within your enterprise. Regardless of whether you start with ESA as a foundation, or begin with another approach to SOA and need to integrate the services and capabilities SAP offers, it is important that your architectural decisions lead toward a common business blueprint and agreed-upon guidelines for technology realization. Because there is no single right way to accomplish this the key is to ensure active communication, and as you learn more about ESA, to be focused on the long-term architectural considerations that go well beyond the more tactical NetWeaver adoption activities.

Rationalizing Your IT Portfolio in Terms of True Cost/Benefit Options

Historically, organizations have made decisions around specific technologies and business application solutions on a case-by-case basis using feature and function comparisons. That seems like an obvious approach, yet it is also why most landscapes have become so complicated, adding in a lot of hidden expenses and reducing flexibility. When you begin to align your IT portfolio against the business value each application and technology product delivers, you can begin to weigh where resources are being applied in non-strategic ways, and, therefore, where ESA may offer benefits through consolidation.

The key with ESA is realizing an infrastructure that is well integrated, standardized, and consolidated has great business value. Hence, the goal is no longer to identify the best products in a vacuum, but rather the best platform and integrated set of business applications that meet your organization's needs.

As you evaluate the ESA strategy and the features that NetWeaver and the mySAP Business Suite applications offer, as well as those complementary solutions that come from SAP partners, it is valuable to take a hard ROI and TCO approach in making IT landscape decisions. Obviously, this does not necessarily mean SAP or its partners will always offer the right choice. It simply means the criteria by which you make decisions should be expanded to include business strategy and differentiation filters.

Summary

This chapter introduced ESA and illustrated how it represents a significant change in traditional SAP landscapes. ESA is, in fact, a major shift in strategy for SAP. While the company is still first and foremost a provider of business solutions, ESA represents a whole new underlying technology architecture for how SAP will deliver business applications. This, in turn, requires a change in thinking on the part of SAP customers, ISV partners, and systems integrators in terms of their own approach to adopting, extending, and maintaining SAP-based solutions.

Following are some key takeaways from this chapter:

- ESA is an architectural blueprint for the next generation of solutions from SAP. It is based on combining an SOA technical blueprint with a business-process blueprint from the company's solution maps.

- One of the major motivating factors for SAP is that SOA liberates business process logic from underlying IT applications so that they can be managed, monitored, and changed much more easily.

- ESA is not something you can buy. Its blueprints are realized through the NetWeaver technology platform, which is the foundation for mySAP ERP and other mySAP Business Suite applications.

- ESA itself is a large topic that spans business, technology, and product considerations. This leads to many misconceptions that prevent building a shared internal understanding about the importance of ESA, which is vital to successful adoption planning.

- Each enterprise's road map to ESA is unique, and there are many organizational factors that influence where and how to begin with ESA.

- ESA cuts across many functions and levels within both the business and IT organizations, and each role has a number of things to consider.

- The most important filter for evaluating the ESA strategy and the capabilities of NetWeaver and mySAP ERP is to take a true business-first approach to defining the potential benefits for your organization.

With this background in place, Chapter 2 examines the evolution taking place within the IT industry and how this led SAP to the ESA strategy.

References

1. Andrew Lawrence, "Re-Inventing SAP," *Infoconomy*, October 21, 2004.
2. Gartner RAS Core Research Note G00129507, David Mitchell Smith, Charles Abrams, Daniel Sholler, Daryl C. Plummer, Michele Cantara, July 12, 2005. Available at `http://mediaproducts.gartner.com/gc/webletter/microsoft4_enterprise/2005/article15/article15.html`.
3. Robert Westervelt, "SAP's new SOA strategy exposes challenges," Search-SAP.com, July 13, 2005. Available at `http://searchwebservices.techtarget.com/originalContent/0,289142,sid26_gci1107957,00.html?bucket=NEWS`.
4. "Enterprise Services Design Guide," 2005. Available at `www.sap.com/platform/netweaver/pdf/BWP_ES_Design_Guide.pdf`.

ESA in Context: The Emergence and Benefits of SAP's "Applistructure"

Chapter 1 introduced ESA and provided some background on why the evolution is so important to SAP's overall strategy. This chapter helps you understand ESA concepts by providing more details on changes taking place throughout the Information Technology (IT) industry. A danger for many professionals who have worked primarily with SAP technologies is viewing ESA in a vacuum. Many believe the approach is unique to SAP or merely an extension to existing SAP landscapes.

ESA represents a radical shift from the architecture of a traditional SAP R/3 landscape. While SAP's approach has many unique elements, ESA is completely consistent with the technology and business changes occurring in the offerings from most major IT vendors. In effect, SAP is moving the company's underlying infrastructure from its proprietary roots into a standards-based SOA technology platform. That change offers many benefits to SAP customers.

Knowing how and why SAP's approach to ESA came into being is important to understanding what SAP NetWeaver offers, and what changes will take place in applications like mySAP ERP. Think of this chapter as a key history lesson behind the evolution of application platforms, as well as in the marketplace for independent software vendors (ISVs) who sell solutions to enterprise IT customers. Interestingly enough, this story will affect you, regardless of how your organization chooses to move ahead with ESA, NetWeaver, or mySAP ERP because this story is about the inevitable collision between technology platforms and packaged business applications. It is about better equipping IT organizations to meet the needs of their business users. And it is about fixing what's broken in how ISVs themselves work together to serve the needs of their customers.

As a result of reading this chapter, you should be able to do the following:

- Understand how technology changes in the IT and packaged application marketplace affect you, regardless of how you move ahead with ESA

- Appreciate the business and technical motivations behind SAP's ESA strategy, and what problems are being addressed

- See how ESA brings together SOA with other IT innovations such as event-driven architecture (EDA), business process management (BPM), virtualization, and model-driven development

- Become familiar with the tug of war between "best of breed" components and application-platform suites

- Understand SAP's notion of an "applistructure" and the implications its capabilities will have on the future of your IT landscape, including the non-SAP applications you create or acquire from other software vendors.

Motivations for the New SAP Architecture

This section explains the basic direction of the IT industry up until the time SAP first announced ESA and NetWeaver. At that time, enterprise-packaged business application architectures, as you have traditionally known them, were about to become a dying breed. Or, as some industry pundits like to say, "That architecture is so last century." How can you be sure of this? Simply because every major packaged application vendor started to reinvent itself, or became an acquisition target of another organization that had the ability to embrace emerging technology platform-based architectures

None of this diminished a customer's need to have ERP, customer relationship management (CRM), supply chain management (SCM), supplier relationship management (SRM), or other business applications. What began to change is how these solutions were created, acquired, managed, and extended. Whether you come from the enterprise architecture side of the house, work more within packaged applications (such as those from SAP), or are part of an ISV selling application and infrastructure solutions, these changes will affect you in very important ways. The following sections describe the challenges new architectures such as ESA will address.

Overcoming the Problems with Packaged Applications

As mentioned in Chapter 1, the first problem with most packaged business applications such as R/3 had to do with the packaging itself. They typically did a good job of automating key business processes spanning ERP, CRM, SCM, SRM, and many more areas. However, they were built using last-generation (and often proprietary) technologies that made them costly to maintain and difficult to adapt to the unique needs of most enterprises. This led to three key issues, as described in the following sections.

High Costs of Customization and Maintenance

If your organization wanted to make a major shift in a key process, enter new markets, or realign its partnerships in ways that go outside the scope of what your packaged business applications intended, you essentially had two relatively expensive options:

- Perform customization inside your packaged applications to provide this new functionality
- Buy or build new applications that meet your needs, and then integrate everything

Often, a solution required a combination of both approaches. More important, the maintenance associated with managing these customization and integration points across multiple vendors became a big line item in many IT budgets. This maintenance is like an entitlement that is very difficult to reduce or eliminate.

It is interesting to note that packaged application vendors such as SAP traditionally tackled this issue by adding more and more features and functions to their products as a way to accommodate an ever-expanding set of business needs. This helped in some ways but, of course, it made the monolithic packages even more bloated and complicated from a software development, maintenance, and changeability perspective.

Difficulty in Addressing Processes That Span Functional Applications

The second major problem with packaged business applications is that they were usually architected to operate in closed silos. For example, CRM solutions managed the demand pipeline and customer service functions; SRM applications streamlined procurement; product lifecycle management products (PLM) sped up the introduction of new products; and ERP packages handled many of the internal operations and logistics for things such as finances and order-to-cash processing. Having multiple products worked great for optimizing standard processes inside each of these functional areas.

As Figure 2-1 highlights, the problem came when you expanded to managing key processes that crossed different functions and packaged applications. If you bought your packaged business applications from different vendors, you had a huge integration challenge to overcome. Even if you acquired them all from a single company such as SAP, there has historically been a lot of data integration and user interface development needed to have them seamlessly support processes across the entire enterprise value chain.

Slow Adoption of New Standards-Based Technologies

The third major issue with packaged business applications based on monolithic architectures involved getting the benefits of new technology innovations. If you wanted to leverage features such as Web and mobile user interfaces, portals, enterprise application integration (EAI), or process management tools, you were often at the mercy of your packaged business application vendors ability to provide these capabilities. Or, if you acquired these capabilities from other technology companies, then, at the very least, you needed your business applications vendors to integrate in some way with those products.

The more closed the architecture of your packaged business applications, the more difficult your challenge in leveraging the last decade's advances in middleware. Being a market leader with many generations of products based on the proprietary BASIS infrastructure made this especially tough on SAP customers. SAP did create bridges to platforms such as Java and .NET, as well as its own proprietary Web and portal-based development solutions, to help bridge this gap.

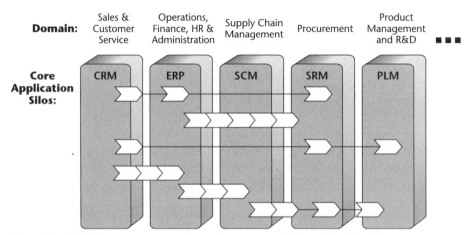

Figure 2-1: Business process requirements span multiple application silos.

Other SAP customers chose to sit still when it came to adopting new technologies. They decided to wait for SAP's own technical infrastructure to mature before using more standards-based Web, EAI, and portal solutions. Many others decided to pursue a "best of breed" strategy to implementing new technologies, as described in the next section.

Overcoming the Problems with "Best of Breed" Architectures

A "best of breed" approach to architecture simply involved picking the best product from a feature and function perspective to meet each need in your organization. This seemed to make a lot of sense at the time. If SAP offered the best manufacturing solution, Oracle had the ideal financial package, People-Soft met your HR needs perfectly, and Seibel had the most comprehensive CRM support, then why wouldn't you choose them? Of course, this is an oversimplification. But, generally speaking, business users who led selection processes for these types of business applications rarely wanted to accept something with less functionality.

Even if you had consolidated around one vendor such as SAP for packaged applications, the same "best of breed" proliferation often happened when picking technology solutions to surround your packaged business applications. The vendor with the best application server, development tools, business intelligence (BI) features, portal capabilities, or content management functions become an ideal choice for many customers addressing a specific project need.

Again, this just made sense at the time, especially since business solutions companies such as SAP were not pursuing a strategy to deliver leading edge middleware alternatives. As technology standards matured and new capabilities emerged, the market for third-party application development, integration, and Web-based technologies took off as a way to complement packaged solutions such as SAP R/3.

The Explosion of Middleware

There have been several major innovations in the IT industry since the mainframe became the center of the data-processing universe. The first revolution was client/server technology, which did many things that included shrinking development timelines, proliferating powerful user interfaces onto PCs, and further abstracting data from applications where it could become a shared asset. You also saw desktop applications such as Office and e-mail suites become the lifeblood for most users, further expanding the desktop's role and distributing information and automation.

Client/server technology also helped fuel the rapid growth of the packaged business applications market. SAP and many other companies carved out a big place in customer landscapes with silo solutions for ERP, CRM, SCM, and so on. These packaged applications triggered the explosion for enterprise application integration (EAI) and other middleware tools and technologies to help everything talk to each other. For many organizations, these business and integration packages now dominate the IT infrastructure.

Of course, Web technologies came along that allowed you to deliver UIs through ubiquitous browser-based technologies. They also enabled you to build applications that more easily extended to customers, partners, and remote employees. As a result, a whole new breed of languages and platforms such as Java 2 Enterprise Edition (J2EE) and .NET, and open source options such as LAMP (Linux + Apache + MySQL + PHP/PERL/Python) emerged as options well suited to enable enterprise Web applications.

All of this combined to fuel an explosion of specialty middleware products that really served as generic, standalone capabilities for things such as the following:

- Java and other types of Web application servers
- Workflow and rules engines
- Business intelligence (BI)
- Portals
- Messaging and integration brokers
- Knowledge and content management
- E-commerce and catalog management
- Mobile gateways and presentation servers for phones and PDAs
- Business Process Management (BPM)

Obviously, this is a vast oversimplification and leaves out a lot of other interesting technology details, including all the new infrastructure components being promoted along with SOA. The point is still clear. Distributed computing has made things a lot more complicated for IT. Worse still is that the right technology or product brought in to meet a business need at any point in time did not just disappear when the next best thing came along. Meeting today's business needs often meant bringing in what amounted to point solutions, whether you intended to or not. Many early Web and mobile projects were really the building of "tomorrow's legacy."

If you are a chief technology officer (CTO) or head of product development at a typical ISV, you face the same challenge from the other side. You are expected to develop products that can be dropped into these complicated IT environments where every customer might have different requirements, products, platforms, and integration points. You also need to proactively focus on evolving your products to support the next big technology standards that customers may demand. Even with standards, these innovations can cause havoc with product planning and release management.

A Cost and Complexity Treadmill

Figure 2-2 shows a very simplified version of a "spaghetti chart" IT landscape that typically resulted from implementing the last decade of "best of breed" middleware innovation and packaged business applications. Notice your cost drivers are spread across the following four main areas:

- Cost of buying or building business applications
- Cost of technology-enabling capabilities
- Cost of integrating everything together
- Cost of maintaining hardware and networking infrastructure

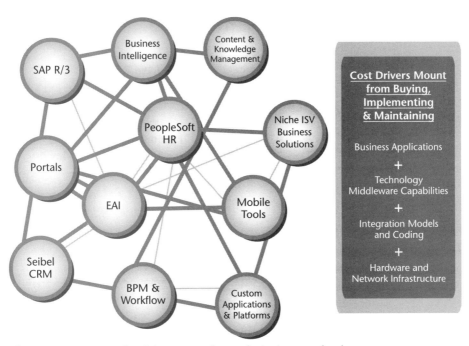

Figure 2-2: An example of the cost and complexity in many landscapes

If your organization tackled all of this rapid technology change, it's very likely that you have the makings of a management, maintenance, budget, responsiveness, or integration nightmare on your hands. Many organizations responded with cost-cutting measures through outsourcing. However, this rarely makes you more productive or responsive to the business in the long run. Outsourcing is a temporary fix, and only then if you have a very disciplined process for managing the outcomes around what you have handed off.

All of this became a treadmill because every innovation was designed to meet the business or technology opportunity *du jour*. Therefore, each piece became additive to the landscape, often without regard to how everything fit together. There was certainly no motivation or justification to change what already existed, unless it was broken. And, very few organizations could afford to really think through the architecture ramifications in conjunction with each project that required new technology. That's typically not how budgets work. The industry has reached the point where a "best of breed" approach to business applications, architecture, and infrastructure is no longer best for most organizations over the long haul.

The reason is all of this technology "progress" usually did not pay big dividends on either the financial statements or on IT's ability to support the business. This point has become a big motivator for SAP's ESA strategy, as explained further in the next section.

> **NOTE** There are many SAP R/3 customers who don't have these problems because they never implemented solutions for EAI, portals, content management, Web, or mobile application development, and so forth. The downside is these organizations are also not getting the benefits of these capabilities to support the business. If this fits your scenario, then ESA may offer the opportunity to add these capabilities to your IT landscape in a much more orderly and cost-effective way, based on business-driven priorities.

Overcoming the Problems with Managing the Business of IT

When Y2K passed and the Internet bubble burst, so, too, did the open IT checkbook many organizations enjoyed. Even those organizations that did a great job of managing all the technology themes of the last decade by adopting "best of breed" solutions still struggle with the complexity of everything in their portfolios. That was the first clue that something was fundamentally broken in the industry.

The Typical IT Report Card

There are very few organizations where the business people have to dream up things for the IT team to tackle because the latter is so effective, responsive, consistently under budget, and has eliminated their project backlogs. It would be nice if business leaders could come up with something new to say in the report card for the typical IT organization. Time and again research continues to show the following:

- Too much of the IT budget is spent on maintaining what already exists, and not enough is spent on strategic business innovation.

- The applications that do exist are not easily integrated or intuitive from an end user's perspective when they do their jobs.

- Packaged business applications offer little in terms of differentiation because competitors can implement the exact same solutions.

- IT often cannot respond fast enough to changing business needs and has trouble meeting deadlines and budget commitments.

These are very real problems. Without leadership inside of organizations, combined with innovation in the industry, this will not change.

Determining the Role of IT in Your Organization

There is another aspect to all of this that may or may not be relevant to your organization. Has anyone in your organization ever asked the question "Does IT matter?" This was the same title of a recent best-selling business book by Nicholas Carr.[1] Of course, the question created all kinds of hubbub among IT practitioners who rushed to defend the profession. Obviously, the question itself taken literally is ridiculous. IT definitely matters in the sense that you cannot run your business without it. Whenever business executives use this line, just tell them, "Okay, let's go unplug all the servers right now and send everybody home." IT does matter in the same way breathing matters. It is first and foremost a utility and a necessity.

What Carr really suggests, and what you should be asking yourself, is whether IT is strategic to your enterprise. A recent meeting with a CIO of a fast-growing, publicly traded company (that was scrambling to modernize its infrastructure) and the author highlighted this point. He was very clear that his job was about "blocking and tackling." In other words, he saw IT's purpose as being a well-run utility in his organization, but not a differentiator or competitive weapon. It was clear he was doing a great job in meeting that goal, and recently received a "CIO of the Year" award for his performance.

Many organizations see things the same way as this CIO. His company's success was based on product innovation, patents, and strong OEM distribution alliances. IT could certainly support these areas, primarily in terms of making the processes more efficient. Of course, there is nothing wrong *per se* with IT maximizing its role around an organization's efficiency of execution, if that is all that makes sense. SAP's approach to ESA has a lot to offer in this area.

On the other hand, there are many organizations in which IT is depended upon to support strategic differentiation. In these organizations, either the products and services are extremely information-centric and can themselves be digitized, or the enterprise has an intense focus on process excellence and agility as a competitive weapon. In the first case, technology-based analytics, integration, transactional execution, and distribution become key. In the second case, business leadership and IT leadership are united in continually looking for ways to reinvent value chains and use information to change how they interact with customers and suppliers.

All this suggests is that every organization must look at two areas. First is how *efficiently* its IT capability supports the business from a total cost and responsiveness perspective. In addition, those organizations that have strategic differentiation objectives where IT really does matter must also consider how *effective* IT performs. Of course, no ISVs would be in business unless they, too, supported one or both or these challenges for their customers.

How SAP's ESA Approach Helps Improve the Business of IT

What does the previous discussion have to do with ESA? It is quite simple. ESA's entire premise is based on improving both the efficiency and effectiveness of IT organizations. By moving SAP business applications to a standards-based distributed technology platform, the cost of maintenance and extensibility can come down dramatically from what was required to manage a typical R/3 landscape. More important, by re-crafting business solutions such as mySAP ERP around an SOA approach, the applications become less of a bottleneck to enabling real business change. Hence, the IT organization can support greater process innovation and more strategic initiatives.

ESA has a number of primary business objectives, including the following:

- Driving down the total cost of ownership (TCO) of maintaining complex distributed computing infrastructures

- Making application solutions and infrastructure components easier to change whenever the business needs dictate

- Making applications easy for people to use by having them support the way people work and their preferred tools and interfaces as opposed to users adapting to the applications

MEASURING THE EFFICIENCY AND EFFECTIVENESS OF IT

When SAP first launched its ESA initiative and the SAP NetWeaver platform, the company also announced measurable goals for tracking how the model would improve the efficiency and effectiveness of IT within its customer base. At that time, SAP illustrated a basic portfolio of IT costs and showed how overall total cost of ownership (TCO) could be reduced. In addition, a shift in the mix of expenses away from traditional maintenance and integration to more business innovation activities would illustrate the effectiveness aspect. The following figure illustrates the TCO objectives announced at that time.

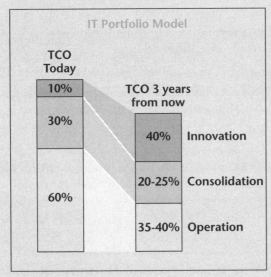

A summary of reducing TCO while increasing the portion of the portfolio spent on innovation (Source: © SAP AG, 2004–2006. All rights reserved.)

The company continues to measure progress toward this goal across its overall customer base. Of course, true TCO measures are unique to each customer organization and take into account a variety of factors specific to their landscape and business environment. SAP worked with the America's SAP Users' Group (ASUG) to develop initial benchmarks and an overall TCO/ROI analysis model that could be used by individual companies to measure their own results. This model covers a number of factors, including costs associated with the following:

◆ Initial investments in hardware and software

◆ Implementation

◆ Ongoing operations

◆ Upgrade and maintenance activities

◆ User experience and operations

(continued)

MEASURING THE EFFICIENCY AND EFFECTIVENESS OF IT *(continued)*

These models are extremely detailed and are available from SAP for both calculating TCO of the overall SAP and IT solution landscape, as well as measuring TCO and ROI associated with specific NetWeaver initiatives. More information can be found at the SAP Developer Network site at http://sdn.sap.com, or by contacting SAP.

- Expanding business intelligence to make information available where, when, and how users need it

- Aligning IT with the business by focusing on the common language of business processes and activities, especially in those organizations looking at IT as enabling strategic process differentiation

- Creating an ecosystem among SAP, ISVs, integrators, and customers in which all work together to tackle specific efficiency and effectiveness challenges in an industry

If you come from the IT side of the house, your challenge when it comes to ESA is to begin to think in terms of these overall business objectives. Regardless of how interesting the technology underneath ESA is, and no matter how much you like or don't like all the new SAP NetWeaver components or mySAP ERP features, try to balance things against what business people care about. This same type of thinking will be applied in future chapters as the adoption road map for ESA is reviewed.

NOTE If you are interested in only the technology side of things, you will quickly find there is much more to SAP's ESA-based strategy that is required to be successful. Just adopting the new technologies in SAP NetWeaver and diving into service-oriented integration alone goes only so far. Having a clear vision and set of business and architectural goals is fundamental to success with ESA.

All of this may sound obvious. But, in fact, it is still counterintuitive for many IT organizations because it means shifting away from the "best of breed" technology approach that created part of today's TCO problems. In other words, optimizing each technology decision on a project-by-project and capability-by-capability perspective led to a surprising result, where the total set of solutions was often less than optimal from a business perspective. It takes a new type of thinking to meet the goals for ESA listed earlier.

Getting back to the business of IT means changing how you manage your portfolio of technologies, tools, and vendors, and applying solid TCO and spending mix analysis to the SAP landscape and beyond. Peek again at Figure 2-2. That's the product-oriented perspective for achieving IT features and functions. Customers don't like it anymore. More important, the software industry itself can no longer sustain this model. So, where is the industry heading? The next section explores the latest trends that are reshaping both technology architectures and business applications.

Industry Consolidation and the Evolution to "Applistructures"

This chapter has made some important points thus far:

- Packaged applications such as SAP's Business Suite will no longer be built or sold in the way you have become accustomed.

- "Best of breed" applications and technology solutions have not proven to be the best answer for many organizations.

- Unless IT and ISV product-development teams begin to think more like their business counterparts, their ESA initiatives will be highly challenged, and are almost guaranteed to have minimal results.

Wayne Gretzky once said, "Go to where the puck is going, not where it has been" (actually, it was his father, Walter, who said this, but that is another story).[2] The only way to know where the puck is going in the IT industry is to ask a few simple questions. First, where is the investment capital heading? Where are the biggest, most influential, and cash-rich companies such as SAP, Microsoft, IBM, Oracle, Intel, and Cisco investing heavily? If you see a common trend, you can probably assume that amount of strategic research and development will influence the market. The related questions are whether their major partners and rivals are heading in the same direction, analysts are endorsing the trends, and, most important, customers are responding favorably through real adoption.

If you have been primarily focused on SAP landscapes and technologies during the last several years, you may not have closely tracked all of the broader industry trends in this area. Let's pick up the history lesson and see how it helps connect the dots relative to ESA.

Emergence of Application Platforms

As mentioned, most enterprises are awash with technology. The client/server and Internet eras led to a whole bunch of new types of infrastructure components that provided capabilities for building business solutions in new ways. Application servers, integration products, portals, data-analysis tools, mobile-deployment environments, and business process–management systems are just some of the examples of these new tools.

With every new category of technology dozens of companies sprout up offering specialized products to meet these needs. ISVs rush to be first to market with a particular feature, and work very hard to gain analyst notoriety as the "best of breed" solution in a particular category. Early adopter customers, in turn, buy these solutions because they have specific business needs requiring a product in that category.

The Benefits of an Application Platform

This proliferation of solutions is always followed by an inevitable round of marketplace consolidation, and that's where things have stabilized today. However, a funny thing has happened this time around on the technology side. The first wave of consolidations left a few "best of breed" vendors standing in each category. There is nothing unusual there. The unique development was that the largest software vendors began to see the advantage of integrating all of these components into a single application development and integration technology infrastructure platform. For the sake of brevity, these will be referred to as *application platforms*, not to be confused with the hardware and operating system connotation associated with the word "platforms."

In essence, this is the same portfolio theory discussed previously. The value of the components working well together is greater (and the TCO lower) than the sum of the individual parts. For example, you might want to develop a business-process solution that runs on an application server, requires a workflow engine, is deployed through a portal, leverages BI information, and shares data with suppliers, customers, and your workforce.

Dealing with a different "best of breed" product for each of these needs is unwieldy, no matter how good they are. It also forces you to build competencies across several niche products, and to deal with the nightmare of upgrade interdependencies. The large ISVs tackling the challenge of building out application platform suites worked consolidate common features of each component into a unified set of interdependent solutions. Figure 2-3 shows the main capabilities of a typical, integrated application platform suite.

Interestingly, the same advantage that accrues to customers is realized by these large ISVs themselves. They can create new products such as a business-process management engine using their application servers, messaging engines, integration brokers, data analytics tools, and portal user-interface technologies. Likewise, other ISVs who create business solutions can build their products around these platforms without having to worry about implementing all of this lower-level technology code.

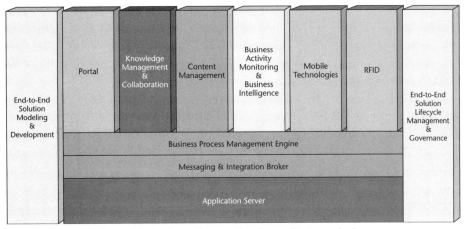

Figure 2-3: Typical capabilities brought together in application platforms

Vendors who sell these application platforms do not necessarily offer the best version of all the components. But, when their breadth of functionality works together well, it becomes a real advantage to customers. The technology vendors most known for initially tackling platform suites include IBM and BEA on the Java side, and Microsoft has its own equivalents with its .NET platform and server products. What's interesting is that SAP now offers a complete set of application and integration platform functionality in NetWeaver. Chapter 3 looks inside the details of the SAP NetWeaver application platform.

NOTE Among other things, SAP NetWeaver offers a complete, standards-based application, integration, and composition platform similar to other market offerings. As you will see, this is a foundational capability needed to deliver on the promise of ESA.

Marketplace Requirements for Platforms

For application platforms to be successful, three things had to happen. First, better alignment of all the parts was an absolute must. Each application platform vendor is moving down the path of better integrating what used to be individual products and technology components (sometimes acquired from other companies) into their suites. Clearly, SAP is following this pattern with NetWeaver. The company is combining existing components, new technologies, and some acquired capabilities in areas like master data management into a unified platform.

Second, the features of the individual capabilities must reach a "good enough" status relative to the "best of breed" solutions. As soon as customers are sure they can rely on them to meet business needs, adoption takes off. The same is true for all the developer tooling that enables you to use the platforms to create and configure solutions.

Finally, the platforms themselves needed to force the commoditization of each segment of the "best of breed" tools. Once a solution is commoditized, customers are more likely to see the advantage of getting that functionality from one of these application platforms, paying only an incremental amount for the feature, and saving money by dropping the "best of breed" components and one-off vendors from their landscapes.

The best example of this is in the area of application integration. When proprietary EAI tools first emerged, vendors were able to charge huge premiums for these solutions because "best of breed" was really the only option for this new style of integration. Now that many standards and features for integration have been made part of application servers and the value-added solutions sitting on top of them, the cost of EAI capabilities has come down dramatically. Likewise the need for proprietary skills has been significantly reduced.

This last requirement could be met only through the emergence of industry standards around each of the components. Hence, the largest software vendors in the world have pushed hard to drive standards such as Web Services for integration, Java Specifications Request (JSR) 168 and Web Services for Remote Portlets (WSRP) for portals, Business Process Execution Language (BPEL) for business process orchestration, Extensible Stylesheet Language Transformations (XSLT) for data transformations, and so forth. Obviously, this just scratches the surface of the many standards available today in order to illustrate the point. Chapters 5 will cover relevant ESA and SAP NetWeaver standards in more depth. Just recognize that there is unprecedented cooperation among the major industry software vendors to define and proliferate the standards that will ensure the success of application platforms, as well as SOA in general.

Note that having an application platform does not preclude you from also adopting "best of breed" solutions for individual components where they make sense for your organization. In fact, these "best of breed" solutions will likely be very interoperable with the rest of your platform because of the evolution of standards. The key is figuring out if you have business requirements where "best of breed" really does make business sense. Chapter 4 describes how SAP is working with other ISVs to enable more solutions to complement the NetWeaver platform.

Maturity of Packaged Business Applications

A similar pattern unfolded in the business applications space where large ISVs such as SAP began to build more integrated solution suites spanning CRM, SCM, SRM, and specialized industry-based ERP systems. Before technical standards existed, an ISV had to create its own version of the underlying application platform technologies as a foundation for its business solution. Obviously, SAP created the entire backbone for its R/3 ERP solution around the BASIS platform and the ABAP language.

As the Internet era came, SAP and other large-packaged application vendors began to acquire or build their own point solutions for Web applications, portals, mobile development, integration options, and so forth. These tools certainly helped meet certain business needs. They did not, however, always support the latest standards, offer the best development tooling, or provide the advantages of an integrated technology application platform.

Today, all but the largest ISVs have ported their solutions to run on market-leading application platforms based on Java or .NET. In fact, standards-based application platforms reduced the barriers to entry and development for many ISVs who no longer had to worry about low-level code. They could simply adhere to the application platform standards and focus more on business features and applications needed by their customers.

As more and more business applications were written on standards-based application platforms, two benefits became clear. First, interoperability was greatly improved. Second, it was much easier to leverage newer technologies such as the Web to improve usability and distribution of the application functions. More and more customers began to demand packaged business solutions that accomplish the following:

- Solve their unique business problems
- Talk with everything else in their landscape through standards, including business applications from other ISVs
- Leverage the features of modern application platform technologies
- Be easily adapted to the unique needs of the customer by using standards

For a packaged application vendor such as SAP, enabling this required both technology change and a significant shift in how business was conducted with customers and partners. If you are familiar with the concepts behind SOA, these goals will sound familiar. Customers were looking for a mainstream technology model that allows all of this to occur. The next section will introduce SOA as a disruptive technology to both packaged business applications and application platform technologies.

Enter SOA as a Disruptive Technology

SOA has become the dominant technology theme of this decade. Every major IT vendor is working on standards in support of SOA-based computing models, and billions of dollars in research and development investments are being made to mature SOA-based solutions. Obviously, SOA is at the cornerstone of SAP's ESA plans and Chapter 5 describes the key technologies behind SOA and Web Services. For now, all that's important is to understand the "big idea" behind SOA.

In its most basic sense, SOA is an architectural pattern based on breaking apart applications into smaller pieces of functionality that have standards-based interfaces. You can then reuse and re-assemble these building blocks into applications for business people to use by invoking the pieces in sequence. Figure 2-4 provides a basic illustration of the idea. While this does not sound like much, it really is a big deal. Enabling SOA is the foundation of changing the major characteristics of how application platforms work, and business solutions are implemented. Obviously, there is much more to SOA than this, but if you recognize a few key points, the changes brought about by ESA become clearer.

■ Business applications no longer must exist as single, precompiled units. They can be composed from these building blocks in whatever unique manner the business process dictates. More important, you can also reuse these building blocks across processes and applications, which saves money and eases maintenance.

■ A bunch of integrated technology standards and infrastructure will be required to effectively support SOA in an industry-wide manner. That's where the evolving set of Web Services specifications come in. Web Services are bringing about a series of technology protocol–based standards that enable SOA to become ubiquitous. Once these standards mature, this approach will help ensure that your business applications can be integrated and changed much more easily.

■ SOA will work best when overlaid with a business architecture that drives what goes into the building blocks in the first place. Organizations that tackle this challenge will have made great strides in better aligning their business processes with their IT implementations, as well as realizing greater reuse benefits.

The fact that SOA is so important to implementing the next generation of business applications explains why SAP has taken a leadership role on many of the related standards bodies. The result will be new business solutions from SAP built on the same SOA technologies and application platform capabilities that all major vendors are working to support.

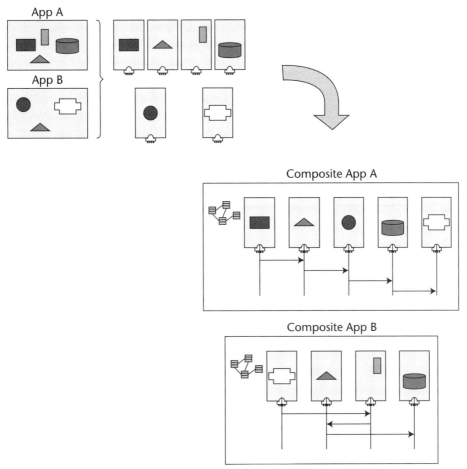

Figure 2-4: Breaking applications into services for assembling composite applications

Business Applications and Platforms Coexist

For a while, the vendors of application platforms and packaged business applications worked together well. As mentioned, smaller ISVs could build on top of leading application platform technologies. Meanwhile, market alliances helped larger packaged-application vendors. For example, SAP and Web-Methods worked together to create an integration solution called Business Connector as a way to integrate with non-SAP applications using XML and Web technologies. It also became easier to extend SAP applications to the Web using Java and .NET technologies without having to learn all the details of proprietary SAP components such as Internet Transaction Service (ITS) and Business Server Pages (BSPs).

This dating period between application platforms and business applications went very well. The question then became what would happen if major business applications such as SAP's Business Suite were re-architected to natively take advantage of all the features in an application platform.

Part of the validation for this architecture came from watching niche vendors release new applications that took this approach. And, as the application platforms evolved to support SOA and Web Services, all the pieces were in place to radically change the marketplace for packaged business solutions.

"Applistructures": Business Applications and Platforms Unite

It is time to bring the history lesson up to date by exploring how all of this has played out in the marketplace, and what the road ahead looks like. Figure 2-5 is a very basic illustration of how ISVs can be categorized in light of this round of consolidations. Having presented this road map with many companies, there are three things you should consider:

- This is meant to be a simple example of a very important point. Focus on the big picture and try not to get hung up on which companies are or are not listed and, for the most part, where any specific company is shown. This is not a feature analysis or ranking diagram.

- The diagram reflects how the marketplace looked at the time SAP first announced the ESA strategy. Seeing how things have evolved reinforces where the market is heading and validates SAP's ESA model. For example, all the companies that are crossed out have since been acquired by other vendors.

- Companies are positioned based on the assets they have in their portfolio, and the strategic road maps they have announced. None of them has fully implemented its entire road map as of yet.

The ISVs in Figure 2-5 are positioned based on two categories. The first is how complete of an application platform they offer based on the components listed in Figure 2-3. It's a simple dividing line in that some ISVs are building multiple application platform components into their suite of products. Others are essentially offering a "best of breed" implementation of a subset of capabilities.

The second dimension is the completeness of business-application functionality and content offered in the ISVs' product suites. This means horizontal and vertical solutions for ERP, CRM, SRM, SCM, and so on. Some companies such as SAP offer products that span the entire business value chain. Others offer solutions for a subset of functions or processes, perhaps to a limited number of vertical markets. The following sections offer some quick observations about what is taking place.

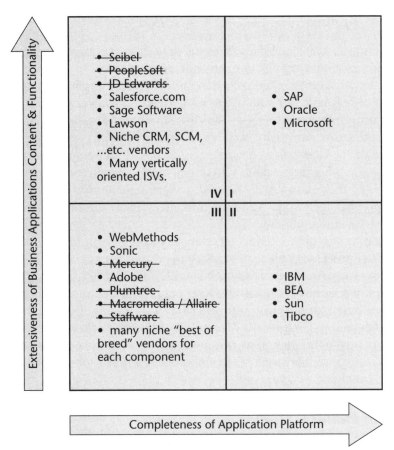

Figure 2-5: The emergence of "applistructure" vendors

"Best of Breed" Technology Market Shrinks

Quadrant III in Figure 2-5 is clearly a very lonely place to be for a large-cap enterprise technology vendor. Point technology solutions that aren't highly "vertical-ized" have been the most challenged and consolidated the fastest. As these solutions become standardized and part of integrated application platforms, it is hard to justify them in your landscape on an ongoing basis, unless you can truly manage to a "best of breed" strategy. Even then, there are often powerful open source solutions that themselves can compete with commercial "best of breed" offerings. There are still dozens of niche players spread across the various platform components and, of course, there has been a spike of new players in this quadrant selling SOA-based "best of breed" technology solutions. However, the cycle continues, and you will see more of these companies be consolidated.

"Best of Breed" Applications Market Consolidates

Quadrant IV in Figure 2-5 is also lonely in terms of large-cap players. Companies with a single business application are not as interesting to enterprise customers as ones with an integrated suite of solutions. Every application vendor must decide how it will compete in an SOA world. The survivors in this quadrant are mainly ISVs who focus on serving small and mid-sized enterprises by competing on simplicity and price. An interesting question is whether the idea of "software as a service" (SAAS) based on new standards-based architectures and hosting models will offer a new value proposition that allows more ISVs in this quadrant to flourish in terms of serving large customers with broad packaged application functionality. This is certainly an area for customers to track and evaluate.

There is also a place for small ISVs who offer very specific solutions tied to a complex business process or vertical industry need that is not met by large packaged vendors such as SAP. These ISVs will find that ESA and SAP NetWeaver offer a whole new opportunity to expand their business that was not available previously. Opportunities for these ISVs to align with the SAP's strategy will be covered in Chapter 4's discussion of the SAP ecosystem. SAP customers are already validating that the greater the relationship between another ISV's solution and relevant SAP Business Suite applications, the more likely they are to buy from that vendor.

The Application Platform Market

Quadrant II in Figure 2-5 represents the application and integration platform vendors that were described previously. They are focused on becoming the foundation of an organization's application development, integration, and SOA infrastructure. These companies will continue to acquire or commoditize companies in Quadrant III as a way of life to round out their portfolios or increase market share. They will also continue to be important vendors to those organizations that select their platform as an enterprise standard.

The big challenge faced by these vendors is to create the SOA platform and set of business-process management technologies of choice for their customers. In addition, vendors in Quadrant II will be looking to define a business-content strategy through a combination of acquisitions, alliances, and internal development to compete with the few vendors in Quadrant I. IBM is perhaps the most interesting player because it is using its strong consulting arm to help define SOA-based application content for its platform infrastructure. For SAP customers, the long-term question is whether to augment your SAP landscape with these platforms, or to consolidate around the new capabilities in SAP NetWeaver. Future chapters will look at some guidelines for making this decision.

The "Applistructure" Market

Quadrants II, III, or IV in Figure 2-5 are essentially the evolution of the industry from the last decade naturally unfolding. SOA and business-process management technologies will certainly shake up individual companies within these quadrants, with those figuring out the right business model obviously having the greatest success. Expect companies to continue to move around through consolidations. Of course, many more "best of breed" and open source solutions could be placed throughout the quadrants as well.

The most significant innovation and change is taking place in Quadrant I. Here is where the marriage between application platforms and business applications is occurring. Figure 2-6 illustrates the basic notion of an "applistructure." The convergence of technology infrastructure, application platforms, and business solutions represents a completely new technology architecture.

Only a few organizations have the potential to amass a product portfolio that encompasses both full-featured application and integration platforms, as well as a portfolio of business content and solutions that span multiple aspects of the value chain. All of these companies have work ahead to fully weave together their platforms with their applications. Each will take a slightly different tact with different timelines based on their roots and current market position.

It's worth noting that, for the time being, Microsoft and SAP are acting far more like partners than competitors in this marketplace evolution. As Microsoft CEO Steve Ballmer recently stated:

> *In large enterprises, there were sort of two basic choices: partner with SAP or compete with SAP . . . We decided we had so much to do and so many ideas and our plate was pretty full with consolidating everything else, that it made a lot of sense to partner.[3]*

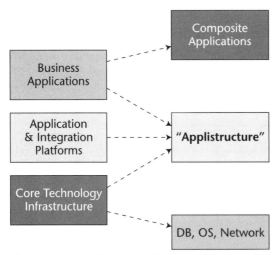

Figure 2-6: "Applistructures" merge all layers of the technology stack.

In fact, this partnership is translating into major innovations for ESA and NetWeaver, whereby the companies are working on a number of research and development projects together. The most significant is Duet, which unites SAP's business processes and structured information with Microsoft Office's widely adopted tools. This alliance will allow knowledge workers to interact with SAP directly from the context of Office applications such as Excel and Outlook. More details on this partnership will be described in Chapter 4.

It's also worth noting that Seibel, PeopleSoft, and IBM saw a similar need to blend business applications and platforms using SOA technologies. For example, all three made significant investments for IBM's WebSphere to become an equivalent of the NetWeaver platform supporting the Seibel and PeopleSoft business solutions. Beyond the technology, Seibel and PeopleSoft also realized an industry transformation to "applistructures" would have a big impact on their overall business models. The end result was both companies being acquired by Oracle. Consider this further validation that SOA is hugely disruptive to the industry, and the combination of end-to-end application platforms and business application suites has been fully embraced by all the market leaders.

It's also a reminder that that SAP is the only company in Quadrant I that grew from a business solutions perspective first, and then built the technology platform to support the strategy. This is why SAP's strategy for ESA is unique from similar SOA-based offerings in terms of having a content-based blueprint for SOA. The features, advantages, and benefits of an "applistructure" will be covered in the next section. For now, just note that understanding this market evolution truly is vital background to understanding ESA and putting it into a larger industry perspective.

Many people describe ESA as a "repackaging of old SAP products," or nothing more than a "marketing fad." Once they see it in the context of a standards-based industry movement, they open up to how different ESA really is for SAP. More important, all vendors are heading down similar paths as a result of SOA. Seeing ESA beyond the traditional perspective of SAP landscapes and products is key to successful adoption and overall IT planning. In effect, the basis of enterprise competition shifts to combining a technology platform with the greatest amount of business content to support enterprise solutions.

The Capabilities of the SAP ESA "Applistructure"

As SAP customers plot their migration to an ESA-based "applistructure" blueprint, it is important to be able to articulate the characteristics of this new model and what benefits it provides. The following sections discuss some of the major features and benefits of SAP's ESA-based "applistructure."

The "Applistructure" Impact on SAP's Business Applications

Just implementing mySAP ERP and other Business Suite solutions on top of an application platform such as SAP NetWeaver makes the applications themselves much better. Your organization can get a lot of value even if you don't use any of the advanced technology capabilities or SOA features in the platform elsewhere. This is because the SAP business applications themselves can leverage the platform capabilities. For example:

- It's easier for SAP to bring its core business solutions to market faster in a way that allows for more incremental upgrades and activation of features you want, when you want them.

- New business solutions can be brought to market outside of the monolithic applications as packaged composites.

- User interfaces are greatly improved, including native Web and portal solutions, as well as options to leverage forms, Microsoft Office, and mobile devices. SAP has also previewed potential replacements to the SAP GUI that uses the same underlying application functionality, but is much richer and simpler to use.

- Data and process integration across the mySAP Business Suite is improved "out-of-the-box," and pre-built integration content is provided for connecting to external applications based on industry standards.

- The applications work natively with the SAP BI, collaboration, and knowledge management capabilities to provide more valuable information to users when and where they need it.

These are just a few of the many improvements in mySAP ERP and other Business Suite applications that occur simply because they are now written to take advantage of the features in the NetWeaver application platform.

The "Applistructure" Impact on SAP's Technology Platform

Obviously, going from a BASIS environment supporting R/3 to a complete SAP NetWeaver implementation supporting mySAP ERP brings about change in your infrastructure. The good news is there are many new things you can do with SAP NetWeaver capabilities, especially if you do not already have alternative middleware solutions in your landscape. Once you have the NetWeaver platform and skills in place, you can take advantage of the following:

- Use of Web technologies, a role-based portal, and Single-Sign On (SSO) capabilities to deliver custom and non-SAP purchased packaged applications

- Brokered Web Service interfaces and easier Java and .NET integration tools to SAP BAPIs, effectively making the business applications more open at the edges

- A full set of standards-based EAI and business process orchestration capabilities for integrating SAP and non-SAP applications

- Knowledge management, content management, and search infrastructure for managing semi-structured and unstructured information inside and outside of SAP

- Standards-based business analytics, reporting, and alerting capabilities for SAP and non-SAP data

- Data consolidation and master data management tools and templates

- Advanced application development and composition capabilities in both Java and ABAP for tailoring SAP applications, or for developing new application solutions

The most important point is that because the NetWeaver platform is part of an "applistructure," you get large amounts of pre-defined business content, templates, and scenarios loaded into the standard application platform. This is a big distinction from acquiring technology platform products from vendors who don't also offer business applications like SAP.

Emerging SOA Capabilities Supporting SAP's "Applistructure"

As mentioned, you get the "applistructure" advantages of improved SAP Business Suite Applications and technology infrastructure, even without leveraging any advanced SOA capabilities. In effect, these combine to overcome many of the problems with packaged business applications and "best of breed" architectures described earlier in the chapter. However, if you want to address the issues associated with aligning IT with business objectives, then more capabilities are required in an "applistructure."

Figure 2-7 illustrates the primary new SOA-based technical capabilities that are at the heart of the next-generation SAP "applistructure." These concepts have been the focus of IT innovations for many years.

The degree to which the IT industry has worked to evolve SOA standards is helping align and enable these features. Today, SAP is the clear leader in bringing to market a complete suite of packaged business applications (combined with a technology platform) that leverages many of these capabilities. Hence, it is hard to compare SAP's approach with the offerings from other vendors. The real test will be the way in which all the application platform and "applistructure" vendors (including SAP) continue to implement, integrate, and mature the following capabilities.

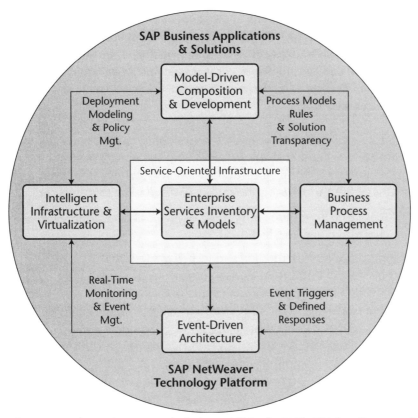

Figure 2-7: The major new technical capabilities in SAP's ESA "applistructure" (Source: © 2006, MomentumSI, Inc. All rights reserved.)

Enterprise Services Inventory

An SOA is only as good as what it contains. SOA-based platforms without meaningful services are about as good as an empty glass is at quenching your thirst. Through ESA, customers will receive an inventory of services and supporting models that come "out of the box" from SAP as part of the "applistructure."

This library of services includes fine-grained business-logic definitions, as well as more coarse-grained process models. These business-oriented services are augmented by a number of technology-enabling services (such as logging, security, and transaction management).

NOTE One of the most difficult parts of SOA adoption is creating meaningful services that can be reused. With ESA, SAP offers a library of business-driven service and process models to help kickstart your inventory. They can also guide the process of adding your own services by demonstrating tangible service models and designs as a reference. Chapter 5 takes a closer look at this Enterprise Services Inventory.

This large basket of pre-defined services is valuable in many ways. In addition, ecosystem partners and customers can extend the library with their own services. This adds to the overall value of the inventory, which, in turn, adds to the overall value of SOA to your organization. Consider the following:

- SAP business functionality is now more open and easier to integrate with at a both a logical and technical level.

- Leveraging useful out-of-the-box services provided by SAP implies that you do not have to build that service yourself from scratch. These services are available for reuse and extension across a number of applications, which translates into real ROI for development and maintenance.

- The SAP portfolio of services gives you a great starting point for defining your own unique services inventory to best support your organization. Consider it a nice reference model for business functions represented as coarse-grained services which are, in turn, implemented and supported by underlying fine-grained services.

- The sharing of common business services across applications from SAP, other ISVs, and the ones you build internally, enables customers to consistently apply business rules and non-functional requirements across the enterprise. Think of it as a basis for improving aspects of your governance model.

Service-Oriented Infrastructure

Of course, the implementation of ESA solutions and management of the SAP Enterprise Services Inventory requires a service-oriented infrastructure (SOI). The goal is to make the integrity of the new environment as robust and reliable as the monolithic applications being replaced. In fact, delivering that level of reliability will be one of the greatest challenges for SAP and other vendors in migrating to SOA. SAP NetWeaver implements SOI capabilities that include the following:

- Registries and repositories to organize and publish services. Think of this as a catalog or Yellow Pages to encourage proper awareness and usage of the services.

- Invoking SOA-based interfaces to mySAP Business Suite applications, as well as future packaged solutions from SAP in a managed way.

- Creating, publishing, or consuming services from non-SAP applications you purchase or develop internally in a managed way.

- Providing the run-time management, execution, reliability, and policy enforcement capabilities for SOA-based solutions and composite applications running on SAP NetWeaver.

These service-oriented capabilities of the "applistructure" are a key enabler of the more advanced platform capabilities.

Model-Driven Composition and Development

One of the main benefits of ESA is the shift away from coding to modeling. This offers a number of advantages, such as the following:

- Reducing the time it takes to implement or change business solutions and increasing reuse

- Providing transparency into the intent of an application or process design

- Improving run-time monitoring capabilities by tying execution information to the solution model metadata

- Shifting certain process configuration and UI definition options to business analysts and end users who can then directly tailor their environment to improve functionality

SAP enables the model-driven capabilities through several design and development features of SAP NetWeaver. The company offers modeling options for processes, applications, integration, user-interface design, and many other areas. Chapter 10 provides an introduction to the many modeling tools in the platform.

Business Process Management

The BPM capabilities of SAP's "applistructure" extract process logic from the underlying application code and allow manipulation through modeling or creation of composite applications. This offers a number of advantages, including the following:

- Process implementation visibility through models

- Effective automation and coordination of online and offline tasks, workflows, and cross-application processes

- Process execution visibility through run-time monitoring

- Analysis of process execution metrics for simulation and optimization
- Real-time business performance management, scorecards, and dashboards based on key process metrics

Chapter 6 provides more details on the BPM capabilities of the SAP NetWeaver platform and their role in the "applistructure."

Event-Driven Architecture

A key enabler of SAP's BPM capabilities is the Event-Driven Architecture (EDA) functions of the "applistructure." EDA provides features such as the following:

- Automatically capturing and responding to events happening at any level of the "applistructure" (business applications, application platform, or infrastructure)
- Allowing unique response at the transaction or activity level based on economic values, customer service indicators, key performance indicator (KPI) thresholds, or other metrics
- Managing the rules for event processing
- Improving capacity to honor service level agreements (SLAs)

As the platform and supporting hardware and network continue to evolve, more advanced event detection and processing will be enabled.

Intelligent Infrastructure and Virtualization

One of the big ideas behind a standards-based SOA is that everything is integrated at the network protocol level instead of via application APIs or data and messaging systems–based interchanges. This will change in a significant way how you think about business applications. Supporting EDA capabilities and SOA-based loose-coupling of solutions requires changes at the infrastructure level. SAP is working with a number of hardware and networking partners to make this part of its "applistructure" more intelligent by doing the following:

- Logically separating solution architectures from physical deployment
- Implementing application-aware networks that can monitor the business context of messages for both economic impact and real-time governance to apply rules "on the fly"
- Moving certain transaction-processing capabilities into hardware layers where performance is much greater to lower TCO, or to enable capabilities that were not feasible because of performance bottlenecks

The area of intelligent, application-aware networks and devices is another aspect of the "applistructure" that you can expect will evolve and change greatly as SOA and related standards mature.

The Value of SAP's ESA "Applistructure"

All the capabilities mentioned earlier are part of SAP's ESA "applistructure." This means NetWeaver supports them through SAP and partner implementations. As mentioned, all of these areas will continue to evolve in more integrated ways as the platform and SOA standards mature, and overall IT industry innovation continues. More important, the mySAP Business Suite and other future applications from SAP and partners will be able to further leverage these emerging capabilities as part of their architecture and design. All of this translates into a number of meaningful advantages.

Figure 2-8 illustrates the business benefits that come from adopting and evolving these SOA-based features of SAP's ESA "applistructure." It's worth noting that success with ESA capabilities such as these does not occur overnight and requires a lot more than just product implementations. Chapter 8 explains more about the process of ESA adoption based on the SAP "applistructure." It is also worth noting that each of the benefits described here reinforces the others. The result is a multiplier effect in terms of value.

Business Alignment Through Process Visibility and Flexibility

ESA helps bridge IT with business goals by improving process visibility and flexibility. Many of these benefits come from the BPM features in the platform as defined previously.

One of SAP's goals for NetWeaver tools within the "applistructure" is to enable the modeling of processes from high-level solution maps, through individual activity steps, all the way down to the real-world implementation components and service interfaces that provide the implementation. If SAP is successful in aligning all of these models, it will make it very clear how a process is implemented on an end-to-end basis. More important, you can better define what the TCO really is for process automation and management within your landscape relative to the strategic value chain activities being supported. This means no more guessing about how processes work, what they cost in IT, or what's needed to change them. Your business model and the execution model of a process have the potential to become one.

For now, there are still gaps between the various levels of process models in NetWeaver, just as there are in the model-driven design capabilities offered by all IT vendors. Even so, your ability to manage the alignment of process is better with the "applistructure" capabilities.

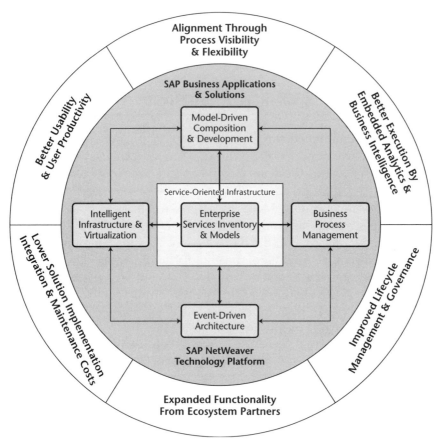

Figure 2-8: The benefits of SOA-based capabilities in the SAP "applistructure" (Source: ©
2006, MomentumSI, Inc. All rights reserved.)

From a higher-level perspective, the SAP "applistructure" improves IT's
ability to support the business by doing the following:

- Providing a platform where processes are intended to be analyzed,
  changed, and extended with models. This reduces the need to bend
  your business to accommodate the SAP-packaged applications, a
  common complaint of earlier packaged solutions.

- Greatly reducing the time to define and implement process changes and
  new applications in IT. The means strategy changes can be realized
  faster, and more tactical projects can see improved ROI. In many cases,
  business requirements that could not be met cost-effectively with earlier
  architectures can now be delivered.

- Providing more options for accessing and analyzing information, configuring processes, and automating certain tasks can be performed by
  business analysts and end users themselves.

- Allowing process analytics and dashboards to provide more timely tracking of strategic KPIs, and better insights into process bottlenecks or high-ROI improvement opportunities.

Chapters 7 and 8 further examine the more strategic aspects of business alignment. This includes describing how SAP's approach to ESA helps encourage managing IT investments and maintenance from a business-value perspective, as opposed to focusing on technical capabilities and costs.

Better Usability and User Productivity

Of all the areas where IT has historically been constrained, enabling user productivity has probably been the most widespread. The main reason is that UIs are almost always tightly coupled with individual applications. And in SAP's case, applications such as R/3 were not known for offering rich, user-friendly interfaces.

The goal of user productivity in the "applistructure" is to put your users first in the context of the processes they perform and the tools they like to work with. Instead of UIs that are simply "heads" on top of functional applications, you can deliver interfaces that seamlessly cut across all types of applications to give your users the data and tools they need, when they need them, all in the context of executing their work. This also means that, instead of restricting users to an SAP GUI or specific application interface you create, UIs can easily be delivered through whatever tools, devices, and formats your users most prefer.

Following are some of the features of the NetWeaver platform that enable greater user productivity:

- Role-based UIs that personalize the presentation formats and information displayed to the needs of your users

- SSO support within integrated UIs, eliminating the need for "swivel chair" integration and multiple login steps

- Process and workflow guidance to systematically lead your users through the process steps they perform, managing their work lists, and alerting them to priority items

- The ability for users themselves to trigger and manage ad hoc workflows and collaboration handoffs

- User-driven alerting to ensure rapid response to critical business events, as well as improved management by exception

- Information and application access available directly from productivity tools such as a user's e-mail system or Microsoft Office, as well as mobile devices including phones and PDAs

- Collaboration rooms and knowledge management repositories for facilitating joint work activities and sharing rich, unstructured information

- Digital forms that are controlled, routed, stored, and directly trigger
  events in applications based on the data within them

As mentioned, mySAP ERP and other Business Suite applications will leverage these technologies. More important, solutions you build or those offered
by other ISVs can leverage the same seamless UI capabilities within the platform. All of this adds up to a more consistent and productive user experience
in terms of process execution.

Better Process Execution Through Embedded Analytics

Information is a critical part of every business process. Typically, standalone
applications that are separate from the day-to-day transaction systems provide
the analysis and reporting functions. This requires users to perform lots of
manual integration, along with frequent switching between different systems
and reports. It can also lead to lots of phone calls and e-mails from those need-
ing information about other functions that actually have the access to the
required data.

Specialized analytics systems rarely contain the most current transaction
data. Sometimes this time delay translates into inaccuracies or process latency.
At the very least, users must rely on specialized tools with their own UIs and
access methods. This means they cannot be assured of getting information
when and where they want it, in the format they desire, using the devices and
applications that they are most comfortable with.

SAP has used the term *embedded analytics,* whereby analytics and reporting
features can now be included seamlessly within the context of any business
application, as opposed to existing in separate reports, dashboards, and offline
tools. These features, when made part of the "applistructure," allow every
business solution to leverage the following features:

- Information needed to answer questions or make a decision during the
  execution of a process is available directly in the context of the UI controlling the process without requiring toggling to other sources.

- Consistent, trusted master data and timely transactional data is readily
  available to support any process.

- Processes themselves are monitored and analyzed to identify performance and simulate the ROI of possible changes.

- Standard management reporting and dashboards to track process KPIs
  are embedded in a user's application interface of choice.

- Perpetual analysis of process data for exceeding thresholds or the
  occurrence of material events can trigger proper alerts or other events.

In short, analytics and reports become much more timely and useful when the information is presented in context with the work being performed. In addition, automated analytics can draw users to places that need attention, enabling more productive "management by exception" to occur. Chapter 15 will take a closer look at the concept of embedded analytics and how this is realized in SAP NetWeaver.

Improved Lifecycle Management and Governance

Lifecycle management deals with the complete, end-to-end management of an application solution. This implies both a top-down approach in terms of managing the application as whole and in terms of the business process model it supports, as well as the more detailed management of individual hardware and software components used to realize the solution. Specific ESA-based "applistructure" features that support lifecycle management include the following:

- Model-driven repository for inventorying all the elements of your IT landscape

- Solution modeling that tracks the logical solution definition and maps it to individual hardware and software components upon which the implementation relies

- Solution monitoring of all systems, interfaces, and processes, including tracking and reporting against SLAs for a solution

- Tools for implementation, testing, upgrading, and maintaining the solution using proven practices

- Opportunities to extend parts of processes and solutions outside your organization, while still managing the SLA against the end-to-end business need

- Open access to the solution management repository using industry standards for integration with help desk, application development, deployment, and other monitoring tools used in your landscape

It should be clear that the lifecycle benefits require a cohesive platform because these capabilities cut across every component and feature. And when these lifecycle management capabilities are combined with the BPM and EDA features of the "applistructure," SAP has enabled a comprehensive approach to improving governance both from an IT and an overall corporate business perspective. In fact, SAP acquired its ecosystem partner, Virsa, and recently launched a Governance, Risk and Compliance business unit.[4]

The SAP ESA "applistructure" enables you to automate more governance capabilities by doing the following:

- Creating a repository of compliance metadata, rules, artifacts, and policies within the "applistructure."

- Automating access management across the landscape.

- Verifying solution models and metadata against governance policies at design-time. Solution designers can also view governance policies and requirements metadata for guidance in creating their own solutions.

- Providing support for mapping logical policy definitions with specific configuration options at solution deployment time and allowing automated verification against solution deployment data to occur.

- Automating compliance checking of transactional activity for run-time governance and compliance features and providing alerts and warnings for follow-up. Ad hoc reporting and analysis are also supported in enhanced ways.

One of the greatest opportunities that comes from evolving SOA capabilities is the ability to abstract more and more governance capabilities from applications, and to manage them as independent assets in the "applistructure." This is very much like the abstraction of business process logic into composites and orchestration environments. As SAP evolves the NetWeaver platform and consolidates features from the Virsa acquisition, this will be another area that significantly matures.

Expanded Functionality from Ecosystem Partners

Recall the earlier discussions around the IT market competitive landscape. It should be apparent that when the basis of competition shifts to "applistructures," the winning value proposition for customers comes from having the most extensive technology capability combined with the largest amount of business content and applications. Not even companies the size of IBM, Microsoft, SAP, or Oracle can support customers at this level on their own. The winners are those organizations whose platforms gain the greatest support from other vendors that can supply additional business content and functionality.

SAP has made a complete turnaround in how it works with other ISVs, systems integrators, and technology companies. Marketing alignment and technology integration have moved from being a byproduct of working together to a strategic necessity for all involved. SAP has invested heavily in building an organization equipped to support these partners in adding value to the SAP "applistructure."

ISVs offering enterprise business solutions that complement mySAP ERP and other Business Suite applications can port their products to run seamlessly on the NetWeaver platform. More important, these same ISVs (as well as consulting firms) can create packaged composite applications that meet a unique business need spanning multiple SAP and non-SAP applications. All of these solutions will be required to pass certification requirements set by SAP in order to receive the stamp of approval that they are consistent with the company's ESA "applistructure."

Last, hardware and technology infrastructure vendors will also be able to certify solutions that add value to the NetWeaver platform and technologies themselves. This offers opportunities for enhancing application development, management, governance, security, SOA mediation, and many other aspects of the platform.

There has historically been a tough tradeoff in those organizations where landscapes centered around R/3. The choice was between getting the best functionality to meet a business need, versus doing everything in SAP. The saying, "If SAP provides it, we'll use it," has become a mantra for many customers, simply because of the ongoing integration and maintenance challenge of picking an alternative. Now you can get the best of both worlds. A third-party solution that's certified and endorsed by SAP for the "applistructure" will be considered a natural extension to the platform. In fact, SAP itself markets and sells certain packaged composite solutions created by other parties.

The extent of the ecosystem is covered in greater detail in Chapter 4. The key takeaway is that an effective "applistructure" has a community that forms around it. This community adds significant value in terms of technical capabilities and business application functionality that can be delivered more seamlessly to customers. Of course, there are considerations (such as licensing, training, support, and so forth), but generally speaking, certified products from other vendors can be acquired and integrated into the SAP NetWeaver landscape faster and more effectively than ever before. SAP also ensures ongoing enhancement and support plans are in place. In a pure "best of breed" setting without a platform such as NetWeaver, this extended research and development could not easily occur.

Lower Solution Implementation, Integration, and Maintenance Costs

Lower TCO for solutions is really a byproduct of all the other SAP ESA-based "applistructure" benefits and capabilities. One area worth covering in more detail is how solution composition helps lower costs.

Composite applications are business-oriented solutions that span multiple underlying applications. For example, you might want a customer-service solution that deals with customer contact information housed in a CRM environment, order history existing in an ERP system, and specialized pricing and promotions available in a customized marketing automation application. A unified solution like this is a composite that exists outside the supporting applications and provides functionality geared to the business user's needs.

In SAP's ESA "applistructure," all the major functionality of the underlying applications will be exposed as services in the NetWeaver platform. This greatly reduces the challenge of tying everything together because integration occurs naturally during the creation of the composite. In essence, application development and integration become one.

Leveraging the composition tools in SAP NetWeaver is just one way to reduce solution development and integration costs. Other ways the "applistructure" helps lower TCO include the following:

- Implementing a common platform and architecture for solutions from SAP, other vendors, and ones you develop internally consolidates skills and infrastructure requirements.

- Using model-based development and configuration techniques, which is significantly cheaper than coding.

- Reusing Enterprise Services and other SAP-provided models and content to yield significant savings.

- Leveraging application and platform consolidation and virtualization capabilities that require less hardware and maintenance in complex SAP landscapes.

- Acquiring pre-integrated packaged composite solutions from SAP and ecosystem solutions to reduce cost of implementation and support, versus dealing with multiple ISVs independently. They also help productize areas that today often require more expensive custom solution development.

Again, it is the combination of all the features in the "applistructure" that makes solution delivery and management faster, better, and cheaper than ever before.

An "Applistructure" Illustration

Figure 2-9 provides an example of how many of the elements of the SAP ESA "applistructure" work together. The simple process flow for this example is as follows:

1. A customer submits an order electronically. This can be via an EDI transaction or through a digital form.

2. The BPM features trigger the order management process upon receiving the order, and the overall processing is now managed by the SAP NetWeaver platform.

3. The order is presented to a customer service representative (CSR) who views it for accuracy, credit approval, and so forth prior to approval.

4. Once approved, the BPM features know to automatically update the customer's CRM profile and enter the order into ERP.

5. The ERP system identifies that the product on this order is available only from suppliers, so an order is placed through an ecosystem partner's supplier network that provides SRM capabilities.

6. The supplier network communicates back a promise date that is beyond the normal lead time. Process analytics identify that this delay will violate the customer promise date.

7. The CSR is alerted to the delay and is presented with alternative delivery dates and other possible supply sources.

8. The CSR determines the best course of action, and communicates to the customer and the account executive what has taken place.

9. The processing of the order continues.

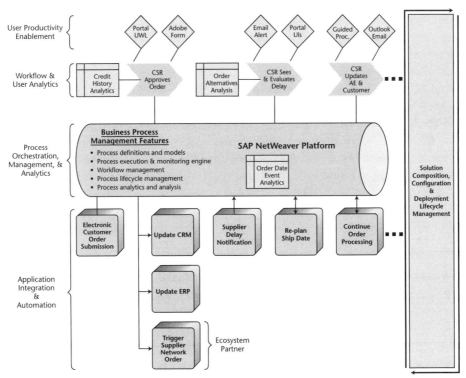

Figure 2-9: An example of how SAP's ESA-based "applistructure" features work together

As you can see in Figure 2-9, many "applistructure" benefits are leveraged even in a simple example like this. First, the BPM features of SAP NetWeaver are used to model and execute the whole scenario. In effect, the high-level process flow logic is abstracted from both the underlying transaction systems and the user interfaces. The platform is able to respond to different events and coordinate both application integration and human interaction steps.

The user productivity and human workflow integration features are illustrated in the tools the CSR uses to interact with the process. A portal interface tracks CSR tasks and alerts, is able to display the order document as a formatted Adobe Form, and provides a single interface into the underlying CRM, ERP, and third-party supplier network data needed to process the order and address the delay. Urgent alerts are also passed to the CSR's Outlook e-mail, which includes context information and a link to launching the appropriate portal workspace for resolution. Finally, a Guided Procedure is used to provide step-by-step guidance for resolving the delay and formatting e-mails to send to the customer and account executive.

Embedded analytics are also a big part of this process. The CSR is provided access to data needed to determine credit approval when the order is first received. And, when notified of the supplier delay, the CSR is provided with additional analytics regarding alternative delivery dates and supplier options to resolve the issue. There are also automated analytics in the process that determined the supplier's promise date exceeded normal lead times, and triggered an automatic alert regarding the delivery issue.

Again this was a simple illustration intended to show the power of the "applistructure" capabilities. Perhaps the most important points are seeing how the SAP NetWeaver platform governed the lifecycle of the solution, and how the user workflow, interfaces, and process capabilities are largely abstracted from the underlying business applications. You will see much more detailed scenarios, along with how they are implemented in SAP NetWeaver and mySAP ERP, in Part III of this book.

Where Do You Go from Here?

Thus far, this book has covered a lot of the business motivations around why SAP has aggressively pursued its ESA strategy. It is also clear that this road map is in line with the direction of most major industry vendors. You have seen that this evolution in the overall IT marketplace represents a goal of merging technology platforms and business applications to shift the focus away from technology products and back toward the business needs of customers.

Your challenge is to look at these trends and determine how you want to proceed. Because you are reading this book, it is assumed that ESA, SAP NetWeaver, and mySAP ERP are all elements you are considering for your architecture, either as a customer, ISV, or consulting partner to SAP. The remainder of this book will help you with understanding the SAP approach and how to shape your ESA adoption plans. It will illustrate how things currently work in the current release of the product platform, and what the future for ESA looks like. This will enable you to plot where and how to build your own strategic road map to ESA, as well as begin your initial pilots and projects. It will also describe what opportunities exist within the partner ecosystem for ISVs and systems integrators to best augment the ESA strategy, and how this can be a win-win-win relationship for SAP, its partners, and, most important, customers.

An "applistructure" eliminates the competitive barriers around individual applications and make the new basis of competition the unified platform itself. The opportunity is simply to realize that you are at the forefront of some big changes, and then find enough people similarly educated in your organization to determine a path that makes the most sense.

A Fork in the Road

As you digest the information in this chapter, you should have discovered that the IT marketplace is about to undergo another round of significant shifts based on industry consolidation and the move toward SOA and related capabilities. Unlike the purely technology-centric innovations of the past, this wave offers the opportunity to tackle the change in a very business-driven way.

Most organizations are still in the process of standardizing and consolidating the functionality of their application platforms down to a manageable number of products. The pieces will be largely consistent with the ones shown in Figure 2-3. And, as mentioned, these organizations are also just beginning to plan and acquire the additional tools needed to support SOA. This means adding things like service repositories, an enterprise service bus (ESB), service intermediaries, and other elements. Whether you consciously define, pick, and plan the components all at once, or end up there by happenstance, does not matter, other than in terms of your TCO and the level of agility you can support.

It is the evolution of "applistructures" that will require a new way of thinking. The unique marriage between business applications and technology platforms that ESA, NetWeaver, and mySAP ERP offer creates all sorts of new opportunities for acquiring solutions from multiple vendors that come with end-to-end business process and solution lifecycle management support "out of the box."

Where and how to embrace the SAP "applistructure" in your architecture is a question you will need to answer. Does the ESA blueprint that combines a technology platform with business content and a series of ecosystem partnerships make sense as a centerpiece for your strategy? Or, are you better off pulling together the same capabilities through a series of "best of breed" offerings and overlaying your SAP infrastructure and service-enabled business applications as needed?

If you are an ISV, the question is how much to embrace the ecosystem. Will your customers benefit from your offering solutions that are a seamless part of the "applistructure," or are you better off taking a more traditional path to partnering and integrating with SAP?

Picking Your Path

Because ESA adoption is business-driven and based on your existing landscape and portfolio, no two road maps will ever be identical. This is both good news and bad news. The good news is that the resulting implementations will be highly tailored to your needs and offer the approach that's most valuable to your organization. The bad news is that it will take leadership, planning, and good organizational management to be successful. And it's these skills that will help you determine the best path for your enterprise, and where and how to adopt ESA for maximum benefit.

In many organizations, this is boiling down to a debate around SAP NetWeaver as an application and integration platform relative to other major platforms and "best of breed" components. Internally, there are battle lines being drawn between the SAP group and the non-SAP group, which is exactly the wrong answer, and is indicative of thinking the old way about architectures. Remember that the key is seeing where the puck is heading in the industry, and to start building your own strategy.

Obviously, this book is about SAP's approach to ESA because, for many organizations, SAP offers a compelling set of solutions that can become key components of an effective SAP landscape and extend across portions of the enterprise architecture. The intent is not, however, to create endless debates around software and architecture principles. And it is definitely not meant to argue that SAP's integration broker is better than another vendor's, or that SAP's portal is the best on the marketplace, and so forth. Ultimately, that's not what SAP is articulating either.

A number of large enterprises are successfully taking an SAP-first approach to SOA. There are also many taking a "best of breed" path toward SOA, embracing SAP as part of the picture in an equally successful manner. There are certainly tradeoffs between the two options. The good news is they are not mutually exclusive. Many large enterprises will create a hybrid of the two as they embrace SOA and "best of breed" options in their non-SAP environments while they look to consolidate certain aspects of their SAP landscape around the NetWeaver "applistructure."

The question goes back to "best of breed" idea in general. If your organization has demonstrated the strong discipline, leadership, and architectural savvy to effectively manage a "best of breed" approach to your infrastructure, then that likely is a path worth continuing into the SOA world, particularly if your business needs demand "best of breed" capabilities. That is often true in certain industries such as banking, insurance, and healthcare, where there is a lot of customization and heavy transaction processing that takes place outside of standard business applications. Of course, having this discipline includes managing the business alignment aspects for IT, as well as the economics and costs of dealing with a complex, multi-vendor architecture.

On the other hand, if your organization lacks the business rationale to pursue "best of breed," then you may be better served through greater consolidation around an "applistructure" platform. This can maximize the business content within your SOA through a model such as SAP's approach to ESA. While that may seem counterintuitive to a pure technologist, it makes a lot of sense to the business. Industries such as manufacturing, chemicals, utilities, and oil-and-gas that are largely dominated by SAP applications will trend toward this approach.

In the end, it is very much like the choice between buying a rack stereo and home theater system, versus integrating a set of high-end specialized components. Each has its place depending on whether you are an audiovisual enthusiast, or someone who is less discerning and just wants an easy solution to listen to music and watch videos. The good news is the technology industry is making it easy to blend these strategies. For example, SAP NetWeaver is one platform, but it can be mixed and matched with components from other vendors where it makes sense, while still taking advantage of all the valuable business blueprints that are part of ESA.

If you are an organization that uses SAP, you will most likely adopt the company's ESA approach and NetWeaver platform in some capacity. At the very least, the enterprise services within the "applistructure" will represent valuable integration points with the rest of your landscape. In addition, core NetWeaver functionality within the portal and business intelligence products will greatly enhance the mySAP ERP and Business Suite applications that you use.

If you are an ISV offering complementary solutions to mySAP Business Suite applications or the NetWeaver platform, you will be equally hard-pressed not to support ESA. The ecosystem approach by SAP embraces embedding third-party solutions into the "applistructure." SAP is actively courting partners who can expand its platform and solution maps. This includes options for running your solution on the platform itself, expanding the capabilities of the technology infrastructure, providing business content to add new features into the "applistructure," or developing packaged composite applications that are woven together based on a combination of services from SAP and those you create.

The remainder of this book provides information and guidance to help build your plans for ESA and NetWeaver adoption, and helps you identify where and how they fit into your architecture. This book walks you through one set of examples, but the real value is in helping you apply the knowledge to your specific landscape. This is both in terms of the NetWeaver capabilities, as well as your overall business and enterprise architecture strategy.

Summary

This chapter should have cemented two things in your mind. First, the road ahead in the industry is about combining technology platforms and business applications into a whole new type of architecture. Second, your specific architectural choices should become increasingly business-driven, as opposed to the pure technology feature-function orientation of the past. As history has shown, the latter is flawed over the long run.

The major takeaways regarding SAP's approach to ESA are as follows:

- Applications and technology platforms are merging, and SOA will bring about major changes in the way you buy and extend packaged business applications. New alternatives will replace the monolithic, pre-compiled solutions that are tough to integrate with and impossible to change at the speed business needs.

- ESA is consistent with all the major IT industry trends and consolidation taking place: specifically SOA, BPM patterns, model-driven development, event-driven architectures, virtualization of hardware and networks, and the combining of technology platforms and business applications into a unified "applistructure" as a new basis for competition.

- The goals for ESA are business-driven and include better aligning business strategy and processes with technology architecture and implementations, making applications easier to use and change, and lowering the overall TCO by consolidating the infrastructure.

- Successful adoption of ESA requires understanding that its scope is far greater than a traditional SAP landscape, and forming cross-functional teams that span business, applications, and infrastructure personnel.

- Part of SAP's plan for ESA includes the creation of a valuable ISV and consulting partner ecosystem that will create solutions that seamlessly align with and extend SAP's offerings.

- Each organization's path to ESA will be unique, and the blueprint lends itself to multiple adoption scenarios for NetWeaver. The key is carefully choosing what components make sense within your particular landscape, given a variety of business and technical factors.

With this industry context in place, Chapter 3 looks at how ESA is affecting the road map of SAP NetWeaver, mySAP ERP, and other Business Suite applications.

References

1. Nicholas G. Carr, *Does IT Matter? Information Technology and the Corrosion of Competitive Advantage* (Boston: Harvard Business School Press, April 2004).
2. Jill Rosenfeld, "CDU to Gretzky: The Puck Stops Here." Fast Company, July 2000. Available at `www.fastcompany.com/magazine/36/cdu.html`.
3. Mike Ricciuti, "Ballmer Says Microsoft Is Different." CNET News.Com, November 8, 2005. Available at `http://news.com.com/Ballmer+says+Microsoft+is+different/2008-1082_3-5938431.html`.
4. "SAP Launches Governance, Risk and Compliance Management Business Unit to Lead New, Emerging Market," SAP Press Release, May 17, 2006. Available at `www.sap.com/usa/company/press/Press.epx?PressID=6247&Query=virsa`.

CHAPTER 3

Enabling ESA: The Evolution of NetWeaver and mySAP ERP

Chapter 2 provided background on ESA in the context of what is taking place across the IT industry. Application platforms and the evolution of SOA, BPM, model-driven development, and related technologies are affecting the delivery of packaged business solutions. The basis of competition is shifting to "applistructures" and value will come from platforms populated with the most extensive set of business content that meets your enterprise's needs. Major vendors such as SAP offer end-to-end solutions that combine the technology and content. The other alternative is to assemble everything using a "best of breed" approach. Of course, many organizations will do a combination of the two.

All of this suggests great change in how applications themselves are created, acquired, and extended. Customers, platform vendors, other ISVs, and systems integrators can benefit from "applistructures" because they offer each of them a common approach for creating solutions. This, in turn, leads to faster time-to-market, greater agility, and better economies of scale for those who leverage the platform investments.

Most important, this new architectural model is the latest evolution in helping improve alignment between IT organizations and their business counterparts. This happens because SOA and related technologies enable business processes to be managed as a first-order concern. In other words, executable process models can be liberated from the underlying applications and managed as independent assets.

SAP's ESA road map is very much in line with this industry path. This chapter describes the details behind the SAP strategy by explaining the transformation taking place in SAP products themselves. Specifically, this chapter addresses how the SAP NetWeaver platform is evolving to support the "applistructure" and what this means to mySAP ERP and other SAP packaged business applications as a new type of packaged composite application delivery model emerges.

As a result of reading this chapter you will be able to:

- Understand the key features of the NetWeaver platform

- See how NetWeaver is evolving into a business process platform

- Appreciate the fact that there are different options for leveraging NetWeaver and mySAP ERP to evolve your landscape toward ESA

- Understand how these changes affect SAP applications, including mySAP ERP and other Business Suite products

- See the key characteristics NetWeaver and mySAP ERP must provide in order for the ESA vision to be fully realized

- Recognize how ESA changes the way in which you extend SAP solutions

- Grasp the value of packaged composite applications and xApps in terms of how new solutions will be delivered by SAP and other ISVs and systems integrators

The Evolution of the NetWeaver Platform: From Components to IT Practices

NetWeaver is the technology platform that makes SAP's approach to ESA a reality. NetWeaver has many underlying features that work together to provide the IT capabilities needed to power the delivery of today's ESA-based business solutions. At the same time, the platform is also evolving to support the longer-term ESA road map and maturing SOA standards. As such, there are many different perspectives to evaluate the platform. This chapter looks at the SAP NetWeaver capabilities and road map from an overall architectural perspective.

It is worth mentioning that SAP itself is evolving beyond the component-oriented view of NetWeaver that you may be familiar with. That view basically organized NetWeaver by the physical component pieces such as EP, XI, BW, WAS, and so forth. The company is now structuring the platform from a top-down solutions-oriented perspective based on a concept called *IT Practices*.

As you will see, having an integrated, functional view of the platform makes a lot of sense in an SOA world because of the way in which the components are blended together to create a unified platform. It also makes it easier on systems administrators managing the physical landscape. However, the shift can also cause confusion for customers because some of the changes are subtle at first.

The following sections walk you through the strategic evolution of the NetWeaver platform. This background will help you see how the different parts of SAP NetWeaver work together, and how the entire platform is evolving strategically over time to enable the realization of ESA. Most important, understanding the evolution will help you recognize the advantages that truly integrated technology platforms such as NetWeaver offer.

SAP Integration Technologies Before NetWeaver

As the need to tie together business processes cutting across multiple enterprise applications grew, customers looked to SAP to provide stronger integration capabilities. In addition, they wanted to take advantage of the benefits offered by Internet technologies and Web-based user interfaces.

Hence, even before NetWeaver, SAP offered a large number of individual technologies, tools, engines, and products for addressing specific integration needs within the SAP landscape. For example, Business Information Warehouse (BW) offered a set of data warehousing and business intelligence and analysis functionality to turn disparate data into integrated, actionable information. The Internet Transaction Server (ITS) and Business Server Pages (BSPs) were technologies that enabled the development of Web based frontends to SAP. Another popular solution was the Enterprise Portal (EP), which could be used to consolidate user interfaces, provide single sign-on to multiple applications, and deliver features typical of a Web-based portal server. Finally, the SAP Business Connector, Java Connector (JCO), and the .NET Connector provided options to integrate SAP and non-SAP applications.

These are just a few examples of SAP technologies that your organization may have used even before NetWeaver was launched. Most of these components were created internally, although some were added through acquisitions and alliances SAP made with other companies.

From a customer's perspective, the multitude of point solutions and technologies started to become difficult to manage. Each could be controlled by a different SAP development organization. That meant release cycles, versioning, and support could be unique to each technology component. If you wanted to build solutions that leveraged the features of multiple components, then your organization had to deal with the complex interdependencies across versions. You may have experienced the challenge of troubleshooting problems and planning for upgrades across the different SAP technologies, components, and products. As Figure 3-1 shows, sometimes it was difficult to determine the cause of the problem when things would not work together.

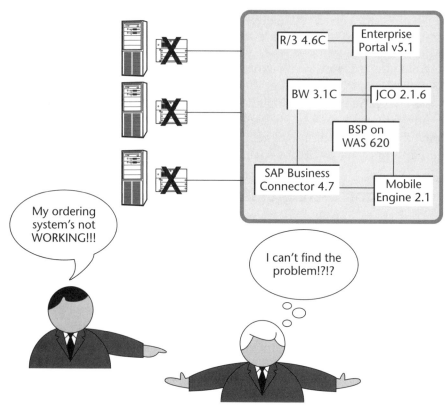

Figure 3-1: The challenge with managing SAP technologies before NetWeaver

The Launch of SAP NetWeaver

When SAP launched the ESA strategy in 2003, one of the first objectives was to consolidate the diverse set of technology components used for integration and development. Having SAP deliver a unified application and integration platform meant customers no longer had to pull together all the pieces themselves. The capabilities of this platform needed to be similar to the generic industry-standard platforms that were illustrated in the previous chapter (see Figure 2.3).

Many of these features already existed as mature products in the SAP portfolio. Others needed to be created or significantly enhanced. Most important, SAP customers wanted the platform to be based on industry-standard technologies including Java, XML, and the evolving set of Web Services specifications.

This was, of course, a big change in direction for SAP, and became the genesis of the NetWeaver platform. The first unified release of NetWeaver (NW2004) brought the components together into a synchronized release, as shown in Figure 3-2.

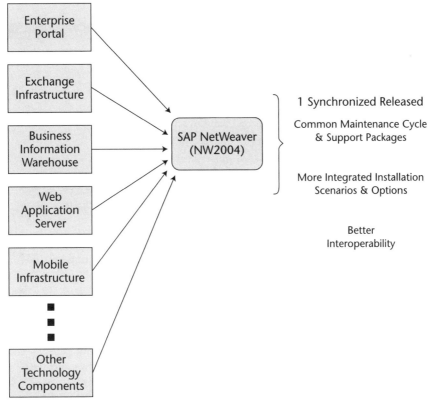

Figure 3-2: Combining SAP technology components into a synchronized release

With NW2004, the major components were released, supported, and upgraded simultaneously with integrated service packs. This meant you could better handle the technical interdependencies and more easily manage multiple components in your landscape. Table 3-1 lists some of the key components within NW2004, along with the features they provided.

NOTE SAP NetWeaver 2004 (NW2004) represented the first unified release of the SAP application platform. Along with its launch, SAP provided the larger road map for NetWeaver. This included the release cycles needed to support the complete evolution to ESA, which are covered later in this chapter.

Of course, NW2004 included many more tools, technologies, and capabilities beyond these components. For example, the NetWeaver Developer Studio was launched as the IDE for supporting Java application development on NetWeaver. SAP's Content Management and TREX search engine features also became part of the platform. In fact, NetWeaver 2004 was like a big pot of technology stew that brought together just about every technology SAP offered.

Table 3-1: Major Components in the Initial NetWeaver 2004 Release

NAME	KEY FEATURES
Enterprise Portal (EP)	Unified, role-based user interface with personalization, single sign-on, and support for knowledge management, and online collaboration features.
Exchange Infrastructure (XI)	An integration broker and business process management solution. Provides standard A2A and B2B integration, as well as Web Services orchestration.
Business Information Warehouse (BW)	Data warehousing, analytics, and business intelligence tools. Handles end-to-end process for extract/transfer/load (ETL), online analytical processing (OLAP), and data mining capabilities.
Web Application Server (WAS)	An application server supporting ABAP and J2EE applications in a secure, highly available, and reliable manner throughout their lifecycles.
Mobile Infrastructure (MI)	Solutions for extending business applications and developing, deploying, and managing new solutions for PDAs, phones, and other devices.
Master Data Management (MDM)	Solution for consolidating, harmonizing, and managing master data. MDM was not technically part of the unified NW2004 release, but it is a key NetWeaver component and will eventually become integrated with the rest of the platform as SAP blends the technologies acquired from A2i with NetWeaver and its earlier MDM development.

The Rise and Fall of the Component View of NetWeaver

As mentioned in Chapter 2, every application platform vendor faces the significant undertaking of combining all their tools and technologies into an integrated platform. While NW2004 represented a major milestone for SAP in terms of synchronizing the release cycles and heavily supporting Java, XML, and Web Services standards, there was a long way to go in terms of having a really cohesive platform. Putting all the parts in one box is not the same as unifying them.

The key for you to recognize is that NW2004 represented only one small step in terms of creating a complete platform that supports SAP's ESA vision. Most IT people embraced this component-oriented view of NetWeaver because it mapped well to the traditional model for managing the IT landscape. In other words, it was more of the same in terms of products and technical features.

Unfortunately, the component-oriented view of SAP NetWeaver has two main weaknesses when it comes to ESA. First, it is heavily technology- and tool-focused, but doesn't provide guidance on how to best put the pieces together to create business solutions. This in turn does nothing to solve the business-versus-IT gap, and creates a barrier to both parties working together on an integrated ESA adoption road map for NetWeaver.

The bigger challenge with this early view of NetWeaver was that the component-oriented depiction of a platform does not reflect the reality of what happens with a transition to SOA. Over time, many of the major platform capabilities themselves become exposed as a shared set of integrated services. These technical services can be woven together to create business solutions. You will see more on this shortly.

Obviously optimizing business processes in an ESA world requires solutions that cut across multiple NetWeaver components to provide comprehensive business functionality. This is why SAP itself has evolved beyond the component-oriented view of NetWeaver that was part of the initial NW2004 launch. SAP is also shifting emphasis away from its famous technology-centric presentation of NetWeaver that was tied to the NW2004 release (see the sidebar "The Closing of the Refrigerator"). The next section describes the new IT Practices view of the NetWeaver platform architecture.

The New NetWeaver Platform: IT Practices–Driven

As mentioned, the monolithic components found in application platforms such as the first edition of NetWeaver can go only so far in supporting ESA. The tools and technology infrastructure itself must evolve to enable the same type of agility and flexibility that you are looking for from your business applications. This almost creates a "catch-22" in terms of explaining an application platform in an SOA world. On the one hand, it is valuable to describe the overall capabilities from a functionality perspective. On the other hand, it can become confusing when you stop seeing the underlying features as standalone, installable products. The following sections cover this evolution in SAP NetWeaver from both perspectives.

Understanding IT Practices and Scenarios

By unifying the platform into a set of cohesive services, your vantage point can shift to a top-down approach. You can start with a business enablement perspective and then drill down to the realization of individual solutions by installing and configuring the supporting NetWeaver capabilities. This is why SAP has spent so much time and energy on repositioning the view of NetWeaver away from individual components. The notion is that *the whole is greater than the sum of the parts.*

THE CLOSING OF THE REFRIGERATOR

Most customers and partners were first exposed to the SAP NetWeaver platform through the following diagram. This view was affectionately called "the refrigerator" because its shape looks like an open refrigerator. It highlighted the launch of the NW2004 release. Although it is a valuable view of many NetWeaver integration functions, this diagram gives the impression of a monolithic view of the underlying components. It also fails to highlight how the capabilities themselves work together to enable a business process solution.

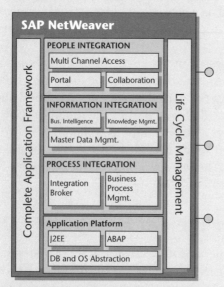

The popular functional view of NW2004 known as "the fridge" (Source: © SAP AG 2004–2006. All rights reserved.)

One SOA principle is the ability to expose business applications as sets of services that can be extended, resequenced, and reassembled to meet the unique requirements of your users and key processes. Interestingly, the same type of thing happens within an application platform itself. The individual product components can also be decomposed into services and then rewoven together into foundational IT capabilities.

That evolution as it relates to NetWeaver makes the "refrigerator" diagram somewhat incomplete because it fails to illustrate the real value of a highly integrated platform from a business and IT enablement perspective. The new view of NetWeaver looks at the platform in terms of the business-oriented capabilities that come from combining the components. As you say goodbye to the NetWeaver refrigerator diagram, just remember that it will take a long time before customers and partners stop thinking about NetWeaver in terms of the underlying technology components that were at the original core of the platform. As subsequent releases of SAP NetWeaver are unveiled, the unification of the platform will become clear.

A simple analogy is to think about your computer. Its value is in all the ways that you use it for business or entertainment purposes. Sometimes it is important to think about the details of the individual parts such as the monitor, the speed of your CD drives, which patch of the operating system you use, the amount of RAM and storage, how you tie it into your stereo system, what peripherals you include, and so forth. But for the most part, you just use it as an integrated system. Hence, we have new ways of describing computers such as "media center PCs," "desktop replacements," "office productivity machines," "ultra-portables," and so on. These categories translate into different physical characteristics and suggest what you will find under the hood when you look at the underlying components.

In the same way, SAP has redefined NetWeaver in terms of a set of IT Practices that represent the major capabilities performed in a typical IT organization. SAP offers a solution map for these IT Practices, as shown in Figure 3-3. It serves as a guide for selecting and implementing the specific features of NetWeaver you need.

IT Practices   **IT Scenarios**

IT Practices	IT Scenarios				
User Productivity Enablement	Running an Enterprise Portal	Enabling User Collaboration	Business Task Management	Mobilizing Business Processes	Enterprise Knowledge Management
Data Unification	Master-Data Harmonization	Master-Data Consolidation	Center Master-Data Management	Enterprise Data Warehousing	
Business Information Management	Enterprise Reporting, Query, and Analysis	Business Planning and Analytical Services		Enterprise Data Warehousing	
Business Event Management	Business Activity Monitoring		Business Task Management		
End-to-End Process Integration	Enabling Application-to-Application Processes	Enabling Business-to Business Processes	Business Process Management	Enabling Platform Interoperability	Business Task Management
Custom Development	Developing, Configuring, and Adapting Applications		Enabling Platform Interoperability		
Unified Lifecycle Management	Software Lifecycle Management		SAP NetWeaver Operations		
Application Governance	Authentication and Single Sign-On		Integrated User and Access Management		
Consolidation	Enabling Platform Interoperability	SAP NetWeaver Operations	Master-Data Consolidation	Enterprise Knowledge Management	
Enterprise Services Architecture	Enabling Enterprise Services				

Figure 3-3: The NetWeaver technology solution map of IT practices and IT scenarios (Source: © SAP AG 2005–2006. All Rights Reserved. Available at www.sap.com/solutions/businessmaps/index.epx.)

Notice that IT Practices are broken down into IT Scenarios. These Scenarios reflect the set of processes within IT that help realize the goals of a given IT Practice. For example, one function of an IT organization is the practice of Data Unification, which among other things enables the business to have a unified information model to support transactions and analyze results. One underlying Data Unification process is the scenario of data warehousing, which consolidates and organizes multiple sources of information. Another set of Data Unification processes deals with creating a consistent set of master data. As you can see in Figure 3-3, there are three IT Scenarios that support master data management processes for harmonization, consolidation, and management respectively.

Scenarios themselves are further broken down into variants that define the sub-processes, tasks, and implementation structure in NetWeaver needed to realize a portion of the Scenario. Think of this as the set of underlying technologies coming together to offer the services required by the Scenario. Following are some important aspects of variants that you should recognize:

- They refer to specific releases and versions of underlying software.
- SAP may designate partners to offer implementations for certain variants.
- There may be multiple installation or configuration options for realizing a variant.
- They contain reference models and links to step-by-step installation guides.

Note that the variants are still removed from where "the rubber meets the road" in terms of what you are actually installing. If you go back to our example of Data Unification, you see that the IT Scenario of Enterprise Data Warehousing contains two variants. One is for modeling and loading the data warehouse, while the other variant deals with operation and usage of the data warehouse. Each of these requires the installation and configuration of different sets of software.

NetWeaver Implementation Units

If IT Practices and Scenarios define the business capabilities of NetWeaver, then what are you actually implementing when you choose one of the variants in a Scenario? Three types of installation units are associated with SAP NetWeaver:

- Usage types
- Engines
- Clients

Usage Types

Usage types are not themselves installable, but instead represent a logical collection of installable software units. They serve three main purposes:

- Attaching specific roles to the SAP systems identified in your landscape
- Organizing the detailed implementation and configuration of underlying software components to realize an IT Scenario
- Providing a logical view of the NetWeaver platform's realization of IT Scenarios

Usage types provide a direct link between the logical role of a system in the NetWeaver landscape and what physical software it requires. Some usage types require the existence of other usage types in the landscape to fulfill their purpose. More details on usage types are covered in the next section.

Engines

Engines are standalone software services. They do not exist as roles for a named system within an SAP Landscape itself, but are instead installable units that support other SAP NetWeaver systems. Following are some examples of NetWeaver engines:

- TREX search and classification services for indexing, searching, and retrieving documents and data
- Web Dispatcher for security and load-balancing of Web applications
- liveCache technology for enhancing and optimizing MaxDB
- Content Server for storing electronic documents and other types of content related to SAP applications

Clients

Clients are another type of installable software unit within NetWeaver. These clients really fall into three categories. First are end-user tools for accessing and using SAP applications. The second type of client is developer tools used to build and deploy new applications. Finally, there are pure technology clients that allow one application to act as a client of another. Following are some examples of NetWeaver clients:

- NetWeaver Developer Studio for building Java and ABAP based applications
- J2SE Adapter Engine that is a standalone tool enabling certain landscapes to connect with SAP NetWeaver process integration capabilities
- SAP NetWeaver Development Infrastructure that helps manage the lifecycle of software projects by providing developers with source code control repositories, integrated build systems, and change control functionality

- SAP GUI and next generation rich clients that will provide role-based front-ends to SAP applications

- Business Explorer for creating and running business intelligence queries from Excel or through a Web interface

- Mobile Infrastructure Client, which is a software layer on mobile devices to provide data storage and a local Web server functions for running disconnected mobile applications

Understanding Usage Types

The switch to usage types can be one of the most confusing concepts for developers and administrators, especially if they worked with the previous component-oriented implementations of NetWeaver. The reason is that components were essentially a direct physical view of NetWeaver implementations, whereas usage types add more of a logical abstraction on top of what gets installed. Before walking through the details, remember the motivations for this change:

- In an integrated, SOA-based platform, components lose their meaning in terms of being able to deliver a complete solution or capability.

- From a developer perspective, SOA enables you to abstract your use of service interfaces from the physical implementation. However, there needs to be a logical ordering mechanism to the services.

- From a deployment perspective, a model is needed to manage the many-to-many relationships between IT Scenarios and the underlying components, engines, and clients.

What really adds to the confusion is the similarity between the names of NetWeaver usage types and those of the former components, as shown in Table 3-2. It is worth pointing out that as of the latest NetWeaver release, MDM was not yet integrated within the overall platform. Hence that component has not yet been replaced with a usage type.

Table 3-2: The Evolution of Components to Usage Types

NW2004 COMPONENT	NEW USAGE TYPE
Enterprise Portal (EP)	SAP NetWeaver Portal (EP)
Exchange Infrastructure (XI)	SAP NetWeaver Process Integration (PI)
Business Information Warehouse (BW)	SAP NetWeaver Business Intelligence (BI) and BI Java Components (BI-Java)
Web Application Server (WAS)	SAP NetWeaver Application Server (AS-ABAP and AS-Java)
Mobile Infrastructure (MI)	SAP NetWeaver Mobile Infrastructure (MI)

The best way to illustrate the de-emphasis of components is to look at the evolution of SAP's business intelligence (BI) capabilities, as shown in Figure 3-4. Before NetWeaver, SAP's data warehousing and query capabilities were mainly contained in the BW component, which was entirely ABAP-based. Today, almost the entire NetWeaver stack is involved in delivering business intelligence capabilities. There is no longer anywhere close to a one-to-one relationship between the business intelligence capabilities of NetWeaver and a component such as BW.

Over time, you can expect further blurring of the lines within NetWeaver as the capabilities continue to consolidate into a set of integrated services. This is why a logical concept such as usage types is needed to abstract the physical structure of components. For example, a Scenario such as "business process management" may ultimately require hundreds or thousands of services spread across the platform to be delivered. Many of these same services will likely be required to realize other IT Scenarios as well. And these services may themselves require dozens of installable units. Usage types simply provide a more lasting and logical way to organize the physical details of what is installed, how things are configured, and the means to administer the landscape on top of the physical service portfolio.

Another analogy may help illustrate this point. Assume someone gives you a favorite family recipe book and a list of meals to cook for the upcoming week. If you follow the plan, the first thing that happens is you return from the store with many bags of ingredients. Some of these (such as eggs, flour, salt, and potatoes) may be used across many different recipes. Some recipes may also call for ingredients that themselves have their own recipe (such as home-made salad dressing or gravy). And finally, some meal plans may reuse the same recipes (such as a salad). However, when someone asks you, "What's for lunch?" you don't rattle off the list of detailed ingredients in your recipes.

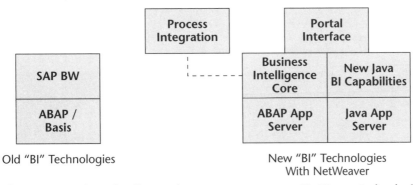

Figure 3-4: Business intelligence features now cut across NetWeaver technologies.

Figure 3-5 illustrates this idea. Notice that the recipes are the logical link between the abstract meal plan and the real-world ingredients. Not only do they define what you need, they also contain all the processes on how to make (configure) the meal. In the same way, administrators and developers need logical ways to organize and manage the underlying services and installable units of the integrated NetWeaver platform.

NOTE The full details of landscape planning for SAP NetWeaver IT Scenarios and usage types is beyond the scope of this book. It is recommended that administrators and interested architects and developers consult the SAP NetWeaver Master Guide for the latest information available, as well as review `http://help.sap.com` to understand more about the physical implementation of NetWeaver. The authors expect SAP to offer more guidance in this area to provide greater clarity on the logical and physical organization of an integrated ESA platform.

Needless to say, there are many new options available to your team for organizing and consolidating your SAP NetWeaver landscape and lowering TCO. Of course, each of these comes with tradeoffs for future flexibility and scaling, and in terms of how you organize your IT organization itself.

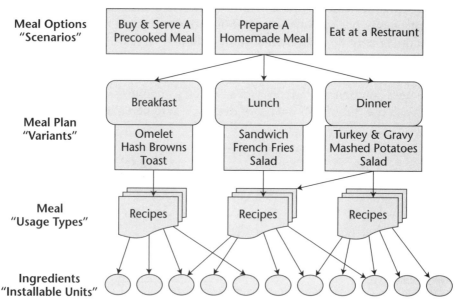

Figure 3-5: A recipe analogy for usage types

Putting It All Together

A final example may help illustrate how all of this fits together. Figure 3-6 shows the relationship between IT Practices, Scenarios, variants, and what ultimately gets installed. Assume you are interested in delivering some of the embedded analytic capabilities mentioned earlier within your applications. Looking at the solution map, you find the IT Scenario *Enterprise Reporting, Query, and Analysis* within the *Business Information Management* IT Practice. Drilling into the Scenario, you find a number of different variants, including one for *Information Broadcasting*. This variant offers services for organizations to "design, deploy, and execute information broadcasting, seamlessly integrating business intelligence, knowledge management, and collaboration into a single, blended experience for the portal end user." Sounds very much like the functionality that you need.

Your system administrators can then use the solution map to identify and install the complete set of components, engines, and clients needed to enable these services. In this case, they would be based on usage types including SAP NetWeaver Business Intelligence (BI), the ABAP and Java Application Server stacks (AS), NetWeaver Portal, and so forth. The key is these administrators can use their own special expertise to determine the physical distribution model across the logical SAP systems and physical hardware hosts. As a developer or architect, your concern is with Information Broadcasting and ensuring the underlying capability is enabled and available to you in the landscape for building a business solution. The physical distinctions between the underlying components, engines, and clients, as well as their installation details, should be less of a concern. That provides greater flexibility to managing the landscape, and allows solutions to be created in ways that are loosely coupled from the deployment. As you will see in later chapters, this is an important principle in an SOA.

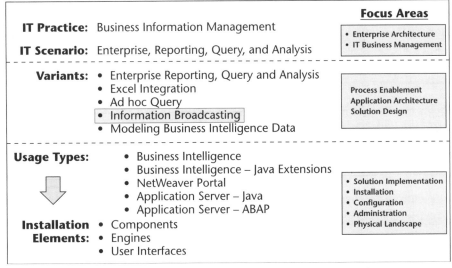

Figure 3-6: Relationship between IT Practices, Scenarios, variants, and usage types

SERVICE ENABLING THE NETWEAVER PLATFORM

Most SOA examples describe business processes being realized through the orchestration of services. For example, a salesperson might have a set of tasks associated with the process of closing an order. This could include performing credit checks, calculating pricing, and getting management approval for special discounts. It is easy to see how each of these tasks could be exposed as a service and then woven together to support the process. Naturally these generic service definitions would have interface definitions and each would have to have underlying implementations in a system that will actually execute when the service interface is invoked.

The NetWeaver platform can be thought of in a similar fashion. In essence, IT Scenarios are analogous to the business process. For example, instead of closing a sales order, you might be performing the *Enterprise Reporting, Query, and Analysis* process. The variants and usage types that realize the business process are, in turn, similar to sets of service definitions. In this case, Information Broadcasting is essentially an umbrella for a set of services that an application developer might like to invoke. And, just as a business service definition such as pricing requires a physical implementation, the variants and usage types are implemented through installable units of components, engines, and clients that handle the service invocations. The bottom line is that, from an architectural perspective, an IT process is still a process and technical level services are still services.

There are two main takeaways from this. First is that in an ESA world, there are many lower-level technical services that work just like the higher level business object and enterprise services that are usually described in SOA examples. These technical services may include a portal interface service that provides presentation logic, a logging service that records activity, a security service that performs authentication and authorization, an analytics service that provides information analysis, a reporting service that formats a set of data, and many more. The second point is that part of the process of unifying NetWeaver is to essentially morph the platform into a set of interoperable services that realize key IT capabilities. All of this helps explain why SAP is shifting the focus away from physical components to IT Practices, Scenarios, and usage types.

All of this seems a lot more complicated than the old component view of NetWeaver, and, indeed, it is in terms of an architectural model for unifying the platform. As mentioned, NetWeaver itself will become more service-enabled. All of the distinctions in the solution map are simply ways of reflecting this SOA-based view of the platform and bridging the business capability, application development view, and the physical installation and implementation models (see the sidebar "Service Enabling the NetWeaver Platform").

If you mine through the NetWeaver technology solution map, you will quickly see that a many-to-many relationship exists between the IT Practices and Scenarios. Likewise, variants and usage types can belong to multiple IT Scenarios themselves. This just further illustrates the level of deep integration that is taking place across NetWeaver.

Another important point related to the IT Scenarios is that SAP will actively partner with other ISVs in the ecosystem to provide solutions for different variants. Browsing the solution map will eventually show not only SAP solutions, but also certified solutions from ISVs whom SAP has worked with to add value directly to the platform.

Chapter 8 revisits the various IT Practices and Scenarios in the discussion of ESA adoption. For now, you have seen the new model for NetWeaver, which better reflects the architecture of how ESA will be enabled. The ESA blueprints are realized when both the business applications and the underlying technology platform shift from monolithic products to flexible services. In both cases, the focus is on the business solution.

With IT Practices and Scenarios, architects and developers focus on the capabilities at the levels they need to deliver solutions. The details of specific components and tools are left to the infrastructure team that determines specific configurations, enables availability requirements, and so forth, based on the Scenarios you need enabled. Again this all adds up to enable deeper integration across the platform.

How NetWeaver Evolves into a Business Process Platform

The previous sections described how SAP NetWeaver is organized around IT Practices and the way it will continue to merge into an integrated technology platform. In this section, you see how SAP has structured its overall NetWeaver releases to support the ESA road map. This section also helps you understand the overall features and capabilities needed to realize SAP's vision for ESA, and what to expect in future evolutions of the platform.

The Emerging Technical Capabilities of a Platform for ESA

Plenty of tools are available from SAP and other vendors that provide the basic features of the original NetWeaver components. Remember that ESA is about enabling the efficient delivery of business process solutions. It is based upon SOA technology blueprints because SOA offers the required architectural agility to best enable this. That flexibility is what allows SAP to take an application such as mySAP ERP and expose its functionality as a set of cohesive services that you can use to assemble your own business process solutions.

But what does the platform need to provide to make ESA a reality? Chapter 2 identified some of the most important technical features and objectives, as summarized here:

- *SOA based* service models
- Common *business semantics* that organize enterprise service models
- *Service-oriented infrastructure* for creating, consuming, and governing SAP and non-SAP services based on standards
- *Unified BPM capabilities* to coordinate end-to-end processes
- *Model-driven development*, for solution delivery speed, design transparency, and flexibility
- An *EDA* infrastructure to detect and respond to complex business and technical events in your landscape
- *Infrastructure virtualization* to cost-effectively deploy loosely coupled solutions
- *Intelligent networking* to take advantage of content flowing through SOA-based Web Services protocols

All of these capabilities exist in SAP NetWeaver to some degree today. Realizing the full potential of ESA requires they mature, evolve with standards, and become much better integrated with the rest of the platform and business applications. One of your organization's challenges is to understand these capabilities, and how they fit together. This will help you drive you enterprise architecture and organizational structure to best leverage these IT trends.

The SAP NetWeaver Platform Road Map

Once you understand the technical features and capabilities of the platform, it is important to see the evolution as to how SAP has been delivering on this vision over time. When SAP announced the ESA strategy, it was clear the massive amount of change would not happen within a single release. SAP defined major milestones for how NetWeaver would become ESA-enabled over the initial four-year ESA roadmap. Figure 3-7 shows these high-level milestones along with the associated SAP NetWeaver releases. The following sections describe the major architectural capabilities that customers, ISVs, and systems integration partners can leverage at each step of the way.

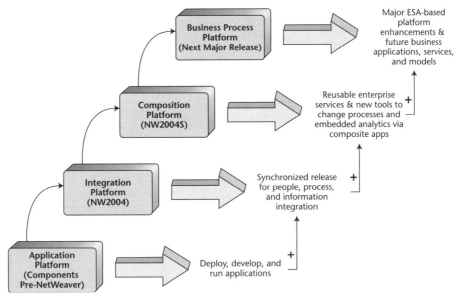

Figure 3-7: The major SAP NetWeaver milestones for enabling ESA capabilities

NetWeaver as an Application Platform

The first milestone was to establish NetWeaver as an application platform. That meant providing new technologies to serve as the foundation for future development. SAP reached this milestone with the launch of the Web Application Server (WAS) as a unified ABAP and Java stack. WAS effectively replaced the original BASIS layer and began to power SAP business applications beginning with R/3 Enterprise.

In addition to WAS, SAP provided standalone components and technologies for things such as Web development, portals, business intelligence, and so forth to SAP landscapes. These solutions could integrate with and extend SAP applications such as R/3, as well as be used for non-SAP application development. Third-party ISVs and IT developers took advantage of these standalone components to build their own business applications. Some customers also saw the potential to consolidate niche middleware components they may have brought into their environments.

As shown in Figure 3-8, the initial application platform components provided a number of useful development technologies for SAP customers A new set of tools and features were now in place within the SAP landscape, including Web Services capabilities for exposing R/3 interfaces.

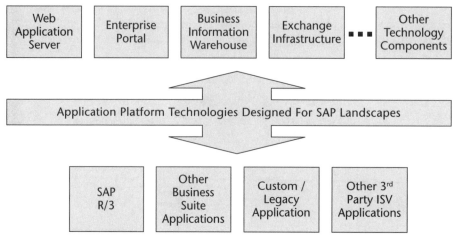

Figure 3-8: The application platform lowered the cost of integrating platform technologies with SAP business applications.

In terms of overall business benefits, SAP essentially addressed certain TCO and IT efficiency challenges for customers. Meanwhile, inside SAP developers began to use WAS and the other components as the foundation for creating the next versions of mySAP Business Suite applications. WAS also became the main application server foundation for delivering an integrated SAP NetWeaver release as described in the next section.

NetWeaver as an Integration Platform

NW2004 represented the integration version of the NetWeaver platform. As mentioned earlier, this was the first edition that offered a synchronized release cycle and installation model for most of the major components. It also greatly enhanced SAP's support for standards. Java, XML, and Web Services capabilities emerged as core features. Components such as Exchange Infrastructure (XI) received major upgrades for providing A2A and B2B integration support.

As shown in the earlier "refrigerator diagram," this edition focused on unifying the pieces to integrate people, information, and processes on top of the application platform. Supporting these components was the release of vast amounts of pre-built integration business content. This included items such as business intelligence packages for different industry scenarios, out-of-the-box data mappings within XI, workflow templates, preconfigured iViews within the portal, and more. Figure 3-9 illustrates the evolution of NetWeaver to an integration platform.

As mentioned earlier, these SAP NetWeaver integration components continued to be used by SAP's own developers who create the mySAP Business Suite and other business applications. For example, EP and WAS provided new

Web-based interfaces on top of some out-of-the-box business solutions. mySAP ERP 2004 was the first version of ERP to make use of many of the application platform capabilities and components to deliver its features.

With this milestone, many customers began to adopt NetWeaver components for integration mainly within their SAP landscapes. The primary benefits were TCO-oriented and efficiency-based because the pre-built SAP integration content and templates drastically reduced the time it took to tie applications, data, and user interfaces together. For many customers, NetWeaver has become the integration platform of choice between their SAP applications, as well as for SAP to non-SAP integration. Some customers have even standardized on NetWeaver for the bulk of their integration needs by integrating multiple non-SAP applications.

In addition to the integration capabilities, SAP and key partners began to use the platform for creating some of the first composite applications (xApps) on the platform. While these early composites tended to be built in a more traditional coding fashion as opposed to leveraging next generation SOA-based composition models, they clearly showed the power of building new, integrated process solutions on top of the platform. mySAP ERP included some of these first-generation composites. SAP and partners also began offering additional packaged composites that delivered targeted business solutions based on combining multiple underlying business systems.

Another important aspect of this milestone is that NW2004 became the platform upon which large numbers of third-party ISVs and systems integrators could certify solutions as being compatible with NetWeaver. Industry analysts are using the level to which third parties take advantage of certification as one indicator of overall market buy-in and maturity of the SAP NetWeaver platform.

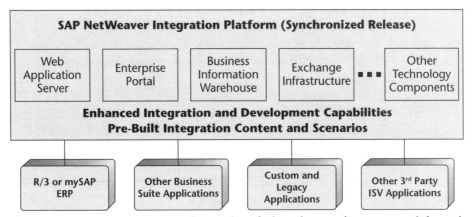

Figure 3-9: SAP NetWeaver as an integration platform for people, processes, information and applications

Although it represented a significant milestone, NetWeaver as an Application and Integration platform merely represents half the ESA road map. NW2004 offered many tactical benefits mentioned previously and served as the foundation for ESA within both R/3 and mySAP ERP 2004 landscapes. Perhaps the biggest advantage came from fixing some of the shortcomings in traditional SAP landscapes by providing more mature, standards-based tools for integrating and extending SAP applications themselves.

Some customers benefited greatly from these offerings, while others saw little advantage to compel them to switch away from their existing "best of breed" integration products and platforms. From an SOA perspective, the NetWeaver platform was now capable of providing and consuming Web Services in both direct and mediated models. This meant that even R/3 landscapes could begin working with ESA concepts for reuse and loosely coupled integration.

NetWeaver as a Composition Platform

The next significant milestone for SAP NetWeaver was labeled a Composition Platform. From a version perspective, this milestone was achieved with the release of NW2004S. It is this release of NetWeaver that powered the launch of mySAP ERP2005 and related Business Suite editions. These applications leveraged many of the new platform capabilities and more advanced, standards-based SOA features. The most important enhancement was the introduction of the first Enterprise Services Repository, as shown in Figure 3-10.

With the Enterprise Services Repository, SAP delivered its first packages of enterprise services content. This content exposed different functionality of the underlying business applications in an SOA manner using Web Services technologies. These enterprise services go beyond the basic Web Service capabilities available with earlier releases of NetWeaver. They expose more complex, coarse-grained functionality. For example, an "order cancellation" service might require a number of complex sub-operations in order to be carried out. All of that functionality can be wrapped neatly into an Enterprise Service with a common, standards-based interface. Instead of mining through BAPIs and RFCs, you can now build and integrate new solutions with SAP at a much more logical and meaningful level.

Another key feature is that these enterprise services are linked into the context of the SAP Business Solution Maps themselves. This makes it easier to find the specific interface operations you need in the context of a business process you are trying to support. Essentially, you can begin with an industry-specific SAP business blueprint and drill all the way down through core processes to an actual Web Services interface defined using the Web Service Definition Language (WSDL). These WSDLs can be consumed and invoked in composite applications your team creates. You can find information on how to navigate the Enterprise Services Repository from the companion Web site for this book, or by visiting the SAP Developer Network.

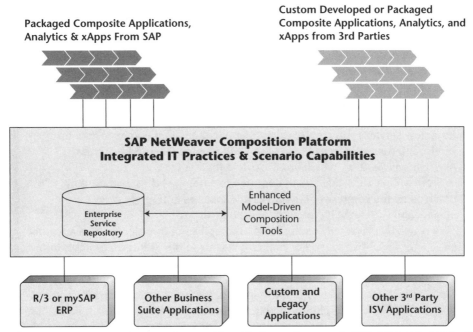

Packaged Composite Applications, Analytics & xApps From SAP

Custom Developed or Packaged Composite Applications, Analytics, and xApps from 3rd Parties

**SAP NetWeaver Composition Platform
Integrated IT Practices & Scenario Capabilities**

Enterprise Service Repository

Enhanced Model-Driven Composition Tools

R/3 or mySAP ERP

Other Business Suite Applications

Custom and Legacy Applications

Other 3rd Party ISV Applications

Figure 3-10: NetWeaver as a Composition Platform (Source: © SAP AG 2005–2006. All rights reserved.)

The composition platform milestone for SAP NetWeaver also provided the developer tooling necessary to create more advanced SOA-based composite applications. SAP delivered major updates to the Composite Application Framework (CAF), Visual Composer, SAP Analytics tools, and a more robust Guided Procedures framework for developing process-driven applications and user interfaces. Essentially, the same development model being used by SAP for new releases of business applications could also now be leveraged by partners and customers for their own development activities.

NetWeaver as a Business Process Platform

The final evolution of NetWeaver will add features to create a complete Business Process Platform (BPP). BPP is actually a term coined by Gartner analysts as the ideal platform for combining business-process content and applications with new technology infrastructures (see the sidebar "What Is a Business Process Platform?"). In essence, achieving BPP functionality is what occurs when the technical layers of an "applistructure" fully merge together.

WHAT IS A BUSINESS PROCESS PLATFORM?

Gartner created a category called *Business Process Platforms* (BPP) as a way to describe the new combination of business application content with SOA, BPM, EDA, process orchestration and model-driven composition technologies. The goal of any BPP is to bridge the business and technology organizations through a unified environment for defining, executing, managing, and changing business processes. The business application content itself will be populated from new services you create, existing applications that you expose with service interfaces, or from the off-the-shelf Service-Oriented Business Applications (SOBAs), which are described in Chapter 2.

Surrounding all of this is an integrated technology infrastructure that provides all the composition features and ensures enterprise class manageability, scalability, security, and so forth.

Because this is exactly what SAP is accomplishing through NetWeaver as the enabler of its ESA strategy, the company has used the BPP term to describe the final milestone for the platform once all these features are fully enabled.

A BPP not only handles the technology infrastructure, but also becomes the place where you define and manage all your business-process architectures themselves. Hence, the choice of which vendor's BPP to standardize on will be a big decision for many companies because leading ones will likely come with baseline models and pre-existing services. This will also affect ISVs who must decide which BPP environments to support, and at what level of process integration they should support them.

Included in the BPP milestone of NetWeaver will be significant enhancements to the scope of the Enterprise Repository itself. Instead of just objects and interface functions, all generic services will be implemented. In addition, full-scale process definitions and supporting models will also be represented as services within the BPP. New SOA-based development tooling that enables enhanced process authoring and management will also be provided. The goal is to enable the platform to handle the definition of business processes from a high-level value chain perspective all the way through the through details of how the implementation is realized in your IT environment in as automated a fashion as possible.

Because all of this will require more SOA-based infrastructure as part of the platform, BPP will deliver more service-oriented publishing, versioning, intermediation, and service lifecycle management features as part of NetWeaver's enterprise services infrastructure. Chapter 5 describes these capabilities in more detail.

A significant feature of the BPP is that some process functionality of the mySAP Business Suite applications will become embedded within the platform itself, as shown in Figure 3-11. All SAP applications can then leverage these services as out-of-the-box integration points.

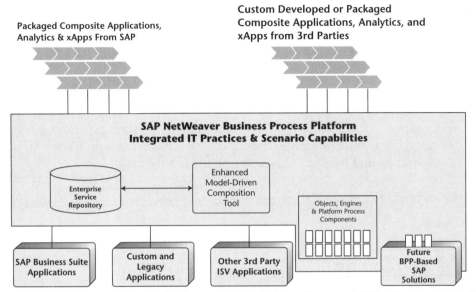

Figure 3-11: NetWeaver as a business process platform (Source: © SAP AG 2005-2006. All rights reserved.)

For example, services for supplier procurement and collaboration could now be seamlessly shared across mySAP ERP, SCM, and SRM applications automatically. You can also include your own processes or those acquired from third-party ISVs in this deployment model by exposing them as services within the platform. As you might expect, it is this evolution to a BPP that can have the greatest impact on simplifying your landscape and accelerating the mySAP Business Suite's transformation to a set of extensible composite applications.

Other Key Themes Within the NetWeaver Road Map

The preceding sections should give you a good feel for the major capability milestones that the NetWeaver platform will go through. Following is a summary of some cross-cutting themes that represent design goals for improving the platform each step of the way. Some of these were touched upon previously, but they bear repeating in terms of overall design goals that will keep improving with every release.

- Less coupling and more cohesiveness across the platform's installation units to act as a full foundation for the business solutions, while allowing maximum deployment flexibility

- Increased support for industry technology standards that continue to undergo rapid change and enhancement

■ Easier installation, upgrades, and configuration through rapid installers

■ Integrated models and business semantics that bridge high-level business-solution definitions through applications and the underlying implementation units

■ Maturing of the SOA technical capabilities with an expanded enterprise services infrastructure

■ Expansion of pre-configured, reusable content including enterprise services, integration mappings, portal business packages, application UI templates, and pre-built business intelligence models

Each release of SAP NetWeaver contains enhancements that support these goals. Over time the platform continues to become better integrated and easier to install, configure, use, and maintain.

The MySAP ERP Applications Road Map

By now, you should have a good idea of where SAP's ESA technology infrastructure is heading with NetWeaver. The next question becomes what happens to the business applications? If you recall your SAP history, the R/2 versions were based on mainframe technologies, R/3 on client/server architectures, and now mySAP ERP and new editions on SOA. As you might expect, the change in platform technology architecture has a big impact on the underlying applications. As the NetWeaver road map evolves, so too will the business solutions themselves.

Evolution of the ERP Technology Foundations

If ever a picture was worth a thousand words, then Figure 3-12 is certainly it. This image shows the architectural progression of SAP's ERP system from R/3 through the latest mySAP ERP 2005 release. As you can see, the decoupling of the business applications is following a parallel path with the SAP NetWeaver road map. The picture makes it looks like things are getting a lot more complicated. In some sense, this is true in terms of the architectural model that comes from breaking apart the monolithic applications. However, what matters most is that things are actually getting a lot easier in terms of consolidating your landscape and having simpler ways to add or extend the functionality of your ERP environment.

What Figure 3-12 really shows is that SAP has been working on loosely coupling the ERP environment since well before the ESA strategy was announced. As you can imagine, there is just so much existing code that this progression (let alone fully SOA-enabling the products) can happen only incrementally. And, obviously, there are dependencies on the NetWeaver road map itself to provide the core technology foundation on which to continue to refresh the architecture of the business applications. In fact, one of SAP's major internal benefits of having a mature NetWeaver platform is the ability to more rapidly change and evolve its business applications.

Obviously, R/3 versions through 4.6c were released on top of the SAP BASIS platform and represented the height of tight coupling and inflexibility of the SAP architecture. Although not much dramatically changed from a customer or partner's experience perspective with the release of R/3 Enterprise, you can see the first steps of using the SAP Application Server as an application platform for ERP, along with technology for managing extensions, became available. With the launch of mySAP ERP, NetWeaver became the foundational application and integration platform supporting the ERP environment. With each edition of mySAP ERP, leveraging of NetWeaver and other technologies to reduce coupling and modernize the functionality of the business applications continues.

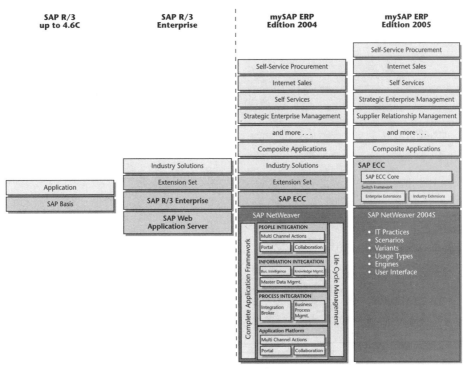

Figure 3-12: The evolution of SAP applications architecture (Source © SAP AG 2004–2006. All rights reserved.)

The mySAP ERP 2005 Architecture

Figure 3-13 focuses on the high-level architectural stack for mySAP ERP 2005. The first thing to recognize is the impact that the ERP Central-Component (ECC) has made. ECC essentially encompasses most of the functionality that was in R/3. In essence, SAP put a box around the legacy capabilities and began systematically decoupling the surrounding applications via smaller components, services, and composites. This decoupling and service enablement will continue to evolve along with each evolution of NetWeaver and the underlying business applications. Think of this as service-enabling the existing SAP environment into a Business Process Platform.

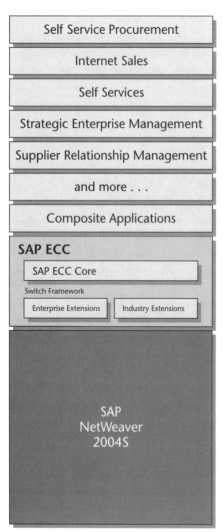

Figure 3-13: A look inside mySAP ERP 2005 (Source © SAP AG 2005–2006. All rights reserved.)

Along with ECC comes a new capability known as the *switch framework*. The switch framework essentially allows the same core ERP codebase to be used in conjunction with various enterprise and industry extensions. This is significant because historically industry extensions had built large amounts of separate code foundations, making it very difficult for SAP to release industry editions in a timely manner when a new edition of the base ERP product became available. The switch framework is just one example where SAP is consolidating and simplifying the core code of ERP while increasing flexibility and options for deployment.

The most important advantage of this new architecture is the way in which it enables new business application features to be created and deployed. Functionality such as employee self-service (ESS), manager self-service (MSS), and Strategic Enterprise Management (SEM) that are part of mySAP ERP are physically implemented outside the ECC core. This makes it easier to control which features you implement and when. These new solutions also take advantage of many of the features of NetWeaver, offering role-based Web and portal application interfaces, advanced analytics, and so forth, making them more valuable to end users. In short, this new model makes it easier to manage your landscape while enabling the creation of more powerful, modern, feature-rich business applications.

Composite Applications

The idea behind *composite applications* was introduced in Chapter 2. It generally refers to a business application that is built on top of multiple underlying systems and services. For example, an Internet retailing system may include order entry and status with the ERP system, real-time pricing and cross-selling from a merchandising system, and product reviews and discussions from a customized collaboration system.

Composite applications have been built for years. However, the term has taken on new meaning with advances in SOA technology. Chapter 14 covers the evolution of composite application development in an SOA world, along with SAP's composite application technologies in more detail.

One key advantage of the new mySAP ERP architecture based on the NetWeaver platform is the ability to easily extend ERP with very feature-rich business applications tailored to your unique processes. SOA-based composite application development offers a standards-based way to assemble these new applications. SAP is exposing the underlying ERP functionality for enhancement using this approach. This means you will be able to draw upon the capabilities of ERP using well-defined service interfaces and models.

This approach is very different from older code-based techniques for creating composites. In the past you usually needed to create a lot of customized ABAP coding inside the ERP system itself to support the composite. Then you often had more coding for new UI development and complicated integration coding to manage states and transaction across all the underlying systems.

SAP and its strategic ecosystem partners are selling new composite business applications that cut across underlying mySAP Business Suite applications and other third-party products. These packaged composites are sold under the brand xApps. Following is a list of some of the xApps that SAP currently offers:

- xRPM (Resource & Portfolio Management) for managing your project portfolio across the enterprise

- xCQM (Cost and Quotation Management) to enable manufacturers to submit more accurate quotes in an efficient manner

- xEM (Emissions Management) for complying with environmental regulations

- xGTS (Global Trade Services) for streamlining cross-border trade processes and managing risk in international trade

- xPD (Product Definition) for turning ideas into products

What makes these products unique is the way in which they are built and sold. As an example, xRPM is a business solution that cuts across the multiple underlying systems, as shown in Figure 3-14. xRPM combines mySAP ERP's Human Capital Management (HCM) employee data, SAP CATS time reporting against projects, mySAP ERP's financial information about project budgets and costs, and project tasks and work breakdown structures from the project management system. All of this information is brought together to help view, analyze, and make decisions across the project portfolio.

An ESA approach to composition will enable easier swapping out of the SAP systems with other third-party applications you may have. For example, Microsoft Project systems are already supported as a means to provide data needed for xRPM. You can envision the need for supporting other HR or financial data sources as well. This is the type of flexibility that a fully ESA-enabled platform architecture and landscape will enable by design as SAP completes its road map.

This same model used by SAP to create composite applications can also be leveraged by other ISVs, systems integrators, and your own internal development teams. The company has delivered tools and reference models along with a certification program for delivering third-party packaged composite applications to the market. This will be covered further in Chapter 4's discussion of the new SAP ecosystem and available from the book's companion Web site. The point is that in the new SAP architecture composite applications will become the preferred way to deliver not only more out-of-the-box SAP business functionality, but also third-party and customer-developed solutions.

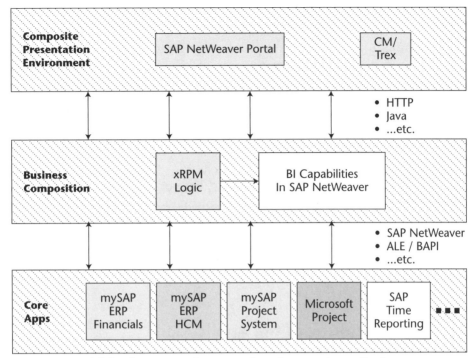

Figure 3-14: High-level structure of xRPM packaged composite application

The Road Ahead for the SAP Architecture

The previous sections have covered the SAP NetWeaver road map and how the mySAP Business Suite applications are evolving into a full-featured BPP. This will happen over time, and SAP's challenge is to incrementally deliver valuable functionality throughout each step of the road map. The advantage to you is the opportunity to ease into ESA adoption today, and gradually evolve your own solutions architecture along with the new releases and capabilities from SAP. In fact, that is probably the best method for any SOA adoption program as the industry standards and product capabilities of all vendors are continuing to evolve.

So, what should you be expecting in subsequent releases of NetWeaver and the mySAP Business Suite applications? The following sections highlight the major themes that will be part of the evolution of the architecture.

Full-Service Enabling of the mySAP Business Suite

SAP will continue to populate the Enterprise Services Repository with more and more robust, coarse-grained enterprise services. These services will become the preferred method for integrating with and extending the underlying ERP and other mySAP Business Suite applications because they are far more meaningful from a business-process perspective and much simpler to work with than detailed BAPIs and other traditional SAP integration methods.

Essentially, SAP is simply service-enabling its applications in the same manner you would with any of your existing in-house or legacy applications and products. In addition, they are making sure the semantics and models associated with these service interfaces are well thought out, published, and governed.

None of this is meant to suggest that the existing BAPI and IDoc integration points vanish in current Business Suite releases, or that the underlying business logic is replaced overnight. The key is that you will have an out-of-the-box SOA-based model of end-to-end core business processes with which to interact with your SAP landscape. For the most part, the BPP release reduces the need to look under the hood at lower-level implementation details and integration points. So, even if you leverage another platform's capabilities such as .NET to create SOA-based composite applications, integrating with SAP will be much easier.

Ongoing Refactoring of the Applications

The trends you saw in the discussion of the mySAP ERP architecture will continue. More and more application functionality will take advantage of specific features of the NetWeaver platform. In addition, SAP will continue to consolidate and simplify the maintenance of the core Business Suite applications around the common technology architecture and service models. Following are some examples:

- *Better user productivity* from composite applications that are organized around work tasks instead of underlying applications. In addition, options to do work from a variety of UIs (including Microsoft Office, Adobe forms, mobile devices, or new SAP rich client interfaces) instead of being bound to a specific business application's front-end.

- *Embedded analytics and business intelligence* giving users information to make decisions and for controlling automated process execution and alerting based on business rules and events. In essence, BI moves beyond reporting to deliver actionable, near real-time information.

- *Process flexibility* to reorganize and change things to meet new business requirements. In some cases, business analysts and users can be empowered to modify screens and workflows in coordinated or ad hoc ways.

- More *process-driven and process-aware applications* that guide human workflow, automate machine handoffs, and automatically respond to critical process events.

- *Lower TCO* through reduced integration complexity including things such as out-of-the-box process, application, and master data integration scenarios across the Business Suite.

- *Consolidation* of mySAP Business Suite Applications around common services, improving installation, reuse, TCO, and maintainability across the products.

- Better design and run-time *governance* at a technical and business level.

- *Ecosystem partner R&D* that brings unified solutions to specific industry business scenarios to market on top of the platform.

Essentially, the applications leverage the power of the technology platform. And, similar to what was accomplished with the switch framework, SAP will simplify the underlying architecture from a maintainability, ease of implementation, and time-to-market perspective. Most important, you can take advantage of these same trends in the solutions you implement or buy from other ISVs and systems integrators.

New Editions of Business Applications

As Figure 3-11 implies, the BPP release of SAP NetWeaver will become the foundation for a whole new breed of SAP business applications. Just as SAP moved from R/2 to R/3, and then from R/3 to mySAP ERP, the creation of the next-generation application platform will allow the company to deliver new editions of business applications built from the ground up on the ESA-based blueprint.

In effect, SAP will give customers choices in when and how to leverage ESA at both the platform and business applications level. At a high level, you can envision three loosely coupled layers that enable ESA. First, the enterprise service models themselves provide the abstractions for processes, services, objects, data types, and so forth. Second is the composite business process–based applications built on top of these models. Finally, the enterprise service models themselves must be supported by actual implementations.

For many customers, those implementations will exist in the ERP or other Business Suite Solutions they have today. In the future, there will be even richer implementations of the models in the next-generation application platform itself. This will allow SAP to offer new BPP-based business solutions for customers of all sizes and across multiple industries that are created from the ground up on the new platform architecture. However, it bears repeating that you can benefit from many of the ESA blueprints using SAP NetWeaver today, regardless of the version of SAP business applications you are running.

Unified Modeling and Development Environments

A rich enterprise services inventory and the overall business process management capabilities of the NetWeaver platform can be leveraged only through powerful tools for solution development and lifecycle management. Historically, SAP has not been known for having a simple set of standards-based, easy-to-use solution management and development environments. Over time, these tools will be enhanced and consolidated. You can anticipate improvements in this area targeted at the following:

- Supporting model-driven architecture and development techniques to better abstract solution definitions from their run-time implementation and configuration

- Digitally modeling end-to-end process solutions with unified metadata all the way from high-level value chain solution maps through detailed process definitions and into actual physical code used in the realization

- Reusing an inventory of common solution artifacts that can be assembled into applications such as process dashboards, three-step approval workflow models, configurable collaboration sites, and so forth

- Unifying the solution development environments (IDEs) based on industry standards, as opposed to the "one tool per component" model

- Integrating the business activity monitoring and lifecycle management capabilities to provide easy and actionable responses to events

- Enhancing the SOA-based composite application development capabilities as described earlier in this chapter

- Empowering business analysts to design and configure business solutions and user interfaces in many scenarios

In short, the road ahead for SAP's business applications architecture has three main focuses. First is enhancing the inventory of enterprise services to cover the entire functionality of the mySAP Business Suite. Second is continuing to morph the applications themselves to simplify the codebase and enhance the functionality with NetWeaver's modern platform capabilities. Finally, easy-to-use tools will make it much simpler to create unique process solutions by extending the existing Business Suite applications.

Summary

This chapter explained how the NetWeaver platform, mySAP ERP, and the other Business Suite applications are evolving to support ESA. Obviously, products as comprehensive as SAP's running in so many organizations with so much history and code behind them are not going to morph overnight into an SOA architecture. Hence, the company has developed an evolutionary strategy around the platform and the applications to migrate to ESA in a step-by-step fashion.

This approach is systematic and can be done in terms of normal product lifecycles. That means customers and partners can get started on the road to ESA today, based on features in the SAP NetWeaver platform that are currently available.

If you have worked with SAP for a number of years, you are seeing many improvements from the old R/3 architecture. If you come from a non-SAP background, you are seeing SAP beginning to support industry standards and deliver tools and technology consistent with other application platforms. Regardless of your perspective, it should be clear to you that your own path to ESA will evolve along with the products themselves.

Some of the highlights of this evolution are:

- NetWeaver is based on a solution-oriented view of IT Practices and Scenarios that help bridge the gap between IT and business users.

- As NetWeaver becomes more fully integrated and service-oriented, the concept of usage types replaces components to better represent the merging of capabilities across the platform.

- The Enterprise Services Repository and inventory provides a completely new model for developing and extending SAP-based solutions to meet your unique business needs.

- The BPP release of NetWeaver will enable the modeling and management of business processes from a high-level value chain through the physical solution implementations.

- mySAP ERP and the Business Suite applications make heavy use of the features of NetWeaver, particularly the people productivity and embedded analytics aspects of the platform.

- Packaged composite applications will become a preferred means of delivering new business functionality on top of mySAP Business Suite solutions by both SAP and other vendors.

SAP's road map for NetWeaver certainly has a big impact on mySAP ERP and other SAP business solutions. Chapter 4 will explain how SAP is developing a customer and partner ecosystem. This enables others to best leverage the NetWeaver road map to create complementary solutions using the same architecture as SAP itself.

The SAP ESA Ecosystem: Enabling Collaborative Innovation

Ecosystem is a scientific term that deals with how all the elements in a community work together with the environment to function as a unit. There has always been a vibrant community surrounding SAP, including systems integrators, consultants, ISVs, and, of course, customers. As mentioned in previous chapters, one of the major components of SAP's ESA strategy is the new way in which the company will work with these groups and the overall technology industry to solve comprehensive business problems. Why is SAP putting so much emphasis on evolving its collaborative customer and partner ecosystem? Because many of the company's stated ESA-based plans will fail unless a vibrant one emerges.

SAP is now coordinating and participating in many new ecosystem activities. These include customers, other application providers, technology infrastructure vendors, systems integrators, and industry experts. The combined capabilities of the SAP NetWeaver platform, the resulting SAP business solutions, and the overall support network for ESA are all being enhanced as a result.

The creation of the ecosystem is significant for several reasons. First, it highlights the major business model change that is occurring in the industry. Remember that SAP is now competing as a complete process platform instead of simply a set of standalone packaged business applications. This gives ISVs and systems integrators a whole new way to productize their offerings around the platform.

Second, it underscores the technology change brought about by SOA. The whole notion of "software as a service" (SAAS) and the merging of technology infrastructure, integration platforms, and business solutions into a unified "applistructure" requires a new type of industry collaboration that was not nearly as feasible under earlier architectures. Most important, the result is a major change in how business applications are conceived, created, acquired, and supported. The whole community can now tackle solving end-to-end business process problems in a seamless fashion. That means customers no longer have to incur all the costs of piecing together the product and service offerings from multiple vendors to meet their needs.

Of course, enabling this type of ecosystem is no small task for SAP. That is why it is important to understand the level of commitment the company is making to cultivate its success. Whether you are an existing SAP customer or partner, or are a new player in the SAP community, you have many options to actively participate. You also have many new ways to take advantage of the collaboration and contributions of others.

After reading this chapter, you will be able to:

- Understand why SAP is committed to developing this ecosystem

- See the full scope of SAP's ecosystem activities

- Evaluate the opportunities available to SAP partners and the new types of integrated business solutions they are creating

- Understand how these changes affect the way in which you acquire SAP-based solutions in an ESA world

- Anticipate future offerings from both SAP and its partners to best plan your landscape and solutions architecture

- Recognize opportunities to participate in and influence the community as a customer or partner along with the key questions you should be asking about the ecosystem

Why an Ecosystem Is Critical to ESA

Chapter 3 showed how NetWeaver evolves from an application and integration platform to a Business Process Platform (BPP). The key word is "platform." What is it that makes any kind of platform successful? The first answer is vast amounts of content running on the platform. For example, gaming systems such as PlayStation and Xbox are popular because of the large number of games you can play on them. Of course, Sony and Microsoft publish their own games, but it is the openness and expandability by others that really increases the value. Similarly, Windows- and Intel (Wintel)–based PCs became a dominant platform partly because of the large amount of software and hardware peripherals that would run on them. One of SAP's challenges is to increase the amount of content on its ESA-based platform.

Integrating End-to-End Business Solutions

A BPP such as SAP NetWeaver delivers the new foundation upon which packaged applications and solutions such as ERP, CRM, and SCM are built. Think of it as the operating system for business applications and process management.

So, how can SAP drive more business content to its NetWeaver-based BPP? First, the platform must support standards that make it easy and cost effective for others to add capabilities on top of it. Second, the combination of new content with the SAP platform must add very clear value to customers. Finally, SAP must simultaneously focus on ensuring that the platform is well-adopted and partners who support it are rewarded for doing so. The last part is especially tricky when it comes to enterprise software because an SAP partner for one solution can easily be a competitor in other areas.

From SAP's perspective, the company knows it must work better with other vendors to support end-to-end process solutions in a more out-of-the-box fashion. Each industry has a set of critical applications that benefit from integration with SAP enterprise systems and data. Trading systems within oil and gas, shop floor applications in manufacturing, and outage management systems in utilities are just a few examples. Think about your own landscape. Where could better out-of-the-box integration between third-party business systems and mySAP ERP or other Business Suite applications reduce costs and enhance processes?

Delivering a Complete Technical Foundation for ESA

Similarly, the world of SOA spans every layer of the technology stack. Everything from hardware, networking, applications, integration middleware, security, and so forth will evolve to support this new computing model and its standards. Again, SAP itself can offer only a subset of the infrastructure, and will rely on other technology vendors to augment the NetWeaver technology platform. SAP will also actively partner with the community on ongoing standards-development efforts that are critical to ESA's success.

So, by working with other ISVs or systems integrators, SAP can effectively share certain R&D efforts with partners who provide complementary solutions on top of the platform in a seamless manner. SAP wins because its own solutions and platform become more valuable. More important, customers benefit from getting more productized functionality that integrates well with their SAP environments. And, of course, the third party has an easier sales cycle when their solutions fit more easily within the existing SAP landscape.

Focused on Customers

Ultimately, all of this partnering succeeds only if customers embrace it. This is why customers themselves will play the most critical role in the SAP ESA ecosystem. They will help drive SAP's new solutions strategy by helping to:

- Identify the most important third-party business content to integrate into the platform
- Influence the enterprise services models for their industries
- Specify the most important features and functions for new types of packaged composite applications
- Recommend the key standards, features, and leading technology vendors that should be part of the underlying platform infrastructure
- Define co-innovation requirements across the industry process and technology solution maps

The result should be significant benefits to customers who can shift some of the cost and responsibility for integration and customization back to the vendor community. This is because platforms such as SAP NetWeaver give them more options to work with preferred ISVs and integrators on solving their unique business problems in a productized way. In addition, customers will be able to have more influence over defining the top priorities that vendors need to solve, and the way in which they solve them.

Figure 4-1 highlights the overall SAP ecosystem scope and how the different parties work together to deliver value. If you have spent a long time working with the SAP community, you will recognize that this is a big change from past practices. The following sections will look at each of these relationships and what SAP is doing to facilitate the creation of a strong ESA-based ecosystem.

Ecosystem-Enabled Business Innovation

SAP has two main efforts underway to organize ecosystem activities for enabling better business solutions. First are Industry Value Networks (IVNs). These networks represent a high-level clustering of stakeholders in a given industry. They focus on defining the most important solution requirements that address well-known industry issues.

The second initiative is the Enterprise Services Community (ES-Community), which supports other ecosystem collaboration efforts including work done by the IVNs. These activities are described in the following sections.

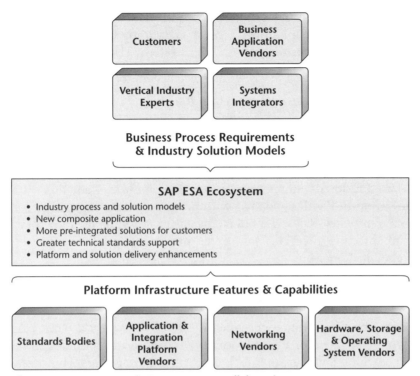

Figure 4-1: Summary of ESA ecosystem collaboration

SAP Industry Business Units and Industry Value Networks

SAP's primary goal remains delivering the best business applications and process solutions that meet the broadest set of customer needs. One of the company's greatest advantages over other large ISVs is its strength in many different verticals. Hence, some of the most important ESA-based ecosystem work SAP is driving takes place in the Industry Value Networks.

These IVNs bring together industry thought leaders from customers, systems integrators, ISVs, standards bodies, and other experts with strong expertise in the vertical. They work together to develop a common understanding of the priorities and opportunities most important to the industry. Obviously, one of the major outputs of IVN collaboration is an analysis of the key business process features and functionality that is not currently well-supported in SAP applications. That analysis becomes a key input to SAP's strategy, and helps the company and overall ecosystem decide where to take action.

The IVNs are led by SAP's Industry Business Units (IBUs) who work with key customers to identify the other participants. IBUs have always been responsible for defining the industry-specific versions of mySAP ERP and supporting the business standards of a given vertical. Now this responsibility extends to identifying industry-specific ESA- and NetWeaver-based extensions to the business process platform, as well as defining the key ecosystem partner solutions that become integral to SAP's strategy. This includes:

- Industry-specific solution maps with an ecosystem focus
- Industry-specific services and models in the ESR
- Industry-specific implementation components (SAP or partner-based)
- Industry-specific composite business applications (SAP or partner-based)

Figure 4-2 summarizes the high-level role of the IVN and IBU in helping define ESA-based industry enhancements to SAP's platform. Remember that the next generation BPP will be loaded with process content exposed as services. The more industry-focused models, the easier it will be for the ecosystem to shrink product lifecycles and offer incremental delivery of new functionality for customers.

Tackling the Solutions White Space

In order to drive the collaboration necessary for the IVN process to work, SAP had to do two things. First, SAP had to identify solutions not provided in the mySAP Business Suite that were of the highest value to customers. This meant building customer buy-in on collaboration in areas considered pre-competitive or non-competitive. Second, SAP needed to explicitly identify the places where partner ISVs would be encouraged to develop solutions (in other words, places where SAP does not plan to internally build a solution in the near term). These opportunities are referred to as "white space" by SAP.

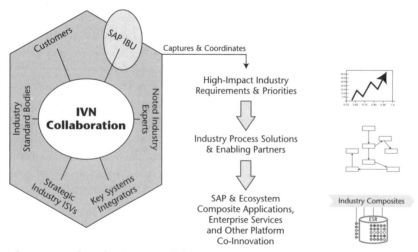

Figure 4-2: The role of IVNs and the IBU in defining ESA-based ecosystem solutions

To do this, each IBU manages an expanded industry Solution Map with a partner focus. These maps build upon the SAP Solution Maps available from the company's Web site that your organization should be familiar with. These extended maps help show the white space opportunities that partners are encouraged to help fill. One example is integrated commodity trading and risk management in oil and gas, as mentioned previously.

There are many scenarios across the more than 25 industries where SAP focuses. Figure 4-3 shows an example of how SAP expands the company's Solution Maps to show partners where there are opportunities to collaborate. Some white space scenarios are completely open, meaning SAP has no plans to develop capabilities in that area. Others are areas where SAP has some intentions but not in the near term. Potential partners can consult with the SAP IBUs to identify the processes where SAP is looking for collaboration from ISVs and systems integrators.

Armed with these road maps, IBU leaders coordinate with the IVN ecosystem to define the key requirements and potential partners for new composite applications as defined earlier. Several examples of IVN-initiated cooperative solutions are starting to emerge (see the sidebar "Some Examples of Industry Value Network Activities"). IBUs also get feedback on industry-specific models needed in the NetWeaver Enterprise Services Repository from the IVN process. They can then leverage the ES-Community, which has processes to help create these models. This is discussed in the next section.

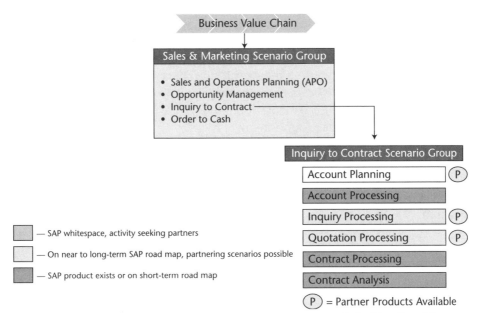

Figure 4-3: An example of how SAP uses solution maps to help identify white space opportunities for partners

SOME EXAMPLES OF INDUSTRY VALUE NETWORK ACTIVITIES

Once of the first IBUs at SAP to aggressively use the IVN model to define an industry blueprint of enterprise services was banking. SAP is working with the CxOs and architects from major banks to identify their strategic technology and application issues. The goal is to create a set of SOA-based services and processes for banking around which SAP will extend the NetWeaver platform and build products. Ultimately, these common definitions and road maps can influence other vendor products as well. Because banking is one industry with many heterogeneous and custom systems, it can benefit heavily from SOA collaboration around non-competitive domains. For example, anti–money laundering is a compliance area that affects all banks and so it makes sense to collaborate around building common models for the related services and processes.

The SAP Chemicals IBU has been very active in finding ecosystem partners to bring new composite applications and solutions to market. It has worked with a customer, a leading systems integrator, and an emerging ISV to launch an industry solution for price and margin management. It is also working actively with other ISVs on areas such as integrating predictive process control analytics with mySAP ERP and the xApp for Manufacturing Integration and Intelligence (XMII) to drive ROI in a number of industry scenarios.

The Enterprise Services Community

The ES-Community provides a collaborative process that helps guide how SAP's out-of-the-box enterprise services inventory gets extended. It is also a key vehicle for customers and partners to understand what services and products SAP itself is focusing on in the near term. This in turn lets customers and partners know where they can augment the platform with their own commercial or custom service implementations and get a jump-start on designing value-added applications around them.

Note that services can fall into two very general categories. The first category consists of services that drive business functionality (for example, areas such as optimized pricing, purchasing, order processing, and so forth). The second area of services describe platform technologies. Domains such as security, networking, RFID, and application monitoring are examples of these more technical services. The ES-Community can help define and enhance both types of services.

In essence, the ES-Community is a set of organizational processes coordinated by SAP to handle activities such as the following:

▪ Governance of the service definition process to ensure a cohesive model and set of business semantics that can be broadly adopted across the ecosystem

- Coordination with SAP's internal product and service definition teams

- Rules and charters defining how subject matter groups are formed and managed across different ESA domains to ensure active participation and transparent decision making

- Knowledge management and distribution for the work of ES-Community teams

- Legal guidelines for business areas such as protection of intellectual property rights

The Need for Coordinating Service Definitions

You can think of the ES-Community as an extension of SAP's own internal process for defining and publishing enterprise services. Organizations are at work inside of SAP defining the enterprise service models that the company will implement. It is then up to the individual product teams at SAP to consume or implement the approved service definitions when creating mySAP Business Suite solutions, expanding NetWeaver platform capabilities, or developing next generation business applications that have not yet reached the market.

Without a process to manage the service definitions, SAP would have a high probability of internal chaos. You can easily envision teams defining multiple enterprise services models that overlap and conflict with one another, as shown in Figure 4-4.

NOTE SAP has found that collaboration around enterprise services requires more than just the service interfaces themselves. Related models such as processes, data types, business objects, and so forth also must be well-defined and governed according to a common set of semantics to make ESA effective. While this chapter mainly refers to service interfaces for simplicity, these additional models also come into play.

In some cases, there may be multiple implementations of a single Enterprise Service definition across different SAP products. As long as the product teams support the defined service interfaces and related models, the process will work. This assumes the governance process makes it clear which product(s) must support which interfaces.

With the ES-Community, SAP is extending this same formal approach to service definition and governance to the overall ecosystem. The process used by the ES-Community as described in the next section.

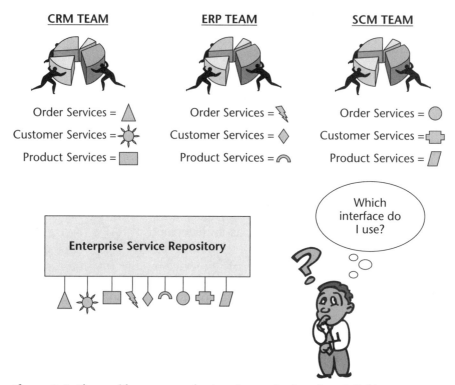

Figure 4-4: Chaos with unmanaged enterprise service interface definitions

How the Enterprise Services Community Operates

As shown in Figure 4-5, the ES-Community serves as a formal bridge between SAP and the larger ecosystem for defining updates to the official enterprise services and implementation from SAP. Members participate because they want to influence how integration with SAP business solutions will take place in the future. Of course, partners are also interested in leveraging the interfaces to create products as early as possible.

The ES-Community was patterned after other successful IT industry community processes that create Definition Groups organized around specific subject areas. However, following are a few things that make the ES-Community unique from general industry activities:

- All ES-Community Definition Groups are currently managed and led by SAP.

- Which Definition Groups are formed, and when they will be governed by SAP, is based on customer demand, requirements identified by the IBUs, or other internal delivery schedules, priorities, and time-to-market considerations.

- The Definition Groups are designed to be results-oriented and have very specific deliverables they are responsible for, as opposed to engaging in general, ongoing collaboration.

- ES-Community Definition Groups have a limited life tied to fulfilling their defined objectives. In general, they are expected to last approximately 3 to 6 months.

- The number of members in any ES-Community Definition Group will vary based on what is needed to deliver results successfully. This can range from a few participants to a dozen or more. SAP also has responsibility for selecting which members will work on which Definition Groups.

- While SAP charges a fee for participation in the ES-Community, there are currently processes for customers to request a waiver on this fee.

As indicated in Figure 4-2, SAP has a formal process by which the ES-Community operates. An Enterprise Services Community Program Office handles the management and operations for the community. SAP has also defined a Leadership Council made up of company executives who oversee the vision and overall operation, and approve major community decisions (such as which Definition Groups will be created). The Leadership Council may also form Advisory Groups of community members who provide advice and best practices for improving how the community works.

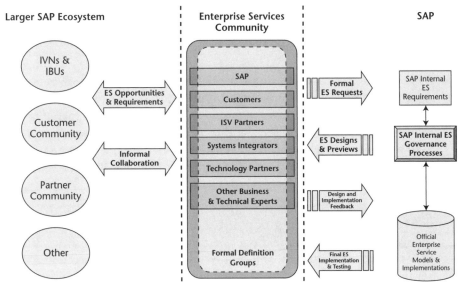

Figure 4-5: The ES-Community's role in influencing SAP enterprise services

Community members get involved through Definition Groups. These groups can range widely in size and scope. SAP will coordinate the membership with a clear set of rules for active participation and will help facilitate the process to ensure results are delivered in a timely manner. In addition to customers, ISVs, and systems integrators, other subject matter experts or industry standards bodies may be consulted with, or included on a Definition Group.

There are two types of Definition Groups. The first helps define new enterprise services. The second reviews candidate enterprise services along with the tangible implementations and products SAP may be planning to ship. These two types of Definition Groups are explained next, along with other key elements of the ES-Community. It is worth noting that there are also options to license SAP's enterprise services for evaluation and commercial planning without participating in formal ES-Community Definition Group activities.

Enterprise Services Community Request Definition Groups

Request Definition Groups are formed to request new enterprise services or changes to existing enterprise services available from SAP. Figure 4-6 shows the high-level phases performed by a request definition group, including the following:

- *Idea Proposal Phase* — This phase deals with the approval and proper formation of a Request Definition Group, including setting the scope and selecting which community members will participate. SAP and community members begin by collaborating informally on ideas for enterprise services. As discussions evolve, the request to form a definition group is made by SAP. If approved, the Request Definition Group is created and staffed.

- *Draft Review Phase* — This phase is where the bulk of the work gets done. Members conduct meetings and workshops to produce an official *Enterprise Services Request document*. This document includes the business case, usage scenarios, and technical information needed by SAP to determine whether the requested service should become part of the official SAP inventory and be made available in the NetWeaver platform.

- *Service Request Delivery Phase* — The Enterprise Services Request is delivered to SAP and the group disbands. At that time, all community members can also evaluate the request under a review and evaluation license. SAP subsequently determines whether the requested enterprise services are implemented as defined, with changes, or not at all. Community members will be informed of the status and progress.

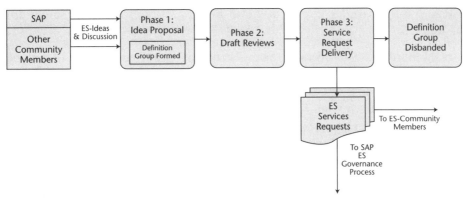

Figure 4-6: The phases of an ES-Community Request Definition Group

Anyone in the community may work informally with SAP and other members to help identify possible Enterprise Services Requests. Obviously, the more critical the request is to SAP customers or SAP's own strategic planning, the higher the likelihood that the company will move forward and consider creating a Request Definition Group.

Request Definition Groups are usually organized in one of three ways. The first type consists of industry-focused groups such as pharmaceuticals or public sector. The second type may be along more horizontal business areas such as manufacturing, marketing, or finance. There may also be technology and platform-oriented Request Definition Groups for areas such as RFID or security.

Enterprise Services Community Review Definition Groups

In addition to requests from the community, SAP will also be dealing with many more enterprise services requests and ideas from its own internal product management and development teams.

As mentioned earlier, SAP has a formal set of internal governance processes to sort through all of these requests and determine which ones will be included in updates to SAP's official enterprise services inventory. Once an Enterprise Service addition or change is approved, it can be included in the ESR and the implementation(s) of the new services can begin as part of SAP's product development process.

Request Definition Groups offer members of the ES-Community the opportunity to participate in the design and evaluation of certain new or changing enterprise services. In addition to influencing SAP's implementation process, participation in Review Definition Groups helps customers (and especially ISVs) prepare their own implementation plans for when the enterprise services are released.

Figure 4-7 illustrates key phases of a Review Definition Group, including the following:

- *Definition Group Creation Phase* — When SAP determines a set of new or changing enterprise services is approved for the community, a definition group is formed. The scope is clearly defined and community members are invited to participate.

- *Draft Review Phase* — While SAP is designing the enterprise services, members of the definition group are given the opportunity to review and comment on multiple design drafts and plans for implementation.

- *Service Definition Delivery Phase* — During this phase, SAP finalizes the design and implements the new or updated enterprise services. ES-Community members have access to final design documentation, as well as a hosted version of the enterprise services once they are fully implemented. SAP also delivers certification tests associated with the new or updated enterprise services.

- *Product Delivery and Certification Phase* — In this phase, SAP ISV and system integration partners can test and certify products they develop based on the new enterprise services.

Third-party products that pass SAP certification are designated as ES-Ready. If current customer demands for SAP certification are any indication, this will become an important classification that customers evaluate when selecting third-party solutions.

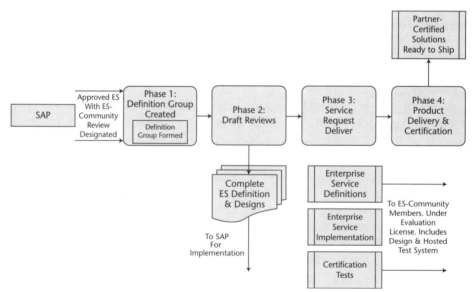

Figure 4-7: The phases of an ES-Community Review Definition Group

Future Considerations for SAP

Remember that one of the big goals of ESA is to have a set of Enterprise Service definitions that are decoupled from implementations. Solution developers can then rely on the interfaces while the underlying implementations can vary over time for greater flexibility (see the sidebar "Enterprise Service Definition Versus Implementation"). By adhering to this "design by contract" mentality, the whole ecosystem can collaboratively innovate in a compatible manner.

ENTERPRISE SERVICE DEFINITION VERSUS IMPLEMENTATION

Most of the initial services ISVs create and enterprises use are implemented through what's called an "inside out" approach. This usually means taking an existing piece of application functionality and exposing the current interfaces as Web Services. There's nothing wrong with this approach. It is a perfect way to get the many benefits of service-oriented integration. In fact, NetWeaver enables all BAPIs and IDoc interfaces to be exposed as Web services in this manner.

But to gain the real benefits of a business-driven SOA, which is what ESA is all about, requires an "outside in" approach to defining services. Using this method, services are defined to meet the requirements of specific processes, activities, entities, and events. In other words, the service interface is created *independently from* (and sometimes *before*) its implementation. The subsequent implementation can happen by mapping to existing applications, developing new code, or a combination of the two. Of course, there can be multiple implementations for any service interface. For example, a "product availability" service could have different implementations for:

◆ Inventoried items

◆ Make-to-order products

◆ Products you private-label from another supplier

The key is recognizing that the interface of the service is best designed outside the scope of any specific application and should be incorporated nicely into the overall set of services that model the business. This effectively decouples the service interface from its implementation. It also encourages the broadest usage of that service.

These are the same goals that the ES-Community helps achieve. Recall that Request Definition Groups deal only with enterprise services requirements, not the implementations. Ultimately, SAP's Enterprise Services Inventory must deliver a comprehensive set of interfaces that are very cohesive and lend themselves to supporting the most flexible set of business solutions. When customers, partners, and SAP product development teams actively design and deliver new composite business solutions that consume those services, this truly becomes a case of collaborative "design by contract." A new development and integration model for SAP-based business solutions is achieved.

SAP has intentionally limited the scope of the ES-Community to help launch it in a manageable way and deliver early successes. The initial scope is still large and deals with how the SAP NetWeaver platform and current and future business applications will be service-enabled. The goal is to enable ecosystem participation and influence on active SAP product development efforts as early as possible.

As the ES-Community processes mature, a stable model for SAP, customers, and partners working together to define enterprise services will emerge. At that point, the authors predict that the role and scope of the ES-Community will need to expand. This is because SAP's ESA benefits extend beyond the boundaries of SAP applications. Any customers developing their own SOA strategies around SAP solutions will need to consider things such as the following:

- What common Enterprise Service definitions and interfaces will you need that will *not* have their implementation provided by SAP? For example, certain shipping services could be implemented by companies such as UPS, FedEx, DHL, and so forth, but the service interfaces are still useful to have in the official SAP service models.

- How do you ensure third-party implementations of services meet a certification standard similar to the current ES-Ready designation for integrating with SAP's enterprise services implementations?

- Which third-party implementations of services should SAP endorse, license, or resell, if any?

- How will Enterprise Service models evolve if they are implemented by multiple third parties so that existing composite application solutions can continue to work?

These are complex questions. Of course, SAP's out-of-the-box Enterprise Services Inventory in the ESR is already intended to be extended by customers and partners for their own use. But, rather than leaving customers and partners to do this individually, it is clear there are certain common industry and technology services that all customers would like in the official model to create composite applications. In the future, SAP may include Enterprise Service interface definitions in the ESR out of the box that actually get implemented by partners or customers.

Hence, the ES-Community (or some other SAP process) will be needed to help define these additional Enterprise Service models and interfaces. In some cases, SAP may work jointly with third parties to provide the actual implementations of agreed-upon model changes. In others, it might leave the implementation open-ended for competition.

It is obviously an interesting question as to whether a new set of services should be implemented exclusively by SAP or by a select set of "go to" partners, or whether they should be open to the community at large. All the variables that go into that decision are beyond the scope of this book. Needless to say, if you are a third-party ISV or systems integrator interested in providing certified solutions on the platform, your organization will likely spend a lot of time understanding all the legal and business aspects associated with the ES-Community today and in the future.

For now, it is worth revisiting the SAP NetWeaver BPP architecture introduced in Chapter 3. Recall that in the BPP release there are new implementation components of certain models in the application platform itself. Figure 4-8 shows how SAP might evolve the platform ecosystem to include specific models for third-party implementations. If you are an SAP customer or partner, it is worth considering how this evolution can affect your landscape, and where and how it makes sense for you to track or participate in the ES-Community or other ecosystem activities.

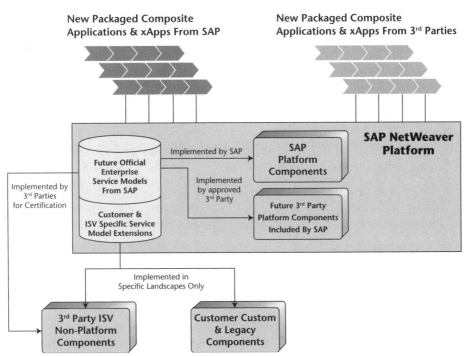

Figure 4-8: How future enterprise services opportunities may be extended to ecosystem partners both inside and outside the SAP platform

The Technology Platform Ecosystem

It is easy to see how the ecosystem benefits when customers, systems integrators, and third-party ISVs offering complementary functionality to SAP business applications participate in the ES-Community. In this section, you will see how SAP's focus takes the ecosystem efforts a step further to expand the core technology capabilities of the NetWeaver platform itself. You can think of this as a technology foundations ecosystem.

As mentioned, SOA and the shift to "applistructures" span every level of the technology stack. Chapter 2 laid out why it is important for you to be thinking in terms of a highly integrated application platform instead of a set of diverse technology components. At a high level, a complete platform should be able to support all the IT Practices and Scenarios shown in the SAP NetWeaver solutions map.

This means two things. First, if your organization standardizes on one or two of the leading platforms such as SAP NetWeaver, Microsoft .NET, or IBM WebSphere, you will need to balance them along with other technology capabilities to enable an end-to-end platform. Second, you can choose to use another vendor's solution to implement part of an IT Scenario instead of one embedded in NetWeaver. The key is to find solutions that seamlessly integrated so that you are not wasting resources on non–value-added integration and configuration activities just to use your platform.

SAP is investing heavily in putting together a technology platform ecosystem to augment NetWeaver. This alignment with major IT providers allows you to:

- Preserve existing investments in other vendor technologies by ensuring they work seamlessly with NetWeaver
- More rapidly adopt new technologies such as specialized RFID, geographical information system (GIS), digital forms, and other areas where focused vendors outperform generic platform providers
- Take advantage of the SOA trend of commoditizing integration and application intelligence into hardware and networking layers
- Leverage innovations in analytics and user productivity enablement from other vendors
- Ensure your end-to-end business processes are managed from a security, high-availability, and integrity perspective across SAP and non-SAP applications

The Role of a Technology Platform Ecosystem

SAP has its own internal product road map for the platform. The company has also picked specific strategic partners for certain core technical areas that augment NetWeaver (for example, Adobe, which is providing integrated XML-based Interactive Forms technology). This makes sense in areas where there are clear industry ISV leaders and a solution requires a lot of joint R&D efforts to be successful.

There will be broader ecosystem opportunities for collaboration in other technology areas. Note that in an SOA world, many lower-level platform concerns can often themselves be modeled as service interfaces. Technology vendors will work together with SAP on developing these common models for the NetWeaver platform using a model such as the ES-Community. Obviously, the technology ecosystem parties will start with industry standards and then augment them to provide advanced functionality where the standards are incomplete or silent. The result will be an additional set of official ESA-based technical service definitions that anyone in the SAP ecosystem can leverage to implement solutions.

You can also anticipate that as SOA technology standards mature, a lot of the lower-level IT integration and plumbing will become further commoditized. Much of it may move into the hardware and networking layers. Because SAP's focus is ultimately on higher-level NetWeaver platform capabilities such as business content and process management, user productivity enablement, and advanced analytics, the ecosystem model is positioned to support both ongoing innovation and consolidation.

It is important that you recognize that NetWeaver, like any composition and process platform, will continue to evolve as explained in Chapter 3. Again, the ecosystem model combines innovation from lots of companies, which can give you more options to meet the specific needs of your landscape.

Leading Platform Ecosystem Partners

Some of the largest hardware, networking, integration middleware, and application development vendors have signed on with SAP to support the ESA ecosystem. Many have very deep, strategic R&D relationships underway, including having licensed the entire ESA platform. Table 4-1 highlights some of the most important technology platform participants.

While ESA may cause greater complexity at first, the collaborative research and development will eventually lead to lower TCO for customers. In addition to the industry leaders listed earlier, many other companies are working at both strategic and tactical levels with SAP to enhance the NetWeaver platform. Some have very broad infrastructure offerings, while others fill in specific niches. It is valuable for your organization to track the evolution of the ecosystem programs over time. Most important, your organization should be working with its key technology partners to understand their NetWeaver strategy and road map, and how it can benefit you. In some cases, you may want to actively participate with them to influence important ecosystem areas.

Table 4-1: Examples of Strategic ESA Partners for the NetWeaver Platform

COMPANY	SELECTED ESA COLLABORATION AREAS
Adobe	Interactive forms, printing, and flex-based Rich Internet Applications
Cisco	SAP application and integration-aware hardware and networks
CA	IT security and systems management services and composites
EMC	Information lifecycle management services for multiple scenarios
Intel	SOA management virtualization, BI Accelerator, and RFID
Mercury	Quality and lifecycle management for services and SOA-based BPM
Microsoft	.NET and NetWeaver platform integration and Office-based composites
Symantec	Intelligent security policy enforcement for SOA-based applications
Veritas	High availability landscape management for SOA and ESA applications

An Ecosystem Infrastructure Example: The Adaptive Computing Controller

This "one platform supported by multiple vendors" approach is a very different model for managing an SAP landscape. The degree to which the following capabilities are integrated will determine the agility and TCO for your environment:

- Hardware
- Networking
- Security
- Integration and service intermediation
- Storage management
- Analytics
- User interface presentation (including portals)
- Monitoring and lifecycle management
- Automated governance
- Application development and quality assurance

As an example, one of the major architectural objectives associated with ESA at the platform level is to deliver on the promise of Adaptive Computing. The goal of Adaptive Computing is to bring the same level of agility and loose coupling to the hardware operating system and networking levels of the computing infrastructure that SOA brings to business applications. SAP will work with ecosystem partners who support its Adaptive Computing Controller (ACC) technology. ACC essentially creates a service-oriented virtualization layer on top of the computing infrastructure.

As shown in Figure 4-9, the ACC allows dynamic resource assignments for business applications across the computing infrastructure. This is one means by which the hardware, networking, storage, and operating system environments become application-aware. These types of resources can now be allocated based on service level agreements (SLAs), economic value of transactions, and other business means, all while lowering the TCO of the infrastructure. This will be covered further in Chapter 5. For now, you should recognize that even the model by which you acquire computing infrastructure resources will change as a result of the ESA ecosystem alliances.

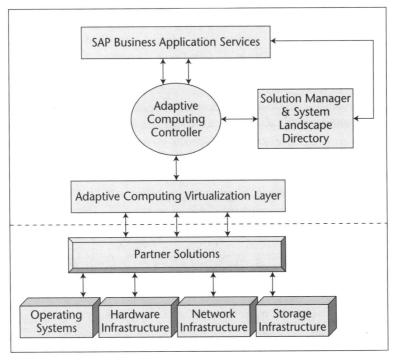

Figure 4-9: The Adaptive Computing Controller helps enable the technology ecosystem.

New Ecosystem Application and Certification Options for Partners

All of this ecosystem work enables next-generation models for SAP applications on the new ESA-based architecture. It also offers customers new options for how they buy business applications and technology solutions to complement their SAP landscape.

Traditionally, acquiring solutions from other vendors offered little in terms of out-of-the-box strategic integration. You typically got products that had some basic API or data-driven integration and perhaps some implementation accelerators. However, most of the real work and cost to tie things together was left to your organization.

With ESA and the NetWeaver platform, there are multiple new delivery models that can improve this situation. Some of these models will require certification from SAP. Others can simply be taken advantage of by any ISV in the same way that you could write a solution for the .NET or Java platforms without getting it certified. Obviously, customers and partners must decide how important these SAP certifications are to selecting a third-party solution.

Figure 4-10 illustrates some of the new partnering scenarios that are described in the next sections. Some require greater investment to deliver more functional value and integration. If you are a customer, these delivery options represent ways of ensuring compatibility with the ESA strategy and SAP NetWeaver platform at a lower overall implementation and maintenance budget. If you are a vendor, they offer options for expanding your product distribution and compatibility.

SAP also has several certifications in place for partners that map to these delivery scenarios, including *Powered by SAP NetWeaver, Packaged Composite Applications* (PCAs), *xApps*, and the *ES-Ready* designation. They differ in terms of technical requirements and the level of business relationship with SAP. SAP will likely continue to evolve the various options and criteria for certification over time. The key is to understand the general NetWeaver-based solution development options as described in the following sections. In addition, you should always look under the hood at which version of an application a partner has certified, along with the specific details of how they achieved it.

NOTE SAP will likely evolve the specific certification and partner categories associated with the NetWeaver platform as it matures. You can research the full catalog of partner solutions at www.sap.com/partners.

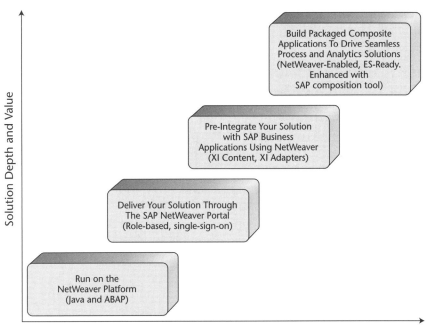

Figure 4-10: New solution delivery options for ecosystem partners

Applications Deployed on the SAP NetWeaver Platform

These are out-of-the-box commercial applications that will run directly on the NetWeaver Application Server. That means they are either written in Java 2 Enterprise Edition (J2EE) or are ABAP add-on applications. In the case of J2EE applications, they will have gone through deployment and functional testing to ensure that the product can run out of the box on the NetWeaver Application Server. Note that this does not mean that SAP tools like the NetWeaver Developer Studio are required to write a Java application. It simply means you can run it on the NetWeaver platform.

The advantage of acquiring applications that can be deployed on the NetWeaver platform deals mainly with landscape consolidation and simplified deployment. Because you will already have the NetWeaver Application Server skills and licenses in-house to support your mySAP ERP and other Business Suite applications, this scenario can offer customers the chance to use the same environment to support third-party applications you acquire. That means you may be able to avoid adding additional infrastructure software or hardware in the form of another licensed or open source J2EE application server for the third-party solution. There may also be some resource utilization, monitoring, and landscape planning benefits that come from having the complementary SAP applications running on the same platform.

Partner Applications Integrated with SAP NetWeaver Portal

Third-party applications can come out of the box with user interfaces exposed through the SAP NetWeaver Portal. This can offer a number of advantages. First, for those companies that standardize on the SAP portal technology as a preferred UI for business applications, these third-party solutions can automatically be embedded in your portal. Second, support for SAP Single Sign-On (SSO) technologies can be provided.

These application UIs can go a step further in terms of being configured to integrate with other SAP content that comes with the mySAP Business Suite. If you recall from Chapter 3, SAP is delivering role-based portal interfaces to optimize user productivity for a number of its application interfaces. Third parties can integrate with these user-driven portals and dashboards by developing Business Packages with expanded roles, worksets, pages, and iViews that build upon existing content.

Finally, third parties can also sell solutions that come preconfigured with integration to SAP's Knowledge Management (KM) capabilities. They can expose existing data repositories through KM, or seamlessly add information and work with existing repositories in the KM environment.

Applications Pre-Integrated with mySAP Business Suite Applications

SAP has always had a number of certification scenarios for third parties to tie into R/3, SRM, CRM, and SCM systems. These interfaces were usually version-specific and focused on tightly coupled information integration based on SAP IDoc and BAPI technologies. Obviously, these interfaces could be wrapped with Java or .NET interfaces as well.

To fully benefit from ESA, these integration scenarios can now be supported by third parties in a much more loosely coupled manner. Basic Web Services integration between mySAP Business Suite applications and the third-party solution can be delivered out of the box. More important, third-party ISVs can deliver solutions that integrate with the more coarse-grained Enterprise Service business interfaces found in the SAP ESR.

These service integrations can be done directly, but are more beneficial if delivered using SAP Exchange Infrastructure (XI) as the integration intermediary. SAP offers a number of content packages with XI that ISVs can use to integrate their solutions. These content packages include objects such as the following:

- Data structures and schemas
- Interfaces
- Mapping programs
- Integration scenarios and processes that map to mySAP Business Suite applications

Third-party ISVs and systems integrators can deliver their own XI content packages for their solution to provide certified NetWeaver-based integration to the SAP applications. They also have the option to create certified XI adapters for their solutions.

Packaged Composite Applications and xApps

Of all the new software delivery models, packaged composite applications (PCAs) may represent the most unique change that ESA and the SAP NetWeaver platform bring about. As discussed in earlier chapters, composite applications are simply application solutions that are built on top of multiple underlying software components. Third parties can build, certify, and sell PCAs themselves. SAP will also co-develop and directly sell certain strategic PCAs with ecosystem partners, usually in conjunction with the IVN initiatives. When distributed directly by SAP, the composite applications will fall under the xApps branding.

Future chapters cover the detailed architecture and anatomy of a composite application. It is worth noting that early PCAs will not necessarily adhere to the purer SOA approaches for delivery because the creation of the ESR and the overall evolution of both the platform and third-party products is still ongoing. Regardless, you should recognize that ecosystem partners will be able to quickly assemble PCAs that have the following characteristics:

- Support "bite sized" functionality that addresses a specific set of high-value business needs from a process perspective
- Run on the NetWeaver platform (Note that some of the underlying third-party application components themselves may not necessarily be running on NetWeaver.)
- Expose their interfaces through the NetWeaver Portal, leveraging all of the role-based features and content mentioned earlier
- Leverage both SAP and non-SAP application components and services
- Come fully integrated out of the box

- May take advantage of Guided Procedures technologies to control process workflow and coordination within the PCA

- May deliver embedded analytics in context of the process or offer analytics-based dashboards

The first advantage of this type of composite application delivery is that it drives new value while leveraging existing application investments. The second advantage is that these solutions have a very fast time-to-market. They are not restricted by major product release cycles as are the mySAP Business Suite applications or other large software components. It is almost like getting the best of all worlds. PCAs offer the rich functionality and ease of delivery similar to custom applications, but they are acquired, integrated, and supported like packaged products.

Because of the discrete size and scope associated with PCAs, the opportunity is open to ISVs of all sizes. Perhaps more interesting is that Systems Integrators (SIs) are also capitalizing on the PCA opportunity. They can now "productize" their industry domain knowledge in entirely new ways. Customers themselves may ultimately be able to use the PCA model to recoup investments in creating their own custom internal solutions by allowing a third party to commercialize them as a PCA. Of course, that will make sense only if the subject matter is not strategic or competitive.

SAP and the Standards Bodies Ecosystem

The previous discussions described the many new ways ecosystem partners can bring solutions to market that enhance SAP business applications and the NetWeaver platform. Another ecosystem activity is based on SAP's involvement with industry business and technology standards organizations.

Technology and Business Standards Organizations

From a technology perspective, ESA and BPP represent a merging of computing infrastructure, software platforms, SOA, and business process management. In those areas alone, dozens of standards organizations and hundreds of specifications and working groups are underway. All of them can affect SAP NetWeaver, partner, and customer road maps in one way or another.

SAP is now very active in playing leadership roles in a number of these organizations. This is quite a change from the company's involvement under the R/3 architecture. Table 4-2 lists *some* of these organizations to give you a feel for where SAP is expanding its standards participation. It also gives you a feel for the many community efforts your organization may want to track to gauge which ones could affect your architectural plans. Future chapters dive into some of the key technical standards that the SAP NetWeaver platform supports.

Table 4-2: Selected Technology Standards Organizations Where SAP Is Active

NAME	FOCUS AREAS
W3C	Variety of Web Service, XML, and other Internet standards
WS-I	Web Services interoperability across platforms and languages
OASIS	Technical and business-level e-business standards
Eclipse	Development platforms, tools, and application frameworks
OMG	Multi-platform model-driven architecture including MetaObject Facility (MOF) and Unified Modeling Language (UML)
WFMC	Workflow and process management standards
Java CP	Community Process for setting Java technology standards

You should also be aware that SAP is partnering very closely with IBM, Microsoft, BEA, and other large platform vendors in developing a host of Web Services–related specifications. Many of these have already been submitted to standards bodies and have made their way into products. Others are still in public review and will be submitted to a standards body after further evolution.

What is important for you to recognize is not only the standards that SAP considers important, but also which ones it works closely with other very large vendors to establish. In particular, pay attention to the ones that are being developed and promoted along with IBM and Microsoft. Obviously, that is a significant amount of combined market influence that likely will find its way into their respective platforms.

Some of these technology standards bodies are also working on more business-level standards, particularly in the area of XML data and process schemas to represent different business transaction models. SAP is especially active in those areas. The company is also working with a number of industry consortiums that have similar efforts underway. SAP is building content packs into the NetWeaver platform and mySAP ERP and other Business Suite products for standards such as the following:

- GS1 product information (UCC/GTIN), EPC/RFID, and data synchronization
- RosettaNet for high-tech supply chain
- HL7 ANSI standards for healthcare
- GCI for retail and consumer products
- ACORD for insurance
- SWIFT for banking
- B2MML and ISA-95 standards for manufacturing
- CIDX for chemicals

Many more horizontal and vertical standards are being integrated in the NetWeaver platform and SAP applications. SAP is also a major sponsor of XML.org, which is hosted by OASIS and is a good source for you to research other specific standards of interest.

Practitioner Community Ecosystem

The final ecosystem SAP has worked to develop is around customer and partner collaboration communities forming around the platform. SAP has always had a rich customer and user community tied to its business applications. With the advent of ESA, SAP NetWeaver also requires a vibrant developer community to be successful just like any other successful technology platform.

The SAP Developer Network

Historically, SAP has been the control center for the vast majority and support information and help related to its products. In conjunction with the launch of ESA, the company created the SAP Developer Network (SDN). By opening up SDN for worldwide participation, it has quickly become the largest source of education and collaboration for software engineers and IT practitioners working with the NetWeaver platform.

SDN contains valuable assets, including the following:

- e-Learning classes, tutorials, and how-to guides
- Developer support forums for questions and troubleshooting around ESA, NetWeaver platform usage types, SAP business applications, and core Java and Web Services technologies
- Blogs from SAP and non-SAP practitioners, including active participation from SAP product managers and architects who give early information on new product developments
- Software downloads for evaluation editions, add-ons, code samples, portal content, and other SAP and non-SAP contributions
- A Knowledge Management library of presentations, articles, and other information

NOTE You can visit the SAP Developer Network at http://sdn.sap.com.

You will likely find you can troubleshoot and get answers to design and implementation questions much faster through the SDN forums because you have not only SAP providing support, but also non-SAP developers from customers and partners actively monitoring and posting ideas and solutions. In fact, a high percentage of SDN content comes from outside of SAP.

Customers will also find this to be a valuable learning resource for developing employees that was not previously available. One additional benefit of SDN is the collaborative way in which the ESA road map and NetWeaver platform strategy are unfolding incrementally. Prior to SDN there was no equivalent comprehensive source of ongoing information that could support the road map.

SAP User Group Communities

In addition to the online developer community, collaborating around ESA and NetWeaver has become a pervasive topic in worldwide SAP user groups. SAP and early adopter customers and partners are continuing to provide more input and training on ESA success factors and platform adoption through their local chapter meetings. In the Americas, SAP has helped to bolster these ties by strengthening coordination with the national Americas' SAP User Group (ASUG) organization.

Today, the ASUG annual conferences now occur during the same week and at the same venues as SAP's Sapphire and Tech Ed events. Now customers and partners can more easily take in the SAP announcements and updates, and then immediately apply them to peer collaboration. ASUG has also expanded its own technology groups to include more coverage of the broader NetWeaver platform and best practices in ESA adoption (see the sidebar "ASUG Enterprise Architecture and ESA Adoption Communities").

ASUG ENTERPRISE ARCHITECTURE AND ESA ADOPTION COMMUNITIES

Driven by SAP customers, ASUG formed an Enterprise Architecture community to explore the broader EA concepts associated with SAP's role in the overall IT landscape. This group is focused on helping customers become better practitioners of EA management, align their efforts with their business counterparts, define their next-generation road maps, and provide influence back to SAP on future directions.

The community itself launched a special-interest group focused specifically on ESA adoption. This group collaborates around experiences and organizational challenges associated with learning and deploying ESA, as well as working with the specific enterprise services and models offered in the NetWeaver platform.

SAP actively supports these groups with advanced briefings, training, and collaboration opportunities with senior management and internal experts. These communities have also received support from selected ecosystem partners such as Microsoft for similar access and advance collaboration. If you are interested in participating, you can find more information at www.asug.com.

All of these broader collaboration communities help customers and SAP partners deal not only with adoption planning around ESA, NetWeaver, and mySAP ERP, but also with the specific questions and challenges associated with their day-to-day activities. This is yet another source of influence for SAP product definition efforts around the new architecture.

Ecosystem Considerations for Customers and Partners

Figuring out the many implications and questions to ask as a result of all the new ecosystem activity can be challenging. Following are some considerations for customers and partners to help you get started.

Implications for Customers

As you have seen, SAP's ecosystem strategy creates a number of opportunities for customers. At the same time, it may also make life in your organization a lot more complicated by raising a bunch of challenging questions. For example, how and from whom should you buy new applications that augment SAP? How should you manage your technology landscape? Where should you influence or use SAP Enterprise Service models versus those you create or buy from other vendors? What happens with licensing? Figure 4-11 highlights these key decisions.

Obviously, this is no longer as simple as having an almost standalone BASIS platform running your R/3 application. If you are like many customers, you probably have separate SAP technology groups from your other application and infrastructure teams because the skill sets are different. Well, now those worlds are about to collide.

The authors have seen many interesting strategy and planning discussions take place on this topic. It is obviously easier to address the more SAP-centric your IT environment is today. The following sections will highlight some of the questions you should be asking as a result of the ecosystem activities.

Working with Other Business Application Solution Providers

As mentioned earlier, SAP is providing the ESA models and NetWeaver platform backbone as a way to run applications written by third parties. Some of these applications may go a step further and be delivered as third-party packaged composites or SAP-branded xApps. The first question you need to ask yourself is how important this is to your organization when deciding on whose solution to buy.

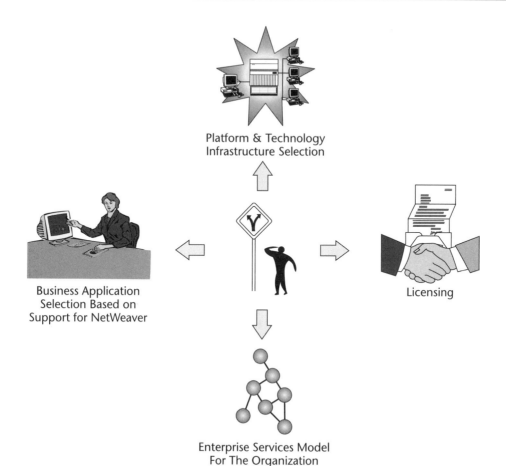

Platform & Technology
Infrastructure Selection

Business Application
Selection Based on
Support for NetWeaver

Licensing

Enterprise Services Model
For The Organization

Figure 4-11: How the SAP ecosystem affects decision making

Keep in mind that this is a question that goes beyond just platform consolidation. The important considerations are how things such as deep SAP process integration, delivery of NetWeaver Portal content, or out-of-the-box integration with the SAP enterprise services model change your decision-making criteria from buying a standalone application and then doing the integration on your own. It really is a new form of purchased solutions.

Following are some of the questions to consider when evaluating a third-party business solution or looking at the ones already in your portfolio:

- How strong is their long-term SAP ESA and NetWeaver delivery strategy?

- How strategic of a partner does SAP perceive them and where do they fit relative to competitors in filling in SAP Solution Map white space?

- How will support for packaged composite applications and xApps work so there is no multi-vendor finger pointing?

- How important is formal SAP certification in selecting a third-party product?

- If the vendor is really a systems integrator who commercialized a solution, how well-equipped is the vendor to evolve and support it as a product?

Because the ecosystem process is so new, you should expect this will be a fluid process for both SAP and partners providing these types of solutions. How well the third parties execute and the market acceptance of what they provide could affect how well SAP supports them and they, in turn, support ESA and the NetWeaver platform down the road.

The good news is that this also means your organization can have more influence over these solutions than you might imagine. Both SAP and the partners have incentives to build meaningful ecosystem relationships. In the near term, certain niche vendors are very open to customers who can actively help them innovate within the SAP environment. Similarly, SAP is looking for customers to help pick key partners and then define and pilot these joint solutions. By being an early influencer, you may be able to drive your specific requirements to a high ROI business need quickly, while also saving money in the long run by getting early-adopter license discounts. The authors have seen several organizations that have taken this path.

Working with Platform and Infrastructure Vendors

The considerations around infrastructure vendors who support the NetWeaver platform are similar to those described for the business application solution providers. Obviously, where they fit in the NetWeaver Solution Map and whether they are a "go-to" partner is of primary importance.

A more interesting challenge is figuring out where SAP's platform will remain tightly bundled versus where it will be easy to use plug-and-play components from other vendors to fulfill all or part of an IT Scenario. Following are some questions for platform ecosystem decisions:

- To what degree do they complement versus compete with SAP?

- How are SOA standards evolving and what things that are core to NetWeaver today could drop to other layers in the technology stack?

- What is a vendor's commitment to joint, ongoing innovation with SAP?

- Where do you want to draw the lines around NetWeaver in terms of your overall infrastructure?

- What are your own long-term IT landscape goals and plans?

Again, these are the complications that the evolution to SOA creates. By cutting across all the layers of the technology stack, even the largest IT vendors will not come close to delivering all the technology that will be required in a SOA-based business process platform. Figuring out how to pull together your various infrastructure components can be a lot easier where the ecosystem partners are working well together.

Addressing Licensing Considerations

One of the most fluid areas for customers will be around licensing. Will ecosystem licensing impacts turn into "death by a thousand cuts" from a cost perspective?

Dealing with these new types of products and new types of solution-delivery models such as composite applications or bundled infrastructure components within the NetWeaver platform can get very confusing. And, because the ecosystem alliances are still so new, you can expect this will be a moving target. Over time, SAP, partners, and customers will need to find models that work for everyone. But in the meantime, you should be thinking about the following:

- How will packaged composite applications be licensed by SAP and third parties? Can they unbundle their product features that you don't need?

- How will enterprise services and their usage be licensed by SAP?

- How will third parties license platform components and service models that extend NetWeaver and populate the ESR?

- How does the adding of ecosystem partner products that run on and integrate with the NetWeaver platform affect your SAP user and NetWeaver licenses?

- If third-party solutions such as Adobe's forms and IDS-Scheer's business process models come out of the box with SAP NetWeaver, what are the restrictions on their use?

- What happens if an ecosystem partner gets acquired by an SAP competitor?

This last point is especially interesting. Chapter 2 described the massive industry consolidation that has been underway for a few years. Companies such as IBM, SAP, Oracle, and Microsoft can be expected to continue to gobble up both business application solution providers and niche technology vendors to extend their platforms. In fact, SAP has demonstrated that certain ecosystem partnerships that work well can often lead to an acquisition. For example, Lighthammer co-developed an xApp with SAP that became the XMII product after SAP acquired that company. Obviously, actively planning for the effects on licensing and vendor management of this continued consolidation is critical.

Tackling Your Enterprise Services Model

One of the major roles of the ecosystem is to help SAP define its certified enterprise services model for ESA. This will cross-cut technology platform services, horizontal business services, and specific industry services. Following are some important questions you should be asking:

- Where should your organization be active in the ES-Community, IVN, or other influence opportunities?
- Is the SAP model taking into account broader industry standards versus being mainly an SAP and SAP customer–specific view?
- What licensing and intellectual property rights and restrictions are associated with the SAP enterprise services models?
- What are the gaps between the SAP enterprise services models and what your organization needs?
- How can you add your internal and partner services to the Enterprise Services Inventory most effectively or alternatively expose SAP enterprise services in other registry and repositories you are creating?
- What service domains are on the SAP and partner road map and how will you evolve along with new releases of official enterprise services models from SAP?

Ultimately, you don't have to address any of these questions overnight. But, if you aren't actively focusing on them in your planning, then you run the risk of having the same type of IT mess many organizations face today, just moved into the SOA world. The SAP ecosystem will be very dynamic during the early years of ESA adoption. To quote a popular infomercial, this means you can no longer "set it and forget it" in terms of buying solutions to complement your NetWeaver platform and mySAP Business Suite applications.

Implications for Partners

By upping the ante with the ecosystem model, SAP has raised the stakes for all partners providing complementary products and services for NetWeaver and mySAP Business Suite applications. ESA will greatly benefit some, and work to the detriment of others. You can expect that all of the mega technology and application vendors will have some degree of support for ESA. The relatively smaller players face a number of interesting questions, as shown in the following sections.

Becoming a "Go-To" Partner

Obviously, if you can become the partner to fill in some defined white space in either an IBU Solution Map or the NetWeaver platform Solution Map, you gain a great marketing and sales advantage. SAP has demonstrated a commitment to work with a number of small ecosystem partners who can offer solutions to high ROI customer problems.

Naturally, SAP will gravitate toward partners that:

- Have an overlapping customer base with a strong track record of success
- Will actively support the ESA blueprints and the NetWeaver platform
- Are more complementary than competitive in features
- Commit to fast time-to-market
- Are comfortable with the licensing and IP models for xApps
- Help increase demand for SAP's platform and business applications
- Can support the demand that an SAP endorsement can drive

The last point is interesting in that becoming the "go-to" partner for a niche with ESA and NetWeaver can tax the delivery capability of smaller ISVs. SAP has experienced this in a couple of cases. So, as you look to build that alliance, be sure to have a plan in place to meet customer needs on an ongoing basis.

There are plenty of opportunities to gain a strategic advantage for partners who actively find the opportunities within an IVN or the platform ecosystem. If you are an ISV or systems integrator who has customers that will help endorse your value proposition to SAP, you stand an even greater chance of carving out an important position in the ecosystem. As you might guess from the previous customer discussion, your specific licensing revenue considerations will be important to understand.

The final consideration is keeping track of the longer-term outcome for your ecosystem partnership. These relationships will likely not remain static. As mentioned, some strategic partners will become acquisition targets by SAP. Others may find themselves becoming more and more competitive with SAP products at some future point. You will also be faced with decisions on how much to invest in other partner and platform ecosystems, and what supporting multiple platforms does to the relationship.

Determining Your Level of Ecosystem Commitment as an ISV

The vast majority of ISVs will not fall into the "go-to" partner category. This means they will be faced with tougher decisions regarding the degree to which they support ESA and NetWeaver. The questions your organization will face include the following:

- How aggressive will your product strategy be in supporting NetWeaver?
- How will you manage your architecture to limit the SAP-specific code needed to take advantage of advanced NetWeaver platform features?

- How important is NetWeaver certification to your customers?

- Are any competitors strong players in the SAP ecosystem?

- Will you invest to develop separate UIs for the NetWeaver Portal?

- Will you develop packaged composite applications?

- To what degree will you participate in the ES-Community or work with the ESR?

- What other platforms will you actively support?

Note that, in the same way that you can deploy applications on .NET or a J2EE application server without getting certified, certification will not be a requirement to support the NetWeaver platform either. In other words, you really do control how much you want to invest in ESA and the NetWeaver platform. The more you can use your own customer relationships to identify the opportunities and expectations, the easier it will be to answer these questions.

Determining Your Ecosystem Role as a Systems Integrator

Consulting firms and SIs can also play very strategic roles in the SAP ecosystem. Not only can their industry domain knowledge help influence the SAP product road map, they may also choose to work with SAP to "productize" their expertise in the form of packaged composites and xApps. Accenture is one firm that has actively pursued these opportunities.

Obviously, there are more tactical ways SIs can support ESA and NetWeaver. At a minimum, ESA done right will lead to major changes in a customer's IT strategy, applications delivery, and infrastructure management processes. SAP will rely heavily on partners to help customers successfully navigate these changes. Some of the larger firms have built global ESA and NetWeaver competency centers in anticipation of this demand.

As a consultant or SI firm, you are faced with questions such as the following:

- What ESA Adoption capabilities and methodologies will you support?

- What NetWeaver platform capabilities will you provide and to what degree?

- How active will you be with IVNs or the ES-Community?

- What other ecosystem partner solutions should you be supporting?

- Will you look to create and sell your own packaged composites or xApps? How will you support them over time?

Examples of ESA Ecosystem Product Collaboration

The following section completes the discussion on the SAP ecosystem by describing examples of ecosystem partners who are working with SAP. They span horizontal business applications, industry white space solutions, and expanded NetWeaver platform technologies. These partners also range in size from small business application ISVs and an established infrastructure leader to an industry giant in Microsoft.

Whether or not these specific solutions apply to your business, the examples will help you understand the types of companies SAP is partnering with. They also show the depth and breadth of new solutions that were made possible by the ESA strategy.

Duet for Microsoft Office and SAP

Duet is a set of composite applications that are jointly developed and sold by both Microsoft and SAP. The companies have built new business solutions that combine Microsoft Office front-ends with SAP back-office applications. The initial process solutions involve employee self-service and manager self-service scenarios, including time management, budget monitoring, leave management, organization management, and report distribution. The companies have also announced upcoming scenarios for recruitment management, travel management, sales management, purchasing, and more. In effect, non-SAP users can now directly interact with SAP systems and processes through Outlook, Excel, and other Office applications to execute standard corporate processes.

From an architecture perspective, Web Service–enabled Office applications are integrating with the Enterprise Service models that expose mySAP ERP and other Business Suite functionality, business rules, and workflows. Figure 4-12 illustrates this high-level Duet integration model. The initial releases of Duet is just a starting point for what is possible from using this type of integration. It is a perfect example of user productivity enablement by letting employees work in the context of a process from inside the tools they are most comfortable with. It also helps automate expensive and error-prone manual processes.

Duet is also a perfect example of how SAP can collaborate with another major IT vendor. These solutions required very deep R&D alliances. The companies have also worked out the joint support structure for the product. This means customers receive consistent support help, regardless of which company they acquire Duet from.

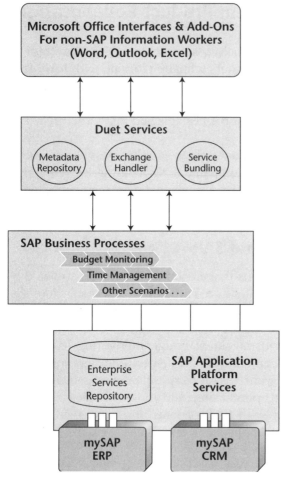

Figure 4-12: Duet architecture uses ESA to expose SAP processes through Microsoft Office productivity tools.

Vendavo Price and Margin Management Solutions

Vendavo is a great example of a smaller ISV that fills in very valuable white space areas within SAP solutions. The company augments the SAP order to cash (O2C) process by enabling optimized pricing calculations for every order.

From an architecture perspective, the company offers standalone products that are certified to run on the NetWeaver platform. It has also worked with SAP to create xApp solutions that automatically integrate with the mySAP ERP and CRM applications.

Vendavo's relationship with SAP validates the ecosystem advantages. Because of its alliance with SAP, the company usually makes the short list of companies who have mySAP ERP and are looking for a pricing optimization solution. And, because the xApp product can be sold directly by SAP, customers receive additional assurance regarding out-of-the-box integration and support from SAP.

Pavilion Technologies Model Predictive Control Solutions

Pavilion is another example of an ISV that works closely with SAP to solve high ROI problems for customers. The company has a patented modeling engine that can accurately predict key process performance metrics. IVNs are applying this capability to define different solutions within their industries. For example, the SAP Chemicals IBU uses the product to help customers predict availability of certain materials that can then be marketed and sold even before they are produced. They can also reduce the cost of quality by predicting when and where quality, samples, and maintenance notifications should occur. Figure 4-13 illustrates some of these scenarios.

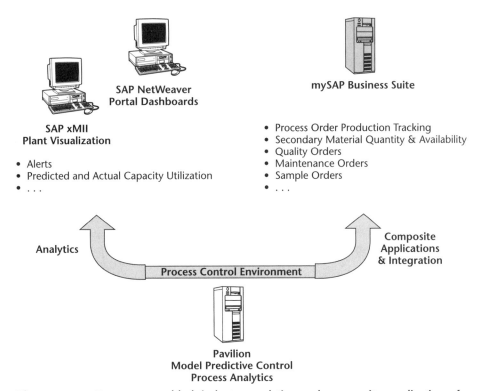

Figure 4-13: Ecosystem-enabled industry analytics and composite applications from Pavilion Technologies

From an architectural perspective, the company is certified to run on the NetWeaver platform and is also developing xApps that tie into mySAP ERP and CRM. Interestingly, Pavilion's solutions also integrate with XMII, which is another SAP xApp. The solution uses Web services and out-of-the-box portal and XI content to integrate with SAP.

The Pavilion products also illustrate the importance of embedded analytics within business processes. The information generated from Pavilion's system can be visualized through XMII and NetWeaver Portal dashboards in mySAP ERP. It can also be used to trigger events and alerts, and to kickoff processes with mySAP ERP. Chapter 10 will explore the Pavilion composite application architecture in more detail.

Mercury

Mercury is a leading provider of technology infrastructure products to improve application quality, performance, governance, and availability. They provide several products that can extend the capabilities of the NetWeaver platform itself. If you look at the NetWeaver Solution Map introduced in Chapter 3, you will see Mercury solutions are especially important to:

- Unified lifecycle management
- Custom development
- Application governance

SAP actually bundles certain Mercury testing products with its NetWeaver release. SAP has also worked with Mercury to define scenarios for "Go-Live" business application checks and other performance evaluations such as load testing on the NetWeaver Portal.

In terms of ESA and business process platform support, the companies are working together on solutions to track overall process performance from a business perspective. That includes things such as SLAs, user experience, and availability checks. Mercury is especially useful in extending these NetWeaver capabilities to expand to non-SAP applications for tracking the total lifecycle management of a process. The products run on the NetWeaver platform and can also be accessed through the NetWeaver Portal.

The ecosystem collaboration between Mercury and SAP is a yet another example of "co-opetition" between the companies because Mercury also offers capabilities that are directly supported by the NetWeaver platform. They have worked together to define the specific areas where Mercury complements SAP's Solution Manager for lifecycle management.

Summary

This chapter describes the comprehensive breadth and depth of SAP's ecosystem efforts. Remember that the basis of competition for SAP is shifting from applications to becoming a broader SOA platform for business processes. The ESA strategy requires active customer and partner support to be successful. And, in order to provide NetWeaver platform-based solutions for end-to-end business processes, SAP needs added business content and products from other ISVs and SIs.

As a customer, the ecosystem offers new opportunities to influence the strategy of SAP and your other vendors. In return, you have new ways of buying and managing more integrated technology and business solutions. From a partner perspective, the ecosystem offers the opportunity to create these new types of products and take advantage of the NetWeaver platform reach that SAP is creating.

Of course, SAP needs ways to help coordinate and support activities of the ecosystem. This includes governance models for controlling the definition and usage of enterprise services, certification options for partners who extend the platform or develop NetWeaver-enabled applications, and open communities for platform and application collaboration.

Following are some of the most important takeaways from this chapter:

- SOA cuts across every layer of the technology stack, including hardware and networking. Vendors must work together on joint R&D to deliver on the promise of SOA.

- SAP is using its IBU-led IVNs to actively work with partners to bring high ROI solutions to market on an industry-by-industry basis.

- The ES-Community is a method by which SAP, customers, and partners collaborate on defining ESA's enterprise services models at a business and technical level and then certify commercial solutions around them.

- Customers should consider vendor strategies around ESA and NetWeaver support when selecting third-party products. There are many new delivery models around the platform.

- Both small and large ISVs can play active roles in the ecosystem, and there are many certification opportunities for SIs to leverage NetWeaver to create composite applications for resale.

- SAP is extremely active in both the business and technology standards setting bodies because supporting standards are required for broad NetWeaver platform adoption.

■ The SDN and groups such as ASUG provide ongoing technical community collaboration to support the platform with education, communication, and support forums including specific communities targeted at enterprise architecture and ESA adoption.

SAP is actively investing to "prime the pump" around its ecosystem. The more SAP shows the industry augmenting the business content and functionality of mySAP applications with support from third parties, the more valuable the NetWeaver platform becomes. Customers win because they can consolidate a lot of the integration noise and cost out of their environment and, at the same time, get more value at the business solution level.

Several industry giants and small players are already on board to bring ESA-based products to market. SAP's goal is to deliver more capability at a much lower TCO through all of the multi-partner platform integration and support. You should be actively determining how this affects your organization.

This chapter marks the end of Part I of the book, which explains the industry strategy and SAP activities behind ESA. Part II takes a closer look inside the technologies, features, and capabilities to help you build your ESA and SAP NetWeaver adoption plans, beginning with an understanding of SOA technologies and SAP's enterprise services infrastructure, addressed in Chapter 5.

Evaluating ESA Capabilities and Building Your Adoption Road Map

Understanding SOA Foundations and SAP's ESA Infrastructure

Thus far, you have seen the big picture behind SAP's strategy for ESA. Technology and integration platforms are merging with applications into a new breed of "applistructures." SAP is making major architectural changes through the implementation of a standards-based SOA platform in NetWeaver, and by morphing its mySAP Business Suite applications to run on top of this new infrastructure. Customers and third parties can extend the SAP platform both for their own use, and in more official ways through helping participate in ecosystem activities such as IVNs and the ES-Community.

As SAP continues evolving its products into an end-to-end business process platform, the underlying architecture will continue to become more integrated, process-driven, and service-oriented. That, in turn, will enable whole new categories of composite applications to be built on the platform. But what does it mean when SAP says its products are SOA-enabled? After all, SOA is a relatively new computing model (at least in terms of its realization by newer Web Services technologies). That means a number of standards and technical capabilities are still in the early stages of development.

A related question is what makes SAP's approach to SOA unique? The short answer is that SAP's ESA road map is driven by the needs of business processes and applications such as mySAP ERP. Tackling things from a top-down business solutions approach is very different than pursuing a purely technology-driven platform strategy. This will be clear as you look inside the components of SAP's enterprise services infrastructure.

This chapter walks you through the basic goals, technologies, and infrastructure associated with SOA. It provides an overview of Web Services and SOA, along with a review of the various industry standards, architectures, and infrastructure required for implementation. The chapter then introduces you to SAP's solutions that support these standards and the company's current SOA-based capabilities. It also provides some insight into the direction SAP is heading to fulfill the overall vision for ESA while evolving with the industry.

This chapter will help you:

- Understand the basics of Web Services
- See the architectural principles and benefits of SOA and the top differences from earlier computing models
- Appreciate the differences between Web Services and enterprise services
- Review technology standards and required infrastructure components needed to deliver an effective SOA environment
- Look under the hood at SAP's ESA infrastructure and how NetWeaver supports SOA
- Understand the function of the SAP Enterprise Services Repository (ESR) as a linchpin to ESA
- Describe how process modeling, application and user interface development, and lifecycle management change as a result of using SAP's enterprise services
- Consider ESA opportunities relative to your current SAP landscape

An Introduction to SOA, Web Services, and Enterprise Services

Whether you like it or not, believe in it or not, or even know enough to care, SOA will become a critical part of your IT environment. Perhaps more accurately, services and service-oriented computing will be widespread in your landscape. As described in earlier chapters, the industry momentum and investments by every major vendor to adopt a service-oriented approach in their products is what makes this inevitable.

The goal of this section is to give you a crash course in SOA principles and, in particular, the Web Services technologies that are becoming a common adoption model for SOA. It will also help you understand the distinction between Web Services and SAP's concept of enterprise services.

Understanding SOA and the Relationship to Web Services

If you get ten architects in a room and ask them to define SOA, you will likely get at least ten answers. That isn't too surprising because SOA encompasses high level principles that, at least today, have no definitive implementation that everyone can agree upon.

There are plenty of places to discuss and debate the notion of "pure SOA" from a computer science perspective. This book will not be one of them. In terms of adopting SAP's ESA-based solutions, you just need a few guidelines that can help you sort through the changes in the SAP architecture and your overall IT landscape that SOA brings about. If you want to dive into more detail on SOA technologies and standards, other books and Web sites are recommended in Chapter 16, as well as on the companion Web site to this book. Just keep in mind there is always a need to balance the pure architectural goals of SOA with practical realization approaches from different IT vendors.

SOA Is a Style of Computing

If you unpack the term "SOA," you quickly see two parts. First is the service-oriented aspects that deal with a simple interaction model based on loose coupling around well-defined interfaces. This usually involves a service consumer interacting with a service provider. Many different message exchange patterns can exist between consumers and providers. Figure 5-1 shows them interacting via the common request-response model.

The second aspect of SOA is the architecture side, which addresses the flexibility, interoperability, quality attributes, and other aspects of enabling, organizing, and encouraging the use of services. The point is that *SOA is an architectural style of computing*. It is designed to achieve loose coupling of interoperable software agents in a technology neutral and highly flexible manner.

> **NOTE** SOA is not something you can buy, install, or implement in a formulaic manner. It is, however, a very beneficial approach to organizing, delivering, and using some of the software assets in your IT landscape.

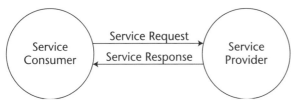

Figure 5-1: The relationship between service providers and requesters is at the core of SOA.

SOA Offers Many Potential Benefits

The potential benefits of SOA in terms of an architectural style include the following:

- Lower TCO in IT through consolidation opportunities and more standards-based integration

- Agility for faster implementation and changes in IT through reuse, modeling, and composite application development techniques

- Better alignment between business processes and their IT realization through more transparent process modeling and monitoring based on services

Success with SOA requires more than just technology. Bringing together business semantics, process content, and the delivery of applications is the key to best leveraging SOA technologies. That is why these things are at the heart of SAP's approach to ESA. Of course, technology standards are still a required enabler. Web Services have recently become an important standard for SOA adoption, as explained in the next section.

Web Services Help Support the Realization of SOA

The next great debate after trying to define SOA and its usefulness revolves around whether Web Services technologies are required for SOA. Many proponents of Common Object Request Broker Architecture (CORBA), Java, and Microsoft distributed object models and messaging systems argue all the benefits of SOA can be achieved through services implemented using these approaches. Others believe there is no practical way to achieve the pure tenants of SOA without using Web Services technologies.

There is no definitive answer to this question, although clearly any approach tied to a single language, object model, platform, or message and transport format builds in tighter coupling and dependencies, as shown in Figure 5-2.

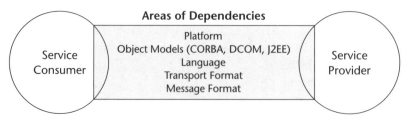

Figure 5-2: The types of dependencies that increase coupling between applications and services

Web Services may not be technically required to implement an SOA, but practically speaking, they are becoming the preferred technical foundation that most IT vendors support. SAP is a leading proponent of Web Services technologies as a foundation for SOA. The company's ESA-based strategy is based widely upon them. This is because Web Services provide the following:

- Standards to describe and call a service based on schemas and contracts
- Language and platform neutrality
- Ability to span different transports
- Full leverage of IP and Internet infrastructure constructs
- Ubiquitous vendor tool support for agreed-upon standards
- Support for incremental adoption and extension

Just keep in mind that Web Services and SOA are not the same thing. You can use Web Services to integrate software without meeting the larger architectural goals of SOA, as described throughout this chapter. In fact, you need much more than Web Services technologies and a desire to loosely couple applications to make SOA work.

How Web Services Work — The Basic Profile

If you come from primarily an SAP ABAP background you may not have worked much with Web Services. This section provides you with some quick background on the technology.

The Web Services Basic Profile

Web Services were launched based on a few simple technology standards to enable language and platform-neutral integration. However, Web Services will work in practice only if all vendors properly understand, interpret, and support these standards in their implementations. In order to ensure industry interoperability, the major IT vendors founded an organization called the Web Services Interoperability Organization (WS-I).

The WS-I publishes agreed upon interoperability standards, along with implementation guidelines, testing tools, and sample applications that help developers ensure their Web Services will be interoperable at an industry-wide level. SAP was a founding member of WS-I and holds a board seat. The company actively supports WS-I standards in its product implementations.

One of the most important deliverables is known as the *Web Services Basic Profile.* Following are three of the key technology standards associated with this profile :

- *WSDL* — The Web Services Definition Language (WSDL) is the standard for describing a Web Service. It defines its location so that you can call it as well as the operations the service supports. This includes the form and information needed to invoke each of the Web Service operations, as well as the form of its responses, if any. WSDLs are XML documents that are formatted according to the specification.

▪ *SOAP* — SOAP originally stood for Simple Object Access Protocol, although its acronym was later dropped by the World Wide Web Consortium (W3C). It is an XML-based communication protocol for sending messages between service providers and consumers. SOAP basically works like a text-based Remote Procedure Call (RPC) for invoking a Web Service. It does not rely on any specific platform or language and can operate on the Internet using HTTP (as well as over other protocols).

▪ *UDDI* — Universal Description, Discovery and Integration (UDDI) is the directory standard for services that defines the service provider, services, bindings, and other specifications. UDDI is also XML-based and contains a construct called `tmodels`, which, among other things, defines the taxonomies of your services so you can perform logical searches. Although the original vision was for a robust public implementation of UDDI, these directories are usually implemented internally by an organization, or securely between trading partners.

WSDL, SOAP, and UDDI are all based upon XML. They are managed by standards organizations such as the W3C and OASIS, and have been around for years. All three represent relatively stable and mature technologies for enabling Web Services.

Web Services Interaction Models Using the Basic Profile

Figure 5-3 shows the simplest interaction model for Web Services based on elements from the WS-I Basic Profile.

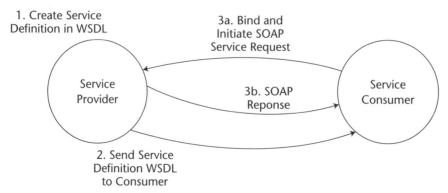

Figure 5-3: A simple interaction model for Web Services

Again you have a service provider that offers some functionality of interest. Examples might be a travel reservation service or an inventory availability service. Next, there is the service consumer. This is some type of application or user interface interested in leveraging the functionality of the service provider. For example, an order processing application might be interested in the inventory availability service as part of its order entry steps.

In this example, the provider and consumer work together as follows:

1. The service provider creates a description of its service using WSDL. The WSDL acts as a contract that tells the consumer what the service does and how to interact with it.

2. The service provider shares its WSDL directly with the service consumer because they know about each other by an unknown means.

3. The service consumer then invokes the service according to the parameters of the WSDL and deals with whatever response comes back, if any, according to the contract.

This is all very straightforward, and SOAP and WSDL are relatively simple technologies. Obviously this example left out the UDDI directory because it is not required. However, a services directory is a very important element in managing Web Services in an SOA. It acts as a "Yellow Pages" for finding services of interest and determining how to interact with them. Notice the previous example implied some unknown mechanism had to exist for the service consumer to know the provider existed, and to secure a copy of the WSDL.

Imagine trying to keep track of contact information for all the people in your organization without a directory. It becomes unwieldy once you get beyond a small number. The same challenge occurs once you get beyond a small number of services in your landscape. The role of a services directory in SOA will be covered later in this chapter. For now, just recognize that if you want to get many of the benefits of SOA, your services need to be organized and managed, which is something a directory helps do. Figure 5-4 illustrates the Web Services interaction model with UDDI included.

Following are the steps in a directory-based Web Services interaction:

1. The service provider creates a description of its service using WSDL.

2. The WSDL definition's location and other basic service information is published to the UDDI service directory.

3. The service consumer queries the directory to find information about the service and where to find the WSDL.

4. The service consumer then invokes the service according to the parameters of the WSDL and deals with whatever response comes back, if any, according to the contract.

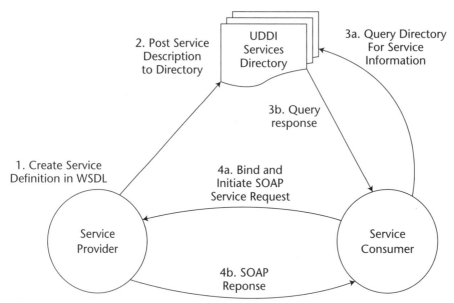

Figure 5-4: Web Services interaction model using a UDDI directory

These basic Web Services interactions are extremely useful for integrating applications, as discussed in the next section.

> **NOTE** A directory is not required for Web Services, as service consumers can directly receive the WSDL from a provider. Ignoring the role of the directory is one simple example of how you can use Web Services technologies outside the architectural goals of SOA. The importance of registries to SOA will be covered further later in this chapter.

The Benefits and Limitations of Web Services

Web Services provide a lot of advantages, particularly in terms of helping standardize and commoditize the technical aspects of integration. There are also many well-known limitations associated with using Web Services. The following sections will describe some of these benefits and drawbacks.

The Benefits of Using Web Services

The primary benefit of Web Services as supported by the Basic Profile is that it enables two pieces of software to talk to each other in a fully platform- and language-neutral manner. From an SAP perspective, this is ideal, because it means applications written in any language can more easily invoke Business Application Programming Interfaces (BAPIs), RFCs, or custom ABAP function modules without having to use connectors or proprietary adapters.

Likewise, an ABAP program can invoke Web Services written in other languages using the same approach. The development tools in SAP NetWeaver provide a number of features that allow SAP applications to be both providers and consumers of Web Services. Chapter 11 illustrates some of these techniques.

This does not mean that Web Services are the correct or best model for all types of integration needs. However, they are a viable choice in many instances. Web Services are especially useful in cases where you are dealing with multiple service consumers. While a service provider has pretty much the same cost and effort to deliver a Web Service as it would for any other interface, service consumers can get a lot of value, including the following:

- Most modern development environments can inspect a WSDL and generate proxy code for the client application automatically.

- If the consuming program is based on a different language or platform, there is no need to use connectors or other types of bridging technologies. Because you may not be able to predict all the types of consumers in the future, given that applications such as Microsoft Office and Adobe Forms are now acting as Web Services consumers, this is valuable for dealing with unplanned consumers.

- The Web Service can be published to a registry, making it easier for clients who might otherwise not have known it was available to discover and leverage it.

- If the service provider integrates with many external trading partners or offers public interfaces, the cost of documenting and supporting partners should be lower because of the common self-describing and standards-based nature of Web Services.

As an example of this last point, Sabre offers Web Service interfaces to its leading travel Global Distribution System. Agents and software product developers can use these Web Services to implement their solutions. Likewise, eBay offers Web Service interfaces for developers who want to build applications on top of its auction and Web store offerings. Yet another example is Xignite, which offers on-demand financial Web Services for mission-critical applications. You can review these services at `https://Webservices.sabre.com`, `http://developer.ebay.com`, and `www.xignite.com`, respectively.

One last benefit of Web Services is that, from a technical perspective, the basic Web Services technologies abstract a service's implementation from its interface. A service consumer need only worry about the interface itself, which becomes the contract it knows the service provider will support. The service provider can then implement the service in any language or format behind the scenes, as well as replace that implementation over time with new ones that support the same interface.

As you will see, this is a very important foundation for SOA, and especially valuable to SAP's approach to ESA. It allows SAP to evolve its underlying application components while keeping common interfaces to business functionality such as "sales order processing" or "open new hire requisition" consistent. If you have an application that consumes those types of services, being able to rely on one interface that works with multiple underlying SAP application versions is very beneficial.

Limitations of Web Services

While the Web Services Basic Profile offers many benefits, it serves as only one building block to achieving enterprise class integration using this technology. In addition, much more than basic Web Services is needed to create an enterprise-grade SOA. Both technology and IT processes are evolving to fill in some of the gaps. This includes areas such as the following:

- Meeting enterprise grade security, transaction management, reliability, monitoring and other non-functional requirements

- Moving beyond point-to-point Web Services interactions between providers and consumers

- Creating services that have greater business benefit and higher reuse value

- Exposing existing applications that were not designed for Web Services in a way that enables your SOA to evolve

- Developing processes to organize, promote and encourage reuse of your Web Services

The remainder of this chapter describes the many ways SAP (and the IT industry as a whole) is filling in these gaps beginning with the notion of enterprise services.

Enterprise Services Versus Web Services

As mentioned, basic Web Services have become very valuable in exposing provider interfaces in language- and platform-neutral contracts to make life easier on consuming applications. However, it quickly became apparent that Web Services technology alone could not fulfill the promise of ESA. Even if technical hurdles such as security and transaction management were overcome, business process and semantic gaps associated with creating useful services remained.

SAP developed the concept of enterprise services as a way to describe an approach to resolving these business semantic and design gaps for Web Services. Although SAP has made the term "enterprise services" a linchpin to its unique approach to SOA, many characteristics associated with enterprise services are being tackled by other IT vendors and customers.

Before looking at the logical distinctions between enterprise services and Web Services, you should recognize that enterprise services actually *are* Web Services in that they support SOAP interfaces, WSDL definitions, and the other elements of the basic profile. This means they can be discovered and invoked just like any other Web Service. However, enterprise services have many additional design characteristics that enhance their usefulness. These are described in the following sections.

NOTE Enterprise services are Web Services from a purely technical standpoint in that they support the WS-I Basic Profile as described earlier.

Characteristics of Enterprise Services

An enterprise service is designed to support a common, well understood business or application-level needs. Note that there is no hard-and-fast rule that distinguishes a "plain old Web Service" from an enterprise service. Again technically speaking they are the same.

An enterprise service simply provides a good level of abstraction to hide underlying implementation complexity while offering some type of functionality that is logically useful in a number of business process or application delivery scenarios. That means a lot more thought is put into designing an enterprise service because you are thinking about the business processes and semantics it must support. You are also planning the enterprise service in the context of other services with which it might interact to deliver even greater business value.

SAP has communicated some of the criteria it uses to identify and design its enterprise services. If you are a customer, you can use this same type of thinking in developing your own enterprise services based on your existing applications landscape. (See the sidebar "Characteristics of Enterprise Services.") Likewise, ISV partners can apply the ideas in designing enterprise services that expose their own product functionality.

SAP has also published an "Enterprise Services Design Guide." You can find a link to this document on the book's companion Web site, or by visiting SAP's corporate site.[1]

The Concept of Service Granularity

Service granularity is an important principle in SOA. Services can perform very low-level tasks (fine-grained) or higher-level tasks with greater complexity (coarse-grained). Making the distinction is important because it affects service reusability, flexibility, and performance characteristics.

CHARACTERISTICS OF ENTERPRISE SERVICES

Enterprise services are Web Services that have a well-defined business purpose in mind. They are designed with some thought as to how they relate to other services in creating a valuable business-driven approach to SOA. SAP has communicated characteristics it considers when defining its own inventory of enterprise services for the mySAP Business Suite and other business applications. Customers and partners can use some of the same thinking to define their own enterprise services. Following are some of the primary characteristics:

◆ Designed with specific business value and integration scenarios in mind

◆ Intended to be consumed by virtually any other technology language or platform that supports Web Services

◆ Are best designed around the business objective from a consumer's point of view, independent from any specific provider applications that may implement the service contracts

◆ Have a well defined and consistent scope as to what the service delivers

◆ May be compound services, meaning they can be designed around multiple underlying services or objects to fulfill a larger business objective

◆ Consider reuse scenarios and cost benefits associated with creating more generic versus specific service definitions

In short, SAP's perspective on enterprise services is that they are well thought-out from the business usage scenarios and consuming applications point of view. This is very different from trying to define interfaces from the standpoint of providing applications. The distinction can make the difference in successor failure with SOA because it ultimately determines the usefulness of a service.

As you might guess, enterprise services are often defined at a higher level of granularity. Figure 5-5 illustrates this concept. In the first example, we have a Web Service for getting an item's list price. Here the Web Service wraps an application's API to invoke a pricing lookup method and return the value. This is a very fine-grained operation similar to exposing a BAPI as a Web Service.

In the second example, you see a more coarse-grained enterprise service for pricing an order. This enterprise service performs a number of activities across multiple underlying systems in responding to the request.

The enterprise service is more valuable because customers have less interest in just seeing list prices. However, it is also more complicated to create and change. As new business rules emerge, it may also be tougher to reuse the coarse-grained service in multiple scenarios. Your design teams will constantly face the granularity trade-offs in defining your unique ESA-based service models.

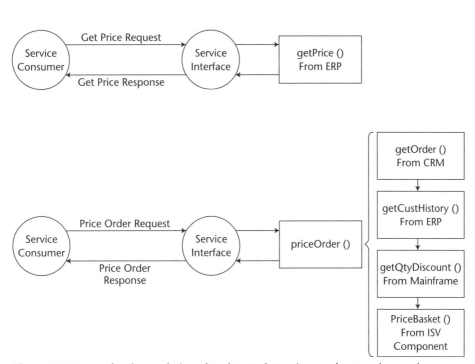

Figure 5-5: Example of granularity related to Web Services and enterprise services

Categories of Enterprise Services

SAP and several other major IT vendors have tried categorizing the types of enterprise services that are needed to support SOA. Unfortunately, no agreed-upon approach has yet emerged. Later in this chapter, you will see more information on the specific models and categories defined by SAP. For now, realize that it is important to think of enterprise services according to their general functional characteristics such as the following:

- *Process services* — Very high granularity services that trigger long-running business processes that can involve human workflow (for example, a recruiting process or new employee hiring process).

- *Business domain and task services* — Services that correspond to specific sets of transactions or business interactions within a function (for example, an Asset Management service, a Payment Processing service or the Pricing service mentioned earlier).

- *Entity services* — Business-level services that support a specific entity (for example, a Purchase Order service or a Customer service). These usually include CRUD (create, retrieve, update, delete) and other entity-related operations.

- *Technical utility services* — Provide support functions such as reporting services, event monitoring services, presentation services, workflow services, logging services, and so forth.

It bears repeating that you do not need to be locked into a specific set of definitions for how you categorize your services. There are models ranging from four to more than ten categories of services proposed. It is just as important to recognize that enterprise services can be defined and organized around the types of business and application-level functions they provide. This is useful in planning your unique service models, as well as trying to rationalize enterprise services provided by SAP with those you build internally or acquire from other vendors. Obviously, if you are an ISV providing services, you will also want to have a categorization model that you support and organize your solution around.

NOTE Many categorization models exist for organizing services. You will want to understand SAP's approach to categorizing its enterprise services and rationalize it with whatever SOA conventions your organization uses internally for all other services.

Because SAP is a business applications provider, the company was really the leader in attempting to put together meaningful models of enterprise services that reflect business entities, domains, and processes. As described in Chapter 4, SAP has established a complete governance process to work internally and with the industry ecosystem on defining the best enterprise service model to support SOA.

The next section provides an example of enterprise services in action.

An Example of Enterprise Services

Consider a company (code name TECH-CO) that is a high-tech manufacturer and reseller of computers and peripherals. The company's core competencies lie in sales, marketing, and customer service, along with the ability to manage a complex distribution and supply chain model. Many of the products TECH-CO sells are commodity items that are available from other wholesalers and distributors.

The problem is in how the company prices an order and determines delivery dates for customers. Both are based on where it sources the inventory.

Historically it filled customer orders from in-house inventory, made-to-order products, and returned and refurbished merchandise. Because prices are so volatile, in some cases it is now actually cheaper to use inventory from third-party wholesalers who drop-ship products to TECH-CO's customers.

Since the company began as a reseller, then later added its own manufacturing and refurbishment capabilities, and then adopted this third-party drop-ship option, not all of TECH-CO's sales channels have access to the entire inventory. This leads to variable pricing and promise dating by channel based on the source of the inventory.

For example, the in-house call center can see all options because reps can toggle between source systems and make the optimal determination for a customer. The distributed sales force automation system is a customer solution that was deployed at a time when the company had only its own inventory or specific manufacturing bundles. Hence, reps are restricted to those options unless they contact the call center. Finally, the custom-developed Internet sales engine supports only on-hand inventory because there are no links to third-party or manufacturing systems. Customers end up calling to find out more options, which adds to the load in the call center.

Figure 5-6 summarizes the TECH-CO challenge. The three sales systems each have their own logic for performing the product availability and pricing calculations. They also have to manage their point-to-point interfaces back to the various inventory systems. And, because of the timing and integration issues, none of the systems have complete access to all the inventory.

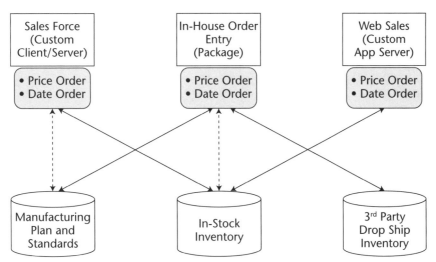

Figure 5-6: Distributed pricing and order dating at TECH-CO won't be solved with simple Web Services.

Even if TECH-CO replaced the point-to-point interfaces with Web Services, nothing really changes from a business perspective. And, even if the company updated all three order-capture systems to account for the full set of inventory, you still have the business logic replicated in three places. That means any changes to the process will remain cumbersome. Because TECH-CO was planning on future strategic sourcing changes it wanted a model that could accommodate things more easily.

Figure 5-7 shows the new approach based on the use of an enterprise service for product availability and pricing. Here all three systems can point to the enterprise service as a means for getting the same information. This means TECH-CO's pricing and promise dating is now complete and consistent across all channels. And, because the enterprise service is also a Web Service, it is much easier to integrate with the three channel systems that are all based on different technology platforms and languages.

Obviously, a lot is going on inside that enterprise service, and work needed to be done to retrofit the existing sales systems to use it. However, the value of this approach continues to be realized. As the company explores adding new channels, as well as the new inventory sources, the flexibility provided by the enterprise service can become very important in terms of time-to-market of these new processes.

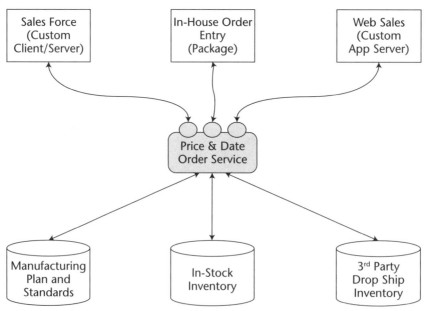

Figure 5-7: Consolidating functionality into a shared enterprise service

Technical Requirements for Services in an ESA World

SAP's approach to enterprise services solves many of the business design and semantic gaps needed to deliver on ESA. However, there are also many limitations associated with the basic Web Services technologies themselves that need to be overcome in an ESA world. Many deal with non-functional requirements such as the following:

- Security
- High availability
- Reliability
- Performance and quality of service (QoS)
- Transactional and process scope and management across Web Services
- Manageability
- Monitoring

Other emerging technical standards are addressing how Web Services are actually used to solve business problems. This includes areas such as Web Services orchestration, which controls the execution flow of multiple Web Services to support a business process objective. Another area deals with technical standards that support a more common industry approach to creating composite applications.

SAP has and will continue to meet all of these needs using standards where they exist. And, of course, like any IT vendor, the company will need to augment semi-complete standards to guarantee these requirements are met in their products. There are now many advanced and emerging Web Service technology standards under development that help tackle these technical concerns.

In short, SAP's enterprise services must provide the robustness, reliability, and usability you need to rely on them as building blocks for mission-critical business systems. The inventory of enterprise services provided by SAP (as well as the SAP NetWeaver tooling that customers and partners use to develop their own enterprise services) is designed with these requirements in mind.

The following section highlights some of the major technical developments that most IT vendors are pursuing to support Web Services–based SOA. Having that groundwork in place will help you better understand the details of SAP's ESA infrastructure supported by the NetWeaver platform. It is also useful in that your organization may use alternative platforms or a hybrid approach for its SOA foundation where these concepts come up.

Web Services Extensions

You have seen that WSDL, UDDI, and SOAP are the basic XML-based Web Services protocols that enable loosely coupled integration. As these standards solidified, an explosion of extensions and new protocol proposals emerged from various vendors to meet the more advanced technical requirements of enterprise-grade Web Services. Collectively, these are dubbed the *WS-** specifications because most of them begin with "WS-" in their names. And while surrounding standards evolve, the Basic Profile itself continues to be enhanced in conjunction with the larger industry initiatives.

Some of these WS-* specifications have become official standards supported by organizations such as OASIS or W3C. Others have become de facto standards that are implemented in major vendor product implementations (including SAP NetWeaver). However, many of them are still early-stage specifications.

Whenever a true supported standard matures, you can anticipate vendors such as SAP will shift away from proprietary efforts to meet the need and support the standard in subsequent releases of platforms such as SAP NetWeaver. This is similar to how the J2EE application server market evolved over time. In the early days, major vendors would offer many proprietary extensions to support needed Java platform functionality. As more and more standards emerged, these proprietary implementations would be replaced with support for the new standards. And, of course, over time, the platform features as a whole would grow (see Figure 5-8).

Because there are dozens of these WS-* specifications in various stages of development, they will not all be covered here. The good news is that you don't need to worry about all the technical details associated with most of them. Once they become native parts of products such as SAP NetWeaver, you can be sure they will likely be abstracted with model-based tools and configurable options in the infrastructure. Only really hard-core developer and infrastructure managers will need to get into the low-level details.

Following is a brief description of the major categories of extensions needed for more enterprise-grade Web Services computing. Within each category is a list of some of the most important specifications that you can consider for further research.

Reliable Messaging

One of the benefits of Web Services is that they can make heavy use of Internet transport protocols such as HTTP, FTP, and SMTP. However, these protocols and the Web Services Basic Profile contain no capabilities to address things such as guaranteed delivery, message sequencing, delivery failure notifications, and so forth.

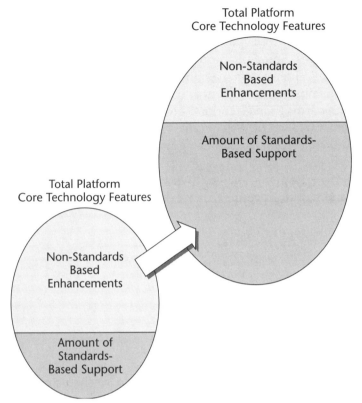

Figure 5-8: Predicted evolution of standards support in SOA platforms such as SAP NetWeaver over time

Obviously, the ability to provide assurances around QoS for messaging must be addressed for enterprise-class mission-critical use of Web Services. And, to support the goals of true loose coupling, the ideal solution will be platform, vendor, language, and protocol neutral. Following are a few of the extension specifications that SAP is working with industry technical committees to help develop:

- WS-ReliableMessaging
- WS-ReliableExchange
- WS-Addressing
- WS-Notification
- SOAP MTOM (Messaging Transmission Optimization Mechanism)

Security

It goes without saying that *security* is paramount to successful enterprise use of Web Services technologies. Some of the concerns related to Web Services include securing messages, identity management, policy enforcement, and supporting trust relationships between client and service.

The WS-I formed a Security Profile working group to deal with transport, SOAP message, and other aspects of Web Services security. As with the Basic Profile, its goal is to drive clear interpretations, guidelines, samples, and tests for achieving true interoperable security. This group relies on a number of standards such as the following. Again, SAP is active with many of the industry technical committees and working groups that are developing these standards.

- WS-Security
- WS-Trust
- WS-Federation
- XML-Encryption
- XML-Signature
- SAML (Security Assertion Markup Language)
- WS-Addressing
- SOAP MTOM (Messaging Transmission Optimization Mechanism)

Transactions

Along with security and reliable messaging, the third most-needed enterprise class attribute for Web Services deals with *transaction processing*. Computer systems have long needed mechanisms such as two-phased commits to support ACID (atomic, consistent, isolated durable) transactions across multiple participants. By definition, combining Web Service interactions into larger units involves multiple software units to support a logical business transaction.

A number of Web Services extensions have been proposed to support transaction management in an SOA environment. These specifications include mechanisms for processing compensating transactions in cases where one party was unable to complete its role in the overall transaction. You should recognize that, like security and reliable messaging extension, these transaction specifications become important foundations to supporting business process standards such as those described in the next section. Some of the more important specifications that SAP is working with other vendors to develop include the following:

- WS-Coordination
- WS-Transaction

- WS-Business Activity
- WS-Atomic Transaction

Policy and Metadata Management

A final area of major importance for extending basic Web Services deals with concepts called *policies and service metadata management*. Policies provide a means for describing the non-functional attributes of a Web Service. For example, you could define a security policy for all your sensitive human resources data, or a QoS policy for certain classes of customer orders. These generic policy definitions can then be applied to multiple Web Services, which should implement the policy. SAP has played a leading role on the technical committee tackling the policy standards.

The ability to apply the policies to Web Services greatly expands the amount of metadata associated with them. Again, SAP has partnered with IBM, Microsoft and others on a standard way to retrieve policy, schema, and WSDL definitions on Web Services. They have created a common request model to find out basic information about a Web Service. Some of the important specifications associated with policies and metadata include the following:

- WS-Policy
- WS-PolicyAssertions
- WS-PolicyAttachments
- WS-MetadataExchange

Figure 5-9 provides a summary of Web Services standards. If you find all of these WS-* extensions to be confusing, rest assured you are not alone. The preceding sections actually barely touch the surface as to what is going on industrywide in terms of turning basic Web Services into an enterprise-grade computing model for SOA. Keep in mind that some of these will continue to mature and become solid standards. Others will likely stagnate or be superseded, never making it to official standards status controlled by groups such as the W3C or OASIS.

All these technologies continue to enhance the capabilities, robustness, and usefulness of Web Services. And as they do, other standards are emerging to help make SOA work at the business process and applications level as discussed in the next two sections.

WS-I Basic Profile

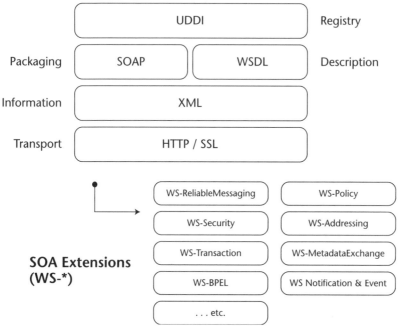

Figure 5-9: Summary of Web Service specifications supporting SOA (Source: © 2006, MomentumSI, Inc. All rights reserved.)

Business Process Orchestration and Execution Standards

Remember that one of the key benefits of ESA is to increase agility within IT for managing, monitoring, and changing of business processes. Chapter 6 explains more fully the capabilities and benefits of a Business Process Management (BPM) environment. One requirement for meeting this goal is the ability to digitize business processes in a standards-based way. This allows your run-time infrastructures to actually execute those digital process models.

There is a Web Services extension called the Business Process Execution Language (WS-BPEL), which was created to support these goals. WS-BPEL is an XML-based language for formally specifying certain types of business process flows and interaction protocols.

Individual Web Services may deal with specific operations, but implementing a number of these operations in a controlled sequence is often required to deliver a higher-level business result. WS-BPEL provides a mechanism for invoking services in sequences to fulfill that larger business objective. A WS-BPEL definition can itself be exposed and invoked as a Web Service. In effect, it is a very coarse-grained Web Service defined with its own WSDL.

A WS-BPEL engine controls the run-time execution to support long-running processes. It not only defines the flow, but it can support transactional contexts across the flow. WS-BPEL is supported today within SAP NetWeaver as the modeling and execution environment for Web Services orchestration.

SAP and IBM have drafted proposed extensions to WS-BPEL for supporting the role of human actors within a business process. These were given the interesting name of BPEL4People. The two companies have also worked together on another set of proposed extensions tied to sub-processes. The goal is to define process snippets that can be reused within and across multiple WS-BPEL processes.

Solution Composition Standards

Another standards proposal from SAP and IBM (along with BEA, Oracle, and other large Java technology vendors) is called Service Component Architecture (SCA). This is a very new concept that builds upon the WS-* extensions for security, transactions, and reliable messaging to offer a model for building composite applications in an SOA world.

SCA provides greater guidance on how to build services for assembly into applications. It is a standard that will make it easier for service providers that are implemented in many different platforms and languages to package their services in more consistent ways. This interoperability can extend into how the services are woven together into applications. It can then also support how the applications are supported at run-time.

There is a related standard known as Service Data Objects (SDO) that these vendors proposed to work hand-in-hand with SCA. SDO provides a simple, standardized mechanism for accessing different types of data needed to support composite applications.

Among other things, SCA and SDO have the potential to offer an interoperable approach to implementing business process–driven composite applications from a collection of services. This is a very new area and is definitely a specification worth tracking to see how it might find its way into the composition products and infrastructure of SAP NetWeaver.

In the next section, you will see more about other standards and approaches that help organize services for reuse in creating composite applications.

Finding and Governing Services with Registries and Repositories

Thus far, you have seen that SOA will not work without the ability to create robust enterprise services that meet meaningful business requirements. In addition, these enterprise services must be supported with technology standards that make them enterprise-grade, and help control how they are actually pulled together to deliver process and application functionality.

But even with all of this technology in place, SOA still will not work in an "if you build it, they will reuse it" model. Organizations must have specific tools to publish and organize their services so they can be better discovered, reused, and governed. This is where service registries and service repositories come in, along with the processes for using them to govern service models. These topics are introduced in the following sections.

Service Registries

As mentioned in the earlier discussion on UDDI, registries are optional components that support interactions between services. If you are just getting started with basic Web Services, it is not always obvious why registries are such an important component within an SOA.

Think about what it must have been like after the telephone was invented and the first exchanges began to pop up in local communities. It didn't take long before the need for a telephone book was recognized. Of course, early phone books did not even have phone numbers because an operator could handle all the connections by name. But, over time, it became important for one person to be able dial another without requiring operator intervention if the phone network would scale. A few years later, the first copy of the Yellow Pages was published. Just like today, it contained directories of businesses organized by the types of services they offered. Whether you use a physical phone book or an online directory, the ability to get the number of someone you want to call and to reach them is a commonsense requirement.

Service registries act much like a phone book. They play a very important part in implementing SOAs because, as the number of services you have in your library expands, your organization needs a way to keep track of them all. Having services isn't of much use if you either can't find them or do not know how to access the ones you do discover.

The basic technology standard for registries is UDDI, which, as described earlier, is a key part of the WS-I Basic Profile. SAP was a big proponent of the early UDDI specifications and provides a UDDI server with SAP NetWeaver for you to use in organizing your services. The key information provided by UDDI registries includes the following:

- Service names
- Basic service classifications
- Description of what the service does
- Pointers to a services WSDL that describes the interfaces and other features
- Pointers to the actual access point for the service

Service Repositories

UDDI is very useful, but it has limits. That is because registries basically describe how to find services, but do nothing to manage the service models themselves. In other words, it will tell you where a WSDL is, but it won't contain the WSDL itself.

This is similar to what happens when you find and dial a phone number from the Yellow Pages. It works only if the home or business on the other end has its own phone hooked up for you to talk with them. In other words, their phone is the actual service enabler that exists for them to interact with you.

The Basic Purpose of Service Repositories

A robust SOA infrastructure requires tools to manage its service models and metadata including WSDLs and policies. Many vendors began to implement repositories to meet this need. Repositories manage advanced service metadata and all the other artifacts related to a service. Virtually any type of service artifact can be managed in a repository. Following are some of the most common elements:

- WSDLs and schemas
- WS-BPEL documents and other business process models
- Service dependencies, versions, and users
- Policies for security, message patterns, and other enterprise concerns
- Access controls
- Service contracts between consumers and providers

While registries are based on the common UDDI standard, repositories are still fairly proprietary. At the core of SAP's approach to ESA is a robust Enterprise Services Repository, which will be described later in this chapter.

> **NOTE** Many ISVs who provide SOA infrastructure are combining the logical functions of registries and repositories into a single commercial product. This really should not matter, as long as they are supporting available standards such as UDDI as appropriate. It's just another example of how SOA infrastructure will be maturing so that you can focus more on the business value that it enables.

How Repositories Help with Governing Services

Used properly, a service repository is very valuable in helping to govern enterprise SOA efforts. First, it helps ensure anyone interested in using a service can find all the key metadata about its capabilities and how to best utilize it. More important, because you can define all your service policies in a consistent, digitized way, it becomes easy to perform automated audits of actual service WSDLs and other elements. This will allow you to check that services deployed by developers actually do adhere to your company policies for security, transaction management, protocol bindings, and so forth. Finally, an effective repository will allow you to govern service versioning and updates because you can see how services interact with each other, as well as the ripple effect of making changes.

Organizations face two challenges when it comes to using repositories for effective governance. First is that current standards are limited, meaning vendors must augment them with proprietary solutions to provide more extensive repository solutions. Second, it is likely that large organizations can easily end up with multiple repositories. For example, you might have a best-of-breed SOA infrastructure solution, or get a repository from a platform vendor such as IBM or BEA if you standardized on their product suites. At the same time, business application vendors may also provide repository models that they use to service-enable their own products. This is certainly a big part of SAP's strategy. The company provides a repository as a critical component in SAP NetWeaver's Enterprise Services Infrastructure.

Because standards such as UDDI and WS-Metadata Exchange are still limited, there is no common model for vendors to support. This can make it challenging in trying to manage a federated, multi-vendor repository that ensures consistency in models and policies. As with any new technology and architectural approach, this will likely improve as Web Services–based technologies mature. Much more on the larger topic of governance is covered later in the book.

Service Intermediaries

There is one more key concept to cover before we dive into how SAP is implementing all of these industry standard SOA principles. It is important to point out that the concept of a client consumer directly calling a Web Service provider is actually not a desirable architectural pattern in enterprise SOA environments.

There are many reasons for this. As you probably guessed, the most important is that this is still a form of tight coupling between clients and services. Too much has to be done at each endpoint with this model.

Many organizations fall into this trap when starting out with basic Web Services integration. They end up replicating services or augmenting multiple clients to support the unique needs of a contract between a single client consumer and service provider.

THE RELATIONSHIP BETWEEN SERVICE REGISTRY, REPOSITORY, AND IMPLEMENTATION

A registry provides basic information about the service and how to find its metadata so you can use it. A repository actually houses the service itself. Keep in mind that services are physically metadata models and artifacts that describe a service's interfaces, policies, and so forth. The actual implementation of a service lies in the software application(s) that the service ultimately binds to. The following picture illustrates these relationships.

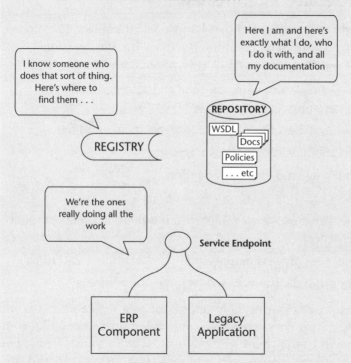

Registry, repository, and implementation relationships

As SOA technology has evolved, many vendors now provide products that integrate a registry and repository. Regardless of the physical deployment model, these products implement the same basic standards and logical functions of a separate registry and repository underneath the covers. The features of the SAP NetWeaver Enterprise Services Repository are covered later in this chapter.

Another main reason for avoiding this direct connection pattern is that there is nothing inherent on either the consumer or provider side to account for all the nonfunctional requirements and business process management capabilities discussed earlier in this chapter. An SOA is based upon the concept of a network of interoperable services. The ability to provide a smart network backbone to support these interconnections from a business perspective is what ultimately makes SOA work. Once service interfaces and policies are defined in common standards-based way, the network can do lots of things for you. It is through *service intermediaries* that these capabilities are best provided.

Functions of a Service Intermediary

An intermediary acts as a traffic cop that handles all the message exchange over the service network. By having an intermediary broker the connectivity between clients and services, you gain advantages such as the following:

- Reliable message brokering with run-time endpoint resolution to enhance loose coupling
- Intelligent, content-based routing with load-balancing and failover
- Authentication and access control management
- Logging, monitoring, and event notification.
- Transformation
- Ensuring actual run-time service interactions adhere to organizational policies (governance)
- Support for business process management, orchestration, and rules
- Adaptive computing decisions based on QoS requirements

This type of functionality is especially important in a Web Services world because you are integrating services whose underlying implementation components are not known to the client. For example, what if you have a client application that wants to make an asynchronous call to a customer master data Web Service, but the actual implementation of that service exists on a mainframe and supports only synchronous calls? A service intermediary can simulate the asynchronous behavior for the client while dealing with the service in a synchronous manner. Likewise, the intermediary can bridge transport protocols (such as between HTTP and FTP), messaging protocols (such as between different versions of SOAP), and so forth.

In short, intermediaries provide run-time governance, process management, and integration support between Web Services. You are probably saying, "Wait just a minute. Aren't these things that traditional messaging, enterprise application integration (EAI), and BPM products also do?" The answer to that question is "yes." In fact, messaging, EAI, and BPM are really enterprise computing concepts that have been confused with categories of products and specific implementation architectures. The same thing is happening with service intermediaries, as described in the next section. For now, just recognize that SOA and even better forms of Web Services integration require some form of intermediation to be successful. Figure 5-10 acts as a simple reminder of this principle.

Architecture and Design of Intermediaries on a Service Network — The ESB Debate

No one will dispute the value of service intermediaries. The debates that crop up in the industry (and perhaps within your organization) surround the implementation architecture, standards, and which specific products to use. Clouding this fact in the SOA space is a relatively new category of product called the Enterprise Services Bus (ESB). Even vendors and analysts cannot completely agree on what an ESB is other than to suggest that it provides the features of service intermediary, is usually based on standardized messaging infrastructures that services can plug into, and that it is very important in Web Services–based SOA.

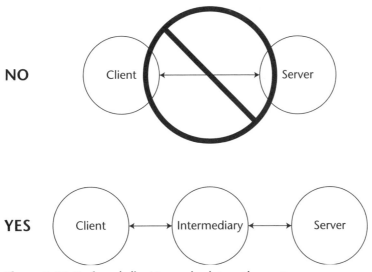

Figure 5-10: Preferred client to service interaction pattern

Perhaps the distinctions between the vision for "new" intermediaries versus "old" integration and BPM models can be summarized as the following:

- Extensive, native support for Java, XML, and Web Services–based standards, including XPath, XQuery, and XSLT, along with key WS-* extension metadata as described earlier

- Support for standards-based messaging infrastructures versus a reliance on a single vendor implementation

- Minimization of proprietary APIs and adapters for bridging to non-XML–based environments

- Extensive run-time governance features and more intelligent insights into business information and events on the network

- Support for flexible, highly distributed deployment options at or near the endpoints

The last bullet is the one currently getting the most attention. A new style of intermediary will act like an application-intelligent router, gateway, or firewall. Just like how those devices work today for data networking, you can easily add new ones in with different features to any point in the network where it makes sense. Figure 5-11 shows an example of next-generation intermediary capabilities distributed across the application network.

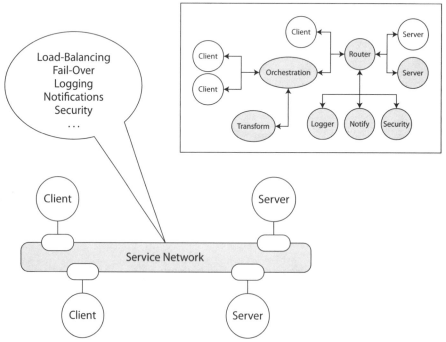

Figure 5-11: Distributing intermediary capability throughout the service network (Source: © 2005–2006, MomentumSI, Inc. All rights reserved.)

Obviously, this model is very different from the hub-and-spoke architectures of centralized EAI and BPM tools. Very few vendors offer such pure ESB intermediary capabilities today, and those that do generally fall into the best-of-breed category as opposed to full-platform providers. Most existing vendors of messaging, EAI, and application platform tools are morphing their products to become effective intermediaries for SOA. Each will have limitations relative to the pure distributed goals of service intermediaries, but that may not be an issue for your organization in the near term.

NOTE From an industry perspective, there is still plenty of confusion around both the capabilities of intermediaries, as well as the ideal deployment and implementation model needed to support SOA. You can expect continued industry innovation, consolidation, standards development, and changes in this area, as well as all the other technical aspects related to SOA discussed in this chapter. As these standards gel, they will make their way into leading platforms such as SAP NetWeaver.

Regardless of the architecture or products your organization chooses, having a highly standards-based service intermediary will be very important to successful enterprise-wide SOA. As these intermediaries become more intelligent, they will be able to make very complex decisions in optimizing service invocations and responses. You can expect industry consolidation and innovation to continue in this area for the next few years.

SAP's Enterprise Services Inventory and Infrastructure

The previous sections have offered a primer in SOA and Web Services technologies from an industry perspective. Figure 5-12 summarizes how these general SOA elements work together.

Because SOA is the foundation of SAP's new architecture, the company is implementing these technologies within the SAP NetWeaver platform. Of course, SAP will also be providing a full library of enterprise services based upon the core business processes found in the SAP Solution Maps and the mySAP Business Suite applications.

The remainder of this chapter provides a brief introduction to how these elements come together in SAP's new architecture. First, characteristics of SAP's inventory of enterprise services will be covered. Next, the way in which all the models and content associated with these services in the Enterprise Services Repository (ESR) is explained. Finally, characteristics of SAP NetWeaver's SOA design and run-time capabilities are described.

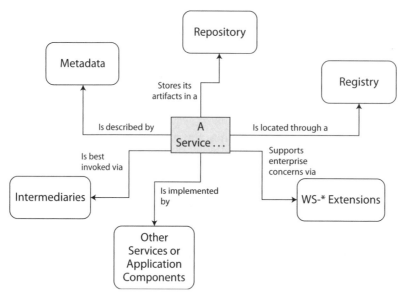

Figure 5-12: Summary of Web Services based SOA elements

SAP's Enterprise Services Inventory

The Enterprise Services Inventory is SAP's official set of models that service-enable the company's business applications. It is what currently differentiates SAP's ESA approach from every other vendor's SOA offerings. By providing this comprehensive out-of-the-box set of services designed in an SOA manner, SAP is providing a whole new abstraction point for its business solutions. Customers can use these services to jump-start their SOA initiatives.

This inventory affects two main areas. First, they represent the new interface model for customers, partners, and SAP itself to build new composite applications that integrate with underlying SAP business functionality. Remember that these enterprise services are deigned from the point of view of business requirements and consuming applications. That means these will be *significantly* easier to navigate and reuse than BAPIs and IDoc interfaces.

Second, they affect the product development efforts inside SAP. The official Enterprise Services Inventory provides the common model for SAP's product teams to create components and applications that support implementations of the services models.

The following sections explain key characteristics of the SAP Enterprise Services Inventory and how it is managed.

How the Enterprise Services Inventory Is Managed

SAP has a complex internal governance process for identifying, specifying, and approving official enterprise services that make their way into the inventory. As shown in Figure 5-13, many sources feed information into this process, including the following:

- Well-known business process requirements defined in the SAP Solution Maps

- Well-known process implementation and application usage scenarios from experiences with mySAP Business Suite applications

- Requirements and input from the customer and partner ecosystem as defined by the IVNs and ES-Community processes described in Chapter 4

- SAP's strategic business strategy and product development requirements

This process meets three main objectives. First, it ensures that the Enterprise Services Inventory is business and usage-scenario driven. Most of the services are defined logically before thought is put into how they are actually implemented. This ensures the services are as compatible as possible across multiple versions of SAP products.

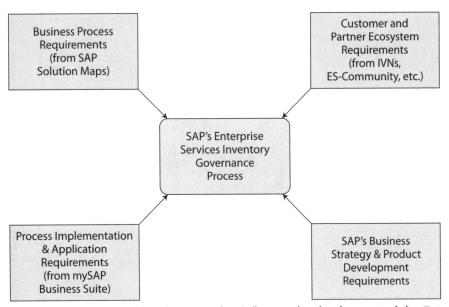

Figure 5-13: Sources of requirements that influence the development of the Enterprise Services Inventory

The second objective is that the enterprise services are managed in a cohesive way. This ensures that common business semantics and an organizational structure exist across all services. That, in turn, makes it much easier for consuming applications to leverage these services in a well-understood manner. Finally, the process limits the amount of duplication of service definitions across industries and product teams that would otherwise crop up if left unmanaged. By mitigating this chaos, SAP is able to ensure its inventory of enterprise services is more consistent and easier to understand and reuse.

As mentioned earlier, you will want to adopt similar processes and practices internally. This will enable you to best extend SAP's official Enterprise Services Inventory with your own models, or those from other vendors in your landscape.

The Relationship of Enterprise Services Inventory and SAP Business Applications

As Figure 5-14 illustrates, SAP's Enterprise Services Inventory is now the core abstraction layer around SAP business applications. For example, an enterprise service such as "Purchase Order Processing" is loosely coupled from the underlying implementation. This means purchase order services can be supported by implementations in many different versions of SAP applications.

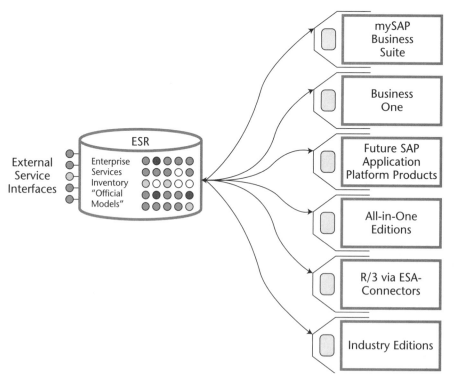

Figure 5-14: Many enterprise services will have implementations supported by multiple SAP business applications

The first releases of enterprise services content was supported by implementations in mySAP ERP and other current releases of the Business Suite Applications. Of course, some of these services, as well as many new ones, will be made available for future releases of SAP business applications. This includes implementations in SAP's editions for small and mid-sized businesses. SAP has also indicated ESA-connectors may be made available for implementations in R/3 as well.

NOTE Not every enterprise service can have an implementation supported in all versions of SAP applications. As you will find in exposing your own applications in an SOA manner, existing products such as R/3 and even mySAP ERP have limits in terms of the service models they can support. Of course, future editions of SAP business functionality are being designed from the ground up for SOA. That means they will have the richest support for the best practices service blueprints and models SAP is creating.

Over time, this abstraction will allow SAP to refactor code underneath its components, or roll out whole new implementations of business application components that are better aligned with the future architecture. In essence, SAP is using SOA internally just as you would in your company. The company can deliver new products faster, better, and more efficiently, while constantly improving what is behind the interfaces without consumers of those interfaces knowing or having to change.

Of course, the enterprise services will also be used as building blocks to create new types of process-driven composite applications on top of SAP and non-SAP application components. SAP developers, partners, and customers can rely on these models for their development because they are abstracted from the implementations. This will make the process of upgrading much easier down the road.

Previewing the Enterprise Services Inventory

Customers and partners that want to preview, explore, and work with the Enterprise Services Inventory prior to upgrading their own landscape have two main options as explained in the material that follows.

The Enterprise Services Workplace

You can browse and explore the Enterprise Services Inventory through the online Enterprise Services Workplace (ES-Workplace) available from the SAP Developer Network. The ES-Workplace allows you to do the following:

- Browse a sample SAP Enterprise Services Inventory and find the WSDL interfaces
- Create sample client applications to invoke services

▪ Look inside the underlying SAP applications to verify the services are exposing and updating data and business logic

▪ Collaborate with other developers and SAP employees on your experiences

The process for navigating the Enterprise Services Inventory in the ES-Workplace is based on SAP Solution Maps. You can drill through various scenarios and processes to find the underlying enterprise services, along with their operations and WSDL contracts. This illustrates how services can be defined in the context of business processes and scenarios. You can find out more about using the ES-Workplace in the companion Web site to this book.

Pre-Built ESA Servers and Environments

An even better opportunity for working with the Enterprise Services Inventory and all the other aspects of ESA is through pre-built server environments. These servers contain a pre-integrated set of the following:

▪ An Enterprise Services Inventory

▪ SAP business application components and service implementations

▪ Sample reference composite applications

▪ SAP's composition tools to work with the services and create your own composite applications

▪ The Enterprise Services Infrastructure including the Enterprise Services Repository and run-time execution environments

As of this writing, SAP has released an ESA Discovery Server, available from hardware partners such as Hewlett Packard. It contains an environment based on current product releases. SAP has also announced it will release another pre-integrated server solution currently referred to as the Enterprise SOA appliance.[2] It will contain much greater content based on the latest ESA product releases, and should be available to you around the time this book is released. You can find out more by contacting SAP.

Enterprise Services Repository

In the preceding discussion on repositories, you learned that these are a critical mechanism for organizing all of your service artifacts and supporting design-time, development, and governance requirements. SAP's Enterprise Services Repository (ESR) is the part of SAP NetWeaver that provides this functionality and holds all the content from the Enterprise Services Inventory.

In fact, the ESR goes well beyond the typical SOA repository you might find from other vendors. It encompasses several types of models in addition to just service interface definitions, documentation, and contracts. It supports the entire set of official meta-models upon which future editions of SAP applications will be built. The ESR grew out of the XI Integration Repository, which has been part of SAP NetWeaver since the initial release of the integrated platform. Of course, it has been extended to incorporate all the new features of the ESR.

SAP will be able to update the content in the ESR independently of new releases to application components. The company organizes ESR content by software component versions and namespaces to ensure that all content can be uniquely identified. In addition, there are tools that allow you to browse through the various ESR models and the relationships between them. Customers and partners can also extend the ESR with their own content solutions by using the same modeling constructs.

Figure 5-15 provides a conceptual view of key models included in the ESR, along with some of the logical relationships between them. These are explained in the following sections.

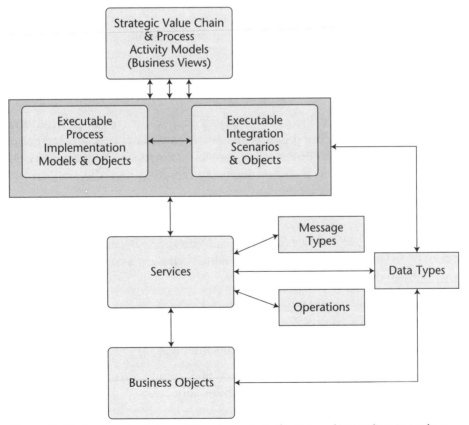

Figure 5-15: A conceptual view of the elements in the Enterprise Services Repository

Process and Integration Models

The ESR contains process models ranging from the high-level business value-chain and activity scenarios through executable process implementations. Application-to-application (A2A) and business-to-business (B2B) integration scenarios and objects support these executable processes. In addition, all of these executable process models and integration scenarios can be reused by multiple applications.

SAP has partnered closely with IDS Scheer (a leading business process automation company) on the structure of these models. SAP customers will be able to use IDS Scheer's ARIS tools natively within the design-time environment to build high-level process models within the ESR. And, of course SAP NetWeaver supports BPEL-based Web Services process orchestration models as part of the executable process models in the ESR. Chapter 6 covers these process models in more detail.

The integration scenarios are modeled using familiar SAP NetWeaver XI integration objects. This includes content for industry standard schemas and mapping objects to handle message transformations from one format to another. Chapter 13 illustrates these integration objects and process orchestration features within SAP NetWeaver.

Services

Services are the externally defined interfaces to SAP functionality based on SOA and Web Services technologies. SAP has developed many of its enterprise service interfaces using an outside-in approach. This means SAP began with the ideal service definitions based on customer use cases, regardless of current implementations in the back-end components.

There are many ways to expose basic Web Services interfaces within the SAP NetWeaver infrastructure. However, the ESR provides a common model for exposing the ones that are part of the official Enterprise Services Inventory. It grew out of the XI integration repository, which relies on a combination of the following three main constructs:

- Operations that define what the service does
- Message types that represent the messages exchanged by the service
- Data types that help describe content semantics

The service interfaces are exposed via WSDL, which forms the contract a service consumer can rely on. One nice thing about service interfaces is they can abstract the data type naming conventions with ones more useful to you and your business partners. They can also eliminate many data elements to include only the ones you need in a particular service operation. This makes the service interface much easier to understand than looking through the format of a BAPI and trying to determine which elements are and are not required.

In short, using service interfaces is much easier than working with typical SAP BAPI or IDoc interfaces from a semantic perspective. Of course, you will need your own governance process to effectively manage these extensions.

Business Object Models

SAP is defining a whole new set of business object models as the organizational structure for future application components. Previous chapters mentioned that certain aspects of the mySAP Business Suite applications will be decomposed into common components that are included as part of SAP NetWeaver itself. Those components will be based on the implementations of these business objects. In effect, the inner workings of SAP application components are becoming much more loosely coupled. This makes for a better foundation for exposing enterprise services because you can rely on well-defined objects underneath them.

The models for these objects will be maintained in the ESR. Like any business object model, these models will define the data elements and service operations of each object. Business objects can be made up of multiple nodes, providing a form of composition to create more complex object types. For example, a Sales Order Object would likely contain a Header node and an Order Line Items node.

A strict governance process inside of SAP will control this business object modeling. These objects will make it much easier for SAP applications to support service-enabled scenarios because they are designed from the ground up to meet the goals of ESA.

NOTE SAP exposes enterprise services that are implemented in current editions of products that were created well before SOA emerged as a common design philosophy. By building a new set of business objects from the ground up with SOA in mind, SAP is effectively laying the foundation to have its entire product line ESA-enabled.

One important point surrounds the interfaces associated with these business objects. SAP has defined four types of interface patterns for the objects:

- Access patterns for performing CRUD operations on the business objects
- Associations for managing relationships between business objects (for example, the relationship between a Customer object and a Sales Order object for that customer)

- Query interfaces for complex searching
- Action interfaces to support specific operations for the object (for example, a sales order confirmation operation).

Both the access and association patterns can be automatically created from the object definition in a very precise way. By using this approach, SAP can ensure that all business objects have identical syntax for these types of methods. This enables the model-driven development tools to interact with the business objects and automatically generate application and UI code. That in turn enables a whole new set of model-driven development tools for SAP-based applications.

Data Types

As mentioned earlier, data types describe business content. SAP's governance structure provides models of Global Data Types (GDTs). These are based upon international and industry standards as much as possible. The goal of GDTs is to create a common set of semantics for defining business information. These GDTs are highly reusable and made available to all components created by SAP. This includes service interfaces, business objects, and integration objects.

Data types are one part of the XI Integration Repository that has been carried forward into the ESR. Current users of R/3 and mySAP ERP can rely heavily on data types as a foundation for creating service interfaces within XI. Of course, a GDT can be reused across multiple service definitions.

Implementation and Composition Tools

SAP NetWeaver provides a number of development tools to support the modeling and management of enterprise services, along with the development tools to compose new applications and business process solutions based on these services. Using the foundations of the ESR models, composite applications can be built in multiple ways. This includes traditional application coding, model-driven application assembly, and BPM implementations. These capabilities are introduced in the following sections.

Modeling and Managing Enterprise Services

SAP offers an Enterprise Services Builder, which is an extension of the XI Integration Builder. The Enterprise Services Builder is used to manage the inventory of the ESR, including the following:

- Navigating and changing the enterprise services business objects, processes, data types, services, and other models to see their definitions and where the underlying implementations exist

- Reviewing the dependencies and contracts between services

- Creating new enterprise services by exposing existing applications and legacy systems in your landscape or modeling, and defining new services that will be implemented with new development or composition

- Generating client proxies for consumers to invoke services, and server proxies to connect the interface to the implementation

- Configuring models according to your unique business requirements

- Handling version management of models

- Defining policies and other non-functional requirements to services

- Providing design-time repository links for analyzing service metadata from application development and composition tools

Using the Enterprise Services Builder environment, you can expand on the official SAP services metamodel to create a services portfolio that best maps to your strategic business requirements. This includes developing services composed on top of existing IT assets in your organization, or abstracting your business partners' systems.

Over time, the repository management tools will continue to be enhanced, and to support faster creation of new models and more complete drill down across and between models. Just keep in mind that you use these types of tools to manage models, not the actual implementations. The implementations exist in other software components that you expose, or new assets that you create to support a model.

Application Development – ABAP and Java

Composite applications can be built from application code in the same way they always have, although there are other model-based tools that allow you to assemble them more quickly and effectively. Those tools will be described in the next two sections. If you want to rely on more code-level constructs, you can use the standards-based development environments and tools for J2EE and ABAP that SAP NetWeaver provides.

These tools provide multiple perspectives for interacting with enterprise services. They link to the ESR, enabling you to browse the models and generate client and server proxies that you can use to link to your implementation code. In the case of creating services using the outside-in approach, these tools can be used to provide the implementations of new models. They also provide wizards for exposing any existing application code as Web Services in a matter of minutes. This allows you to create applications that both provide or consume services very easily.

Composite Application Assembly

Today, there are no universal industry standards for creating composite applications. While you can build them using application code, it's more tedious and less effective in realizing the agility benefits from SOA. If you were an early Internet developer, you remember using text editors to hand-code HTML and implement application scripts. Today, there are many tools for automating and accelerating these activities.

In the same way, SAP is providing composite application development tools that allow you to work more efficiently. These tools are very model-based, work closely with the design-time repository in the ESR, and include a number of pre-built building blocks that can be configured to support your unique application needs. These options include the following:

- Composite Application Framework (CAF) for building rich composite applications that support ad hoc process workflows and manage multiple underlying component interactions, persistence requirements, and creation of new business objects to support the composite

- Web Dynpro for building complex, role-based user interfaces using the Model-View-Controller (MVC) design patterns, and handling linkages to complex services and application logic

- Visual Composer (VC) for rapidly assembling role-based user interfaces based on core services in the ESR. This tool is targeted at IT analysts who do not require deep coding backgrounds

All these tools are available today and can be used in conjunction with existing SAP application landscapes to meet development needs for new composite applications. You will see these tools in action in Part III of the book.

One problem that results from a lack of standards for composite applications is that developers create very inconsistent UIs across applications. The pre-built templates from SAP can help address this issue. Following are some of the UI building block accelerators that can be linked to ESR content and configured for quick deployment in a consistent look and feel:

- Guided procedure templates for lightweight process workflows, such as a "three-step approval process" or a "five-step data entry task"

- UI generation patterns, such as "header-detail" screens, "search and display results," "hierarchical tree navigation," dashboards, and so forth

- Work center services for pushing tasks to users in the context of a process managed by their role-based UIs

- Display and update screens for business objects

Over time, SAP will be able to enhance these tools to support next-generation application development models based on new versions of the SAP NetWeaver application platform. This is because the models in the ESR will become more and more precise in terms of the syntax and organization of ESR artifacts. That, in turn, provides you with even greater degrees of auto-generation and configuration from application models and more pre-built out-of-the-box content for your applications. And, if a standard such as SCA becomes a de facto technique for composite application assembly, you can bet the SAP NetWeaver tools will evolve to support the specifications because SAP is helping define them.

Enterprise Services Run-Time Infrastructure

The previous section described the tools developers use to manage the ESR and create new applications. As you probably noticed, there is a heavy emphasis on design-time models for these new applications. Those models require a reliable, robust run-time environment that provides end-to-end solution lifecycle management. These capabilities are delivered with run-time capabilities in the SAP NetWeaver Enterprise Services infrastructure.

SAP NetWeaver includes a run-time that supports the Web Services Basic Profile. Using features within the Application Server layer, you can expose any ABAP or Java/J2EE function as a Web Service using wizards, as shown in Chapter 11. The environment also helps generate proxies for both clients (to access the service) and the server side (to expose the implementation).

In addition to the basic point-to-point Web Services interface support, SAP NetWeaver has been offering service intermediary functionality since the launch of XI. The service intermediary capabilities of the platform include the following:

- Reliable messaging
- Routing
- Transformations
- WS-BPEL based Web Services orchestrations
- Policy support for security, QoS, and other SLA characteristics
- Run-time management and monitoring of services
- Dynamic endpoint resolution to abstract developers from physical service details via the System Landscape Directory (SLD) models

The SLD also helps to support the virtualization aspects of SAP NetWeaver. This is a precursor to more flexible run-time environments and intermediation for SOA. These point-to-point and mediated Web Services capabilities are supported in SAP landscapes ranging from R/3 and mySAP ERP, and will be extended to future releases of the application platform.

Figure 5-16 illustrates how SOA starts to bring together the worlds of application development and infrastructure. Notice that much of what had been traditional developer responsibilities is now shared with the infrastructure team. This creates new roles within IT because the infrastructure teams are responsible for configuring solution support in the intermediary. They must obviously adhere to the policy design requirements provided by a developer. For example, a developer may specify a service must support strong authentication. The infrastructure team will then use the Enterprise Services run-time environment to define how that policy will be met, such as with X.509 certificates.

The NetWeaver platform itself is continuing to consolidate into an integrated set of features, as described in Chapter 3. This includes combining the messaging environments of the Application Server and XI into a unified bus. SAP's active role on the technical committees defining a number of the SOA-based Web Services standards is also affecting the platform. You will continue to see NetWeaver offering greater support for the WS-* and related specifications as they mature. In the meantime, SAP can use existing platform technologies to provide the security, transaction control, reliable messaging, and lifecycle management elements of the infrastructure.

The continued commoditization and consolidation of Web Services–based SOA infrastructure is a good thing for SAP. More and more intermediary functionality will become standardized within the SAP NetWeaver platform. Some of this support may even drop into hardware-based intermediation layers, such as the R&D work SAP is doing with many vendors around "application-aware" networks. These are useful trends to monitor and plan around.

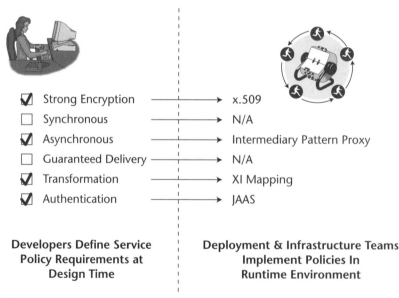

☑ Strong Encryption	⟶	x.509
☐ Synchronous	⟶	N/A
☑ Asynchronous	⟶	Intermediary Pattern Proxy
☐ Guaranteed Delivery	⟶	N/A
☑ Transformation	⟶	XI Mapping
☑ Authentication	⟶	JAAS

Developers Define Service   **Deployment & Infrastructure Teams**
Policy Requirements at   **Implement Policies In**
Design Time   **Runtime Environment**

Figure 5-16: Separating concerns between developers and infrastructure specialists

The point is that, from SAP's perspective, ESA is about delivering business solutions. The underlying technology plumbing must be a given in terms of robust capabilities and ease of use to allow you to focus more on the business issues. The ecosystem discussion in Chapter 4 explained how SAP is working with the major hardware and networking vendors to tackle this opportunity in support of the SAP NetWeaver platform.

One other important aspect of the enterprise services run-time capabilities deals with the service-enabled generation of user interfaces. As described in the previous section, applications make heavy use of modeling based on top of UI elements and business objects and services. These models require a rich rendering environment that is supported by the infrastructure. You can think of these UI elements as one type of service consumer that requires specialized support from the platform.

Summary

This chapter serves as a crash course in SOA and the emerging Web Services technologies the industry is working on to support successful adoption. If you felt that there were many similarities to earlier object and component models for driving reuse, you were right. Two primary differences with SOA are the ability to model more coarse-grained business solutions as services, and the general goal to make the network itself a key player in service interactions to support complete language and platform neutrality. This is one main reason Web Services have become so important to SOA. However, the emergence of a complete set of generally accepted Web Services standards is still a ways off.

Because SOA is the foundation for the new SAP architecture, you saw how all of these trends are coming together in SAP tools, technologies, and approaches for supporting ESA within SAP NetWeaver. To deliver on the promise of ESA, SAP has created a complete Enterprise Services Inventory that combines Web Services technology with models based on the business requirements of processes and applications. It has also implemented a full infrastructure to support ESA-based design and run-time needs. This includes some of the more unique capabilities SAP offers for creating business-driven composite applications based upon enterprise services.

Some of the most important takeaways from this chapter are:

■ Enterprise services are technically Web Services that expose a meaningful unit of business functionality. SAP differentiates itself based on having semantically modeled a complete set of enterprise services that are included in the Enterprise Services Inventory.

■ Many extensions to basic Web Services technology are still under development. SAP is very active in the standards community and, as new specifications emerge, they will be supported within the SAP NetWeaver platform.

▪ A services repository is a key infrastructure component for managing and governing your enterprise services artifacts.

▪ Enterprise SOA initiatives benefit greatly from the use of service intermediaries that broker the communications between services and provide all the non-functional support in a scalable and manageable way.

▪ SAP's Enterprise Services Repository extends the XI integration repository to include models of services, processes, data types, and a new set of business objects that will be implemented by SAP as the foundation for future business applications.

▪ SAP provides Web Service intermediation through a combination of XI and Application Server capabilities. These features will continue to be consolidated into a unified services run-time platform within SAP NetWeaver.

▪ SAP offers a full complement of tools for creating composite applications from enterprise services using model-driven development, and traditional application coding techniques. The model-based development capabilities will mature as the ESR metamodels become more standardized.

It's important to understand the larger industry SOA initiatives because your organization may pursue a non-SAP strategy for its core SOA infrastructure. Other organizations may choose greater adoption of the SAP NetWeaver platform as their underlying SOA environment. Of course, many companies will pursue a hybrid of the two options for SOA infrastructure.

Chapter 6 introduces how SAP is leveraging ESA technologies to deliver more robust Business Process Management capabilities.

References

1. *Enterprise Services Design Guide,* SAP whitepaper, 2005–2006. Available at `www.sap.com/platform/netweaver/brochures/esa.epx`.
2. "SAP Leads Industry in Driving Customer Evolution to Enterprise SOA," SAP press release, May 30, 2006. Available at `www.sap.com/Company/Press/Press.epx?PressID=6336`.

ESA and End-to-End
Business Process Management

If SOA is the technology foundation for SAP's ESA road map, business process management (BPM) is the sister principle from a solutions perspective. SOA and BPM work hand-in-hand to deliver value. Chapter 2 introduced the concept of BPM as a key industry trend associated with the realization of ESA. This chapter provides a more complete look at what BPM is all about, and how its capabilities are realized in SAP NetWeaver.

Unfortunately, the term BPM is often misunderstood because it is applied loosely to mean many different things. BPM sometimes describes a general set of IT capabilities. In other cases, it implies a category of products as defined by industry analysts. In still other cases, BPM refers to specific technologies and features. BPM encompasses all of this and more.

You can best think of BPM as a formal approach to managing and improving your business processes on an end-to-end basis. BPM really began from a business perspective where many important methodologies such as Total Quality Management (TQM), Six Sigma, Performance Management, and Business Process Re-engineering (BPR) exist to address the challenge of improving processes. With the emergence of EAI and more standards-based technologies such as Web Services, it didn't take long for the IT industry to develop new ways to transform these BPM practices. A best-of-breed category of software systems called Business Process Management Systems (BPMS) emerged.

At the same time, many related software categories also began to add BPMS style features in different ways. As the industry consolidates, the end-to-end functionality of a BPMS will become a seamless part of most major software platforms such as SAP NetWeaver.

In fact, enabling organizations to change how they manage business processes on an end-to-end basis is one of the most important outcomes of adopting ESA. As a result of reading this chapter, you will see:

- The goals of automated BPM systems and the value of a platform-based approach to achieving them
- The major features and capabilities that a BPMS platform delivers
- How SOA relates to BPM
- Key technology standards and methods for enabling BPM
- How SAP NetWeaver delivers end-to-end BPM capabilities
- Other efforts by SAP to improve the practice of BPM by establishing a community focused on business process expertise

An Introduction to BPM

Business processes are fundamental to the operation of any business, yet their execution can obviously get very complicated. Consider the set of high-level processes supporting the operations of a consumer products manufacturing company. The company works with various resellers and distributors to get products to market. Many processes are needed to enable the resellers to select and order goods from the manufacturer. Those processes must meet expectations for delivering predictable product quality and timelines of when goods will arrive.

The manufacturer must set up its entire supply chain, manufacturing, and logistics processes to meet these requirements. They must also work directly with end customers to promote their brand, handle product inquiries, address warranty claims, and so forth. Every step of these processes must be done reasonably efficiently for the company to be effective. This is no easy task, considering that these processes cut across all functions inside the organization, and require interaction with multiple third parties. So, where does BPM fit into all of this? First, you need a working definition of the term.

The Difference Between BPM, BPMS, and a BPP

Of course, many process management activities are done today without any specialized software. In addition, many important business management practices such as Six Sigma and TQM support effective process management.

The point is that BPM is really a much bigger topic than just the automation aspects tackled in this book. The sidebar "BPM, BPMS, BPP — What's Behind the Abbreviations" makes some formal distinctions between the terms.

IDS Scheer is a leading BPM software and solutions provider that has entered into a strategic partnership with SAP to bridge the business and technical worlds of BPM. The company has a full suite of business-oriented process modeling tools that support a number of portfolio management and improvement frameworks. Figure 6-1 shows a high-level view of how the business and technology aspects of BPM come together. You will see more on the IDS Scheer capabilities integrated with SAP NetWeaver later in this chapter.

Because this is a book about ESA and SAP NetWeaver, from here on out the term BPM will be used synonymously with the concept of a BPMS, which refers to a new set of automated capabilities and techniques that allow you to best define, execute, support, change, and retire business process–driven solutions.

NOTE For the purposes of this book, the terms BPM and BPMS will be used synonymously, meaning BPM will refer to the platform capabilities that automate the management of business processes. Of course, there are many non-automated ways to manage processes, and many other management methodologies that are involved with optimizing your business process portfolio that are beyond the scope of this book.

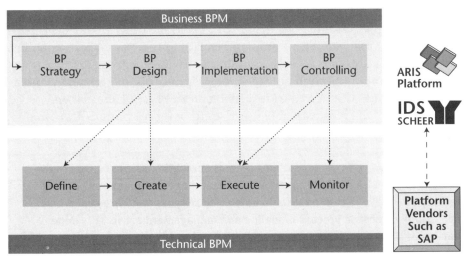

Figure 6-1: The relationship between the business and technical sides of BPM (Source: © 2006 IDS Scheer AG. All rights reserved.)

BPM, BPMS, BPP – WHAT'S BEHIND THE ABBREVIATIONS

The industry has so overloaded the term BPM that it can take on many meanings. BPM is often used synonymously with terms such as BPMS or BPP. Here is one way to look at the distinctions:

◆ *BPM* can be thought of as all the activities that go into defining, supporting, enhancing, and retiring business processes, including both the technical and non-technical aspects.

◆ *BPMS* refers to the set of technical capabilities that enable you to perform BPM activities most effectively. You can assemble these technical capabilities from multiple products, or get them from a unified platform such as SAP NetWeaver.

◆ *BPP* was described in Chapter 3 as the future of applied BPM that comes from combining all the characteristics of an ideal BPMS with actual process definitions, content, and supporting business applications. This is the goal of the SAP NetWeaver road map, and a BPP is what results from creating the complete "applistructure."

Confusing this even further is that some companies (including SAP) sometimes use the term BPM to refer to related, but lower-level, concepts. For example, there are specific integration scenarios within SAP NetWeaver XI that are referred to as BPM. These are based on the WS-BPEL technologies introduced in Chapter 5. Where technologies and products such as WS-BPEL and XI fit in is explained later in this chapter.

A good question is where SOA fits into all of this. Some people see SOA and BPM as competing concepts, one driven by IT and the other by business people. In fact, they are incredibly complementary. SOA is really about enabling agility within IT through loosely coupling software components and standardizing integration through new technology protocols and advanced metadata. You can think of SOA as the ideal enabler for BPM. Put another way, BPM provides some of the most valuable use cases for why adopting SOA within IT is important. You will see more on this in the next section.

NOTE SOA and BPM are sometimes seen as competing concepts. One of the reasons is that SOA forces IT to understand and model business processes in entirely new ways to create reusable enterprise services and next-generation applications. Because process modeling and management are usually done outside of IT, this can lead to internal politics and turf battles over who controls the effort. You should consider how to ally the two camps when doing your own ESA adoption planning.

From Functional Silo Applications to Process Management with ESA

Vendors such as SAP, Oracle, and many others built packaged software products to automate business processes like the ones needed by the consumer products manufacturer described earlier. As shown in Figure 6-2, these products clustered into categories such as ERP, CRM, SCM, SRM, and so on. Each of these products addresses part of the overall process requirements, mainly from a functional perspective.

The information in these systems must interact. For example, accounting data in the ERP system must be consolidated with procurement data from the SRM system. Traditionally, the overall business process is achieved through coding within the applications, a patchwork of integration logic between various systems, and lots of human interaction and coordination.

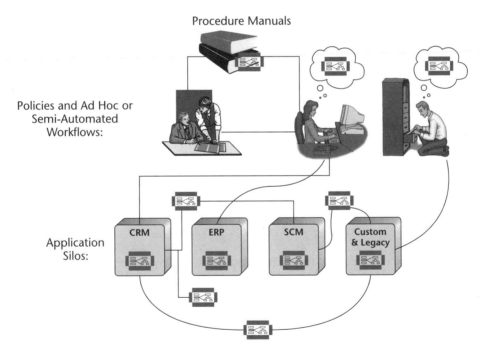

= process logic embedded in applications, integration or human interaction

Figure 6-2: Business processes embedded in application and integration code, along with manual coordination

While this is certainly better than the situation that existed before packaged applications such as ERP became common, the many limitations of this approach have become obvious. Point-point interactions between systems mean less flexibility in IT to adapt to changing business-process requirements. In addition, all the human integration and coordination means processes are harder to track from a performance perspective, and even harder to mine for useful process analytics.

As shown in Figure 6-3, the goal of SAP's ESA-based solutions is to allow you to improve upon this situation in the following ways:

- The overall process logic and flow is extracted from the individual application and integration coding, and defined as its own easy-to-understand model.

- Integration can be simplified through the use of reusable enterprise services.

- The people executing the process are given automation tools in the form of composite applications, abstracting them from all the details and nuances of the underlying systems, and organizing their work around process tasks with the right information provided at the right time.

- The management and monitoring features of SAP NetWeaver can coordinate process execution and provide better exception handling for people and systems.

The point is that people can be given tools to do their work much more seamlessly, the supporting IT enterprise systems can become more flexible, and the overall process can be managed and monitored in well-automated ways through an ESA-based approach to BPM. The benefits of BPM as enabled by ESA are explained in the following section.

NOTE BPM is unique in that it liberates processes from applications. It does this by creating digital process models that can be translated into actual execution models supported by many features in platforms such as SAP NetWeaver.

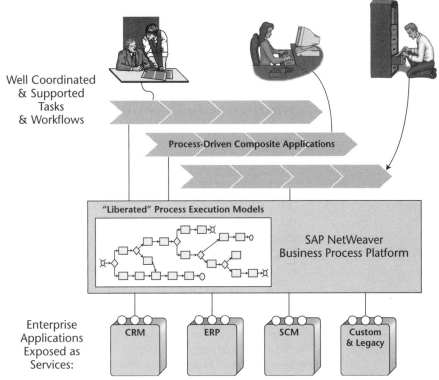

Figure 6-3: SAP's ESA-based BPM capabilities can transform processes.

The Benefits of BPM Solutions

There are many reasons to leverage BPM when delivering IT solutions. Some of the most important are described in Table 6-1.

Not surprisingly, SAP has put a lot of work into defining how these capabilities and benefits can be realized through SAP NetWeaver, mySAP Business Suite applications, and the new xApps it creates internally or with partners. You will see more on SAP's end-to-end BPM capabilities later in this chapter. For now, you can think of these benefits as a checklist you can use to guide how you define your own BPM-based solutions.

Table 6-1: Benefits of BPM

BENEFIT	DESCRIPTION
Clear visibility into how processes work	In many organizations, processes are modeled and described in static documents and binders. IT teams then develop solutions based on those models. Over time, enhancements to applications, new policies, and other process changes are often implemented without updating these official process definitions. At some point, the actual understanding of how the process works is lost, forever embedded in code or people's heads (see the sidebar "How Valuable Are Digitized, Executable Process Models?").
Ensure consistent execution	Having explicit process definitions guiding users in a BPM environment means that you can ensure consistent flow of execution regardless of who is doing the work. SAP's ESA solutions take this a step further by embedding analytics and procedures in the context of both automated and end-user execution to improve consistency even further. This can greatly reduce the impact of turnover and high training costs from changing the process
Manage by exception	Instead of looking at all activities to discover problems, the BPM system itself can detect problems and bring process bottlenecks or issues to people's attention automatically through various means of alerting and escalation. This lowers the time it takes to solve problems, and better allocates resources to where they can have an impact.
Analyze and simulate process changes	A BPM engine can track process execution over long periods of time, including all the resulting analytics. You can leverage this historical record to model and simulate process changes (such as raising approval thresholds or eliminating steps). A truer indication of the expected ROI of any process change can then be intelligently determined.
Operational agility	Process models are much easier to change than code. Model updates can be deployed very quickly into real-world execution. BPM also enables more business-level configuration and modeling along with triggering ad hoc workflows in an organized way.
Better linkage to business strategy	Clearer visibility into process models and rules, as well as the ability to create automated scorecards and analytics around near real-time information, helps give all levels of employees the visibility to improve alignment between process execution and strategic goals.

HOW VALUABLE ARE DIGITIZED, EXECUTABLE PROCESS MODELS?

The authors recently completed an application consolidation project to replace a handful of aging custom systems. The goal was to deliver very similar process functionality in newly developed solutions to provide some enhancements, but mainly eliminate the platforms, infrastructure, and maintenance associated with the current applications.

We began the project by looking at the existing process documentation. There were so many exceptions between that documentation and what was really happening in practice that the process details needed to be redefined almost from scratch. Even many of the users and process owners did not know what was taking place inside the applications. Ultimately, a lot of legacy code analysis was required to identify the real business rules and automation steps. The project team estimated almost 40 percent of the delivery cost could have been eliminated if an accurate model of the existing processes and rules had been available. An even worse situation occurred on a similar project where the enterprise no longer had any source code for the custom application being replaced.

Enabling Capabilities for BPM

Now that you understand the basics behind BPM, it's important to understand how developing BPM-based solutions is related to, yet different from, other technologies and solution architectures. As you saw in the previous section, BPM makes the process itself a first-order construct in designing solutions by liberating it from underlying applications. These process models themselves can then be digitized into executable models controlled by a platform such as SAP NetWeaver.

This concept is combined with a number of IT capabilities that deliver all the features of a BPM platform. The best way to understand these capabilities is to look at how the market itself is evolving. Pure-play BPM vendors offered best-of-breed solutions that rolled together a number of capabilities. The goal is to create products focused solely on enabling end-to-end BPM. Customers liked the idea, but began to demand BPM capabilities that work better with their existing application and integration platform products, as well as supported industry standards.

It didn't take long before several different categories of IT vendors claimed to deliver BPM solutions. If you look at Figure 6-4, you can see all the various standalone IT product categories that must come together to deliver on the promise of BPM.

The following sections describe the related technical capabilities required to deliver BPM on an end-to-end basis.

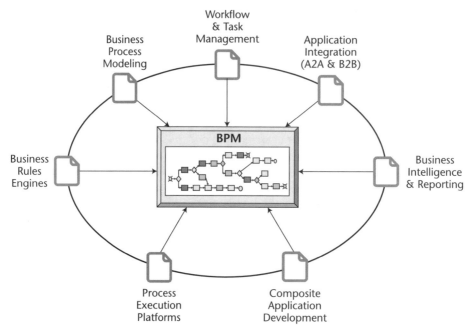

Figure 6-4: Different IT capabilities coming together to enable BPM

Process Modeling Tools and Repository

Obviously, BPM systems require tools to model and store process definitions. Early BPM vendors usually delivered proprietary graphical modeling tools that focused on creating process definitions specific to their run-time engines.

Because business analysts have a number of standard notations they use to define processes (such as swim lanes, flowcharts, UML, and so forth), more effort has been put in place to support common process-modeling techniques. This makes the BPM system more accessible to non-IT people. The key is to be able to then translate these common process models into an executable format. Today, this often requires that analysts and developers work together to tweak the models and tie things properly into the IT landscape.

NOTE The Holy Grail for BPM process modeling requires a set of interrelated industry standards that can span from a strategic value chain definition of a business process all the way through the detailed implementation and execution models. These standards will also need to encompass human workflow and offline process activities within the modeling and standards. While proprietary solutions still span this stack, SAP has been very active in working with standards communities to solve this issue. One area where SAP is especially involved is the Business Process Modeling Notation (BPMN) specifications from Object Management Group (OMG). BPMN may become an important part of a model-driven BPP.

When the digital representations are linked directly to implementation elements, you end up with a "What You See Is What You Get" (WYSIWYG) version of processes. This is quite different from most organizations' process definitions, which really do not reflect the actual implementation of the process in the real world.

The concept of a repository was defined in Chapter 5; it is the place where all the process models are stored, versioned, and governed.

Process Execution Engine

A *process execution engine* acts as the mission-control center for processes at run-time. It can take the digitized process models and then coordinate the flow of execution for all process instances. A process execution engine is responsible for things such as the following:

- Knowing the state of all processes at any point in time

- Capturing and correlating process events and initiating the appropriate response

- Coordinating handoffs of process tasks to different services, applications, or end users for offline processing

- Addressing technical errors and breakdowns during process execution

In an SOA world, this turns out to be fairly difficult to accomplish because all of the interacting software elements are loosely coupled. Two key computer science concepts that support the process execution in an ESA world are worth noting. The first is *process orchestration*, which is a special type of service composition that describes a process flow existing within a domain of control. Think of these as similar to private or "black-box" processes that can be exposed as enterprise services themselves. Consumers of the process do not need to worry about the actual internal steps.

The second is referred to as *process choreography*, which identifies the publicly observable message interactions and sequence used between peer services to support a business process. In other words, no central point of control is specified.

Understanding the details between orchestration, choreography, and related concepts is important only to the extent that you understand what they are intended to accomplish. First, loosely coupled executable process models are preferred over tightly coupled and declarative ones in an SOA world. In other words, if you go to all the trouble to create flexible enterprise services and then tie them into inflexible processes, what have you really accomplished?

More important, processes that cut across services need mechanisms to deal with things such as managing process states for long-running processes that include asynchronous and synchronous steps. In addition, conventions such as compensating transactions and other mechanisms must exist in a process execution engine to deal with transaction scope and reliability across the various loosely coupled services.

> **NOTE** The low-level distinctions between process orchestration and choreography can get confusing, but these are important concepts that will influence standards such as WS-BPEL and other Web Services extensions to enable more robust process execution engines. As mentioned, WS-BPEL is already a key part of SAP NetWeaver's Process Integration (PI) usage type (formerly XI), and SAP is working to help develop future standards and extensions.

There are many features in SAP NetWeaver that work together to support these process execution requirements for BPM. More important, SAP continues to help define industry standards that can be leveraged in future editions of the application platform.

Workflow

The difference between *workflow* and BPM has blurred in recent years because both concepts deal with organizing and controlling the flow of work. Generally speaking, workflow capabilities deal more with human interaction and support as opposed to application integration. Workflow tends to focus on providing support for areas such as the following:

- Controlling the flow of tasks within a specific application, as opposed to process steps across multiple disparate systems that come together for BPM

- Dealing with simple patterns for exchanging tasks between multiple people, or between people and an application

- Handling pre-defined document- and data-driven task coordination

One of the biggest challenges for BPM is to efficiently account for these intra-application workflows, document-driven tasks, and human coordination activities. Again, there are multiple features in SAP NetWeaver required to deliver this capability and one of the challenges for the company has been to tie its application workflow capabilities into the SAP NetWeaver platform's BPM environment. This includes support for industry workflow standards such as XML Process Definition Language (XPDL) and Wf-XML, which are developed by the Workflow Management Coalition (WfMC). You can find out more about these standards at www.wfmc.org.

Business Rules Management

Business rules engines have become popular again as a result of BPM. Rules management provides a way to digitize corporate policies and then use them across multiple applications. Examples include rules for purchasing authorization limits, pricing discounts, expense reimbursement policies, and so forth.

Managing rules has become increasingly important to automated BPM for three reasons. First, it enables better business activity monitoring as discussed later in this chapter. Second, rules are critical to defining process flows and the related execution, meaning BPM cannot work without them. Finally, one of the best ways to make a process more efficient is to change rules that create bottlenecks or inefficiencies without adding much value. Rules must be able to be defined and changed easily in the context of BPM. Ideally, business analysts can do this themselves.

NOTE Rules are important constructs within ESA. Many rules can be exposed as more fine-grained services, which are then used directly by applications or BPM execution engines. These same rules can also be included in more coarse-grained enterprise services through composition techniques, making them a key part of higher-level business functionality.

Integration Capabilities

BPM solutions must be able to integrate with all types of underlying applications and systems that execute the actual process tasks. These applications can exist inside or outside of your organization and include the following:

- Packaged business applications such as mySAP ERP and other Business Suite solutions
- Custom and legacy applications and databases
- E-mail and messaging systems
- Workflow systems and rules engines
- Multiple UI technologies for interacting with the process, including custom composites you create

This means BPM solutions support many EAI capabilities such as adapter creation; database connectivity; common APIs; file, XML, and Web Services integration; and so forth.

As mentioned earlier, integration is a key area where SAP's ESA-based applications and BPM come together seamlessly. Before ESA, BPM systems had to have intimate knowledge of the design, granularity, and structure of applications such as R/3 in order to include them in process execution correctly. With ESA, the key becomes exposing well-designed enterprise services to the BPM environment for both modeling and seamless integration.

> **NOTE** The marriage between ESA and BPM comes together through the creation of well-designed enterprise services with which the BPM environment can interact. SAP's Enterprise Services Inventory is designed with BPM in mind because the service models are tied to process models in the repository, and the enterprise services themselves are being created to hide integration dependencies and potential side effects from the BPM design and execution systems.

Business Activity Monitoring

The technical monitoring of processes to uncover issues such as loss of connectivity between systems or an unknown change in integration points is an important feature of the process execution engine. However, a real benefit of BPM is that all the process metadata can be used to monitor activities from a business context itself. This can provide much greater insight to people performing the process, and allow them to identify and resolve issues very quickly.

This type of tracking is called Business Activity Monitoring (BAM). BAM provides the ability to monitor individual and aggregated process data from a business perspective. Individual process states are constantly evaluated. If concerns pop up from a business perspective, the BPM system can quickly draw attention to the issue. BAM is key to delivering the management-by-exception features of BPM and enables things such as the following:

- Immediate alerts and notifications for orders that will miss their planned ship date

- The ability for users to look inside specific activities and quickly uncover any delays or issues

- The creation of manager dashboards to show work backlogs and allow reallocation of resources or tasks if needed

The possibilities are endless in terms of the value that can come from monitoring activities in the context of business processes.

> **NOTE** One of the unique aspects of SAP's ESA solution is the ability to provide a comprehensive set of tools for taking BAM information and funneling it to users at the right time, using their preferred UI technology (Office, SAP NetWeaver Portal, mobile devices, and so on), and then allowing them to take action within that context.

Process Analytics and Simulation

While BAM provides process analysis to support the day-to-day execution of work, process analytics and simulation provide insights into how the process as a whole performs over time. Advanced capabilities can look at the historical process execution data to calculate metrics such as the following:

- Time delays between receiving an order and its approval, or from approval to when it is shipped
- Number of exceptions that occur with processing claims, and the reasons why
- The cost of executing a warranty claim versus the amount of the claim
- The number of times approvals are escalated to second-level managers for amounts slightly above current approval limits

Again, the possibilities are endless. Being able to gather, analyze, and view process-related statistical data enables decision-makers to identify problem areas in the process designs themselves.

In addition, the historical process data can then be evaluated against new candidate process models to estimate the impact of possible changes. In this way, a business analyst can evaluate multiple different process variables to see which ones will have the greatest ROI *before* committing to a change in procedures or systems.

UI Development and Delivery

The final capability associated with BPM is the ability give users a way to interact with the process in meaningful ways. While SAP's ESA-based approach is able to push process information into existing application UIs and tools preferred by the user, in some cases, new UIs are needed to provide simple workflows or screens.

Most BPM systems offer the capability to create some type of composite application or user screens to support their processes. Because SAP offers a complete platform in NetWeaver, there are multiple options to define and implement a broad set of composite UIs in the context of process execution. These are discussed later in this chapter.

This section provided background on the many capabilities needed to realize end-to-end BPM. In the next section, you will see how SP is putting all of the pieces together in its BPM solutions.

How SAP Delivers End-to-End BPM Capabilities

SAP NetWeaver offers tools and features that span the entire platform, allowing you to create BPM-based solutions. Figure 6-5 introduces the conceptual view of SAP's end-to-end BPM support, which is covered in the following sections.

> **NOTE** SAP offered most of these capabilities beginning with the NW2004 release of the integration platform. The early versions of these capabilities are based on several different components, and require a lot of manual configuration and integration. Future releases of the ESA-based platform will bring all of these capabilities together into a highly unified design-time repository (the ESR) with integrated modeling tools, a consolidated UI framework for creating composite applications, and a more fully integrated NetWeaver run-time execution platform. In addition to the technical integration, semantic integration tied to the business content itself will also be included in the Enterprise Services Inventory.

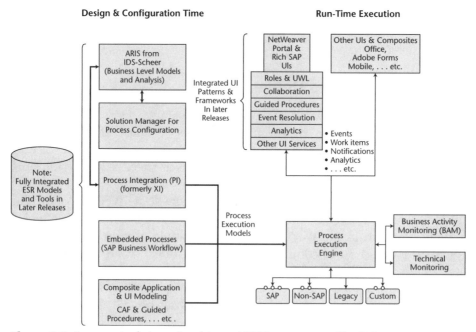

Figure 6-5: A conceptual view of end-to-end BPM as supported by SAP

Design-Time BPM Capabilities

SAP offers an end-to-end set of process modeling capabilities that span from high-level business value chain definitions through detailed process-execution models.

High-Level Process Modeling and Configuration

As mentioned, IDS Scheer and SAP have collaborated to create a complete set of integrated process models and tools to support ESA. High-level business process modeling and configuration are done using a combination of ARIS and SAP Solution Manager as follows:

- ARIS is used to define company value-chain process maps and scenarios.

- ARIS can import relevant SAP reference models from Solution Manager.

- ARIS enriches these models with organization modeling, rules, integration strategy, and other value-added views and enhancements.

- Processes are then synchronized back to SAP Solution Manager, which can then configure the lifecycle management aspects, solution monitoring, and other SAP content properly.

Figure 6-6 summarizes the activities associated with high-level process modeling and configuration between ARIS and SAP Solution Manager based on initial releases.

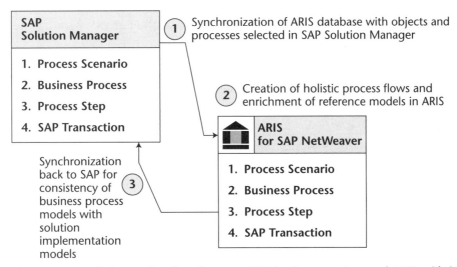

Figure 6-6: Basic integration flow between SAP business content and ARIS with initial releases of SAP NetWeaver (Source: © 2004–2006, IDS Scheer AG. All rights reserved.)

While current product releases require more manual integration and synchronization steps, future product direction from SAP and IDS-Scheer includes announced plans for a version of ARIS embedded within SAP NetWeaver to manage the integrated process models within the ESR.

From the ESR, analysts and developers will be able to access the models through an integrated design-time environment, or from their IDE of choice to work with the process models. Figure 6-7 shows an example screenshot provided by IDS Scheer that shows how embedding ARIS capabilities within NetWeaver might look.

Process Execution Modeling

There are three basic categories of executable BPM models used in SAP NetWeaver today:

- The process orchestration and integration models that coordinate the overall process flow run-time activities across all the participating applications and services
- The workflow models that tie to process execution done within a specific SAP application component
- The executable process logic modeled within the UIs that people will use to interact with the process

Each of these is covered in the following sections.

Process Orchestration & Integration

Process orchestration and integration models are implemented through the SAP NetWeaver Process Integration (PI) usage type. This is essentially the same features that were part of the original XI component, and include capabilities for modeling WS-BPEL solutions and plenty of Web Service and traditional A2A and B2B integration content. The business-level configuration in SAP Solution Manager can be extended with these process integration and execution scenarios.

Again, IDS Scheer offers capabilities to help define integration models using its rich toolset. These models can be translated into BPEL and then imported into the SAP integration repository for further changes and final deployment as run-time models.

Also recall from Chapter 5 that SAP, IBM, and others have developed proposals to expand WS-BPEL models to include human interaction and better sub-process constructs. As these definitions mature, you will likely see them make their way into the PI capabilities of SAP NetWeaver.

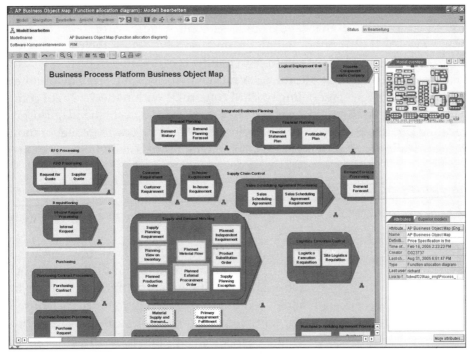

Figure 6-7: An example of ARIS embedded in future editions of SAP NetWeaver to provide integrating modeling capabilities for the ESR (Source: © 2004–2006, IDS Scheer AG. All rights reserved.)

Workflow

SAP Business Workflow is a mature technology that existed long before NetWeaver, and is now part of the Application Server usage type within the platform. It is a full-fledged workflow system that supports WfMC standards and allows you to create execution models for processes that run within a specific SAP application component.

Like any workflow system, you can define and route tasks to user groups, trigger notifications that include information on what to do, track progress, and override or intervene on important tasks that pass their deadlines. These workflow models become critical aspects of end-to-end BPM within SAP NetWeaver.

Guided Procedures and Composite Application Modeling

A third category of creating process execution models is similar in nature to workflow, but deals with aspects outside of any individual business application component. The whole idea behind composite applications and xApps is to give users much better interfaces that can help guide them through a structured set of tasks for completing their work.

SAP currently offers a set of technologies called Guided Procedures that allows you to build in this type of process control logic within a composite application UI. It also offers the ability for users to define their own light-weight ad hoc workflows at run-time to handle coordination of certain tasks.

Future releases of the application platform will include a UI framework that enables more powerful modeling of BPM constructs within the design of composite applications. That, in turn, will put more power in the hands of users executing processes in terms of managing their tasks, accessing collaboration features, dealing with process events, leveraging process analytics, and more.

The Future of BPM Modeling

As mentioned, the end-to-end BPM capabilities of SAP NetWeaver will become much more highly integrated in future releases. The company has provided plenty of insight into its future vision of how ESA will transform the way in which BPM is performed. As long as you understand the key concepts of BPM and the primary characteristics the integrated platform must offer in terms of the types of design models required, you will have a much easier time taking advantage of any specific implementations. For further insight into how the design-time aspects of BPM modeling will change, see the sidebar "A Unified Modeling Environment for ESA."

Run-Time BPM Capabilities

If you refer back to Figure 6-5, you can see how the Design-Time models translate into the BPM run-time environment. The executable models for process orchestration, workflow, and process-based composite applications will obviously be supported. Some highlights in terms of run-time BPM support include the following:

- The process orchestration features can handle the integration with all underlying applications. Ideally, this will be through well-defined enterprise services, but in many cases will require traditional EAI functions as illustrated by the legacy component that has no service interface.

- An integrated set of technical and business activity monitoring exists today in areas such as Solution Manager and XI/PI. These, too, will be significantly enhanced and integrated in future releases of the application platform.

- Many different UI technologies can interact with the BPM environment, including ones developed on both SAP and non-SAP technologies. Obviously, UIs based on SAP NetWeaver capabilities will be able to more easily take advantage of these BPM and BAM features to interact seamlessly with process events, alerts, notifications, and more.

A UNIFIED MODELING ENVIRONMENT FOR ESA

Chapter 5 provided insight into the types of models that will be coming in the Enterprise Services Repository and Inventory. In addition, SAP will be providing a whole new set of integrated modeling capabilities to manage all of the process and service models in the ESR.

The company has provided some insight into what this unified modeling environment might look like. In fact, there is a useful FAQ tied to all the BPM capabilities in SAP NetWeaver that was made available on SDN. It had this to say regarding the upcoming unified modeling environment:

> . . . the future BPM solution will offer a modeling environment with a unified data model and repository, covering all business process and technology-related information. The modeling environment will offer various role-specific views (Business Analyst, IT consultant, developer, and so on) to support different abstraction levels of process visualization, design and monitoring . . . The Unified Modeling UI with its different clients will be based on a common UI framework based on ARIS modeling UI look and feel. SAP NetWeaver process repository will bring versioning, change management and software logistics.

You can read the full FAQ about current and future BPM capabilities on SDN at the following URL: www.sdn.sap.com/irj/servlet/prt/portal/ prtroot/docs/library/uuid/f0485648-0a01-0010-97a6-f865bf6f3fad. A link is also available on the companion Web site to this book.

In terms of this last point, we mentioned in Chapter 5 that UI patterns and frameworks would be part of the SAP ESR. In addition, having well-modeled business objects and services in the application platform will allow you to generate much more intelligent UIs that understand the business process semantics in which they operate. SAP is creating a rich UI framework that brings together capabilities such as the Universal Work List (UWL), Guided Procedures, collaboration, SAP Analytics, and other composite application features. These capabilities will be able to be modeled in the context of business processes, making them an integral part of task management within end-to-end BPM.

Currently, the SAP NetWeaver Portal offers the primary role-based UI environment, content, and work centers to embed these BPM features into an end user's experience. The company has also announced a next-generation UI initiative referred to as "Project Muse." This can be thought of as a next generation SAP GUI that offers many of the same role-based features and simplified composite UI advantages of working in the SAP NetWeaver Portal, but through richer, more interactive desktop and mobile clients.

Intel and Adobe are partnering with SAP on developing Project Muse and you can find out more information on SDN at https://www.sdn.sap.com/ irj/sdn/weblogs?blog=/pub/wlg/3748. The main point is that UIs based on current and future SAP technologies will have extensive BPM and BAM capabilities inherent in them, including the ability for analysts and end user to do some of their own UI configurations to enhance the process execution experience.

Business Process Experts Community

One final area related to BPM deals less with technology and more with a community initiative launched by SAP to help customers and partners take better advantage of all these new capabilities. SAP is working to organize a community for what it calls *Business Process Experts*. This community will be at the forefront of helping thought leaders take advantage of all the BPM opportunities that come from a transition to ESA and the SAP NetWeaver BPP. The following sections provide insight as to the purpose, people, and resources that will be part of this community.

Defining the Business Process Expert

You can think of a Business Process Expert (BPX) as either a very technically savvy business analyst, or an applications consultant, solutions architect, or IT project manager who has a great understanding of the business. These are the "techno-functional"–type people who have the aptitude to do well working with modeling and configuration BPM tools to create solutions on top of SAP's ESA platform.

Based on the description of end-to-end BPM defined earlier in this chapter, you can envision a BPX would be involved with tasks such as the following:

- Defining process requirements and improvement opportunities
- Developing process models, including both business and certain execution level views
- Configuring the end-user experience for working with the process
- Developing lightweight analytic composites, dashboards, and other process-based analytics
- Analyzing business process metrics to perform analysis and simulations of process changes
- Defining and possibly configuring changes in underlying business applications to support the process

NOTE BPXs do not do formal coding, but they are the type of people comfortable operating as power users in tools such as Microsoft Office. They are usually the ones who build things such as complex Access-, Excel-, or Notes-based applications that become critical parts of process execution.

Ultimately, a BPX is responsible for supporting the entire process lifecycle for a given process or business solution domain. SAP has organized this lifecycle into five key phases, as explained in the next section.

The Business Process Management Lifecycle

Figure 6-8 illustrates the phases SAP includes in its process management lifecycle. Much of the content in the BPX community can be organized around these phases to provide guidance to members in the context of overall activity goals. Following are the phases:

- *Analyze* — The analysis phase identifies process requirements and needs from the baseline of today's activities.

- *Design* — The design phase involves a consideration of different options and candidate solutions for meeting requirements and developing the "future state" business process model.

- *Implement* — During implementation, the BPX is involved with activities ranging from project initiation through a "go-live" transition into support, including all the BPM-based steps involved with realizing changes.

- *Operate* — While the process is operating, the BPX and the user community are actively using the BAM capabilities to execute their process work. In addition, the BPX may be involved with slight tweaks to the process models and configuration to address any obvious operational issues.

- *Optimize* — In the optimize phase, a BPX tracks the overall performance of the business process, gathers user and manager feedback of what's not working or can be improved, simulates potential process changes, and documents improvement opportunities to feed into another round of the analysis phase.

Figure 6-8: The BPM lifecycle, which helps organize content for the BPX community

In addition to providing content, tools, and templates to support the process lifecycle, the BPX community will include plenty of other features to support process innovation.

What the BPX Community Can Offer

Although still in a pilot phase, the BPX community already offers a lot of content in a number of areas. The road map for the community includes, among other things, the following features:

- Process forums and content organized around horizontal business solution and vertical industries (such as procurement, sales order management, or integrated field service in the oil and gas industry)

- Process best practices templates, KPI models, analytics templates, and other baseline content

- Online education and tutorials on various SAP composition and process modeling tools (such as ARIS, Visual Composer, Guided Procedures, and Solution Manager)

- Collaboration forums, blogs, and resource downloads similar to what you would find on SDN supporting all the areas mentioned earlier

By the time this book is released, the BPX community should be nearing completion of the pilot launch and moving into full-blown release in conjunction with the launch of the first ESR content from SAP. It is possible that this community might evolve to include formal education and certification elements as well. This BPX community is likely one that you or others in your organization will want to track. You can find more information at `https://www.sdn.sap.com/irj/sdn/developerareas/bpx`.

Summary

This chapter provided a look into the features, advantages, and benefits of end-to-end BPM capabilities that complement and leverage the features of an SOA. It also introduced the many design and run-time features available in SAP NetWeaver that enable BPM throughout the platform, along with insights into where SAP is heading in future releases.

Following are some of the most important takeaways from this chapter:

- BPM provides some of the business scenarios that can take advantage of the IT agility offered by SOA.

- The most important characteristic of BPM is that digital process models can be liberated from underlying applications, giving you better visibility and control over how processes are designed and implemented.

- Many process models become run-time execution models that allow process monitoring and analysis at both a technical and business level.

- Execution models cover three general types, including process orchestration across all actors and systems, application workflow in underlying applications, and process or workflow elements (such as Guided Procedures) used to create new composite application UIs for the process.

- SAP, in conjunction with its partnership with IDS Scheer, offers a complete set of end-to-end BPM capabilities that initially span multiple components within the NetWeaver platform. The two companies are working together to integrate the process modeling capabilities in a unified environment.

- A more integrated, process-driven UI framework will also be available to create more process-driven composite applications using SAP technologies, while other UIs and composites can still interact with the processes using their own framework.

- SAP has launched a community for Business Process Experts that provides a wealth of tools for those people who can best balance the technical and functional aspects of BPM-based solutions using the NetWeaver ESA platform

In Chapter 7, the focus shifts from technology capabilities to a review of enterprise architecture practices and the role they play in successful ESA adoption.

ESA Adoption: The Role of Enterprise IT Architecture

You should now be familiar with ESA's goals and the impact in IT that a shift to SOA technologies and end-to-end management of business processes can bring about. There are many paths and options for succeeding with ESA. In fact, the road map for every organization will be unique because the details of your specific business drivers, processes, existing IT landscape, and especially your organizational structure and culture will have a huge impact in terms of how you pursue ESA.

Some organizations will include ESA within the framework of larger business process improvement or SOA programs. Others will use ESA as the mechanism to drive these efforts. One thing is certain. The more strategic benefits of the ESA approach cannot be realized from doing business as usual within IT. And simply adopting SAP NetWeaver technologies for implementing individual projects is only part of the process. A successful enterprise IT architecture (EA) program is the best way to deliver better long-term alignment between business and IT organizations, along with the process agility gains discussed in earlier chapters.

Of course, there are tactical benefits from using service-oriented integration and application-development techniques, and this can be a great place to begin piloting ESA adoption, as discussed in Chapter 8. However, those efforts will eventually hit a wall in many organizations if not incorporated into a larger EA initiative.

It should be no surprise to you that the discipline of EA has become increasingly important in recent years. This usually happens with most major technology transitions such as the one business process–driven SOA is bringing about across the industry. In fact, you will likely see a major shift in the entire EA discipline as a result of SOA's impact on business process management.

As a result, people who can play an enterprise architect role are currently in very high demand. At the same time, the understanding of what EA is and the approaches for practicing it are not unanimously understood or implemented. Different organizations see the function's purpose very differently. And the value that business leaders, IT executives, and even implementation teams within IT get from EA initiatives can vary widely.

The purpose of this chapter is to introduce the concepts of EA and explain why they are so important to successful ESA adoption. As a result of reading this chapter, you will be able to:

- See the many areas affected by ESA that are best addressed by EA planning for more strategic adoption.

- Establish a baseline for discussions around defining what EA means within your organization, along with how you go about performing it successfully.

- Understand factors that can make or break an EA initiative including ones associated with ESA adoption.

- Gain exposure to some existing industry frameworks and methods for supporting EA activities.

- See how ESA and end-to-end BPM adoption will ultimately transform the organization and processes within IT.

The Purpose of Enterprise Architecture

As the term "ESA" implies, EA needs to be a key part of the strategy to be successful. How EA gets done varies widely by organization. The size of the enterprise, the way the function is organized, and, most important, the value placed on EA within IT (as well as your business) makes a huge difference.

This section provides you with a baseline on the topic. Its purpose is to define the role of EA and how it applies to ESA adoption. Because the subject of EA is so vast, and its purpose and practice varies widely across organizations, this will certainly not be a definitive reference on the subject.

EA is still a discipline that is more art than science. In fact, you or your team members may find some of the perspectives offered here, as well as many industry recommended practices, simply don't apply to your specific situation. That is certainly okay. If it triggers discussions in your organization to arrive at the right model for how EA practices will support your ESA adoption efforts, then the chapter has served its purpose.

NOTE The companion Web site to this book offers a number of links to EA resources, assets, and approaches you might find useful for establishing an EA initiative in support of ESA adoption.

Classical Enterprise Architecture

Although EA is traditionally a function performed mainly within IT, its purpose is to support the needs of the business. EA provides the strategic context for IT decision making. Think of this as the stewardship plan for IT to manage assets in a way that balances efficiency with maximum business agility.

The City Planning Analogy

A well-known analogy compares the role of EA to the role of city planning. This helps explain the purpose of EA and distinguish it from more project- and application-specific architecture activities. City planning provides things such as the following:

- A master plan that outlines projected needs and changes in line with the overall city vision
- Zoning that divides the city into units for specific purposes to meet needs
- Building requirements that define the safety and material standards that new construction must adhere to
- Decisions on how major infrastructure (such as roadways, utilities, and public safety) will be provided to citizens and businesses
- A set of processes and support structure new construction projects must follow to be in line with the city plan, along with ways to track and enforce compliance

Remember, city planners have to do all this with an extremely long-term view and guaranteed uncertainty about changes in infrastructure, technology, social trends, external government mandates, and so forth. This is very much how IT planning works, as business requirements, processes, and technology in general are all guaranteed to change in unpredicted ways.

Within a city, companies, organizations, and individual citizens have a great deal of freedom to develop their property underneath planning guidelines. This is similar to the way in which IT project teams need some freedom to deliver their solutions on time and within budgets. The city plan also accounts for the fact that malls, homes, hospitals, and neighborhood parks all have unique requirements that the plan must support. Likewise, transaction systems, business intelligence capabilities, and integration solutions all have unique roles the IT architecture must enable. Figure 7-1 compares the elements of a city plan to that of an IT EA.

Without city planning, chaos will eventually ensue when change occurs. Individual citizens and companies have no incentive to invest in support of the common good. Without the economies of scale of shared infrastructure, many beneficial projects will be too expensive to pursue. And, as many communities discovered, future expansion to things such as roadways, sewage systems, high-speed communications, and effective zoning are much more difficult to implement when things grow in an ad hoc way. Master planned communities find these changes are much cheaper and easier to bring about.

The same considerations are true in IT. The lack of successful EA functions is often why organizations end up asking questions such as the following:

- Why are our most important projects far exceeding their schedules and budgets?

- Why do we have 14 different business intelligence products that don't work together?

- Why can't we pick an enterprise portal solution for the company?

- Why can't we change this business process faster?

With an effective EA function, all the parts of the organization work better together and that ultimately shows up in faster, better, more effective IT support for the business.

Ultimately, EA activities serve two purposes, as shown in Figure 7-2. First and foremost they must ensure IT strategic planning and investments (IT supply) is best aligned with business objectives (IT demand). Second, these plans and investments must add real value to implementation teams that are ultimately responsible for delivering IT solutions. In short, EA helps close the gaps related to IT's *efficiency* and *effectiveness* in supporting business innovation.

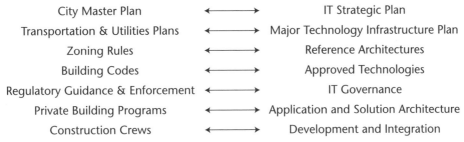

City Planning		Enterprise IT Architecture
City Master Plan	←——→	IT Strategic Plan
Transportation & Utilities Plans	←——→	Major Technology Infrastructure Plan
Zoning Rules	←——→	Reference Architectures
Building Codes	←——→	Approved Technologies
Regulatory Guidance & Enforcement	←——→	IT Governance
Private Building Programs	←——→	Application and Solution Architecture
Construction Crews	←——→	Development and Integration

Figure 7-1: Comparing the role of EA with city planning

A REAL WORLD CITY PLANNING EXAMPLE

One of the authors actually experienced the power of successful city planning firsthand while living in one of the top ten fastest growing counties in the United States. Some cities in the area grew as much as ten times their size in a decade. And with continued high rate growth projections, major havoc was occurring. Elections brought in new leaders who hired city managers and staff with backgrounds in dealing with this type of growth.

These city managers had the dual challenge of competing to attract business and deliver projects in their own communities, while collaborating in regional planning for major infrastructure. Many planned transportation, public safety, and community projects were halted across the region because they would not have kept up with the growth projections, and did not involve alignment with other cities and counties. These projects were replaced with more suitable coordinated projects in line with the area growth that allowed greater economies of scale, lower tax investment, and better service across the board.

Meanwhile, each city still controlled its own zoning ordinances, economic development initiatives, and streamlined business policies to drive some of the specific rules of its own expansion. None of this would have happened without first committing to mature and responsive city planning efforts across the region. As you can imagine, the authors have seen many fast growing companies go through this same transition in their IT environments. At some point, the shift to coordinated planning must occur.

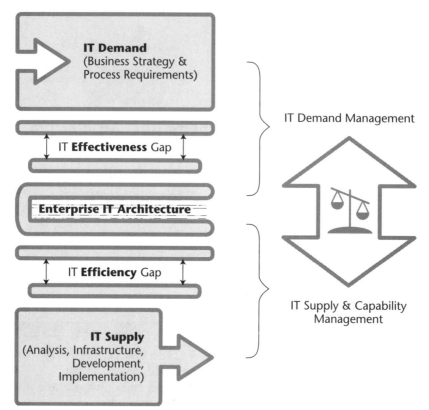

Figure 7-2: EA balances IT supply and demand to make things more efficient and effective.

What Enterprise Architecture Delivers

EA activities result in a number of deliverables, as shown in Figure 7-3. There is no exhaustive list, and different EA approaches have their own view of the outputs. Some of the more traditional EA deliverables along with their purpose are summarized in Table 7-1.

EA is obviously far more than a technology exercise, and is really valuable only if driven by the business. There are two important things to consider when it comes to EA deliverables. First, they should not be static views but ongoing models tied to changing business needs and evolving technology opportunities. Second, they are really only valuable when put into use and support the common good of the business and IT implementation teams.

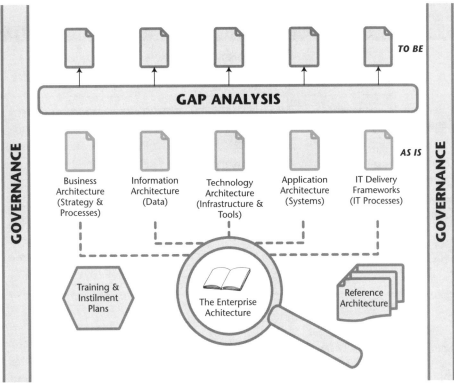

Figure 7-3: Major EA artifacts

Table 7-1: Typical Deliverables of EA Programs

FRAMEWORK	DESCRIPTION
Business Architecture	Critical elements of the organizational strategy and processes and how they drive IT demand, as well as how IT supply is aligned with these needs.
Information Architecture	The critical data and information needs of the organization and how they are delivered and managed logically and physically within the IT assets.
Application Architecture	The portfolio of IT systems and subsystems for supporting the needs of the organization, including their interrelationships and their roles in realizing business processes.
Technology Architecture	The IT infrastructure, security, management, networking, and other capabilities required to support the organization.

(continued)

Table 7-1   *(continued)*

FRAMEWORK	DESCRIPTION
Gap Analysis	Current versus future state analysis of various architecture elements, and plans for transitioning to the future state.
Reference, Template, and Candidate Architectures	Best practices templates, recommendations, decision guides, and models for use by IT implementation teams in delivering business solutions.
IT Delivery Process Frameworks	Best practice recommendations for project solution lifecycles to increase successfully delivery and include and influence elements of the architecture.
Instilment Plans	Method for communicating, training, and supporting the organization in its use of EA.
Governance models and processes	Approach to ensuring EA deliverables are adhered to across the organization, and guidelines for when compliance is and is not required.

How Enterprise Architecture Is Typically Practiced

Although EA activities are supposed to deal with strategic business alignment, the authors have found most organizations use EA to manage their major infrastructure project portfolios and address primarily technology issues. This usually means:

- Working with vendors to select platform infrastructure and tools
- Providing guidelines on which technologies, products, and languages to use, and when to use them
- Establishing hardware, networking, desktop, and security standards
- Evaluating new technologies and looking for areas of benefit to seed adoption
- Trying to resolve the issues in the current EA faced by application and solution architects

All of this is valuable. However, EA is on a more strategic collision course with business needs for one simple reason. Historically, business strategy and process models were fairly static. This meant you really could focus mainly on technology issues when it came to EA. Now, the rate of change in processes is speeding up.

Likewise, IT capabilities themselves can support greater agility through things such as business process–driven ESA adoption. If EA teams are focused only on technology, products, and service-oriented infrastructure activities, the benefits will fall far short of what is possible. New types of thinking are required in today's EA activities. You will see more on this later in the chapter.

At What Level Do Enterprise Architecture Activities Take Place?

While the word "enterprise" implies the entire organization, EA activities are not always performed at that level. Obviously, the scope of EA in a Global 1000 company is much more complex than that of a midsize or small enterprise. There may be dozens of EA initiatives spread throughout the organization. Smaller organizations will have simpler structures for architectural decision-making across the enterprise.

At the other extreme, the term "architect" is often applied to individuals whose scope of work deals with a small number of technologies and applications. For example, Sun offers a "Sun Certified Enterprise Architect" designation that tests expertise with a specific technology platform (J2EE) and how to best apply it to meet individual application needs. Likewise, at last year's SAP TechEd conference, a relatively high percentage of attendees tagged their role as "architects" during registration. It is likely that many of these architects operate at the level of individual applications and projects, dealing more with the "guts" of how a solution is implemented.

Unfortunately, there are no hard-and-fast rules for where to draw the line as to the scope of EA. For the purposes of this book, EA activities can occur at multiple levels within the organization, provided they meet the following minimum level of scope:

- Span a portfolio of applications as opposed to a single system.
- The portfolio is meaningful at a *significant* business level (which could be the whole organization or a specific sector, subsidiary, business unit or department).
- EA decisions affect infrastructure product selection, standards, design patterns, and so on, across this entire portfolio.

Alternatively, the portfolio at which EA activities take place could be tied to a business domain or set of processes such as manufacturing, customer-facing demand management, or supply-chain domains. For the remainder of this book, just remember that the term EA can apply to multiple levels of influence within your organization that meet the criteria of decision-making around a portfolio of applications.

The distinction is relevant when it comes to ESA adoption. Many organizations begin with pilots that involve using an SOA-based platform such as SAP NetWeaver to perform service-oriented integration and application development. Although valuable, this is merely a small part of ESA adoption. The role of EA is to help create and manage the larger vision and plan for the business.

Why Enterprise Architecture Initiatives Are Critical for Successful ESA Adoption

EA tends to go in and out of vogue with major technology transitions. Each new computing wave usually involves heavy investments in infrastructure, as well as new skills and implementation methods. This triggers the desire for more EA activities to plan and execute on these decisions, and to instill the changes across the organization. Once things mature, the desire for EA investments has historically diminished until the next major transition drives a new round of bigger IT investment.

As mentioned, historically, EA activities tend to be more technology adoption-focused as opposed to business-focused. You have probably seen this in your organization.

What Changes with ESA — The Big Picture

First and foremost, the "applistructure" means an SAP landscape is no longer just a standalone business application suite, but also a generic technology platform. This requires a shift in thinking at an EA level to answer questions such as the ones in the following sections.

Where Does SAP NetWeaver Fit In?

In larger organizations, EA groups generally viewed SAP as a business application that was just one piece of the portfolio, and often a proprietary black box at that. SAP teams have historically had little participation in EA decisions around distributed computing models, application and integration platforms, and Web-based technologies.

At the same time, SAP groups built their own EA capabilities for decision-making around the SAP landscape. They focused on things such as upgrades, activating new modules and features, and determining how to best manage the

SAP applications and infrastructure environment. In essence, the interaction between SAP and non-SAP architects took place mainly at the edges, where integration between SAP and the rest of the IT landscape was required.

Even if this model does not change overnight, just by adopting SAP NetWeaver, introducing ESA-enabled mySAP Business Suite applications, and leveraging ISV ecosystem partners and xApps requires a whole new set of EA-style decision-making by SAP teams.

Going forward, SAP teams must have the skills to be able to look further out into the overall EA decision-making process. Likewise, enterprise architects must be able to look inside the SAP landscape, which now includes service-oriented applications, a composition platform, and a library of reusable enterprise services. Together, both sides must develop a whole new set of guidelines within the SAP landscape, as well as across the enterprise. Figure 7-4 summarizes the major ways SAP NetWeaver and ESA adoption influence EA decision-making.

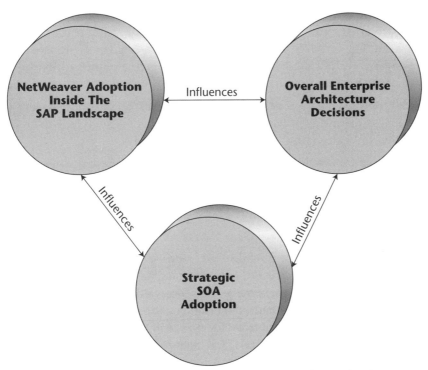

Figure 7-4: The cross-EA influences of SAP NetWeaver and ESA adoption

How Does ESA Change the Thinking Around EA?

SAP's ESA approach is one option to bring IT much closer to the business. As discussed in earlier chapters, ESA is based on a number of industry trends that are transforming classical IT processes, technologies, and organizational boundaries. Figure 7-5 shows how just a few of these major IT trends come together under ESA. These include the following:

- Business Process Management (BPM) and integration aligns business process definitions from the strategic value chain all the way through the run-time IT execution components, and includes human workflow and offline activities.

- SOA is based upon composition of shared services running on top of application-intelligent networks.

- Event-Driven Architectures (EDA) that create a different interaction pattern that allows software to dynamically respond to complex business and technical events that occur.

- Model-driven architectural approaches deliver application solutions using less code, reusable design elements, and having the designs themselves directly reflect the run-time elements in a platform-neutral way that the business can understand.

- User centricity is an approach for having applications naturally reflect the business processes of users, and includes concepts such as guided workflow, embedded analytics, rich interfaces, and so on.

- Process-driven lifecycle management and infrastructure services models map the logical and physical environment interdependencies, and interactions, essentially creating a live representation of many architectural elements.

NOTE As service-oriented, process-driven, and model-based approaches to architecture standardize and improve, it becomes possible to create much more dynamic views of your EA that link strategy and process definitions with IT realizations. As all these areas of innovation continue to evolve and converge, classical approaches to EA will need to evolve as well to take advantage of the opportunity, govern the adoption process, and manage risks associated with changing standards and products.

These are obviously *huge shifts* in the IT industry that cannot be adopted haphazardly. EA teams in many organizations are currently working to define how all of these come together in their environments. From an ESA perspective, this is even more interesting when you have a complex landscape that spans both SAP and non-SAP platforms for meeting these needs.

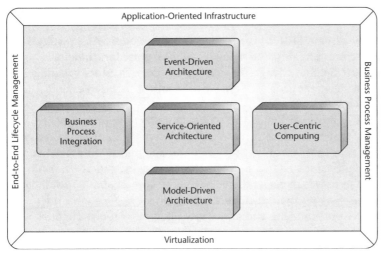

Figure 7-5: ESA represents a convergence of many major IT trends that affect EA decisions.

Each of these areas opens up a whole new class of decisions that expand the role of EA facilitation and enablement. At a minimum, ESA done right raises the bar on the business strategy and process architecture elements of EA. They become much more dynamic than classical EA models accounted for (see the sidebar "The Shift in EA to a Business-Driven Architecture"). Once business owners wake up to these possibilities this will create the ripple effect in IT processes and create a need for more dynamic EA.

The good news is that all of these concepts are actually harder to grasp than they will eventually be to implement. By their very nature, the model-based tools for building applications, establishing EA policies, and managing the infrastructure help automate many classical EA activities and deliverables. It will take time for SAP and other tools vendors to close all the gaps and mature things. But once they do, the speed of EA work, and the ability for the outputs to be actionable, can grow.

The remainder of this chapter deals with EA goals and objectives. Chapter 8 provides more specific details on how ESA adoption is best done by combining program-level EA considerations with pilot- and project-level activities. In either case, starting small and delivering wins early and often are vital.

NOTE Beginning with a strategic end in mind does not mean you need to "boil the ocean." You still want to start small with ESA and build momentum as you go. At the same time, you must recognize where things are heading in the industry, as well as in your organization, to avoid hitting the most likely roadblocks.

THE SHIFT IN EA TO A BUSINESS-DRIVEN ARCHITECTURE

Classical EA usually assumed static process and strategy models. As a result, IT organizational structures and decision making could be more functional and technology-focused. Now that changes in strategy and processes are speeding up, those business alignment gaps are starting to manifest themselves and affect decision making.

For example, the authors worked with a global manufacturer in the healthcare industry that had built a successful "Web team" in its IT organization as a means of adopting that technology for customer and partner interactions. This group made all decisions related to Internet technologies and handled all the development. But now that everything is becoming Web-enabled (including their SAP enterprise systems, their document management applications, their business intelligence environment, and all partner integration tools), there is confusion from an EA perspective on how to consolidate platforms, build a successful reference architecture, and support the business processes.

Similarly, many organizations have built integration groups as they adopted EAI tools and standards. With SOA and ESA, integration and application development become unified. Centralized integration organizations and tools no longer fit with the process-oriented model. Unfortunately, changes such as this that affect both technology and IT organizational structure take much longer to accomplish.

Chapter 6 described the "secret sauce" for ESA as the ability to effectively digitize business processes. This allows you to liberate them from underlying, monolithic applications, and replace them with agile, more user-friendly and analytics-driven composites. The change this will have on application architectures cannot be overstated. It is unlike any other transactional, data analysis, or user-presentation technology innovation that has come before. Unfortunately, many organizations have not yet awakened to this fact.

Increasingly, organizations are requiring a business-driven architecture approach for managing this transition. The following figure illustrates the major alignment activities associated with effective, business-driven ESA adoption.

A real and tangible coupling can now exist between strategy, processes, and IT assets. Previous chapters described how SAP's high-level SAP Solution Maps can be traversed through process specifications down to the implementation components and interfaces in the IT landscape. This is one of the main benefits of ESA and the SAP NetWeaver platform strategy. EA initiatives must evolve to address this need.

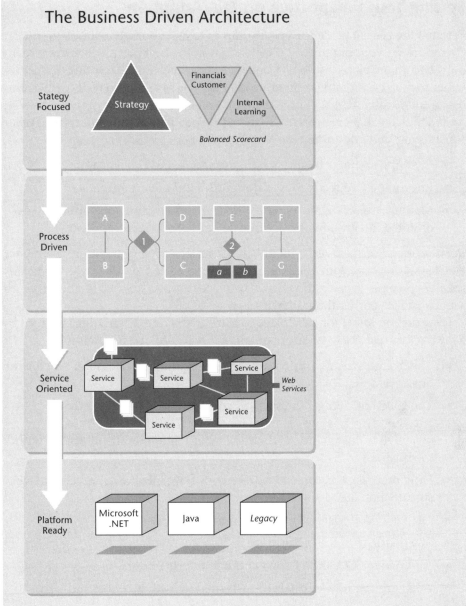

Major alignment activities in the business-driven architecture (Source: © 2005–2006, MomentumSI, Inc. All rights reserved.)

Setting Your Perspective on ESA Adoption

Perhaps the easiest place for you to start is to ask yourself a simple question: "Why should your organization tackle ESA in the first place?" There are really only two main places to look to answer this question. Adopting ESA must either make your organization more effective, or save it money. It really is that basic, and ideally, ESA will do a combination of both.

At a high level, there are usually three perspectives organizations take when considering ESA adoption:

- Enabling strategic business transformation and process agility

- Improving IT effectiveness through EA and governance

- Making project delivery more efficient through new tools for service-oriented integration and composite application development

These perspectives vary greatly in terms of scope and potential impact. Ultimately, success with ESA requires a combination of all three. Practically speaking, some organizations are better equipped to tackle the strategic aspects of ESA earlier than others.

How do you know the best place to start? To a large extent, this is driven by a few factors relative to your organization, including the following:

- The overall size of your organization and number of different sectors or business units.

- The speed of change and growth characteristics of your industry and the value business leaders place on IT for meeting strategic objectives. This includes IT's track record and overall credibility with the business.

- How process- and customer-driven your organization has become, versus functional and silo-based.

- The way EA decisions are made, budgeted, and enforced.

- The maturity of EA initiatives.

- Alternative SOA and IT consolidation efforts underway.

- What group or individuals are assigned to lead the effort and why.

By working through an analysis of these factors, the logical way to define your ESA adoption scope, budgets, and approach will emerge. Your organization will have a natural capacity for how much to take on and where to start. Just keep in mind that although tactical, project-oriented approaches can be quite successful, you will eventually hit a wall. At that point, a more strategic planning and governance-oriented approach will be needed to achieve the next levels in ESA adoption.

How SAP NetWeaver and ESA Affect the Architecture

Adopting SOA or ESA along with a new technology platform such as SAP NetWeaver will obviously have a major impact on your EA. Not only does ESA span the existing elements of an EA, whole new considerations emerge.

The most important areas your EA efforts must address to get the most benefit from ESA adoption include the following:

- Capturing business needs and expanding the role of business process portfolio management in the overall EA.

- Effectively aligning the new technology infrastructure in SAP NetWeaver with your current technology architecture for delivering IT Practices.

- Balancing current platform capabilities with planned evolution by SAP.

- Developing decision trees for when and how to use SAP NetWeaver to solve specific objectives.

- Expanding reference and candidate architectures, providing training, and enhancing processes for solution architecture teams to account for the new capabilities (for example, when to use ABAP versus Java, or when to use SAP NetWeaver Portal instead of a classical Web application).

- Deciding how the SAP ecosystem and third-party NetWeaver certifications and composite applications affect your purchasing decisions.

- Expanding your information management architecture to include enhanced master data management and embedded analytics within new composite applications and processes.

- Managing and governing a whole new portfolio of enterprise services across multiple composite applications.

The last bullet point is perhaps the most significant. One of the biggest advantages of moving to SOA and ESA is the "network effect" that comes from building a portfolio of useful enterprise services. When this portfolio is well-designed, managed, and governed, reuse of the enterprise services is high. Chapter 8 looks at the elements that make an enterprise service useful to others. It is not something that happens by accident. Failure to plan at an EA level for managing and governing your enterprise services is, as the adage goes, planning to fail with ESA.

NOTE Chapter 5 described how SOA technologies can enable more automated governance around services and composite applications. This is possible because using your organization's pre-approved enterprise services means there is already a level of assurance contained in the content and structure of the service itself. Recall that SOA standards also enable explicit descriptions of non-functional policies they support, which allows for ongoing monitoring of design and run-time interaction. Finally, the model-driven aspects of composite application development and Business Process Management enable compliance analysis and monitoring at the solution level.

Of course, you can ignore EA considerations and just begin adopting NetWeaver and pursuing service-oriented application development and integration initiatives. As mentioned earlier, you will eventually hit problems with this approach, not unlike the ones shown in Figure 7-6.

Figure 7-6: Adopting ESA without a plan reaches limits eventually.

ARCHITECTURE DECISIONS AND MANAGEMENT AT SAP

As mentioned in earlier chapters, SAP is creating whole new sets of business processes, objects, services, and other models that must be shared across all mySAP Business Suite and Composite Application (xApp) development teams. In addition, product solution teams must be delivering on the evolving SAP NetWeaver infrastructure using the new development tools that support user-centric computing. Can you imagine the architecture and governance approach required to accomplish this?

Product teams need training and guidelines on how to use the new models. Decisions must be made in terms of what tools and technologies should be used to deliver new functionality on top of the platform. For example, when should the Composite Application Framework (CAF) be used and which scenarios should be developed using Microsoft Office and Duet? All this activity also creates lots of feedback to the groups in charge of the official business object, process, and services models to ensure that they are useful across multiple applications.

Now, take it a step further. Recall that these exact same models and tools are also being shared with customers and partners who can use, influence, and sometimes help change the overall official models and platform capabilities through the ecosystem. Finally, individual customers and partners will be adopting the infrastructure tools and models, and then tailoring everything for their unique needs.

In effect, everyone is shifting to the same development approach within the SAP landscape. When you adopt the SAP NetWeaver platform as the foundation for ESA-based mySAP ERP or other Business Suite applications and composites, your organization will need to make a lot of similar choices.

A good example is what is happening inside of SAP itself. The company is dealing with many of these same challenges in delivering ESA (see the sidebar "Architecture Decisions and Management at SAP").

As mentioned, large organizations with strong EA groups will find it toughest to include SAP teams in the EA function. Traditionally, SAP architects were part of an EA council, but only to the extent that R/3 or mySAP ERP and other business applications played in the landscape. The role of the SAP teams now shifts based on the degree and scope that SAP NetWeaver is bringing to the landscape. The new out-of-the box services, the process management capabilities underlying mySAP ERP, and the SOA-based infrastructure require consideration and alignment with other options.

Why Enterprise Architecture Activities Succeed or Fail and What This Means to ESA Adoption

Whether you have been part of creating an EA or were responsible for using the outputs from an EA program, you have likely seen how difficult it is to perform this function successfully. Even when the deliverables themselves are done right, the EA program often can fail because of other issues.

This section identifies some of the main reasons EA efforts succeed or fail. Many of these are commonsense, but people either don't think about them, underestimate their impact, or simply don't like performing certain aspects of the job.

Understanding the issues can help you better plan for the role of EA in support of your ESA adoption activities. You can also reach out to others in your organization to perform some of the activities that would otherwise have been overlooked.

Determining the Right Level for Enterprise Architecture Decisions

One of the biggest challenges with successful EA programs is ensuring that work is performed at the right levels. Often, this means EA decisions should be made that do not span the entire organization. Some guidelines on what sphere of influence an EA program should cover were mentioned earlier.

ESA adoption will likely occur in a manner similar to how you make all EA decisions. The three basic models organizations use for managing EA are as follows:

- Centralized under a Chief Enterprise Architect
- Distributed across business units or domains
- A federated model, where multiple groups collaborate on some architecture decisions and decide which can be left to local levels

Using the city planning analogy again, you can see how decision-making can cascade to multiple levels. Cities themselves must make decisions in accordance with federal, state, and county plans and rules. For example, federal and state conservation and transportation rules must be adhered to at the city level. Likewise, a neighborhood association within the city can make many of its own decisions on how to plan the community, and to which rules homes in the neighborhood must adhere to as well. Finally, the individual homeowner can make decisions on what to build as long as it adheres to the hierarchy of decisions from above. Figure 7-7 illustrates the different levels at which IT architecture decisions are made in an organization.

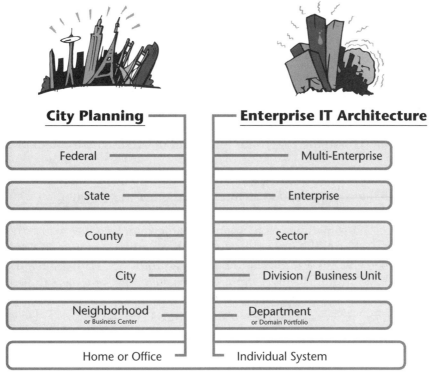

Figure 7-7: Allocating decisions to lower organizational units

A good rule of thumb is to make EA decisions at the *lowest* level possible that makes sense. In other words, if a decision can be made at a lower level in the organization without it affecting any meaningful business objectives, then it should be delegated.

The questions for you are how low should each ESA adoption decision be made in your organization, and how do you go about distributing and assigning this decision making? Getting this right is one of the first steps to successful ESA adoption. It is a decision that can become very complicated in larger organizations that historically are not used to SAP teams participating in platform, SOA, and Business Process Management decision-making. The degree to which classical EA teams work with SAP architects on successfully understanding and scoping the changes brought about by NetWeaver and SAP-based composite applications is critical.

Getting the Right Input to Support Enterprise Architecture Decisions

Even when EA decisions are distributed down to the right level in the organization, many EA programs still fail because they are done in a vacuum. This can lead to EA plans that are too technical, too theoretical, or too incomplete to be useful. It is also a risk even when the EA team is making good decisions because the users of the EA may not be brought in to the plan.

The first group to actively include is *business owners* who are responsible for the project and process portfolio around which you are performing EA activities. They must see how the results of EA decisions affect the business over the long haul, because they will likely be the ones with influence over the budgets. If they understand why some projects require added time or investment to support longer-term objectives, they are more likely to be supportive. This is especially true as IT and the EA groups have built up credibility through past performance.

Similarly, enterprise architects must solicit input from *project teams*, including solution architects, application architects, and other implementation team members. EA activities that don't take into account these groups are subject to great sabotage. And sometimes what seems sensible at an EA level really isn't when you look at it from the perspective of practical implementation. If *development teams* perceive the EA efforts to be way out of touch with reality, the chances of success are slim. Timely input from trusted *solution teams* can help avoid these mistakes and bridge the gaps between groups.

As you approach ESA adoption, there should be a list of people you plan to include to review and validate decisions before they are made firm. You cannot succeed without understanding what is important to them and addressing their concerns and pain points in your ESA plans.

Ensuring the Enterprise Architecture Deliverables Are Useful, Usable, and Actionable

Sometimes EA teams forget their work is simply a means to an end. The investment is only valuable if it actually gets used. This is much like the city planners. If the city doesn't encourage growth and new development, or has rules that are too difficult to understand and follow, then expansion and compliance will be limited.

Similarly, there is plenty the EA team must take into account beyond getting the input described earlier to ensure value comes from their work.

Making Enterprise Architecture Artifacts Actionable

EA decisions are often easier said than done. The outputs must be created at a level that can influence downstream decisions. This means creating actionable reference architectures and candidate architectures, as well as providing training for adoption teams. For example, the switch to a new architecture based on an integrated platform such as SAP NetWeaver, SOA-based design patterns, and intelligent infrastructure is a big change that requires guidance to go with the decisions being made. Sometimes this can be as simple as publishing tools such as decision trees, process guides for implementation teams, and sample artifacts. For example, Figure 7-8 shows a highly simplified decision tree for picking the right GUI technology for an application need.

In fact, one of the advantages of the model-driven aspects of the ESA vision for NetWeaver is that the out-of-the-box end-to-end process management models described in Chapter 6 can be tailored into ready-made candidate architectures that are highly reusable. And, because many of these models reflect the physical and logical aspects of your production environment, performing change analysis on portions of the architecture can be done automatically.

Ensuring Enterprise Architecture Artifacts Are Available

One of the common pitfalls the authors see when auditing many EA efforts is that the artifacts are scattered and out of date. This typically comes from thinking EA decisions are static events tied to major technology transitions. Nice binders are published and e-mails are sent. Of course, over time, people, technologies, and processes evolve incrementally and the EA artifacts get lost in the shuffle.

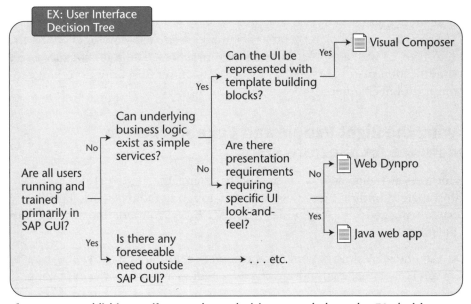

Figure 7-8: Publishing artifacts such as decision trees help make EA decisions more actionable.

The reality is a successful EA effort is ongoing and incremental. By having a publishing plan and process for sharing EA information widely, you provide the method to enable more frequent change. This could be as simple as offering relevant EA portals with appropriate alerting of changes. As mentioned earlier, more modern, model-driven IDEs will include links to repository information, including self-describing architectural policies and guidelines. This means application architects and developers will have certain elements of the EA efforts available directly in the context in which they work.

Of course, there's no sense getting carried away with tools and over-automation. The point is ensuring that the EA information is available to those who need it in whatever format can be sustained. With ESA adoption, this ongoing sharing of information will be vital to dealing with the continued evolution of SAP NetWeaver and the mySAP Business Suite applications, as well as ecosystem partner offerings that become part of your landscape.

Communicating Enterprise Architecture Decisions and Results

Perhaps the most overlooked aspect of EA decisions is having a supporting marketing effort to communicate results. Giving project teams a forum to share successes that were supported by EA initiatives is critical to increasing credibility. Business owners also need to hear successes such as how a commitment to reuse lowered the cost and timeline for subsequent projects, or how new user productivity features improved ROI of a business process by a significant amount.

The communication plan becomes a valuable feedback loop for evolving the architecture, as well as spreading new best practices. The role of a successful communication plan is covered in the discussion on ESA adoption pilot programs found in Chapter 8.

Having the Right People and Collaboration in Enterprise Architecture Roles

Performing EA successfully begins with having the right people involved. Unfortunately, finding those people is very tough in today's market primarily because being good at EA activities requires a broad combination of skills such as the following:

- An understanding of your organization's critical drivers, as well as how to run IT as a business, and use this information to guide decision-making.

- Strategic thinking ability with a pragmatic appreciation of downstream execution concerns.

- Knowledge of technology and active pursuit of new trends such as SOA, Web 2.0, Saas, MDA, application-aware networks, BPM, and so on, with a critical eye.

- Active collaboration with peers inside and outside the company and ability to borrow best practices from others.

- Ability to communicate exceptionally well and facilitate, train, coach, mentor, and especially listen to others.

- Role as consensus builder and influencer, but not afraid to make or enforce unpopular decisions.

- Knowledge of classical and emerging EA frameworks.

- Self-motivation and continuous learner. This means appreciating change and not being invested in yesterday's decisions as the right answer to solve tomorrow's problems.

Unfortunately, there are no generally accepted certifications, training programs, or career backgrounds that guarantee success in an EA role. As one CIO commented, "I just know them when I see them."

Larger organizations often require teams to perform EA work. So, in addition to picking the right individuals, you also must consider the harmony and complementary skill sets of the overall team. Keep this in mind if you are building a new team for ESA adoption that reaches outside your typical EA structure. Its also useful to ensure that key players associated with ESA adoption participate in regularly scheduled EA council meetings if you conduct them.

Many organizations put their architecture decision-making in the infrastructure group because hardware, networking, and security were the areas that traditionally spanned project portfolios and had the clearest benefits for standardization and economies of scale. With ESA, application, process, and business architecture decisions become much more important. You should definitely keep this in mind when beginning to pursue ESA if your organization adopted the infrastructure-centric approach to EA decisions.

Enforcing Enterprise Architecture Decisions

Cities have laws to enforce their planning decisions and specific rules to govern exceptions and changes. At some point, your organization will have to make the hard choices on when and how to enforce EA decisions. This often falls under the domain of governance. If you make too many exceptions to your plan, or leave too many decisions in the hands of application architects and project teams, then you risk undermining the whole process. EA practitioners usually hate the enforcement aspect of the job (who wouldn't?). As mentioned earlier, it is important to have team members who are skilled at this for when the situation dictates.

Unfortunately, this means that not only do EA efforts require support from senior IT leadership, the IT leaders themselves also must have support from business leaders who may push to overrule decisions in the interests of their local projects. And don't let this slip away when you hand off implementation projects to outsourcing or offshore firms (see the sidebar "The Clash Between EA Governance and Outsourcing").

Obviously, EA decisions are best supported when made using all the best practices described earlier in this chapter. If scoped well, made at the right levels, and properly communicated in an actionable way, then compliance concerns are usually discovered earlier in the project lifecycles when they can be addressed most effectively. New ways to automate governance audits through the modeling environments and management tools in SAP NetWeaver have also been discussed.

Ultimately, your organization must decide whether to put a "consequences model" in place that has teeth to it. Of course, everyone involved has to be pragmatic. Enforcing an EA decision that does not make good business sense in a specific circumstance is silly, but it happens all the time. Sometimes teams can win the battle but lose the war when it comes to successful EA programs by becoming too bureaucratic. This is especially true with ESA adoption. Platforms such as SAP NetWeaver and applications such as mySAP ERP and the Business Suite now cross into new territory beyond the traditional SAP landscape. It will take a while for decision-making to catch up, especially in larger organizations.

And instead of using only "sticks" associated with governance and enforcement, it is even better to have "carrots" in place to encourage compliance. This can include formal efforts such as the way in which you set up cost allocations and recharge models. In many organizations, classical models do not apply well to ESA and SOA adoption. You must invest time to think about how to encourage reuse and process management, not penalize those teams that take advantage of it. Of course, informal recognition and factoring compliance into the HR reviews for application and solution architects are other good ways to encourage cooperation.

Gaining Leadership Support for EA-Related Activities

The previous discussion assumes that EA activities are valued at a meaningful level in your organization. If that is the case, you have a head start on strategic ESA adoption. But, just as some cities can languish because of a lack of leadership and planning, some businesses have not yet awakened to the fact that ESA represents a major transition for IT that requires a new level of EA coordination.

THE CLASH BETWEEN EA GOVERNANCE AND OUTSOURCING

For some reason, organizations seem to more easily overlook governance and enforcement activities when dealing with their implementation partners. This happens for lots of reasons. For one, the decision to outsource certain projects is often made by individual business units outside the scope of IT. Even within IT, the focus on approved vendor lists and procurement is often disconnected from internal EA programs, project implementation processes, and decision-making.

As organizations gain more experience with outsourcing and offshoring of development, they are beginning to reconsider how handing off project outcomes can better work within internal governance models. This includes the following:

◆ Creating a governance handbook for vendors

◆ Having a certification and audit program in place

◆ Defining and implementing a consequences model

◆ Recognizing and rewarding partners for successful compliance and including them in feedback loops

◆ Requiring training and oversight programs for partners as a cost of doing business with your organization

The last bullet is especially interesting. The authors have seen organizations begin to require partner investments into their EA initiatives because, as customers, they should be gaining from ongoing and expanded relationships.

As you outsource or offshore significant portions of your SAP development and maintenance, this is an important consideration for your ESA adoption initiatives. It will either become a great opportunity or a big threat to long-term success. You definitely do not want inconsistent technology platforms, environments, service portfolios, or non-standard model-based development to spread across your organization.

At the end of the day, your business and IT leadership either values EA work at some level, or it does not. You are unlikely to change that fact overnight. But even if it doesn't, there are some things you can do to influence successful ESA adoption. Consider some of the following options, which are all about building momentum for your efforts:

▪ Take a minimalist approach and do not try to "boil the ocean" or copy models from organizations with much more mature EA efforts.

▪ Get peers in your organization involved and create informal networks of architects who look for common reuse opportunities tied to services or even SAP NetWeaver infrastructure for justification across multiple projects where you lack common platform capabilities.

- Strive toward quantifiable metrics to track. Many EA initiatives struggle because of fuzzy metrics.

- Think strategically while acting tactically to lay some groundwork. There are often ways to embed longer-term benefits in short-term projects without a lot of fanfare if you find the opportunities with high ROI and short payback.

- Actively participate with peers from other organizations (such as the ASUG EA Group and ESA SIG) and communicate what they are doing in your own organization.

Everyone knows a healthy diet and exercise are good things, but not everyone does these things. If the business and IT leadership are not pushing for strategic EA programs to drive ESA adoption, then you can still get the benefits of SAP NetWeaver adoption for end user productivity and embedded analytics in the short run.

Eventually, even those organizations that claim to be "wall-to-wall" SAP and don't think they need EA efforts will hit a barrier in the same way a city cannot grow forever without planning becoming an obvious imperative. If you focus on generating wins early and often, you will begin to see opportunities build. And, when it comes time to allocate resources or enforce decisions tied to EA, you will know if you are making progress.

Figure 7-9 summarizes some of the principles for succeeding with EA activities. A great list of EA anti-patterns (that is, what not to do) was published by Scott Ambler and can be found at `www.agilemodeling.com/essays/enterpriseModelingAntiPatterns.htm`. A link is provided on the book's companion Web site, and the authors highly recommend giving this a look.

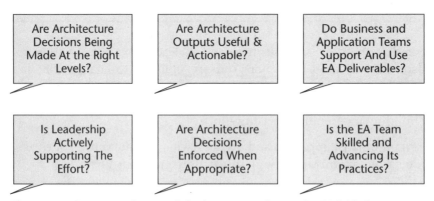

Figure 7-9: Summary of some of the key success factors for EA initiatives

Enterprise Architecture Frameworks and Related Tools, Methods, and Processes

Classical EA activities have been practiced for decades. Over the last several years, a number of frameworks, methods, and processes for performing the EA functions have been published in the public domain. Some of these have been broadly adopted by many organizations, becoming de facto standards for supporting EA initiatives. In addition, automation tools for managing EA artifacts including ones based on these frameworks have also emerged in recent years. These tools are helpful in helping to ensure that EA deliverables become living resources that are easier to evolve and more useful to stakeholders.

This section will help you understand the purpose of these frameworks, tools, and processes. It will also provide brief introductions to some of the more popular ones available. If your organization is interested in evolving your EA initiatives, you can use this as a launching point for places to seek further information.

If you come from primarily an SAP background, you may discover some of these are in use in your organization today. Understanding your company's overall EA approach will help you better participate from an ESA-adoption perspective. And, if your organization does not use a framework or have mature EA processes, you may want to research some of them further to see if there are portions you want to adopt or use. As mentioned, the companion Web site for this book contains a number of links to resources and additional information on these frameworks.

The Value of EA Frameworks

An EA Framework is simply a set of tools to help you create and manage your EA assets in an organized way. Figure 7-10 identifies some of the major elements for an EA framework.

Obviously, benefiting from best practices and not having to tackle an EA program from scratch is useful. These frameworks make it easier to provide a common set of semantics and training across your organization for performing EA activities. They also make it easier for EA professionals across organizations to work together to advance the discipline. In some cases, these frameworks are serving as a baseline for certification efforts to track the depth and breadth of people working in the EA space underlying methods and tools. They help ensure that you don't leave anything out or accelerate through what can be a complex process.

Popular EA Frameworks and Methods

There are a number of EA frameworks, guides, and methods available to choose from. The good news is they don't require an "all-or-nothing" choice. Most organizations with mature EA programs pick parts from several of them, and build out an approach that makes the most sense internally. Others might use just a few of the processes and templates to get their EA initiatives started.

Obviously, these frameworks and methods are not created equal. The best question for you is to decide how formal your program will be. Some frameworks are designed to be especially agile and simple to use. Others are much more thorough and apply to very large organizations performing extensive EA initiatives. Table 7-2 lists three of the most popular EA frameworks that you may have encountered or wish to review.

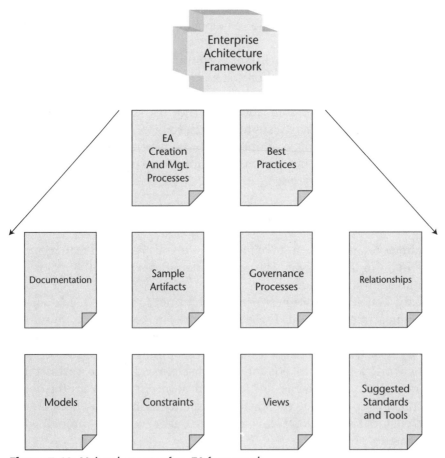

Figure 7-10: Major elements of an EA framework

Table 7-2: Three Widely Adopted EA Frameworks

FRAMEWORK	DESCRIPTION
Zachman	This is a popular EA framework launched in 1987 and now available from the Zachman Institute for Framework Advancement (ZIFA). It organizes analysis according to multiple perspectives (scope, enterprise model, system model, technology model, components, and working system) and six abstractions (data, function, network, people, time, and motivation) for each. These abstractions cover the who, what, when, where, why, and how, resulting in a 37-cell matrix. More information is available at `www.zifa.com`.
TOGAF	The Open Group Architectural Framework (TOGAF) has been available since the mid-1990s and contains three main components. First is an Architecture Development Method (ADM) that explains how to develop an EA for meeting business requirements. Next is the Enterprise Continuum, which is a virtual repository and includes a number of reference models and architectures. Last, there is a Resource Base with guidelines, templates, and other accelerators for using TOGAF. More information (including online documentation) is available from `www.opengroup.org/togaf/`.
FEA	The United States Office of Management and Budget developed the Federal EA (FEA) as a means to create interrelated "reference models" to facilitate investments and increase collaboration within and across federal agencies. It offers a number of useful guidelines, principles, templates, and sample deliverables that apply to both public and private sector EA initiatives. For example, case studies, references, and tools cover areas such as security and privacy, geospatial usage and analysis, and records management. More information can be found at `www.egov.gov`.

Figures 7-11 and 7-12 show the high-level scope covered by TOGAF and FEA, respectively. These classical EA models all have heavy emphasis on business strategy and process modeling. As mentioned previously, the authors have found that in practice many organizations rarely master business strategy and process architectural views, and mainly focus on issues related to data, technology platforms, and infrastructure.

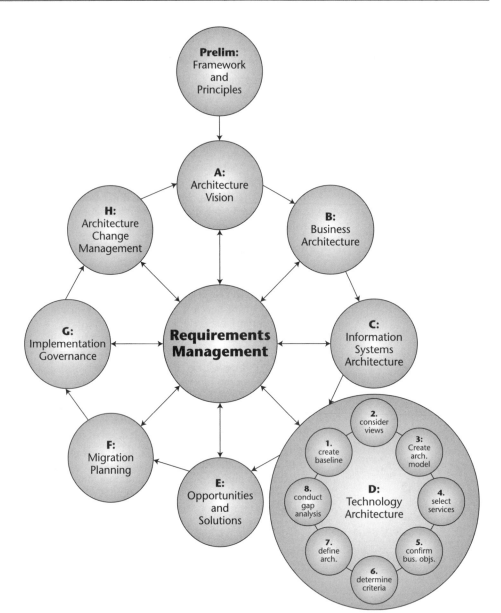

Figure 7-11: The TOGAF EA framework (Source: © 1995–2006, The Open Group. All rights reserved.)

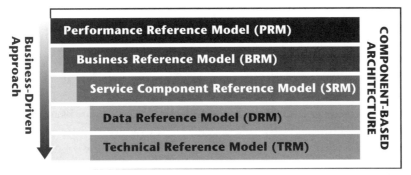

Figure 7-12: The FEA framework references models (Source: Office of Management & Budget. Available from www.whitehouse.gov/omb/egov/a-2-EAModelsNEW2.html.)

Lighter Weight Enterprise Architecture Considerations

The well-established EA frameworks and methods are very extensive. For many small and midsized organizations, it is daunting to think about how to apply them. Similarly, if your EA initiative occurs at lower levels in the organization (such as a departmental or single business unit), these classical approaches can also be tough to apply.

A movement is underway to take a simplified approach to EA activities. The goal is to not ignore EA altogether, but rather to tackle it at "bite-sized" levels that align with the way your organization works.

One example is the Enterprise Unified Process (EUP) created by Scott Ambler of Ambysoft, Inc. EUP is an extension to the popular IBM Rational Unified Process (RUP). RUP became a de facto industry standard methodology to software development that aligned well with the rise of object-oriented and component development technologies. While RUP deals well with best practices surrounding the use of individual projects and applications, EUP *extends* RUP to bring more enterprise-class considerations into the lifecycle. EUP adds two phases to the RUP model. One addresses how to deal with solutions already in production. The other considers processes for retiring a solution when it becomes obsolete. EUP also adds disciplines and workflows related to the following:

- Enterprise business modeling
- Portfolio management
- Enterprise architecture
- Strategic reuse
- People management

- Enterprise administration
- Software process improvement

These elements are all part of classical EA initiatives, but Ambler offers an approach that tackles these initiatives in a more "bottom-up" manner. As you will see in Chapter 8, many similar considerations are key parts of a successful ESA adoption process, especially if you start at more tactical, project-driven levels. You can learn more about lighter weight EA models and the EUP at `http://enterpriseunifiedprocess.com` or by reading some of the books on the topic.[1,2]

Enterprise Architecture Maturity Measurement

One advantage of all the industry focus on EA is that the discipline is moving from art to science. An outgrowth of the standard frameworks has been the shift to finding ways of assessing the maturity of EA programs and efforts. Examples include the following:

- The NASCIO Enterprise Architecture Maturity Model, which state and local governments can download to assess their efforts
- Analyst firms such as Gartner offer valuable guidelines, techniques and benchmarks for evaluating EA initiatives, along with their own EA frameworks and solutions
- The Institute for Enterprise Architecture Developments (IFEAD) Extended Enterprise Architecture Maturity Model (E2AMM)

The purpose of these initiatives is to help you track the impact of your EA investments and suggest options for improving your processes and results. This is a good thing because too often EA initiatives are plagued with fuzzy guidelines where you can claim success without delivering meaningful value. These maturity models focus on areas tied to successful EA adoption. As mentioned earlier, this includes the following areas among others:

- Effectiveness of the IT architecture process itself
- Strategic link to the business
- Senior management involvement
- Actionable use by application teams
- Successful compliance and governance
- Impact on IT investments and acquisition strategy

If you want a quick way to test your EA modeling efforts and get a great look at what does not work, you can check out the anti-patterns mentioned earlier.

Enterprise Architecture Tools

Another advantage of enterprise-wide maturity in EA disciplines is the emergence of automated tools to support the efforts. A number of vendors offer EA modeling capabilities. These tools are rapidly evolving to support the models and processes from Zachman, TOGAF, FEA, and other EA frameworks. The IFEAD offers an excellent guide and evolutions of tools[3] according to their support for:

- EA modeling
- IT portfolio management and business strategy alignment
- Program management
- System architecture
- Software engineering

Having better automation for EA models goes a long way in ensuring that the results are well-communicated. Tool vendors can also seek certification of their products, which allows your organization to trust whether they support any of the popular EA frameworks that you might be interested in adopting.

From an SAP perspective, the company has a strategic alliance in place with IDS Scheer to embed the company's ARIS modeling capabilities within SAP NetWeaver as part of the ESA strategy. ARIS supports a number of popular EA frameworks. It also allows business process models to be extended with IT architectural elements such as organizational units, applications, data, and systems landscape.

When combined with SAP's own modeling capabilities for system landscapes, the business-to-IT Solution Maps, and model-driven application development, a complete end-to-end capability for managing EA models emerges in support of ESA. You can expect to see even tighter integration across these models as the SAP NetWeaver platform evolves.

> **NOTE** The ARIS solution from IDS Scheer supports many popular EA frameworks. You may want to investigate the degree to which these capabilities are supported and licensed in the ARIS modeling environment embedded within SAP NetWeaver for managing process models in the ESR.

Enterprise Architecture Training and Certification

Yet another advantage of emerging standards in the EA community is richer and consistent training based on the most popular frameworks. You can find plenty of sources who provide EA training based upon Zachman, FEA,

TOGAF, and other popular models. All of this leads to a more consistent body of knowledge and improvement in the EA profession.

Recently, a number of industry-leading software vendors and firms have come together with The Open Group to develop certification programs for architects. These certifications are designed to identify people with the skills needed to be effective in contributing to EA programs. They are currently expanding the accreditation of the program to third parties who can offer training and exams.

Another group offering certification and training programs for EA disciplines is the Federal Enterprise Architecture Certification Institute, which trains and certifies firms and individuals in the FEA framework. You can expect SAP to expand its own EA-related training offerings as it relates to creating successful skills for ESA Adoption.

Summary

This chapter described from two perspectives the role EA has on ESA adoption. First is how the many themes related to SOA and ESA dramatically affect the EA of any organization, and second, how just adopting the SAP NetWeaver platform requires change both inside and outside of the traditional SAP landscape and IT organizational boundaries.

Generally speaking, the role of EA is to balance the efficiency and effectiveness of IT against the needs of the business. The discipline of EA has evolved rapidly in the industry. There are several frameworks available that can guide the effort. However, even these classical EA approaches must adapt to the fact that ESA enables business process and strategy models to become much more dynamic.

Whether your organization uses formal EA approaches or prefers more informal, lighter weight techniques, some level of EA decision-making is required for ESA adoption. Some of the most important takeaways from this chapter are:

- SOA, Business Process Management, model-driven architectures, and user-centric computing are major technology themes that are converging. All of them have a big impact on EA.

- ESA brings all these trends together and affects EA decision-making both inside of the SAP landscape and across the organization.

- Enterprise architects must account for the changes ESA and SAP NetWeaver bring about in terms of their overall road map.

- Within the SAP landscape itself, EA skills are needed to successfully adopt SAP NetWeaver and address the many technologies and capabilities the platform offers.

- The discipline of EA is very complex. It requires a commonsense approach and attention to a number of factors that go well beyond technology to be successful.

- A number of generally accepted EA frameworks are available today. As a result, tools, training, and certification programs have evolved to help you grow your organization's EA capabilities based on best practices.

Chapter 8 looks at how to create an ESA adoption program in your organization that builds upon the principles of EA.

References

1. Scott Ambler et al., *The Enterprise Unified Process: Extending the Rational Unified Process*, Prentice Hall, February 2005.
2. James McGovern, Scott Ambler, et al. *The Practical Guide to Enterprise Architecture*, Prentice Hall, November 2003.
3. J. Schekkerman, *Enterprise Architecture Tool Selection Guide, v 3.0*, Institute For Enterprise Architecture Developments. January 2006. Available at `www.enterprise-architecture.info`.

Planning Your ESA Adoption Program and Pilot Projects

Chapter 7 discussed the role that enterprise architecture plays in supporting ESA adoption. Some organizations embrace this concept and build strategic road maps to systematically guide their ESA efforts. Others prefer to dive right into pilot projects using the SAP NetWeaver platform to gain experience with service-oriented infrastructure, development, and integration techniques. Of course, a combination of the two is ideal. Combining strategic planning with some healthy proof points is a great way to increase your chances for success with ESA.

As mentioned many times in this book, no two companies will have the same road map to ESA. Some organizations are initially motivated to look at ESA by their plans to upgrade to mySAP ERP or other Business Suite applications that introduce SAP NetWeaver into the infrastructure. Others have a stronger interest in how SOA can improve the efficiency and effectiveness within IT. And there are those who find that an ESA approach offers the best opportunity to solve a high ROI business problem. No matter why you get started, your organization will face some common challenges in adopting ESA.

There are many good approaches and practices that help in creating and managing an ESA adoption road map. This includes both running the overall program and managing individual pilots and projects. Ultimately, you will have to decide which approach fits best with the way your organization makes decisions around applying new technology and solving business process problems.

The purpose of this chapter is to provide the "food for thought" that can make your path to ESA more successful. As a result of reading this chapter, you will be able to:

- See the main elements that go into an ESA adoption road map
- Evaluate the strategic business and IT drivers that can be used to build the vision for your ESA road map
- Understand how to plan and execute a program that spans multiple pilots and projects
- Consider how ESA may evolve the IT organizational structure and individual roles to better align activities with the business
- Evaluate considerations that go into balancing ESA adoption, based on the SAP NetWeaver platform with other SOA initiatives
- Appreciate the importance of governance for successful ESA adoption
- Understand some of the characteristics of valuable enterprise services

The Role of an SOA Adoption Program

A business-driven architecture aligns strategy and processes and enables them through an agile IT capability. Obviously this type of transformation does not take place overnight. Figure 8-1 highlights where an adoption program fits into the process.

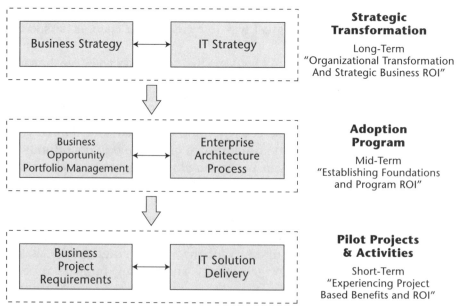

Figure 8-1: Where an ESA adoption program fits into IT planning and execution

Your business and IT strategy provide the vision and guiding principles for the type of long-term transformation ESA can enable. The EA function helps ensure that the combination of technology, IT process, and organizational change evolve so that the longer-term benefits of SOA are realized.

Unfortunately, IT planning and budgeting do not always operate at a long-term strategic portfolio level. The purpose of an ESA adoption program is to put special emphasis at an EA level to kick-start the transformation and manage it in a consistent way so that those long-term benefits are achieved. At the same time, the program also helps ensure you deliver recognized value to individual projects along the way.

> **NOTE** The purpose of an ESA adoption program is to help the EA teams put special emphasis on what is much more than a technology transition effort. The program sets the foundations for consistent and sustainable adoption by bridging short- and long-term business and technical objectives with individual project needs.

This chapter uses the terms "SOA adoption program" and "ESA adoption program" somewhat interchangeably. While the adoption processes are very similar, the difference is that SOA adoption is typically a more generic, vendor-neutral approach to SOA, versus ESA adoption, which is centered specifically around SAP's capabilities and SAP NetWeaver as the foundation. Both have common business and technology components to them (see the sidebar "SOA Versus ESA Adoption Program Terminology").

A formal SOA adoption program serves as the launching point for making systematic change. It is typically sponsored by a combination of business and IT executives, and is often assigned to EA teams to be the primary facilitators. Of course, many other business and IT personnel also get involved in the process. Chapter 7 described the basic goals, purpose, and success factors for a typical EA function. These same things apply to successful execution of an SOA adoption program. The primary purpose of the program is to instill SOA across the enterprise, creating the necessary standards, experience, and meaningful change to allow a business-driven architecture to become a way of life.

> **NOTE** In this chapter, the term "enterprise" has the same scope that was defined in the discussion of enterprise architecture in Chapter 7. Your ESA adoption efforts can be targeted at a sector, divisional, subsidiary, or similar level in the organization, and can be run in a centralized, federated, or decentralized manner.

SOA VERSUS ESA ADOPTION PROGRAM TERMINOLOGY

In many ways, adopting SAP's vision for ESA is simply a specific instance of more general SOA adoption. ESA has the advantage of providing all the SAP content (including models for processes, services, data types, business objects, and so forth), as well as composite applications built on the architecture. ESA also implies a specific set of tools and technology infrastructure in SAP NetWeaver to provide your foundation, whereas general SOA adoption programs have more complex tasks associated with defining what the technology landscape will look like. In essence, SAP gives you a head start on the process, but it's one that is obviously not vendor-neutral.

Part of the source of confusion comes from the fact that there are top-down and bottom-up approaches to both SOA and ESA adoption. *Top-down programs* have a heavy business strategy and process analysis component that drives strategic adoption. *Bottom-up activities* are more project-focused and technology infrastructure– and governance-driven. While SAP's approach to ESA adoption makes it easier to focus on the top-down aspects, there are plenty of other excellent SOA adoption methodologies that do the same thing.

In this chapter, the terms "SOA adoption" and "ESA adoption" will be used somewhat interchangeably. The general phases, activities, and best practices associated with vendor neutral enterprise SOA adoption programs are the same as those used for an SAP-centric approach. Where there is a need to specifically distinguish between the two, it will be made clear.

Typical Phases in ESA Adoption

Figure 8-2 illustrates the typical phases organizations go through when adopting SOA from a strategic business-driven architecture perspective. As mentioned, the early phases are driven by an EA team that helps create the necessary standardization required for SOA to pay off over the long-term. This is important because the benefits of SOA come from strategic reuse, consolidation, process flexibility, and alignment. Those are all things that span multiple projects and organizational boundaries. Failing to recognize this means your SOA adoption efforts will provide a fraction of the potential benefit.

Phase 1 involves launching your SOA adoption program. Your strategy and goals are defined, the right team is identified, and a plan is put in place. Instead of trying to attack all the elements of SOA and ESA at once, EA teams are best served by breaking up the adoption program into "bite-sized" pilots and projects that can deliver meaningful results early and often.

Phase 2 involves experimenting and piloting service-oriented enablement, integration, and development to solve business problems on a project-by-project basis. Notice that a successful SOA adoption program may iterate through multiple pilot initiatives that help to refine your plan. This is because SOA adoption is not a linear process, but rather a path to maturity. The key is that you are establishing a sound SOA infrastructure, set of processes, and a governance model.

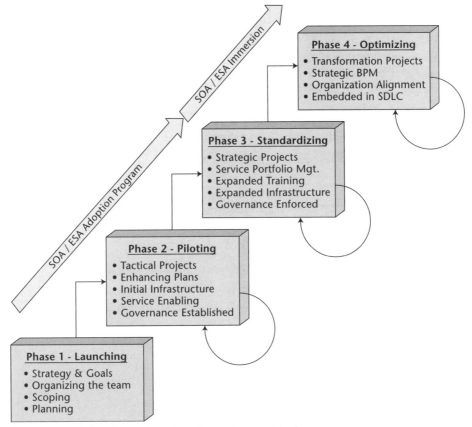

Figure 8-2: Major phases in enterprise SOA and ESA adoption

Phase 3 involves standardizing SOA as a business and IT alignment model across the organization. Training and facilitation across teams and service reuse become common practices in the organization. If your foundations were set correctly, the SOA infrastructure and governance models can expand to enable more strategic business transformation projects. Again, this phase often involves several iterations of projects and programs across the organization.

Phase 4 matures the effort. Organizations in this phase see SOA as just another way of life. The need for a specialized adoption program ends, and more general IT management and EA processes take over the instilment efforts. In essence, strategic business process management and organizational transformation capabilities become the norm.

NOTE Success with ESA ultimately comes when service reuse, process-driven solution implementation, and the related benefits become a way of life in the organization. This is not too far off from the cycle things such as relational databases, client\server solutions, EAI, and Web-based computing went through. They are hardly novel today.

The Basic SOA Adoption Program Process

Figure 8-3 shows the generic process for launching an SOA adoption program. This covers phases 1 and 2 described previously. As you can see, strategic goals for SOA adoption are defined as the "proof points" that will guide the effort. These can be a combination of business and IT goals that show possibilities such as the following:

- Reducing development costs and timelines
- Consolidating and simplifying infrastructure and retiring outdated components
- Improving business analytics from operational to strategic dashboards
- Performing faster product introductions
- Streamlining customer and supplier integration and support
- Creating a single-view of your customers for improved decision-making and multi-channel access
- Supporting merger and acquisitions consolidation activities

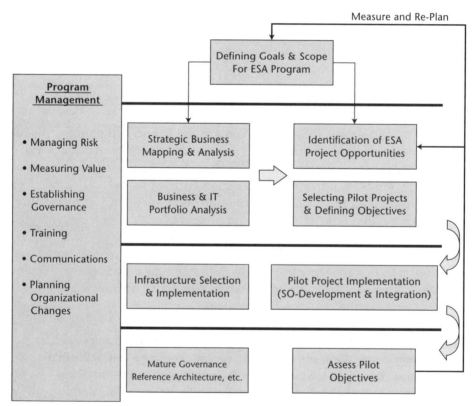

Figure 8-3: A standard SOA and ESA adoption program process

The EA team facilitating the process then works closely with the business to identify the best opportunities for specific SOA-based pilot projects. These pilots are then implemented with two goals in mind.

First is to deliver the business objectives associated with the project as you would with any other IT initiative. The second purpose is to establish the SOA infrastructure, reference architecture and processes that facilitate future projects. Again, the idea is that the exponential payback from SOA comes over time from increasing reuse of services, a simpler and more agile IT environment, and the leveraging of that agility by the business.

The activities are repeated many times with different pilots and projects in mind. Each iteration serves to mature your SOA adoption capabilities. Notice that program management activities (including training, communications, risk management, and so forth) evolve throughout the process.

SAP's ESA Adoption Program Service Offering

There are many methodologies available for guiding SOA adoption. The vast majority work similarly to the process described earlier. The main distinctions between them are the level of formality and scope assigned to business strategy and process analysis, and the degree to which technology and business interests are blended.

As mentioned, there are three main areas that make SAP's approach to ESA adoption unique from a typical SOA program:

- ESA implies SAP NetWeaver will be a key part of the SOA infrastructure and development processes, at least within a portion of your IT environment.

- ESA comes with an out-of-the-box portfolio of enterprise services, business process models, and implementation templates to give you a head start on ways to best align SOA technologies with business processes.

- ESA and the partner ecosystem offer a portfolio of packaged composite applications based on the new architecture that you can acquire and deploy "off-the-shelf" to get started, essentially offering another form of reference architecture.

Basically, taking an SAP-centric approach just implies that you are using the SAP applications, infrastructure, and reference models, as opposed to other vendor tools and products. And, of course, adopting SAP NetWeaver, using SAP enterprise services for integration, and implementing partner xApps alone do not mean you have succeeded with ESA. The bottom line is that strategic SAP ESA adoption road maps are very similar to what you would see with any other SOA adoption plan.

SAP'S ESA ADOPTION PROGRAM

SAP launched its ESA Adoption Program to help customers make the shift to NetWeaver technologies in conjunction with longer-term planning for future ESA offerings. The program is offered by SAP and trained consulting partners, and follows the familiar SAP Customer Engagement Lifecycle (CEL). It was designed to be tailored in three key ways:

◆ By customers in conjunction with their own priorities and EA practices.

◆ By partners who have their own business strategy, process and SOA methodologies.

◆ By enhancement of the program based on customer experience and SAP's own realization of its multi-year ESA road map.

You can see the major phases and activities of the SAP ESA Adoption Program in the following diagram.

Discovery	Evaluation	Implementation	Operations
Grasp the Vision	**Build Your Own Roadmap**	**Go Live**	**Grasp the Vision**
• ESA and SAP NetWeaver Vision Value Session • ESA Opportunity Workshop • TCO Discovery Session	• ESA Enabling Roadmap Workshop • ESA Roadmap Workshop	• Plan Services • Build Services • Run Services	• Continuous Operations and Governance • ESA / NetWeaver Community • Become an ESA leader in your industry

The SAP ESA Adoption Program (Source SAP, AG.)

The program is focused on practical adoption through a consistent, step-by-step approach that's been tested across multiple engagements. Similar to most SOA adoption methods, the program supports multiple iterations of priority project opportunities that increasingly demonstrate the value of ESA and SAP NetWeaver.

The *Discovery phase* is intended to create a shared understanding across the organization for what ESA is about, and identify candidate project opportunities with immediate business impact. The NetWeaver IT Practices and Scenarios map is used to help facilitate alignment between business and IT during this phase.

The *Evaluation phase* delivers a long-term road map, along with short-term plans for executing on the best pilot project opportunities.

> During the *Implementation phase*, NetWeaver's Enterprise Services Infrastructure is established to deliver the project and provide the proper foundation for the next phases in your road map.
>
> The *Operations phase* includes processes for continuous improvement including feedback for projects in subsequent iterations.
>
> Supporting the program is a full set of training, templates, sample deliverables, and other accelerators. These can be very valuable tools for your team chartered with driving the ESA adoption effort, and can augment your existing EA methodology. If the EA discipline is new to your organization, or will be newly practiced within your SAP groups, these tools can help them establish a more structured business-driven foundation.

SAP has created its own ESA Adoption Program as a commercial services offering. It is available from both SAP directly, and from trained system integration partners (see the sidebar "SAP's ESA Adoption Program").

Naturally, SAP's ESA Adoption Program has a heavy SAP NetWeaver–specific enablement component associated with it. Through the use of the IT Practices and Scenarios maps described in Chapter 3, this program helps organize your efforts by providing the following:

- An identification of specific business priorities that are ideal candidates for tackling with an IT Practices–based enablement approach

- Guidance on the most effective implementation and use of SAP NetWeaver to lay the foundation for ongoing ESA initiatives

- A focus on pilots with real business impact, as opposed to taking an "if you build it, they will come" approach to ESA

- A set of phases very familiar to your SAP staff that is organized around the company's Customer Engagement Lifecycle (CEL) model

Even if your focus is mainly within the SAP landscape, it is important to think about how your efforts will be aligned with other SOA and EA efforts in your organization. Some of these considerations are examined later in this chapter.

Crafting Your Adoption Program

An SAP-centered ESA adoption program is ideal if your overall SOA goals are centered mainly around service-enabling your SAP environment, implementing the SAP NetWeaver infrastructure, and generally improving your SAP teams' capabilities from an ESA perspective. This usually happens if a large portion of your landscape is based on SAP, as is the case in many companies.

ESA Adoption in Conjunction with mySAP ERP Upgrades

It is especially useful to undertake ESA adoption in parallel with any mySAP Business Suite Application implementations or mySAP ERP upgrade planning. The reason is you are bringing SAP NetWeaver and all the SOA capabilities into your environment by default. Unfortunately, the authors have found many organizations underestimate the opportunities ESA and SAP NetWeaver offer when tackling these landscape upgrade projects. That means that they miss out on many benefits that would have naturally come from added education and planning for ESA. During an upgrade, you have the opportunity to do the following:

- Improve on the integration points your non-SAP applications have with SAP using NetWeaver and enterprise services, or perhaps consolidate those applications with easier-to-maintain composites.

- Identify specific enterprise services that benefit your organization and implement them as part of the configuration and customization activities.

- Include greater analytics within your SAP applications and processes during the process re-engineering phases that usually occur in conjunction with upgrades.

- Take advantage of all the new composition, development, and integration tools within SAP NetWeaver that will become part of your landscape by default.

In fact, many organizations begin planning and piloting with SAP NetWeaver and ESA in advance of their upgrades. This helps you better plan how to take advantage of all the additional application-level capabilities you get when the upgrade activities actually occur.

Defining Your Unique Program

While an SAP-centered ESA adoption program may be beneficial in many situations, some companies wish to roll the SAP-specific aspects of ESA adoption into a larger SOA program with broader strategic business and IT alignment efforts. These organizations often find they need to complement SAP's ESA Adoption Program with either their own EA processes or other third-party approaches.

As mentioned, most system integrators and consulting firms will combine the SAP ESA Adoption Program with other classic EA methodologies and their own vertical expertise, business process analysis capabilities, or SOA technology transformation techniques to create a hybrid offering.

No single approach offers the right answer. The authors have found two things are most important. First is organizing a program that is best in line with the amount of change you are trying to create. If your organization does better tackling business projects already in the portfolio, then an approach heavily oriented to rigorous IT and business strategy analysis, or long-term technology architecture and infrastructure planning, may not be an ideal place to start. Likewise, a more tactical project and technology-driven approach to SOA and ESA may be undersized if you truly plan to drive strategic business and IT changes at an enterprise portfolio level from the start.

The second factor is that, regardless of the size of the effort, you *must* have the right balance between technical and business objectives and involvement to be successful. Too much of either will derail your program. Either you won't reap the flexibility benefits of SOA on future projects, or you will end up with over-architected capabilities that the rest of the organization is not quite sure what to do with.

In the end, the specific program chosen will have much less impact on your success than the team you assign, leadership you provide, and buy-in to the goals and objectives that are established. Organizations that get hung up internally looking for a formulaic approach to be the "right way" to adopt SOA or ESA are missing the point. Remember that everyone's road map, investment models, and value proposition are different.

Establishing a Strategic Business Process Perspective for ESA Adoption

Before you dive into the planning and execution details of your ESA adoption program, it's important to ensure that your organization has an overarching vision for what you want to accomplish with ESA. This will guide your efforts and help drive the details of the program.

Developing this vision comes from evaluating two main areas. First is increasing IT agility across your business process portfolio. The second area is targeted at aligning IT costs with business process value.

To understand how to apply these opportunities to your organization it is important to understand why they have been so hard to achieve in the past. More important, you must be able to create a shared understanding as to how SOA, and specifically SAP's ESA-based solutions, can fundamentally change things.

Shifting Your Focus to Business Processes and IT Investment Alignment

There is a fundamental flaw in the way IT historically supports business processes. In essence, IT has focused on creating "built to last" solutions to problems that are guaranteed to change. That may sound silly, but if you think about it, that is exactly how things usually work. The rigidity comes from having had three options for delivering solutions, all of which are relatively distinct and inflexible:

- Building a custom solution using on top of an open development platform such as Java, .NET, LAMP (the open source bundle of Linux, Apache, MySQL, and Perl, Python, PHP, or Primate), or another development environment

- Buying a business application solution from an ISV such as SAP and dealing with all the customization and integration requirements

- Handing off the process to a business process outsourcer (BPO) who also handles certain IT aspects of the solution

Each of these has had a unique set of benefits and drawbacks. The cost of trying to do a combination of the three has been relatively high, and each organization that has done so had to bear the costs of integration themselves.

Over the last decade, organizations have tried to tackle this issue. From a custom development perspective, agile methodologies and better tools improved the IT process, but they still involve delivering incremental business functionality on top of an ever-expanding foundation of code.

Architecture and design patterns have also evolved to make applications more maintainable from a general development perspective. But architects must still build in flexibility from a functional perspective. Unfortunately, it's difficult for the business to anticipate where all those changes might occur. Engineering a lot of functional flexibility that might not be needed down the road can add a lot of cost and time to projects, which business owners often don't want to bear.

Packaged business application providers such as SAP have made their products highly configurable to ease some functional change. However, their focus has to be on enabling the most common practices, which means little flexibility exists to easily meet the unique business needs of an organization. More often than not, business processes are altered to match the business applications, rather than the other way around.

Likewise, BPOs offer flexibility in areas common to lots of companies, but tend not be cost-effective in meeting the unique requirements of any one. And, if business needs dictate changes to an outsourced process, your organization has given up a lot of schedule and budget influence to the BPO.

NOTE Almost all traditional options for implementing business processes were inflexible. This "built to last" approach will no longer work. It makes changing high-value business process more expensive and timely, which affects a business flexibility and decision-making. Alternatively, they leave you overspending on maintenance around processes that no longer add as much value. Understanding the lifecycle of business processes is critical to ESA adoption, as explained in the following sections.

Why Business Processes Change

The key to solving this problem is to understand why processes are guaranteed to change. There are four basic reasons:

- There are a number of process exceptions that cannot be envisioned when designing a new process solution.

- Business requirements evolve that require incremental modifications to a process.

- Business strategy shifts, or events trigger major enhancements to a process or creation of entirely new variations on a process.

- The value of a process to the organization changes over time.

The first two happen all the time. If the IT systems are flexible, you can automate some of these changes. More often than not, a bunch of expensive manual activities supported by patchwork automation (such as spreadsheets) are used to initially deal with exceptions. These start out as modest, hidden costs. In many organizations, those costs can expand rapidly, eventually triggering new automation projects to bring them under control. The authors have dealt with several companies trying to address process issues around returns management, billing disputes, warranty claims, and so on. All of these involved unanticipated exceptions to the normal order to cash process flow that was initially implemented. Eventually the patchwork of manual procedures and office automation efforts to deal with them became unwieldy.

> **NOTE** A great place to look for "low hanging fruit" ESA opportunities is in all the manual activities and patchwork automation that grows over time to deal with unanticipated process exceptions and ad hoc workflows. It is no coincidence that these types of things are at the heart of many Microsoft Office–based Duet scenarios.

While the third area doesn't happen as frequently, strategic business shifts can require major IT change to support new processes. For example, new distribution models, entering new markets, merger and acquisition (M&A) into new lines of business, and so on may have a significant impact on IT that cannot always be anticipated.

The last area is perhaps the most interesting one for enterprise architects to think about. SAP has worked with author and strategy guru Geoffrey Moore, who examined the fundamental paradox between IT investing and business process changes. Thomas Davenport has also done extensive amount of research and publishing around the intersection between IT and business process effectiveness that has many parallels to ESA and SAP NetWeaver. The authors recommend enterprise architects, business process owners, and others on your team review some of their work as part of setting your own program vision and strategy.[1, 2, 3, 4]. You can also find links to some of their work on this book's companion Web site.

The Notion of Core and Context Processes and the Influence on IT

Moore has uncovered two basic premises about business processes that should affect the thinking of every SOA and ESA strategic plan:

▪ Processes either support business differentiation (in the sense that they drive customer decisions and other key metrics) or they don't. The belief is that there are many very important processes you perform that do not differentiate your organization (see the sidebar "How Can Really Important Processes Not Be Core?").

▪ Processes have a natural maturity lifecycle, but organizational structures and IT implementations and investments usually neglect this fact, making infrastructure retirement difficult even when the ROI is clear.

HOW CAN REALLY IMPORTANT PROCESSES NOT BE CORE?

Moore refers to processes that create value by differentiating your organization as "core" processes. Processes that do not provide differentiation he describes as "context."[5] What is confusing is that many context processes are still critical and must be performed successfully. The key is in how you invest in them.

A simple analogy is your own process you use to commute to work. It's obviously critical in that, if you don't show up, you won't remain employed for long. However, it's a context process because good attendance alone is probably not going to transform your career. So, your goal becomes making this process as efficient as possible. You can either shorten the commute (working at home is really ideal), or make the most of your drive, train, plane, or bus time by what you listen to or read, making calls, and so on.

In most organizations, it's easy to see how processes such as payroll, financial reporting, office supply and services procurement, facilities management, and so on, are necessary and important, but probably do not create strategic differentiation. What gets confusing is that even processes such as manufacturing and customer service are often context processes in many (not all) organizations. It is expected that you can produce, ship, and service what you sell at an acceptable level.

Consider an example. The president of a major airline once commented on all the requests his company gets to improve the reservation and in-flight experience for customers. He determined which to pursue by commissioning market research to see which changes would actually boost fares or create a meaningful preference for his flights. It turned out that customers said they were not willing to pay for or consider the vast majority of those "good ideas" when choosing one airline over another. While critical, these are still mainly context processes. Route, schedules, availability, dynamic pricing, and on-time predictability remained the most important core processes for the airline.

The ability to discern between processes that provide meaningful differentiation and ones that do not is becoming an important part of business and IT strategy, as well as a guiding model for SAP's overall ESA vision. The goal is to better align IT investment with differentiated processes, while making context processes as efficient as possible to manage and maintain. What makes this tricky is the way in which processes evolve. As you will see in the next section, this is a very important aspect of SOA and ESA adoption planning.

The Lifecycle of Business Process Differentiation

The concept of "S-curves" has been around in management theory for many years to explain the law of diminishing returns. It is interesting to combine the idea with process lifecycles and how they create differentiation.

Figure 8-4 shows the normal lifecycle of a new process that creates differentiation. You can see there are diminishing returns from the amount of differentiation you can create. Eventually, the amount of differentiation levels off as your implementation scales to full capacity and competitors start to catch up.

Figure 8-5 shows what happens as the process matures. Differentiation of the process declines and your focus shifts to optimizing its execution, and then finding ways to cut costs internally or outsourcing the execution to someone with greater efficiency and economies of scale. If, at some point, the process loses its importance, you may decide to eliminate it altogether. Some examples of maturing processes that carried heavy IT investments for early adopters include things such as the following:

- Entering an order securely on a Web site
- Running customer loyalty and discount card programs
- Automating receipt matching and electronic payments
- Offering ATM banking services
- Booking reservation for travel

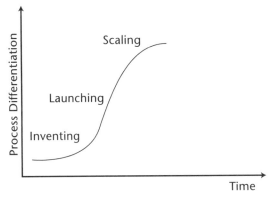

Figure 8-4: Launching and scaling a differentiated process

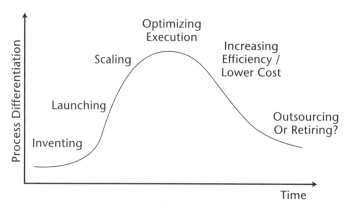

Figure 8-5: The full process differentiation lifecycle

All of these have become commoditized capabilities, where the process must work extremely well, but does not offer much differentiation. Interestingly, late adopters can usually find packaged IT products and services that enable these processes, while early adopters are stuck maintaining their unique legacy environments.

Figure 8-6 overlays the IT investment model against the general process lifecycle. As mentioned earlier, creating built-to-last IT solutions eventually leads to maintenance costs that are tough to reduce. Functionality enhancements can spike the costs, while certain outsourcing, maintenance, and infrastructure options try to hold expenses in check. Unfortunately, the IT solution usually cannot drive out cost fast enough when the differentiation of the process declines. This is why as much as 70 percent of IT spending has been estimated as necessary to cover maintenance and operations of existing applications and infrastructure.[6]

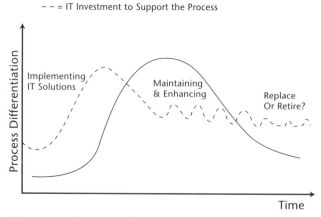

Figure 8-6: The General IT investment and maintenance model for a process

As Figure 8-7 shows from a business perspective, you may find new innovations that can breathe differentiation into existing processes. If the process requirements change to the point where the cost of IT enhancements becomes prohibitive, a new IT solution is identified and implemented on a project ROI basis. All that means is that you run through the same lifecycle again until things mature or the next innovation comes along.

How ESA Adoption Can Better Align IT Investments with Business Processes

ESA improves business process agility by eliminating the tradeoff and inflexibility associated with having to choose between building, buying, or outsourcing solutions to business processes, and then ending up with a hard-to change-solution. SAP's strategy is to make these options complementary by supporting all three with a common platform. Because ESA is based on SOA technology, it allows you to compose business processes that can take advantage of all three types of capabilities. More important, you can selectively change your compositions over time to reduce IT costs, or enable new functionality needed by the business.

Essentially, you start with the out-of-the-box functionality of the mySAP Business Suite applications configured to meet your needs as closely as possible. Because SAP applications are built upon an open composition platform in NetWeaver, you can then tailor your implementation or create new solutions that are loosely coupled to the packaged applications. As SAP and its ecosystem partners implement new functionality as composite applications and xApps, you selectively adopt and implement features in pre-integrated, "bite-sized" chunks as business needs dictate. And, finally, the open integration features allow you to hand off parts of a process to a BPO vendor in a controlled manner. SAP NetWeaver provides the lifecycle management features to coordinate the process execution and manage SLAs with those vendors.

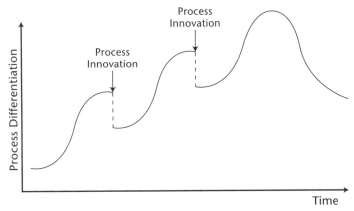

Figure 8-7: Innovating existing processes for new differentiation

NOTE A guiding principle in scoping any SOA adoption program is to simultaneously drive out IT costs from non-differentiated processes while increasing the flexibility and support for your key differentiated processes. SAP's ESA approach enables differentiation in a way that is better connected to underlying package applications that you standardize on to lower TCO.

The bottom line is that a well-run ESA adoption program enables IT to better support process agility by allowing you to customize in areas that create differentiation without sacrificing the efficiency of using purchased applications or process outsourcing of specific tasks that do not. Moving from "built to last" to "built to change" solutions (or "throwaway applications," as some like to call the new composition model) allows you to more easily match IT budgets to the processes they support. The buildup of big maintenance entitlements is reduced with effective ESA adoption The next section will look at how these capabilities specifically influence your ESA adoption process.

Selecting Major Themes for ESA Adoption

For purposes of your ESA adoption program, you can now evaluate some of the following themes as global goals for guiding your program and for helping to select the best pilots and projects. You cannot tackle all of these objectives at once, although good pilots will allow you to combine them to some degree. As you will see later in this chapter, part of building a successful road map is prioritizing when and how you will address each opportunity.

Optimizing Key Business Processes

If you refer back to Figure 8-5, the question becomes how you can best increase the capability of processes that offer the greatest differentiation value, while reducing the costs of context processes that don't. By using your highest process ROI opportunities to guide your ESA adoption program, you can ensure that business goals are driving the effort. This comes from collaborating with your business process owners and analysts to do the following:

- Identify and classify key processes according to business strategy and differentiation drivers.

- Map IT costs and capabilities associated with supporting those processes today to determine areas of possible over-investment and under-investment.

- Evaluate the potential benefit to these processes from the composition, productivity, process management, and other business-enabling capabilities of ESA.

- Identify major opportunities for enabling new differentiation or optimizing process efficiency and ROI.

To some extent, you are doing this already in managing your current IT project portfolio. The goal is to extend that effort by building a larger vision between business and IT through a shared understanding of new ESA-enabled capabilities in SAP business applications and the NetWeaver platform.

Part of your ESA adoption program will include digitally modeling these key processes and identifying the underlying services needed to support them. You can then work with SAP and its ecosystem partners to determine the ones you can acquire, and those that you need to create or extend to enable differentiation.

Consolidating Applications & Infrastructure

A second major theme in ESA adoption is to drive out IT costs through consolidation. ESA enables you to continually innovate on top of a changing or consolidating landscape by providing the abstraction layer of enterprise services. The savings in licensing, integration, maintenance, infrastructure, and overall simplicity can be used to fund ongoing process improvement initiatives. Consolidation opportunities emerge from the following:

- Replacing multiple instances and custom (or "best of breed") business applications tied to other platforms with mySAP Business Suite solutions or packaged xApps from SAP and ecosystem partners.

- Evaluating where application platform, integration, and composition capabilities of SAP NetWeaver can reduce the number of middleware products used in your environment.

- Improving master data management by liberating control from disparate applications into a consolidated shared services approach supporting multiple SOA and ESA adoption efforts. Note that data access and management processes make great reusable services.

- Service-enabling legacy applications to preserve their life, while enabling systematic retirement without having to do a large rip-and-replace initiative.

- Eliminating duplicate business functionality through use of shared services.

- Using application and infrastructure consolidation, along with virtualization techniques, to consolidate hardware and infrastructure.

For large organizations, consolidation may mean reducing thousands of applications and infrastructure components by a meaningful percentage. You will still be left with multiple platform and integration environments. However, small and mid-sized organizations whose landscape is largely based on SAP may find they can use ESA to consolidate a larger percentage of their applications and infrastructure around the SAP NetWeaver platform over time.

Just remember that the goals here are to drive out the cost of supporting context processes by reducing the number of vendor packages and infrastructure solutions in your environment, and to eliminate the integration taxes that have no business benefit.

As long as the work is getting done acceptably, you are better off driving out redundant costs versus trying to perfect the execution of those processes. That's because the value of investing IT resources in these processes is limited. Of course, you can always go back and use composition techniques to enhance the process after consolidation if the need arises.

NOTE Going from "great" to "good" is counter-intuitive to everything you and your team have been taught. However, when it comes to an ESA adoption program and to seeking benefits from consolidation, this is sometimes exactly the right approach. Doing something "good enough" at a lower cost is often better than being excellent at a disproportionably higher investment and maintenance that sucks up valuable resources. Unfortunately, each business area is constantly trying to optimize capabilities, even if the overall value is not there.

Modernizing IT Capability

The third theme associated with ESA adoption is based upon elevating your overall IT capability. In addition to enabling business processes and reducing infrastructure costs, your ESA adoption program should transform ITs efficiency and effectiveness in areas such as the following:

- Business process management and modeling
- Event-driven architectures
- Establishing an enterprise services inventory and SOA infrastructure
- Model-driven design and composition

- User productivity enablement
- Embedded analytics

These are all relatively new capabilities that have self-evident benefits much like Internet and client/server computing evolutions offered. One way to pursue this during SOA and ESA adoption is by having a deep understanding of how your organization delivers the IT Practices and Scenarios described in Chapter 3. While these IT processes are a means to an end, improving the overall capability of IT must be tied to a business motivation and payback to be successful. That's why the incorporation of these goals into an overall ESA adoption program is the most effective way to tackle improvement in a business-driven manner.

Figure 8-8 illustrates how you can begin to formulate the vision and goals for your ESA adoption efforts based upon these themes. You start by looking at the different opportunities and the degree to which they support these areas. Some may address multiple areas, giving you a multiplier effect in terms of benefits. Second, you look at the alignment between multiple opportunities to see how tackling them in a related way might reduce overall costs of implementation. In this way, each phase can have a number of aligned projects that cut across all the themes in a well-aligned manner (see the sidebar "An Example of Establishing a Vision for ESA Adoption).

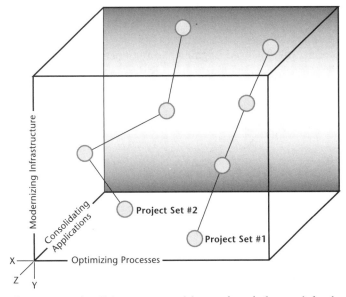

Figure 8-8: Identifying program vision and goals from reinforcing projects

AN EXAMPLE OF ESTABLISHING A VISION FOR ESA ADOPTION

An organization in the healthcare industry had an IT environment that became unwieldy. The major shared enterprise applications were a collection of purchased applications and homegrown solutions created before the market for packaged products in the industry had matured. In addition, multiple platforms and technologies were used across the enterprise for differentiated and context systems in various business units. Each of these was requiring support from IT, which had trouble managing the diversity.

The company took a three-step approach to addressing the situation. First, it upgraded its major corporate ERP and SCM applications to a common foundation. This process alone consolidated a number of applications and platforms, and created the new integration platform, services environment, and master data management backbone for the enterprise.

The second step was the creation of a reference architecture and frameworks for composing applications in the new environment. The company went through a number of pilots using this new approach to tackle some of the differentiated systems requested by the various business units. It then trained the organization on the new standards and techniques to be used going forward.

The final step involved tackling the rest of the hard-to-maintain applications in the portfolio. For those applications that offered little differentiation, the company looked to ecosystem partners for packaged solutions. Even if one didn't exist, it talked with ecosystem vendors about partnering to create new commercial packaged applications that fit the reference architecture. In a few cases, the company was able to get a solution built in this manner. The partner provided lower implementation costs and then productized the solution for other companies. This ensured ongoing maintenance and support for the solution. When third-party options didn't exist, custom solutions were created according to the new platform-based reference architecture model to eliminate some of the remaining platforms tied to hard-to-maintain applications.

Launching Your ESA Adoption Program

Once you've decided to move ahead with some type of ESA adoption program (either as part of a strategic IT transformation effort as described earlier, or simply to better organize your SAP NetWeaver implementation projects), you can begin to follow the general process shown in Figure 8-3. The following sections describe the major activities that lead you through the selection of pilot projects.

Picking the Initial Program Management Team

Perhaps the most important step is determining who will be on the core team that will run your adoption program. This is usually a virtual team at first that has a number of roles to be played, including the following:

- Executive sponsor(s) with influence that is commensurate with your program goals.

- ESA adoption lead based on how your company makes EA level decisions.

- Key line-of-business stakeholders who can help create the business vision and want to influence the effort. This could be a business process owner, strategic process analyst, business unit IT project portfolio manager, and so forth.

- A technical SWAT team with an aptitude for SOA and an ability to deliver fast implementations of prototypes, proof-of-concepts, and implementation patterns.

- Other IT leaders including additional enterprise architects if your approach is federated, current SAP application and infrastructure owners, and so on.

Obviously, the bigger and more diverse the team, the more complicated decision making becomes. That means the slower you can move. The key is to pick a team that's broad enough to get buy-in and avoid sabotage. You may want to divide your team into a core program management group supported by active advisory teams to avoid having things get too big.

The characteristics of good team members are similar to what makes a good enterprise architect, as described in the Chapter 6. In general, these are people who:

- Understand your business drivers and what is important to key stakeholders

- Have a balanced understanding between the concepts and technologies associated with ESA and their practical application to your business

- Have a track record with real results in leading and supporting successful business and technology transition programs

- Have a great attitude and are good at facilitation and dispute resolution

- Are comfortable with change and have a desire to grow

- Can attract and involve others from the business and IT during the program and pilot project execution

Much of this is common sense, but you would be surprised how often these things are overlooked when picking a team. The chemistry is critical to being able to work through the many different decisions, conflicts, and politics associated with ESA adoption. Remember that there is no one right way to do this stuff.

It's also important to ensure that key team members are given enough time to do the job right. Just assigning ESA adoption program responsibilities on top of already full plates is rarely successful. Perhaps more important is tracking how the amount of time required grows as you move through the program, and adjusting accordingly. This has become an issue in many organizations, and has disrupted the momentum behind several SOA and ESA adoption programs.

Setting Goals and Planning Your Program

With the team in place, the next step is to define the specific goals and plan for your program. This is best accomplished through a series of facilitated training exercises and workshops, as discussed in the following sections.

Team Briefings and Training

Because ESA covers so many different dimensions, it is important that the adoption team have a shared understanding of all the elements. Because your core adoption team will likely come from different business and technical backgrounds (as well as different experience levels with SAP), you will gain a lot of value if you provide training as part of the kickoff projects.

Whether you use SAP or another internal or external group to facilitate the exercise, it is important to run through education briefings that cover the following:

- SAP's ESA strategy and road map
- Understanding IT Practices and Scenarios
- Previewing the SAP NetWeaver platform
- Fundamentals of SOA, business process management (BPM), composition, and model-driven architectures and how they come together in SAP NetWeaver
- Key issues, activities, and impacts associated with SOA and ESA adoption programs

The briefings can be tailored for both business and technical audiences, so both groups experience the level of depth and breadth they need to move ahead. By taking the time to cement a thorough, shared view of ESA, your adoption team will be much more productive. You can also develop lightweight versions of these briefings for the extended team and other interested stakeholders to keep them informed and engaged in the process.

Goal Setting, Scoping, and Planning Workshops

Once the team has the full understanding of ESA's potential, the work begins to craft the specific adoption plan for your organization. This will be used to drive the scope, goals, and plan for your adoption program. During this activity, it is sometimes as important to decide what you will *not* be tackling in your adoption program, in addition to what you will be focusing on.

As Figure 8-9 shows, there are very different value and complexity tradeoffs between addressing ESA adoption at a project, portfolio, or enterprise level. The larger your scope, the more exponential the gains can become. However, it is also more difficult to execute at a more global level, and requires greater vision, leadership, and commitment to be successful. The good news is that tactical adoption techniques can also add value. They are easier to adopt at local levels in the organization and can pave the way to larger successes if managed well. Unfortunately, they also have less strategic impact because of the limited scope, and you will eventually have to tackle the larger issues.

NOTE Ensure that your scope and goals map to what your organization really can support. That includes both executive sponsorship and execution capabilities. Sometimes adoption teams set grandiose goals that are far removed from what is feasible.

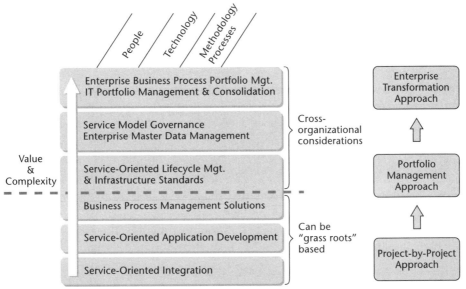

Figure 8-9: Value and complexity increases at different levels of ESA adoption.

If your plan is to dive into a project-by-project approach without really trying to coordinate a larger program, then you can jump ahead to identifying a pilot project. Depending on a number of factors (including how your organization makes and budgets infrastructure decisions, and has the discipline to continuously innovate from one project to the next), this may or may not be the best path. At the very least, you can get started with basic service-oriented development and integration projects and enable features of SAP NetWeaver in your infrastructure for future reuse. Eventually you will hit a wall, but if this is the best place for your organization to start, then that's where you should begin.

There are many management-consulting methodologies for business and IT strategy and process analysis that can support your planning exercise. While the details are beyond the scope of this book, you should recognize that you begin by working through the key strategy and process-oriented themes associated with ESA adoption, as described earlier in this chapter.

By analyzing your organization's business and IT strategy, you will find many areas where ESA can be used for optimizing context processes, innovating core process differentiation, consolidating applications and infrastructure, or modernizing IT capabilities. One interesting observation the authors have made is that even though IT is often perceived as the bottleneck to business transformation, getting to this strategic process analysis is actually very hard for business teams as well. As with IT, they are often organized functionally, and do not have a more holistic view of processes and how to transform them in this way.

Some of the typical processes with strong candidates for enterprise services include the following:

- Large numbers of external customer or partner interactions
- Multi-channel access points where you want users to have a consistent experience, regardless of the system or touch point used to interact with the process
- High degrees of exceptions, manual interactions and tasks
- Tasks that are common to multiple processes where the potential for reuse is high
- Significant change backlogs in IT because the solution spans multiple underlying applications, or is tied to a brittle infrastructure environment

It is easy to see how a process-driven, services-oriented approach can improve each of these scenarios.

The better your EA practices and IT planning function, the easier this step will become. In many organizations, a well-designed IT plan and project portfolio will help guide the effort because your organization has already done the work to identify and prioritize near-term business priorities. That is not to say that your broader analysis of business strategy, key processes, and IT plans won't uncover other options. The key is to let the process happen naturally. ESA adoption is iterative. You can always evolve the program during subsequent phases, pilots, and projects.

NOTE Looking at your current project portfolio, IT plan, and the "wish lists" of the business is yet another good way to find "low-hanging fruit opportunities" for ESA adoption. It is amazing how often this is overlooked when companies do SOA planning.

Generally speaking, all SOA adoption programs will have similar technology and IT process objectives, including the following:

- Establishing the SOA infrastructure (including security, intermediation, management, and so on)
- Establishing foundations for an ongoing governance program
- Service-enabling existing applications
- Understanding how to best digitally model business processes, activities, and services for execution
- Understanding ideal roles and practices for composite application development and other organizational and software development lifecycle (SDLC) changes
- Enabling and facilitating reuse

These, too, become part of your plan and scope, and will be covered in more detail later in this chapter. Together with the business objectives, you have plenty of filters in place to pick your initial pilot projects and opportunities.

Selecting and Running Pilots and Projects

Your planning and scoping exercises should have identified a number of candidate projects. As shown in Figure 8-10, one way to evaluate them to select a pilot is by looking for the "low-hanging fruit" opportunities. Here, you can see five opportunities classified by their perceived value and the relative time to benefit. Keep in mind that value comes from two dimensions. First is the immediate project or process benefit to the organization. The second is the future agility and reuse benefits you get from implementing the new services.

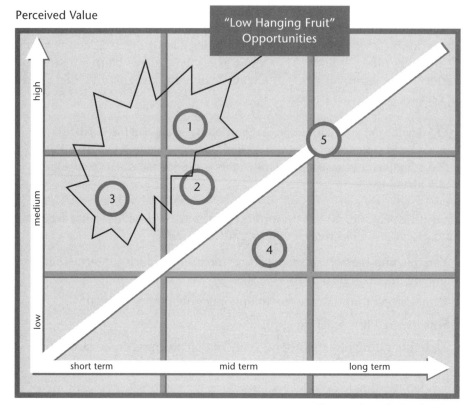

Figure 8-10: Finding "low-hanging fruit" ESA opportunities

Obviously, a number of other factors go into picking an ESA pilot. Table 8-1 lists some of the main factors your team should consider in picking an ideal pilot or project. You can use this as a checklist against your own potential opportunities.

Managing and Executing Pilots and Projects

Once your pilot projects have been selected, budgeted, and approved, the ESA adoption program management team helps facilitate the implementation efforts as described in the following sections.

Table 8-1: Considerations for Selecting an ESA Pilot Project

CONSIDERATION	FACTORS TO EVALUATE
Strategic versus tactical value	An ESA pilot should address an important business problem. Being successful with tactical projects may provide good experience, but the greater the business value delivered, the greater the visibility for your program and the better the ESA proof point. Likewise, revenue-enhancing projects are better than cost-reduction efforts. However, you should not pursue a mission-critical project with your initial pilot.
Complexity and time to value	The goal with early pilots is to deliver value early and often. Tackling something too complex may require too many people and increase implementation time. Similar value and visibility with less complexity is preferred.
User-facing versus integration pilots	While SOA is ideal for solving tough integration needs, no one can really see the results. Pilots that provide a differentiated user experience offer more perceived benefits.
Internal versus external usage	Services used inside the organization have lower risk and complexity. However, a number of good business cases associated with services are available for external consumption.
Future reuse potential	Creation of services and agility that can deliver both immediate pilot benefits, but also near-term value to follow-on projects, are generally better than those without a clear reuse horizon.
Transactional versus query-oriented services	Transactional services exercise more aspects of SOA technologies including security and lifecycle management. However, they also carry greater risk and complexity.
Budgeting model	SOA pilots include cost associated with delivering business value and additional budget for the shared infrastructure, program management, and other activities designed to benefit future projects. The manner in which budget decisions are made can influence the selection of pilots that will best allow these activities to occur successfully.
Breadth of ESA experience gained	A pilot that touches on more IT Practices can provide greater experience in evaluating ESA process changes, organizational readiness, service-enablement of existing applications, process management, composition, user-productivity enablement, and so forth. The trade-off is greater risk and longer time to value. By prioritizing the important IT Practices for your organization, you can select a pilot that provides the ideal experience.

Source: © 2005–2006, MomentumSI Inc. All rights reserved.

Engaging and Training the Implementation Team

The first step for the program management team is to prepare the project implementation team. This includes ensuring that team members clearly understand the goals of both the project and its relationship to the overall ESA program. In addition, training on ESA-related capabilities is required. Topics such as the following should be covered:

- ESA and SOA principles and patterns
- Service-enabling existing applications
- Service-oriented integration
- Architecting, designing, and implementing effective services
- SAP NetWeaver capabilities and implementation (including working with the Enterprise Services Repository)
- Creating and maintaining loosely coupled composite applications using SAP NetWeaver

Many of these topics are covered in Parts II and III of this book. The ESA program management team will act as facilitators and ESA subject matter experts for the project.

Implementing the Pilot Projects

The execution of pilot projects involves delivering the business value while meeting the goals of your overall ESA program. Activities include the following:

- Analyzing the business project and ESA program requirements and goals
- Modeling the business process and solution architecture
- Designing the landscape and infrastructure
- Installing and configuring the necessary SAP NetWeaver usage types to support your ESA pilot
- Identifying out-of-the-box services, objects, and data types available in the Enterprise Services Repository
- Identifying and deploying additional services from service-enabling other applications, creating new service interfaces and implementations, or acquiring services from ecosystem partners
- Designing, implementing, testing, and deploying your pilot solution

One of the most important roles of the ESA program management team is to control project scope. It's easy to have business or technical architecture teams want to expand the effort. In addition, the team members act as coaches, mentors, and reviewers throughout the implementation.

The ESA program management team must also ensure that as many best practices are employed in creating new services and other models so that they are as reusable as possible. Figure 8-11 highlights some of main characteristics that improve the chances for reuse of an enterprise service.

ESA Adoption Program Management Activities

In addition to directly supporting pilot projects, the ESA adoption management team carries a number of responsibilities to guide the overall program across multiple projects and better establish ESA capabilities throughout the organization. The main responsibilities and objectives are shown in Figure 8-12 and described in the following sections.

Performing Post-Project Reviews

One of the most important roles the ESA program management team performs is executing post-project reviews on each pilot and project. This provides the strong feedback loop to re-plan subsequent ESA adoption activities.

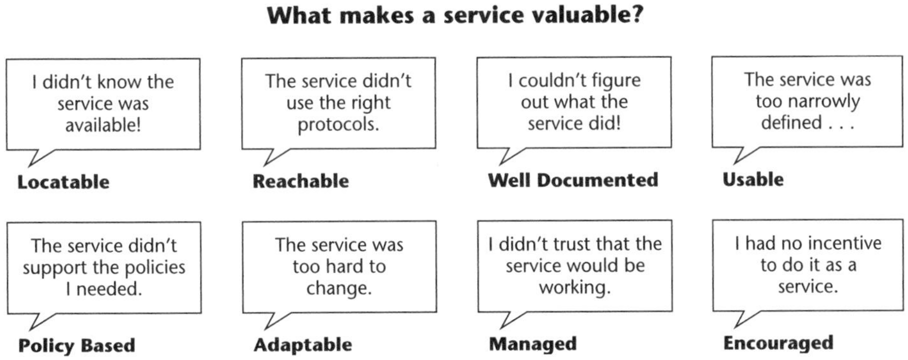

What makes a service valuable?

I didn't know the service was available!	The service didn't use the right protocols.	I couldn't figure out what the service did!	The service was too narrowly defined . . .
Locatable	**Reachable**	**Well Documented**	**Usable**

The service didn't support the policies I needed.	The service was too hard to change.	I didn't trust that the service would be working.	I had no incentive to do it as a service.
Policy Based	**Adaptable**	**Managed**	**Encouraged**

Figure 8-11: Characteristics of reusable enterprise services (Source: © 2005–2006 MomentumSI, Inc. All rights reserved.)

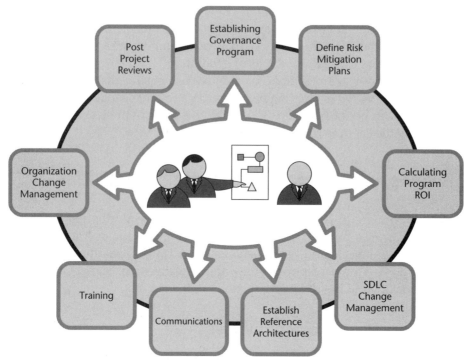

Figure 8-12: Major program management responsibilities for SOA and ESA adoption

The ESA program management team must formalize this effort and perform tasks that include the following:

- Evaluation and publishing of pilot and project results against business and technical objectives

- Interviewing the pilot and project teams, as well as the infrastructure for feedback from their experiences

- Determining cumulative benefits from the program

- Analysis of what did and did not work well in the project lifecycle (including pros and cons of the candidate project itself)

- Evaluating shared service, process, and other models for reuse potential, and encouraging re-factoring as appropriate to promote for use in future projects

- Making official recommendations to executive sponsors and other pilot and project teams that will guide the next iterations of the ESA adoption program activities

The degree to which future planning is improved from past pilot and project results is a measure of how well this activity is being performed.

Running the ESA Communications and Training Campaign

One of the most overlooked roles of an ESA program management team is the ongoing communication and training campaign for the rest of the organization. It is a role IT people often do not like performing. However, it is vital to building momentum and sustaining support for your program.

There are three main benefits that come from an effective campaign. First, benefits remain top of mind for key stakeholders. Second, new pilot and project opportunities that you may not have considered emerge from elsewhere in the organization and improve on the overall ESA adoption plan. Finally, unintended service and infrastructure reuse can occur outside the boundaries of the program as other teams become aware of the opportunity. These include the following:

- Publishing measurable business objectives (either activity-based or ROI calculations, if possible) for past pilots and projects, as well as the overall program

- Sharing business user experiences and feedback on ESA wins for improving their processes

- Documenting IT efficiency gains (such as reduced delivery time or implementation of capabilities that were not previously possible in your landscape)

- Keeping an ESA adoption portal up-to-date with white papers, artifacts, best practices, discussion forums, and so forth, as well as distributing key information and announcements

- Performing formal and informal education sessions on SOA and ESA across the organization

Of course, you will have to continue to manage scope and ensure that interest you generate does not disrupt the strategic program plan. One of the easiest ways to make that happen is by establishing sound ESA governance practices, as described in the next section.

Enabling ESA Governance

ESA governance is a broad topic that includes many organization-wide considerations across the entire solutions lifecycle. Figure 8-13 illustrates the major domains of model management and design-time, deploy-time, and run-time governance covered by an ESA governance program.

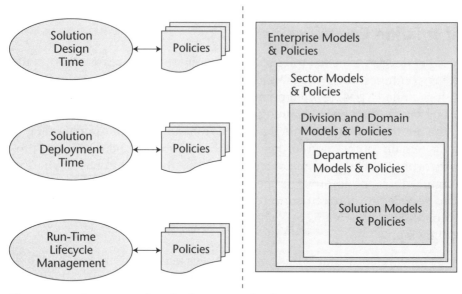

Figure 8-13: Governance domains in an ESA adoption program

Managing the Enterprise Models

Perhaps the most important ESA governance area is managing the portfolio of models themselves. SAP has developed a comprehensive internal program to ensure a consistent set of models for business objects, services, process, data types, and so on. They manage this effort across internal product development teams, as well as throughout the IVN and ES-Community ecosystem.

Your ESA adoption team is responsible for guiding this same level of model governance across the organization. This is the only way to prevent the chaos of competing models with high maintenance and limited reuse. Of course, this is no simple task. You have many different types of service models, as described in Chapter 4. In addition, if your organization has a federated or decentralized approach to EA, these models may be managed at different levels within the organization. Therefore, your governance program must address questions such as the following:

- What is the appropriate level in the organization to control different models?

- How do you best incorporate new services from SAP, the ecosystem, and other third-party vendors?

- How do you handle service model versioning and retirement across distributed service consumers (including changes to interfaces, policies, and so forth)?

- How do you manage and publish these key organizational models so that they are actionable?

Obviously, tackling this in an ad hoc or informal manner is one way to ensure long-term failure of an ESA adoption program. You can actually leverage the best practices of SAP's enterprise services community itself in establishing your own internal program. Not only does SAP publish and share the process, customers and partners can actually participate within it to see how it works. Other vendors and system integrators can also help you set up governance programs based on best practices.

Managing the Infrastructure

A second major governance domain deals with the infrastructure and tools used. As mentioned in Chapter 5, a number of standards are associated with SOA, but the area is still emerging. That means vendors must implement proprietary solutions to common problems until the standards community catches up with a unified approach. Hence, picking an infrastructure that is consistent and compatible is important.

With ESA, SAP NetWeaver will obviously become a big part of the infrastructure. But because SAP has made the environment intentionally open, you may have other products in your infrastructure that you want to use to complement ESA adoption. This means assembling a governance portfolio that covers areas such as the following:

- Service repositories
- SOA testing
- SOA management and monitoring
- Intelligent networks and hardware
- Service intermediation
- Business process modeling and management
- Composition and composite application development tools
- Allowable user interfaces (including mobile devices, office productivity applications, digital forms technologies, non-SAP portal frameworks, and so on)

In cases where you offer multiple options, reference architectures and decision trees should help your application teams determine which infrastructure component to use in a given situation.

NOTE Wherever there are implementation options, it is vital to publish decision-making guidelines that are actionable and easy to use in order to get your ESA adoption efforts off on the right foot. This is especially important when it comes to defining user interface platforms and composition tools because ESA enables so many new options in this area.

Governance in Design and Implementation Activities

ESA governance plays an important part in solution design, deployment, and run-time environments. Recall that one of the unique aspects of SOA and ESA is the heavy use of digitized models. This is different from past computing paradigms, because it provides a lot of digitized information about services, compositions, and processes that your application teams are creating.

Not only can you identify governance standards, there are improved ways to automate the auditing process of static models and run-time interactions across intelligent networks. For example, you can identify all service consumers and the routes and policies they are using to access a service. That is very beneficial in communicating a service change to all constituents.

Obviously, this is a huge advantage in making monitoring a feasible part of governance programs. Hence, part of an ESA adoption team's responsibility is to establish governance in these areas. This includes guidelines for the following:

- Service and other model metadata requirements and standards
- Documentation
- Naming conventions
- Identity management, authentication, and security
- Modeling standards and semantics
- Non-functional policy implementation
- Service provider and consumer contracts
- Usage of registries and repositories
- Usage of intermediaries
- Hardware and network utilization
- Testing

- SAP NetWeaver certification expectations and ecosystem support for choosing xApps and other third-party ISV products

- Lifecycle management and monitoring support, along with error handling

In addition to the automated capabilities, traditional publishing of actionable reference architectures, decision trees, and other EA practices goes a long way toward embedding governance into design and implementation work. Mentoring, reviews, and approval processes should also be created to support design and implementation teams.

Instilling Governance

ESA program leaders should not look at the automated infrastructure as just one step in effectively instilling governance across the organization. There are three things a program management team must do to ensure the governance program evolves successfully along with the rest of the ESA adoption plan.

First, you must have a strong communications program. ESA leaders must ensure that governance decisions are well-communicated, easily accessible, and actionable. Chapter 7 describes the common artifacts enterprise architects produce and how they can distribute them to be more effective.

Second, ESA program leaders must ensure that executive management is behind the governance program and will ensure that there is "teeth" to appropriate enforcement. If policies are consistently overruled, application teams will quickly come to view governance decisions as optional guidelines instead of requirements. Clear procedures should be in place for dealing with exceptions and determining the best course of action when they occur. This process cannot be arbitrary.

> **NOTE** Your governance program should have a clear consequences model, and there should be at least some level of public enforcement with executive support if it is going to succeed.

Finally, the governance program must take on a life of its own that extends beyond the ESA adoption program team's responsibilities. Milestones must be identified within the program to determine when it is appropriate to establish a formal ESA governance group that will outlive the ESA program management team driving initial adoption. Of course, some of the key team members leading ESA adoption may end up in the governance office. Some organizations have gone a step further to establish full-blown ESA competency centers that include governance as one aspect of their responsibilities.

IT Project Lifecycle and Organizational Changes

No matter how good your technology implementation, or how good the design of governance processes or management of initial projects is, successful ESA adoption will eventually require changing the way people and processes are organized. The ESA program management team is responsible for helping guide the cultural changes associated with scaling ESA over time. The following sections describe some of the activities that take place to make this happen. Eventually, these responsibilities would also shift to an ongoing ESA competency center because they involve instilling significant, long-lasting organizational change.

Changes in the Project Planning, Management, and Delivery Methodology

Many of the productivity and flexibility advantages of ESA come from increasing the level of reuse of services, processes, and other models over time. Unfortunately, changing the way business and IT solution teams work to encourage reuse is very challenging. The way in which solution teams are traditionally organized and motivated is at odds with this goal. There is little incentive to think about your next set of projects, let alone issues in other people's projects, when implementing a current solution.

Following are some of the considerations and process changes the ESA program management team should be facilitating across the lifecycle to achieve longer-term success with ESA:

- Changing the traditional "build versus buy" decision to include reuse and composition as solution alternatives, as well as extending SAP or other ecosystem partner composites
- Switching to process and portfolio planning models that allow project schedules to account for reuse planning
- Developing the funding and incentive-based recharge models for infrastructure, service creation, service operation, service reuse, and other key ESA economics
- Collaborating across project teams and organizational units to find and evaluate reusable assets for your projects, as well as to request changes to services outside of the team's control
- Extending testing scenarios to determine how one project's use of shared services and models may affect other applications and solutions using those same assets
- Better engaging EA models and support throughout the project lifecycles (including post-project implementation feedback)
- Extending ESA process policies to outsourcing partners

The last bullet point is especially interesting. The authors have seen organizations that heavily outsource implementation activities and struggle with propagating the changes SOA and ESA bring about to their partners' project lifecycles. The extent to which outsourcing partners fail to support ESA propagation in their delivery lifecycles can greatly hinder your adoption program success.

Successful companies have begun to require their vendors to fund part of the adoption program as part of their investment in the relationship. This includes training their teams on your EA and ESA requirements, and committing to adhering to your governance considerations as part of their delivery lifecycles and SLAs. Obviously, the stronger the relationship you have, the easier this is to achieve and the more likely you will reap benefits from the co-investment over time.

NOTE Because reuse benefits come only after there are multiple consumers of an enterprise service, there must be an incentive model to ensure that services are published and designed for reuse. Similarly, there must be incentives to promote taking advantage of existing enterprise services. This is especially difficult to accomplish when you are outsourcing projects, which is something you should actively manage.

Identifying New Roles and Responsibilities

As the ESA adoption program matures, it will become clear that roles and responsibilities within both IT and the business community need to change as a result. In some cases, there is increased specialization. In other areas, broader and expanded skills are required to be successful. While most ESA and SOA methodologies agree that new roles and responsibilities are required, they may vary in terms of the specific definitions. Here are some of the common considerations:

- It will become clear that IT is ultimately better organized around service portfolios and processes to better align with the business. This will help with aligning budgets, schedules, governance, and decision-making around process and service portfolios as well.

- Enterprise service modelers may no longer have full application development responsibility. They become experts at service composition and provide service implementations, interfaces, and contracts into the portfolio for others to use.

- Application service implementers work on providing service-oriented interfaces on top of existing applications or developing new service implementations according to specific interface contracts. These services can then be used by application assemblers or service modelers who build larger compositions.

- Application assemblers must understand how to create composite applications from a portfolio of services, including managing multiple tiers of application models and collaborating with others to address gaps in existing service interfaces and implementations.

- Business analysts and process experts can use the higher-level modeling tools within SAP NetWeaver to develop and configure some of their own models from the service portfolio that can become executable applications, dashboards, and so forth.

- Infrastructure teams dealing with intelligent, application-aware networks have greater influence over the functional monitoring and non-functional execution aspects of end-to-end business processes.

- Repository managers become the focal point for governance of the enterprise models and processes.

Obviously, culture and politics will create resistance to these types of changes. To move beyond project-oriented economics and gain the exponential benefits of ESA adoption, the organization will eventually need to address these considerations. ESA program management teams can facilitate this by educating senior management on the timing and impact of these types of changes, along with working with HR on creating job descriptions, training, and the ideal evolution plan.

It's worth noting that SAP has been advocating splitting the CIO role itself into two responsibilities that are consistent with the changes ESA brings about. One role is more technology related and involves setting up the infrastructure, composition capabilities, and other enabling elements of ESA. The new role would be tied purely to process innovation and managing the higher-level models and portfolios aligned with the organization's key strategies.

Controlling ESA Adoption Risk

Implementing ESA through initial pilots and projects is fairly easy to control because the early issues and gains are tied to those specific initiatives. As you shift into more sustained ESA adoption at a program level, issues become a lot more complicated. Decisions and activities span multiple aspects of the organization. That creates plenty of risks that threaten a successful long-term program.

Some of these have been touched upon in earlier sections, but it's important to revisit them and ensure your team has an effective management and mitigation plan in place.

While good ESA program management teams identify and track these risks, the most successful teams proactively plan for and do something about them.

If you work with a consulting or IS partner who has helped managed ESA adoption initiatives, that partner should be able to provide you with a full complement of risk identification and mitigation best practices and tools to avoid problems such as the following:

- Eroding program sponsorship and budgets
- Over-architected infrastructure and governance programs
- Under-architected infrastructure and governance programs
- Sabotage from project implementation teams and competing EA groups
- Lack of tolerance bands that anticipate deviations and negotiations in the governance plans
- Lack of preparation to handle training and communications demands in your program
- Failure to get beyond project-by-project focus to program and portfolio management levels
- Lack of incentives for one group to manage or update their published services on behalf of another
- Service creators crashing solutions that reused their assets during a modification phase
- Excessive service duplications instead of real reuse
- Duplication of application development approaches for composition
- Failure to proactively plan and budget for infrastructure, tools, and standards evolution

Of course, there are no formulaic approaches to managing risk. Having the right people on the team who can deal with multiple personalities and organizational politics is very important. In fact, team selection itself may be the most important risk for you to manage.

Measuring ESA Adoption Value

The ESA program management team should have an active measurement program in place to track value over time. Often, SOA and ESA teams have fuzzy metrics in place beyond tracking the schedule and budget of the program itself, and perhaps the number of services used. This makes it difficult to gauge real success. To the degree that you can track and prove real value, it becomes easier to expand the program over time, and to move into more strategic adoption phases.

NOTE One of the biggest challenges with measuring value from SOA and ESA is that there is a network effect that takes place. Often, the greatest value will not come until the next project or even the next-next project that demonstrates the value of reuse, agility, and new capabilities. Measuring the delayed and secondary value proposition is an ongoing program management responsibility.

As mentioned earlier, there are two sources of value from ESA adoption. The first comes from savings and productivity benefits within IT. The second deals with the business value that comes from new ESA capabilities and enabling processes.

ESA Economic Value Within IT

While many organizations measure ESA value from the number of services created and used, the real value proposition comes from the level of reuse of governed services. Figure 8-14 illustrates a simple example of reuse economics. While the first scenario delivered only three shared services, they were reused an average of four times each. The second scenario had more services in production, but the reuse factor was significantly less. Obviously, more advanced calculations are needed around the ROI of each service implementation, as well as the savings from each client reuse to evaluate the total benefits.

The main point is savings can quickly add up. For example, if each reuse in the first scenario led to a savings of $80,000 in defining requirements, development, testing, and deployment, you are looking at almost $1 million in benefit.

In addition to reusing services, there is also the opportunity to gain economies of scale from leveraging business process models, as well as new ESA-enabled infrastructure that supports new or enhanced IT Practice capabilities.

Figure 8-15 shows a simplified scorecard for tracking the economic benefits that come from leveraging ESA infrastructure, capabilities, and implementations over time. Each area can be expanded into much greater detail. Notice that not only should you measure value from the enterprise services and other models your organization creates, but also from the ones that come from SAP and other ecosystem partners.

Other metrics to develop for tracking ESA's economic value within IT include the following:

- Improvements in meeting SLAs
- Productivity gains in improved project time to value, costs, and reduced error rates over time from SAP NetWeaver infrastructure, model-driven architecture techniques, and so forth

- ROI from consolidation of applications and infrastructure
- Reduction in IT backlog

Obviously, any other IT metrics you track today can be monitored to see the impact ESA has on them. Having a simple scorecard, you can prepare and publish over time is very useful to your executive sponsor communication program.

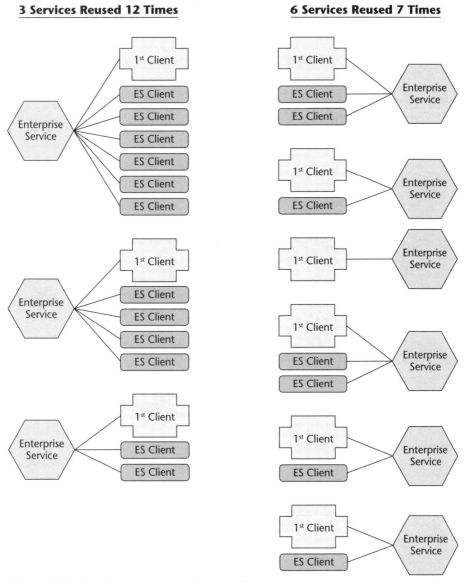

Figure 8-14: Simple reuse economics examples

Enterprise Services	# in Production & Governed	# of Client or Project Uses	Net Gain / Loss of Implementation Or Consolidation	Avg. Net Benefit Per Use
SAP Services				
Other 3rd Party Acquired Services				
Partner Services				
Internal Process Services				
Internal Domain & Task Services				
Entity Services				
Internal Technical Utility Services				
etc.				
BPM-Enabled Scenarios				
Order to Cash Scenarios				
Channel Management Scenarios				
Workforce Management Scenarios				
etc.				
New IT Practices Capabilities Enabled or Enhanced				

Figure 8-15: A simplified SOA scorecard (Source © 2006, MomentumSI, Inc. All rights reserved.)

ESA Economic Value Within the Business

While the IT benefits of ESA adoption can often justify the program by themselves, the more important metrics to publicize are the benefits to the business. While many projects you tackle using ESA techniques and infrastructure could be implemented in other ways, some solutions simply were not feasible without the IT Practice Capabilities and enterprise services available from a platform such as SAP NetWeaver.

You must work with the business to value these projects in the same ways you always have in managing the IT portfolio. In theory, the business process improvements will provide greater productivity benefits in terms of ESA-enabled capabilities, such as the following:

▪ Process visibility, activity monitoring, management by exception, and simulation features

- Productivity enablement within the users' tools of choice

- Embedded analytics, Guided Procedures, and other workflow that facilitate human interaction with processes and reduce error rates

- Model-driven process changes and dashboard analytics that can be controlled largely by business process managers themselves

To the extent that you are using these features in your ESA adoption initiatives, you should see increased lift in ROI.

A second area to explore is xApps and other packaged composite applications you acquire from SAP and partners. Some of the ROI on implementing those off-the-shelf products comes from their pre-integration with the ESA infrastructure in your landscape. Chapter 4 mentioned a couple of these areas, including Vendavo's optimized pricing solutions and Pavilion's model predictive control scenarios to proactively anticipate and address high ROI process events.

Other common business scenarios for which organizations are seeing greater benefits from SOA and ESA adoption include areas such as the following:

- Data unification and master data management programs that reduce semantic errors throughout your processes, as well as lower manual maintenance and transformation tasks

- Managing multiple customer and supplier interaction points through platform-independent shared service interfaces

- Offering new digitized products and services

- Enabling BPO of tasks and sub-processes in the context of your overall process management

- Enabling customer, employee, and manager self-service solutions

- Solving process that have been historically difficult to automate, such as new product introductions, M&A consolidations, returns management, billing disputes, and so forth

Not only are these great projects to consider for ESA adoption, but they also help you track and measure the business benefits from your program. As with tracking the IT benefits, you want to ensure that you have a complete and consistent scorecard that you evolve over time and share with executive sponsors. This will help you move beyond anecdotal statements such as "better process agility," "cheaper integration," "faster time to market," and all the other good concepts that you cannot really value without measuring.

Summarizing the Results of ESA Program Management

Figure 8-16 summarizes the transformations that occur from successfully managing your ESA adoption program. There are four major benefits:

- The creation of new capabilities that offer things you couldn't provide the business previously
- Greater efficiencies and simplification within IT that allow you to execute faster, better, and cheaper than before
- Better alignment between IT and the business
- Creation of sustaining processes for instilling ESA across the organization

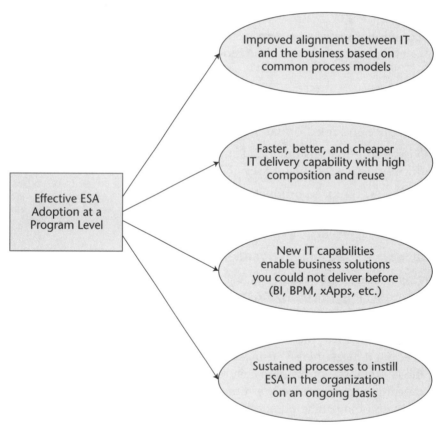

Figure 8-16: The results of a successful ESA program

Balancing General SOA Adoption Practices with SAP-Centric ESA-Based Adoption

As mentioned previously in this chapter, organizations whose landscapes are largely SAP-based will find that the company's ESA adoption model is a great guide for all SOA adoption efforts. However, those enterprises that have very diverse IT application landscapes, decentralized technology planning, and multiple application and integration platform standards will have to factor in additional considerations when pursuing SAP's approach to ESA. The same is true for any SAP customer whose EA teams are encouraging a more generic, vendor-neutral approach to SOA.

This can lead to a number of questions, such as the following:

- How do I need to adjust an *SAP ESA-centric plan* today based on my current versions of SAP applications and SAP's own maturity of its ESA strategy and the NetWeaver platform?

- How do I incorporate SAP's ESA solutions into a *vendor-neutral SOA plan*?

- If my organization takes a *hybrid approach* between general SOA and SAP's approach, where should the lines be drawn and what are the implications?

The following sections distinguish the major characteristics of these three approaches and take a brief look at the types of decisions that must be made around service governance, infrastructure, and composition approaches.

Characteristics of an SAP ESA-Centric Approach

Here, your decision has been made to largely standardize on SAP's adoption approach, tools, and infrastructure solutions for SOA; and consolidation plans are in place. Third-party solutions are usually acquired from companies that are actively participating in the SAP ecosystem and have worked with SAP to deliver certified solutions that complement the SAP NetWeaver platform infrastructure capabilities.

Other tool and technology choices may be made to fill in short-term gaps while waiting on SAP to deliver the next generation of the SAP NetWeaver platform, and your organization to complete its upgrade road map. There will be a conscious plan that these investments are tactical and will be retired when mature SAP capabilities are made available. Examples here might be a pure-play BPM product, enhanced metadata repositories and governance tools, intermediaries, SOA testing products, and specialized composition tools.

Characteristics of a Vendor-Neutral Approach to SOA

Organizations taking this approach have chosen to build an SOA infrastructure that will support multi-vendor platforms. They tend to have very heterogeneous environments and many legacy applications vital to the SOA solution. These companies also tend to be very strong in managing custom application and integration efforts, and supporting high-availability infrastructures.

One of the keys to success with this approach is a strong, mature, well-coordinated and governed EA capability. These organizations will likely pursue best-of-breed platforms and pure-play products that support the greatest degree of SOA capability. From a repository standpoint, they will also pursue as vendor-neutral a set of organizational process and services models as possible.

The ESA adoption efforts for these groups will generally be limited to using the SOA-based interfaces provided by SAP into the business applications. Their goal is to build an enterprise-wide SOA model of the business that abstracts out packaged applications, and they generally treat their SAP systems no differently than any other existing IT asset.

Characteristics of a Hybrid Approach to Adopting ESA and SOA

A hybrid approach is usually adopted by organizations having large SAP footprints that they have traditionally complemented with another vendor's platform (such as IBM WebSphere, BEA WebLogic, or Microsoft .NET). They tend to have two development camps today, with clear lines between what gets done inside of SAP versus within another platform.

As these organizations move to SOA adoption, this model persists in the short run, with both camps relying more on service-oriented integration and intermediaries to communicate between them. Typically, politics play a large role in the attempt to standardize on one platform or the other for areas such as Portal and BPM. As SAP NetWeaver and competing platforms continue to mature into integrated SOA composition environments, making these decisions will become more important.

In terms of model creation and governance, the SAP definitions can accelerate the process in both camps because they provide a large inventory to use as a starting point. The key will be consistently governing the enterprise evolution of models, regardless of which platform defines and manages a specific model or its implementation. This is covered further in the next section.

NOTE The authors have seen the choice of approach vary quite a bit along industry lines. Industries such as manufacturing, chemicals, energy, utilities, and others (where SAP has a long-standing position of strength) tend to gravitate toward a more ESA-centric approach. Meanwhile, industries such as financial services and healthcare (which have large numbers of heavily customized solutions, as well as multiple technologies and platforms) tend to lean more toward a technology-based, platform-neutral approach to SOA to handle their heterogeneous environment.

Major Considerations in Balancing SOA- and SAP-Based ESA Adoption

The three main areas where the approach to SOA adoption has the greatest impact on your program are as follows:

- Creation and governance of service models
- Composition creation and deployment environments
- Service-oriented infrastructure

Governance of Service Models

As mentioned, the value you get from your SOA efforts will be severely capped if you are not able to properly manage a coherent set of services that gets reused across projects. In fact, many SOA programs have stalled or failed altogether when they got beyond an easily managed number of services because the organization did not adopt a governance strategy.

Obviously, you will have a large number of services and processes provided by SAP. The adoption approach you take will have a big impact on how you manage them, and what you do with the additional models you create internally.

Another challenge occurs in organizations that have multiple packaged applications in addition to those from SAP. Because virtually all vendors are working to service-enable their business solutions, these companies are faced with trying to integrate multiple service libraries from different vendors. Of course, the level of granularity, required metadata, and semantics varies between them, leaving it to the organization to resolve the differences.

Table 8-2 highlights some of the considerations regarding managing your services meta-model under the different approaches.

Table 8-2: Balancing SOA and ESA Adoption Approaches for Model Management

SAP ESA-CENTRIC APPROACH CONSIDERATIONS	SOA-CENTRIC APPROACH CONSIDERATIONS	HYBRID APPROACH CONSIDERATIONS
Use SAP NetWeaver as a platform to create services out of existing assets and evolve from XI integration Directory to the Enterprise Services Repository.	Select a primary repository for where services and other models will be managed.	Develop strategies for working with multiple repositories spread across different scopes.
Extend from SAP's base of published enterprise services.	Develop a governance process for your preferred services model and build them in a vendor-neutral manner.	Rationalize the ESA services inventory with other existing assets into a hybrid repository.
Participate in SAP ecosystem efforts as reviewer or requester of new services.	Expose third-party applications such as SAP's according to your internal model and in your preferred repository.	Determine criteria for which platform will be used to create and control which service models.
Acquire services from third parties working closely with SAP ecosystem.		Acquire services from third parties working closely with SAP or other platform ecosystems where it makes sense.

Composition Environments

SAP NetWeaver offers a number of tools and technologies for creating and exposing applications and user interfaces that consume ESA services. Following is a brief list of platform capabilities that will be covered in Part III of this book:

- *SAP NetWeaver Application Server and Portal Development* for constructing role-based user interfaces and business logic to support composites
- *WebDynpro* for building model-driven UIs that can be deployed in a variety of formats
- *Visual Composer* for business and systems analysts to quickly compose simple composite applications from existing services and models
- *Composite Application Framework* for building rich composite applications, including support for Guided Procedures capabilities
- *SAP NetWeaver Process Integration and Management* capabilities for invoking and consuming services in A2A and B2B environments

Because SAP NetWeaver is an integrated SOA platform, these capabilities can be combined to create extremely rich composite solutions. Obviously, other platforms such as Microsoft .NET, IBM WebSphere, and a number of best-of-breed composite application development and BPM tools exist that provide similar functionality, and can work on top of the SAP services.

Your approach to ESA versus SOA adoption will largely determine which composition development and deployment technologies you focus on. Table 8-3 contains a summary of the decisions about where to train people, build methodologies, and implement infrastructure for creating SOA-based client applications.

SOA Run-Time Infrastructure

Of all the areas where balancing SOA and SAP-based ESA adoption considerations takes place, the area of SOA Infrastructure selection is probably the most difficult. Standards are moving very quickly in this area. More important, vendor capabilities vary widely, as do the overall architectural models.

As described in Chapter 5, you can attribute this to the fact that the market is immature for robust SOA infrastructure. And as mentioned previously, the WS-* standards are still limited such that the majority of enterprise class support for non-functional requirements is non-standard. This means that vendor design and run-time infrastructures are very dependent upon one another.

Table 8-3: Balancing SOA and ESA Adoption Approaches for Composition

SAP ESA-CENTRIC APPROACH CONSIDERATIONS	SOA-CENTRIC APPROACH CONSIDERATIONS	HYBRID APPROACH CONSIDERATIONS
Use SAP NetWeaver to build and deploy service-based composite applications.	Where appropriate, select best-of-breed SOA-based composition and BPM tools.	Provide joint training and support for multiple platforms based on reference architectures.
Leverage SAP's xApps and third-party Certified Packaged Composites as they are released.	Enable developers to create clients that call SAP services on their platform of choice (for example, Microsoft Visual Studio).	SAP-centric development focuses on SAP NetWeaver.
Make interim decisions on the importance of advanced BPM tools while waiting for next-generation releases from SAP.		Non-SAP–centric development has a defined toolset of choice that you are probably already using.

Obviously, in SAP's case, using SAP NetWeaver for client composition requires SAP's infrastructure platform be used in production. The same is true with most of the other leading application vendor development platforms, as well as some best-of-breed products. You can also expect that vendor implementations will evolve over time as partnerships are created and evolve with other vendors, IT industry consolidation continues, and standards emerge.

Following is a quick reminder of some of the capabilities associated with an SOA run-time infrastructure:

- Messaging and service intermediation, including ESB
- Run-time registry, repository, and policy management
- Legacy enablement
- Service network monitoring
- Functional load and integration testing
- Orchestration engine
- Composite application lifecycle management engine
- XML transformation and acceleration

The problem you face in this area is that some of the choices are expensive to implement and carry a high switching cost. This has kept some organizations from moving beyond the "grass roots" level of SOA adoption. Table 8-4 summarizes some considerations associated with SOA run-time infrastructure decisions taking place in many organizations.

Table 8-4: Balancing SOA and ESA Adoption Approaches for SOA Infrastructure

SAP ESA-CENTRIC APPROACH CONSIDERATIONS	SOA-CENTRIC APPROACH CONSIDERATIONS	HYBRID APPROACH CONSIDERATIONS
Use SAP NetWeaver as service infrastructure within or between SAP deployments.	Use lightweight service infrastructure for communication between platforms/ESBs.	Develop specific case-by-case scenarios in your reference architecture.
Use SAP's Enterprise Services Repository as it is released for SAP-based enterprise services and xApps.	Implement enterprise-wide strategy to effectively handle multiple service repositories at run-time (SAP and non-SAP).	Augment SAP NetWeaver with infrastructure from other client implementation tools you have selected.
Augment with third-party best-of-breed products in the short run, with plans to retire when SAP or ecosystem partner product becomes available.	Design and implement enterprise-wide service infrastructure strategy optimized to your business.	

Some "Rules of Thumb" for Decision-Making

While this section touched upon some of the main areas affected by juggling different SOA and ESA adoption approaches, you can see how essentially every part of your adoption road map will be affected, depending on whether you take an SAP ESA-first, SOA-centric, or hybrid approach to adoption.

There will be plenty of passionate debates around the "best" way to tackle the problem and make each decision. Unfortunately, there is no clear right or wrong choice. Perhaps the best advice is to think about the mid- to longer-term ramifications of different decisions. This means recognizing the following:

- Today's "best" products in terms of features and functions are not always the right choice from an overall perspective. Which have the features and functions you need?

- Choices should be made with a longer adoption horizon. This means anticipating industry consolidation, the evolution of standards, and especially the long-term road maps of the major platform vendors in terms of when they will have an acceptable level of features that are critical to your organization.

- Most organizations are going to have multiple vendor service inventories and possibly repositories to deal with.

- No single decision is going to address all considerations. Invoke the 80/20 rule and then worry about what to do with the exception cases. For example, consolidating from ten platforms to three and having two major repositories with little overlap is still great progress.

- Selecting the best solution to address immediate, high-ROI business projects does not mean that same solution has to become an organizational standard. Some problems are worth solving today without having to force a long-term EA decision.

- Solutions that can leverage existing skill sets and legacy environments are often better than ones requiring a wholesale retraining of staff.

Larger organizations will likely federate these decisions into different zones, including one for the SAP landscape. Small and mid-size enterprises, and those organizations performing large IT consolidation projects based upon SAP, can avoid some of the extra infrastructure and governance challenges of multiple platforms and products. In those cases, they will find it easier to more quickly move into the strategic ESA adoption phases.

Summary

This chapter provided a comprehensive introduction to the elements in an ESA adoption program, along with best practices and considerations on how to run one successfully. Program-level management is needed to ensure a consistent set of enterprise architecture goals and practices is used to kick-start and sustain your transition to ESA.

Remember that long-term ESA adoption is not a one-time event. It is really a transformation in the way IT is run from top to bottom. This chapter walked you through the process of establishing goals, forming a team, strategically identifying and executing pilot projects, and instilling the longer-term ESA capabilities over time.

Following are the most important takeaways from this chapter:

- ESA adoption value is tied to business and IT strategy, and is realized incrementally and exponentially over time.

- An effective adoption program is required to provide consistent and well-coordinated execution to enable SOA and ESA as part of your enterprise architecture initiatives.

- The major themes for running a consistent program involve finding opportunities, right-sizing investments for both differentiated and context processes, driving savings from IT application and infrastructure consolidation, and implementing new IT capabilities with specific business impact.

- A governance program is critical to successful ESA adoption. This program must cover the reusable models, as well as design, deployment, and run-time activities associated with each project and solution.

- ESA program management teams have a number of responsibilities for managing adoption risks, as well as measuring and communicating value.

- ESA adoption will require changes to the IT solution delivery lifecycle, as well as an evolution of organizational roles and skills to support the transformation.

- If your organization is taking a non-SAP–centric approach to SOA adoption, additional considerations and activities are required to effectively blend in SAP's ESA models and NetWeaver into the larger effort.

In Chapter 9, you will see some examples of both customers and ecosystem partners who have created solution architectures based on their ESA adoption strategies, and have kicked off pilot project or product development initiatives.

References

1. Geoffrey A. Moore, *Living on the Fault Line — Revised Edition: Managing for Shareholder Value in Any Economy*, Harper Business, August 2002.
2. Geoffrey A. Moore, *Dealing with Darwin: How Great Companies Innovate at Every Phase of Their Evolution*, Penguin Group, December 2005.
3. Thomas H. Davenport, "Competing on Analytics," *Harvard Business Review*, January 2006.
4. Thomas H. Davenport, "The Coming Commoditization of Business Processes," *Harvard Business Review*, June, 2005.
5. Geoffrey A. Moore "Investing IT Resources for Competitive Advantage — An Interview," *SAP NetWeaver Magazine*, Winter 2006, p. 13.
6. "Governing IT in the Enterprise," Forrester Research, Inc., July 30, 2004. Available at `www.hp.com/hpinfo/newsroom/feature_stories/2004/04maximizeit.html`.

Analyzing ESA-Based Solutions Architectures

Thus far, you have seen the business motivations and goals for SAP's ESA strategy, along with the major IT industry technology trends and planning principles that help enable its realization. This chapter brings Part II to a close by taking a look at example scenarios that show how to bring ESA to life to solve real business problems. Its goal is to illustrate how the many ESA-enabling concepts come together to create a solutions architecture.

It is important to note that, while these scenarios are designed to show some of the current and future ESA capabilities, the authors have based them around real-world business process needs identified by SAP's customers. In many cases, SAP and its ecosystem partners are already working to productize these opportunities using ESA design principles. That means leveraging existing business application components and services to create new solutions much faster and more flexibly than ever before. These new solutions will take advantage of the user productivity, process management, and more agile composition and integration capabilities of SAP NetWeaver.

And, as the capabilities of ESA continue to grow in terms of the Enterprise Services Inventory surrounding the mySAP Business Suite applications and SAP NetWeaver platform, even more advanced compositions can be created. In Part III of this book, you see some of the SAP NetWeaver tools and technologies that illustrate how scenarios like these can be implemented.

As a result of reading this chapter, you will:

- See examples of how ESA principles can be applied to address specific business process scenarios

- Understand why traditional methods of addressing these opportunities are less efficient and effective

- Review solutions architectures that combine SAP applications, ecosystem partner solutions, and custom development to illustrate how all three leverage the same development model

- See how the various SAP NetWeaver IT Practices and Scenarios work together to enable the solution architectures

- Have a foundation for Part III of this book, where some of the ESA capabilities in SAP NetWeaver tools and technologies are demonstrated

Introducing the Business Scenarios

This chapter contains business scenarios that demonstrate the value of ESA. In this section, you will see the background and requirements behind each of the solutions, along with the general ESA considerations that went into their planning. Subsequent sections illustrate the specific solution architectures associated with each scenario to help you see how ESA features in SAP NetWeaver can be used to address opportunities like these.

Summary of Process Needs and Opportunities

The scenarios covered in this chapter have historically been difficult for SAP customers to address because they involve high levels of integration, and traditional technology options were not simple or cost-effective to use to create a solution. As you will see, an ESA-based approach offers the following advantages:

- Accelerate time to value while leveraging current IT investments
- Reduce maintenance costs
- Improve reuse
- Enable the underlying processes to change more easily in the future
- Improve the productivity of users who interact with the process

The first scenario expands upon an example from Chapter 4's coverage of the ecosystem. It involves improving the integration between a manufacturing environment and corporate systems. Here, predicting events through advanced data analytics can improve the ROI of several business processes. ESA-based alerting, integration, and analysis capabilities can embed this information throughout those processes.

The second scenario involves a company that needed to create front-ends for customers and knowledge workers to interact with their SAP data and processes. ESA and SAP NetWeaver provided options to improve the usability of these interfaces and to increase process flexibility and reuse.

The final scenario involves improving supplier management and integration with supplier networks. This is a common need for many SAP customers, as well as suppliers themselves. An ESA-based approach can help all parties manage the many-to-many relationships that can become a process-and-integration nightmare, especially for the high volume of tier II and tier III suppliers.

Note that, in some cases, SAP may offer products that compete with capabilities of the ecosystem partners or custom-developed solutions covered in these scenarios. This actually highlights one of the major benefits of the ESA strategy. Whether it is because of unique functional requirements, licensing, or simply a prior choice or preference, many SAP customers may not select an available SAP business solution to resolve these types of scenarios. Regardless, the value of ESA and the SAP NetWeaver platform can still be leveraged by customers and partners to enable whichever solution they choose.

ESA Benefits Over Traditional Approaches for These Scenarios

As mentioned earlier, there really was no ideal or cost-effective way to address these scenarios using traditional technology options without sacrificing usability, maintainability, and process agility at some level. In fact, the ESA designs in all three scenarios were created to replace manual and semi-automated procedures and integrations that were not effectively solving the real problems. Following are some of the typical issues encountered by using traditional IT approaches to enable these processes:

- Information delays caused by having no alerting or event management capability meant exception management was reactionary instead of proactive.

- EAI and file-based integrations required heavy amounts of custom coding and maintenance, often resulting in brittle point-to-point interfaces that are easily broken.

- Process logic required heavy amounts of custom coding and maintenance, and was buried inside of applications of procedures documents, making things very inflexible for meeting new business needs.

- Lots of "swivel chair integration" was required by users as they toggled between multiple systems and reports to find information needed to execute and manage their process workflows.

- Reuse was limited to the API level. For example, even when BAPIs or custom SAP function calls were exposed as Web Services, the low level of granularity did not provide much reuse benefit from one solution to another.

What made these challenges difficult to overcome without an ESA-based approach is that all of these scenarios rely on multiple underlying systems. The solution landscapes are made up of packaged applications from SAP, other third-party products or hosted services, and custom applications and legacy systems developed by the customer. Integrating most of the functionality from these diverse systems in an intelligent way that does not compromise adaptability is tough, especially when you cannot control all the required components. ESA offers the advantage of creating flexible solutions on top of the existing landscape through easier integration and composition techniques.

Scenario #1: Enhancing Processes with Manufacturing Analytics

As described in Chapter 4, Pavilion Technologies is working with the SAP ecosystem to define value-added solutions for the manufacturing industries. The company's core solutions create advanced model-based analytics across manufacturing processes. This helps manufacturers optimize their processes by reducing variability, minimizing transition times, achieving performance consistency, and increasing production to maximize efficiency.

These advanced analytics can also be leveraged by mySAP ERP and other Business Suite applications to enhance a number of business scenarios. From an ESA perspective, Pavilion, SAP, and their joint customers are working together with the Chemicals IVN to identify high ROI areas that can be best solved with composite applications. Some examples of these business opportunities include the following:

- Predicting quantities and availability of *secondary transition materials* (off-specification material created while a manufacturing process shifts from one product grade to another) so that they can be marketed and sold even before they are produced

- Ensuring secondary transition materials can be efficiently reflected in corporate inventory as soon as they are produced

- Predicting optimal times for quality samples by technicians to reduce costs and increase the timeliness and effectiveness of samples

- Predicting optimal or unanticipated maintenance requirements and placing notifications and orders at the appropriate time

The companies have designed a composite application for *Model Predictive Intelligence* (*xMPI*) to begin addressing these opportunities. It can provide predictive information in real time to the mySAP Business Suite applications to facilitate highly dynamic decision-making. This is a type of embedded analytics that can help increase the effectiveness of operations and improve profitability.

A key to maximizing value with xMPI is that the composite application leverages the same predictive models that are actually used to control plant operations. Another tightly integrated composite the companies have designed will continuously optimize the plant based on applying dynamic business objectives to real-time operating conditions. This composite is referred to as *Model Predictive Control* (*xMPC*). An example scenario for predicting secondary material quantity and availability realized through these two composite applications is illustrated in Figure 9-1.

If you do not work in a process manufacturing industry, it's not critical that you understand all the details of these chemicals industry business opportunities. The key is recognizing that the value comes from integrating high volumes of real-time production information with corporate systems, and then embedding actionable information and analytics inside the processes to optimize results. That is the heart of what ESA enables, and it is likely you can find parallel opportunities within your own industry for analytic engines such as Pavilion's.

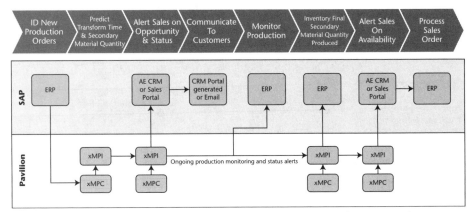

Figure 9-1: A sample manufacturing analytics business scenario for xMPI and xMPC

The Overall Composite Solutions Architecture

One key to enabling an ESA-based approach was the work done by Pavilion to tailor its own applications architecture. As you can see in Figure 9-2, Pavilion designed and extended its product suite using SOA principles.

The Pavilion applications are developed in Java and run on standard J2EE application servers with SQL databases handling the persistence. From an integration standpoint, the company supports a number of manufacturing industry interfaces such as a digital control system (DCS) and programmable logic controller (PLC) to enable it to integrate seamlessly with process control and information networks. Pavilion also supports Java, Web Services, XML, Java Database Connectivity (JDBC), Open Database Connectivity (ODBC), and many other common application development integration standards.

To support xMPI, the company also created a set of loosely coupled enterprise services that provide additional abstractions to support semantics such as Business to Manufacturing Markup Language (B2MML), and some of the related mySAP ERP integration scenarios. These services enable the Pavilion platform to offer additional service-oriented integration features beyond just low-level API-based Web Services to support the development of ESA composites. Through this architecture Pavilion analytics can easily be used across various presentation and integration points.

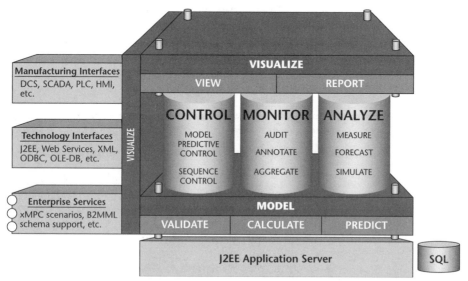

Figure 9-2: Pavilion's SOA-based product architecture (Source: © 2005–2006, Pavilion Technologies, Inc. All rights reserved.)

These capabilities were leveraged to create the initial xMPI solution. Figure 9-3 illustrates elements of the overall architecture for xMPI designed by SAP and Pavilion in conjunction with key chemicals industry customers. As you can see, the following ESA principles were implemented using SAP NetWeaver to create this composite:

- Service-oriented integration between mySAP ERP and Pavilion to track production order status and trigger inventory updates for secondary materials

- Service-oriented integration between Pavilion and SAP xMII to enable Pavilion analytics to be exposed to the overall xMII shop floor analytics engine and dashboards, as well as the ability to persist xMII analysis back to Pavilion as needed

- Business process orchestrations within SAP NetWeaver to facilitate the process flows between the underlying applications

- Support for SAP NetWeaver XI B2MML business content to use the ISA-95 industry standard semantics

- Use of SAP alerting and SAP NetWeaver Portal presentation services to trigger notifications of secondary material availability to sales and the updating of employee dashboards for quality orders

Figure 9-4 shows how SAP NetWeaver XI technologies were used by Pavilion to create additional enterprise services to support the xMPI scenarios. Process orchestrations were modeled using WS-BPEL, as explained in Chapter 6. Recall that these orchestrations can be invoked as Web Services themselves.

While this composite application implements several ESA-based capabilities of SAP NetWeaver, you can expect subsequent xMPI releases to more fully embrace the platform. For example, in the future, the Pavilion services could be published in the SAP ESR as partner extensions. Or, over time, Pavilion and SAP may work together to enhance the official SAP enterprise services models to represent these capabilities. This will allow customers to easily access the underlying Pavilion services for modeling and implementing their own composites.

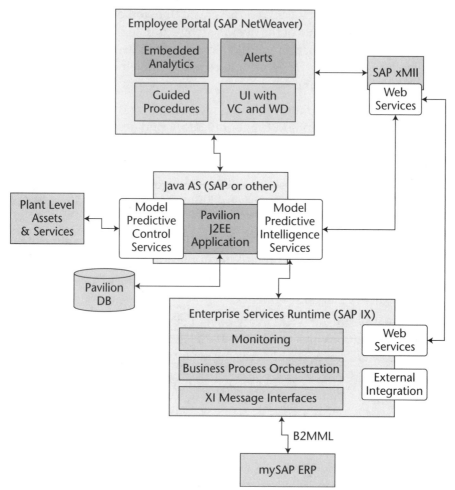

Figure 9-3: The high-level architecture for xMPI (Source: © 2005–2006, Pavilion Technologies, Inc. All rights reserved.)

In addition, xMPI can be enhanced based on capabilities of SAP's CAF and Visual Composer composition tools. This will allow capabilities such as Guided Procedures and more role-based content packages within the SAP NetWeaver Portal or future UIs such as "Project Muse" to be employed.

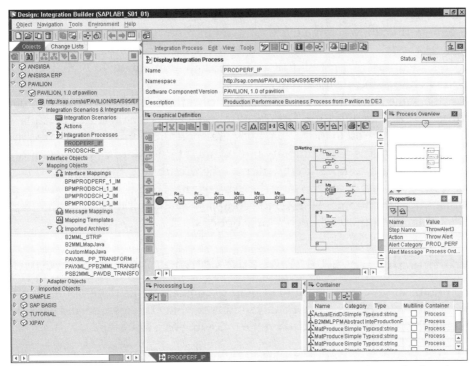

Figure 9-4: A sample process orchestration to implement an enterprise service interface

Scenario #2: Providing Information Workers and Customers with Front-Ends to SAP

The next solutions architecture is derived from the experiences of a global manufacturer implementing applications for pricing master data management and customer self-service processes. This organization has standardized on SAP R/3 for all key ERP functions, and a non-SAP CRM system for sales and contact management processes. Like many enterprises, it spent the last several years surrounding the enterprise applications with multiple custom-developed (or purchased) client/server and Web-based systems to address different processes.

Over time, maintenance costs began to rise. In addition, core processes were becoming difficult to change in existing applications to support new strategic business models the company wished to pursue. The typical IT planning process identified a portfolio of projects with immediate ROI that could address some of the business gaps.

At the same time, the organization began to think more about its longer-term enterprise architecture. Historically, application architectures and platform choices were left to individual business-sponsored projects supported by functional IT groups. The company now wanted to standardize on a common development and composition platform when refreshing these applications. Knowing SAP NetWeaver would be part of the IT landscape following a planned upgrade to mySAP ERP, the company evaluated it along with other commercial platforms and open source options.

Defining the Development and Composition Architecture

The organization developed a road map to consolidate its development and composition architecture. After analyzing its current IT landscape and considering multiple options, it landed on the following as a first step:

- The primary Web application development platform would be based on Java technologies, and the primary application server would be SAP NetWeaver AS.

- A reference architecture for lightweight, loosely coupled Java applications using frameworks such as Spring, Hibernate, and Struts was defined.

- The SAP NetWeaver Development Infrastructure was selected as the source code control, build, and transport mechanism.

- The existing Tibco EAI solution would continue to be leveraged as an integration intermediary, with a focus on developing reusable service-oriented integration points.

- Custom business services based on ERP would be implemented in ABAP, and these services would be exposed to other composition environments using Web Services, Java wrappers, and occasionally EAI adapters, as appropriate.

- A subset of Microsoft Office and .NET development and composition technologies would be used for delivering certain types of rich user interfaces.

In addition, the company put a road map in place to evaluate a number of other options. This included SAP NetWeaver Portal (especially for manager and employee self-service applications), and the addition of tools such as Web-Dynpro and the SAP CAF as future implementation standards.

ESA-Based Solution Architectures

The next step was to put the new architecture in place to address projects in the IT portfolio. Solution architectures for two projects are described here.

Managing Master Pricing Information

The first project deals with maintaining master prices. Pricing analysts evaluate data from multiple internal and external sources, including order and price exception history. Statistical packages also provide additional insights. Ultimately, analysts rely heavily on Excel-based tools to make their final base pricing decisions. These pricing updates need to be published to customers and the CRM system, and stored in SAP R/3 for order processing.

As shown in Figure 9-5, the company leveraged the Microsoft Office Information Bridge Framework (IBF) in the solution architecture. IBF allows developers to connect Microsoft Office front-ends to enterprise applications such as SAP. As you probably guessed, IBF is a core technology used to develop the Duet business solutions discussed in Chapter 4. You can use the same technology to create your own Office front-ends to SAP.

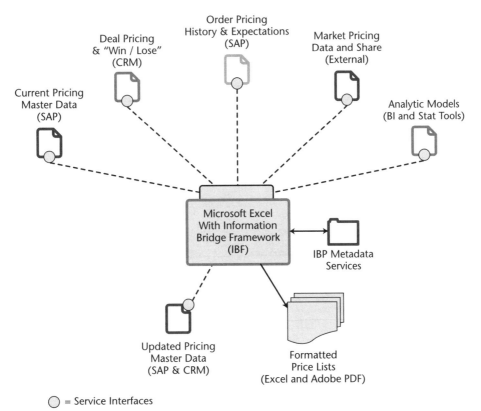

Figure 9-5: The solution architecture for managing master pricing data

In this example, Excel can leverage a number of services to populate information for the pricing analyst. Once pricing decisions are made, service-oriented calls back to SAP and the CRM system can be used to update the official pricing master data. At the same time, other Excel templates can then retrieve the official pricing data and format customer-specific price lists as spreadsheets or Adobe PDF documents.

Customer Self-Service

Figure 9-6 shows the solution architecture for the customer self-service front-end applications. SAP and other back-end information sources can be exposed as services to the composition environment. These services can then be used to implement a number of customer scenarios (including order entry, order updating, checking product availability, processing warranty claims, monitoring order status, price checks, and more). Many of these activities used to require calls into a customer service center, where agents did the lookups and entry within SAP. In fact, this architecture allowed the same information to be accessed by internal employees who were not traditionally SAP GUI power users.

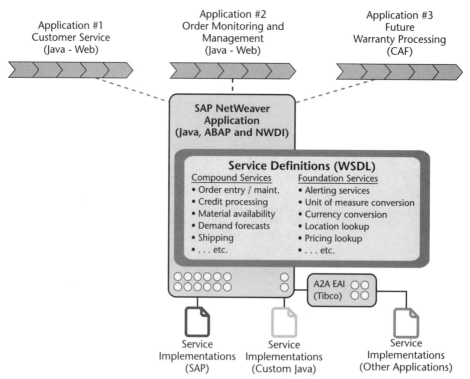

Figure 9-6: Architecture for customer self-service front-ends

The important point to recognize in this architecture was the level of reuse of services across the scenarios. Careful planning went into defining common services for locations, materials, orders, availability checks, and claims. New functions could leverage these in subsequent projects.

Future considerations include expanding these applications for access from SAP NetWeaver Portal, particularly for internal users. More important, the service models would need to be re-evaluated as SAP formalizes similar services in its official enterprise services models for mySAP ERP 2005. A governance process will be required to dictate how decisions on harmonizing these models will be made.

Scenario #3: Integrating Suppliers for More Efficient and Effective Procurement

This scenario is based on experiences working with several SAP customers and ecosystem partners who specialize in supplier management and collaboration solutions. As mentioned in Chapter 8, supplier integration is one of the most ideal scenarios for ESA-based solutions. This is because you are dealing with multiple integration points in a many-to-many scenario.

In other words, customers must manage multiple suppliers, and each supplier must integrate with multiple customers. Because these are all external B2B integrations, each party has little control over the platforms, technologies, or integration sophistication of their trading partners.

The Self-Service Procurement Challenge and the Role of Supplier Networks

One area that is especially problematic for SAP customers is employees requisitioning and acquiring products and services at local levels. This usually involves purchases outside the strategic supply chain. Unless controlled and governed, there is no way to ensure overall corporate purchasing programs are followed, preferred vendors are selected, and volume pricing opportunities are taken advantage of. Many ecosystem partners offer "best of breed" spend management solutions to address this problem, as does SAP through the mySAP SRM application. There are other organizations that tackle this challenge through custom-built composite applications that integrate with their R/3 or mySAP ERP environments.

Figure 9-7 shows the high-level business scenario map for self-service procurement in mySAP SRM. This process can help get localized purchasing coordinated at a strategic level, which offers many benefits. However, notice that the scenario map still involves direct communication between buyers and suppliers, meaning that the challenges of dealing with each supplier still exists. The SRM system may enable B2B connectivity. However, you are still faced with having to manage all the integration points along with the related supplier content and other data. This is often not cost-effective for SAP customers when it comes to interactions with a high number of tier II and tier III suppliers for non-strategic products.

So, regardless of whether you use a best-of-breed solution or SAP SRM, or create your own custom application or composite for spend management, there are still opportunities to improve the external integration with suppliers. One way to address this issue is through integration with an existing supplier network such as the one offered by Perfect Commerce. Perfect Commerce's Open Supplier Network is one of the largest supplier networks in the world. SAP customers work with Perfect Commerce to integrate with the millions of product SKUs, existing catalog content, and connectivity to the thousands of suppliers in the network.

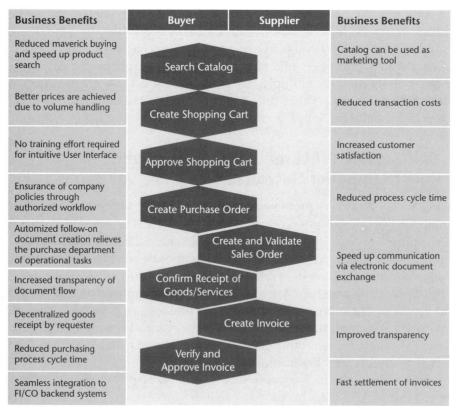

Figure 9-7: The SRM Self-Service Procurement scenario map from SAP Solution Composer

Figure 9-8 takes a closer look at one scenario where applying services and other ESA principles to integrate with the Perfect Commerce network has proven valuable. Note that this scenario is presented from the buyer's viewpoint, where the buyer relies on the Open Supplier Network to avoid having to know anything about the supplier's order-processing or invoicing systems.

Other potential benefits of using ESA for integration within the supplier network setting include the following:

- Offering a platform-neutral set of Web Services–based integration points to consolidate integrations for buyers and suppliers.

- Composing more complex enterprise services that can be used in other BPM and composition environments such as SAP NetWeaver.

- Consuming and invoking services in the buyer's corporate applications. This makes it easier for buyers to integrate their ERP systems with the supplier network, and then seamlessly switch to other integration points such as a mySAP SRM system if they later implement that capability.

- Exposing transaction data as services that can be consumed by buyers and suppliers in the network for creating embedded process analytics around spend management, order efficiency, and so forth.

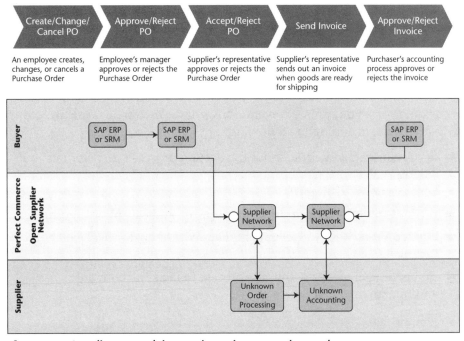

Figure 9-8: Supplier network integration using enterprise services

- Using a process orchestration model to bring aboard new suppliers requested by buyer organizations, facilitating the complete workflow and setup between the two entities.

- Alerting and other configurable process monitoring solutions can be applied on top of the services in the network.

Perfect Commerce achieved SAP NetWeaver certification by implementing several service-oriented integration points to SAP business applications using the platform. A services-oriented approach allows both mySAP ERP and SRM customers to take advantage of the supplier network capabilities faster, easier, and with more flexibility than ever before.

A Hypothetical ESA-Based Solutions Architecture for Supplier Networks

Using ESA proved to be a great way for a supplier network provider such as Perfect Commerce to act as an intermediary between buyers and suppliers to facilitate everything from PO processing and approvals through invoice processing and settlement.

This section builds upon the supplier network concept to describe an ESA-based solutions architecture for a hypothetical scenario called the WaveCross supplier network. This scenario will be used along with others to illustrate some of the features of SAP's NetWeaver platform throughout Part III of this book.

Figures 9-9 and 9-10 show the candidate technical solutions architecture for the WaveCross supplier network. The goal is to leverage multiple features of SAP NetWeaver to integrate the WaveCross solutions with SAP and other back-end applications. It also allows WaveCross to create richer composite UIs for customers. As you can see, several ESA principles can be implemented in SAP NetWeaver, including the following:

- Service-oriented integration for transaction processing, including "outside-in" enterprise service models and "inside out" creation of Web Services from existing APIs

- Business process orchestration, monitoring, and exception alerting

- Guided Procedures to facilitate human workflow approval elements of the process

- Embedding analytics within the process to facilitate both automated and human interactions

- User productivity enablement by the ecosystem partner for providing role-based portals and Visual Composer composition points for the buyers and suppliers in the network to develop their own ad hoc analytics user interfaces

As mentioned in earlier scenarios, a number of areas would need to be considered with this type of solution. First, the WaveCross services would need to be harmonized with future models from SAP in the official Enterprise Services Inventory. In addition, customers and WaveCross would have to determine the degree to which SAP NetWeaver should be used to support its own SRM application features and user interfaces. The greater the use, the more ESA-based features that can be seamlessly integrated into the user productivity and BPM environments of their SAP customers. Of course, WaveCross and SAP could also work together to commercialize an xAPP around this process.

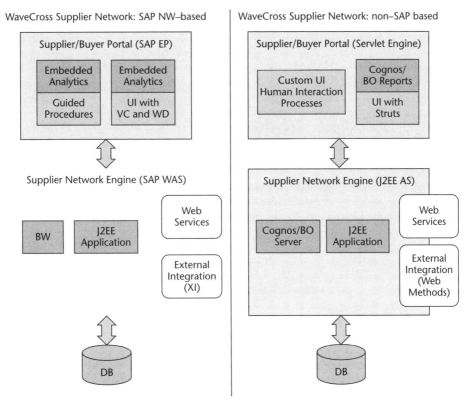

Figure 9-9: Hypothetical supplier network integration architecture developed using SAP NetWeaver

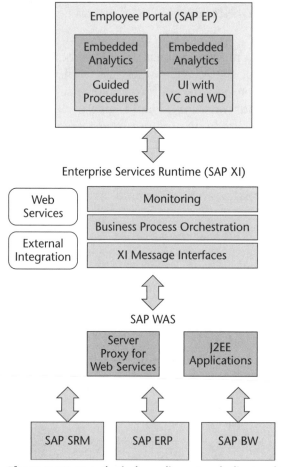

WaveCross Supplier Network Client: SAP NW–based

Figure 9-10: Hypothetical supplier network client architecture enriched with SAP NetWeaver

The Role of These Solutions in ESA Adoption

It is worth noting that each of the scenarios described in this chapter represents an ideal ESA adoption project. The first example involved collaboration between SAP, customers, and a strategic ecosystem partner that wanted to identify high-value process ROI scenarios that could be solved with composite applications. All parties are part of an SAP IVN and are active in helping define SAP's ESA long-term strategy for their industry.

The SAP customer upon which the second scenario is based made the decision to standardize its composition platform on SAP NetWeaver. This customer had specific business process issues that were part of its project portfolio, which became ideal candidates for using the new approach. Part of the solution approach was to create the initial reference architectures, governance strategy, and initial services that could be used for future adoption efforts.

The third scenario is based upon an ecosystem partner that both complements and competes with SAP. This organization has a number of clear integration scenarios with mySAP Business Suite applications that are best implemented using an ESA-based approach. In addition, the composition tools of SAP NetWeaver are ideal candidates for their joint customers to improve user productivity and leverage more embedded process analytics capabilities.

In short, these scenarios represent early potential ESA adoption program pilots and projects as described in Chapter 8. They were discrete projects that solved a clear business need with real ROI. They also represented "low-hanging fruit" in that the projects weren't overly complex or expensive to deliver. Finally, the adopting organizations (and, in some cases, SAP and its partners) worked to add value beyond the specific projects by doing the following:

- Creating reference architectures around SAP NetWeaver's ESA-based capabilities
- Identifying and creating services for future reuse
- Productizing commercial composite applications in areas that fill in SAP white space so that customers can get the dual benefits of a custom-like solution that is pre-integrated, supported, and enhanced as a product

Summary

This chapter illustrated how ESA principles can be used to solve different types of business problems. You saw three SAP NetWeaver-based solution architectures and how they were used to meet specific process requirements and opportunities. The first scenario involved using model-based analytics, alerts, and role-based interfaces to show how process industries can influence sales, quality, and maintenance activities more proactively.

The second scenario involved creating reusable services to compose a variety of customer self-service applications and pricing master data management solutions. Here, the focus was also on creating a reference architecture for future composition based on SAP NetWeaver and Microsoft Office to support the ideal user-productivity scenarios.

The final scenario showed how ESA and SAP NetWeaver capabilities can be used to improve supplier integration through the use of supplier networks. This scenario involved the greatest amount of B2B interactions. This scenario was also extended with a hypothetical architecture to show possibilities for a supplier network vendor and SAP to work together to create rich, end-to-end BPM orchestration, workflow, and analytics-based applications. Part III of this book uses this idea to illustrate some of the development and composition capabilities in SAP NetWeaver to support this WaveCross supplier network scenario.

Some of the most important takeaways from this chapter are:

- There are many ways to leverage the SOA, BPM, and user-productivity features of SAP NetWeaver. It is critical to have a clear business case driving which features to use and when.

- Projects such as these are great candidates for ESA adoption pilots and projects because they offer more efficient solutions to business problems than traditional application and integration coding.

- Ecosystem partners will play a key role in accelerating the realization of ESA because they have clear integration scenarios that can benefit.

- Each solution architecture should solve not only a current process need with real ROI, but also consider longer-term plans for leverage and extension.

- As SAP completes its ESA road map and fills out its official Enterprise Service Inventory, solutions such as these will need to be re-evaluated to ensure the interfaces used adhere to your internal governance process.

This chapter concludes Part II of the book. Part III dives more deeply into SAP NetWeaver to illustrate how some of these solutions can be implemented. Other implementation scenarios that highlight additional ESA principles will also be shown. Part III begins with Chapter 10, which provides an introduction to some of the key development and composition tools in SAP NetWeaver that will be illustrated in this book.

Realizing ESA Through SAP NetWeaver

An Introduction to ESA-Development with SAP NetWeaver

This chapter begins Part III by providing an overview to some of the key ESA-enabling development tools and technologies available in SAP NetWeaver. NetWeaver offers a number of options to create and run applications that use enterprise services, as well as to define, build, and govern the enterprise services themselves. Note that there are many other SAP capabilities that enable ESA beyond what are presented here, and the company has plans to continue to enhance its suite of solutions. As mentioned previously, you can also work with SAP enterprise services using the SOA-based design and composition tools available from other platform vendors.

This chapter focuses on a few NetWeaver capabilities that are then demonstrated in detail in the rest of Part III. From a provider perspective, the range of NetWeaver tools helps you to develop back-end services, create business-level services and processes, and add your services to the ESR. From a consumer perspective, there are multiple tools to help you find and consume services, build UI components, and assemble composite applications that present information and processes to users.

This chapter provides an overview of some of the most important NetWeaver capabilities that can be used in implementing ESA-based solutions. The focus is on creating composite applications with a focus on process orchestration and UI development. Subsequent chapters provide details on how to use many of these key tools through concrete examples and scenarios.

Following are the key development technologies that are introduced in this chapter and then demonstrated through examples later in Part III:

- *SAP NetWeaver* — The core platform functionality itself
- *NetWeaver Developer Studio (NWDS)* — The Integrated Developer Environment (IDE) for building Java/J2EE-based applications
- *Web Services infrastructure and wizards* — Part of the SAP Web Application Server and developer tools used for exposing Web Services
- *eXchange Infrastructure (XI)* — The integration and intermediation platform and associated design-time tools that are now part of the PI usage type
- *SAP NetWeaver Portal (SAP Portal)* — Includes the Portal Content Studio (PCS) and Portal Development Kit (PDK)
- *Composite Application Framework (CAF)* — Used for building composite applications and enabling end-user–driven business processes
- *Web Dynpro* — The technology for building UIs based on models
- *Visual Composer (VC)* — The modeling tool to create analytics applications and other UIs based on services in a user-friendly manner that can be leveraged by both analysts and developers

Following are some additional SAP technologies that enable ESA, which are also covered in more detail in later chapters:

- *Solution Manager* — Platform and tools for configuration of business processes
- *ARIS for NetWeaver* — Tool for modeling business processes

An Overview of ESA-Based Development

Figure 10-1 provides a high-level view into ESA-based development. There are essentially three main elements to consider:

- The repository of services and models
- The back-end applications and components that provide implementations of services
- The development and composition tools used to create services, develop service implementations, and deliver new applications and composites

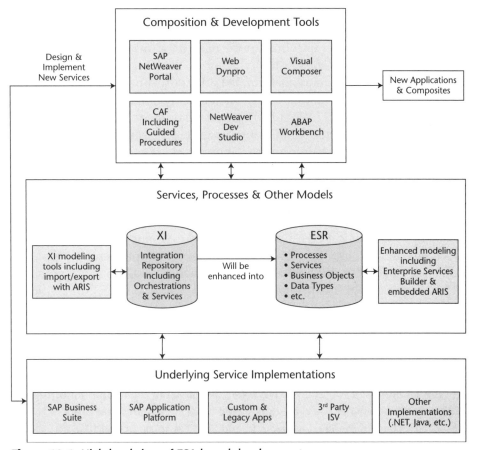

Figure 10-1: High-level view of ESA-based development

As mentioned in Chapter 5, current releases of SAP NetWeaver leverage the XI Integration Repository (now part of the PI usage type in NW2004S) for managing executable process and service models. A number of design-time tools support creating and configuring the items in this repository, which will allow you to use the service mediation features of the platform at run-time. In addition, ARIS process models are supported through synchronization features.

Future releases from SAP will expand the XI repository into the full-fledged ESR. This includes the new business object models, processes, enhanced global data types, and future aspects of the Enterprise Services Inventory. With the release of the ESR will come enhanced modeling tools, including the Enterprise Services Builder and embedded versions of ARIS modeling capabilities. Whether you are starting with XI or the ESR, the concepts are the same in terms of managing your services for use in creating composite applications.

Ultimately, these enterprise service models must be supported by some implementation code. In some cases, this could be through orchestration or integration logic defined in XI. But, for the most part, implementations will be in back-end applications such as R/3, the mySAP Business Suite, future application platform implementations from SAP, other third-party ISV products, or custom and legacy development using virtually any language or platform.

The third layer shown in Figure 10-1 is development tools used to create applications. These include familiar products such as the ABAP Workbench, the NetWeaver Developer Studio, WebDynpro, and the SAP NetWeaver Portal. In addition, there are newer composition tools designed with the ESA world in mind, including CAF and Visual Composer.

These tools can access enterprise services to create new Java- and ABAP-based applications using traditional architectures, as well as more loosely coupled composite applications. Obviously, the ABAP and Java development capabilities are also used to create and expose new implementations of services. As a final reminder, SAP offers additional development technologies, and you can use other platform products such as Microsoft .NET and Office to create composite applications or service implementations as well. The next section introduces the NetWeaver platform architecture that supports this high-level development model.

NOTE Unless noted otherwise, the demonstrations and coverage for the remainder of Part III will apply to NW2004S, which is the foundation for mySAP ERP 2005. This includes the repository based on XI capabilities that are installed as part of the PI usage type. In addition, the focus in Part III is on demonstrating Java-based development technologies because these will be newer to most SAP professionals.

The SAP NetWeaver Platform Architecture

As discussed in previous chapters, SAP NetWeaver is a comprehensive application and integration platform. The core delivery platforms for ESA-based services and applications that use those services are all part of the SAP NetWeaver technology stack (see Figure 10-2). This chapter focuses on three core platform features: the SAP Web Application Server (WAS), SAP XI, and SAP Portal.

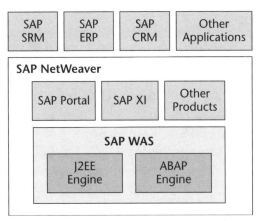

Figure 10-2: SAP NetWeaver platform architecture

XI and SAP Portal themselves run on WAS. SAP back-end application components such as mySAP ERP, SRM, CRM, and the rest of the Business Suite run on the NetWeaver platform. The higher-level development tools and technologies are built on top of these core capabilities. Note that the Web Dynpro run-time, CAF Core services, as well as J2EE- and ABAP-based Web Services, are hosted in SAP WAS. The ESR and enterprise services are hosted on SAP XI. Finally, the CAF Guided Procedures Run-time and portal content are hosted on SAP Portal.

WAS provides the complete foundational infrastructure for developing, deploying, and running all SAP NetWeaver components. It incorporates the ABAP Run-time and the J2EE Run-time. The ABAP Run-time incorporates advanced application server features (such as data access abstraction from specific vendor databases and the concept of a controlled run-time that helps developers focus on business logic rather than infrastructure issues). While the ABAP Run-time, by itself, is rather compelling, only developers working on SAP solutions and products are familiar with it.

One of the big advantages of SAP NetWeaver is its reach to a more critical mass of developers than J2EE technology has amassed. To enable these Java-aware developers to create applications on SAP platforms, SAP built WAS to support both run-times. All technologies that can be leveraged to build ESA-based applications are deployed and run on WAS. The set of technologies include Web Dynpro, SAP Portal, VC, CAF, and XI, as shown in the next section.

Development Tool Architecture

The SAP NetWeaver suite of development tools is based upon a varied set of technologies (see Figure 10-3). The design-time tools for Web Dynpro and Web Services are available for both the Java and ABAP platforms. The Portal Development Kit (PDK) is available for the Java and .NET platforms. The XI tools are a combination of Java- and ABAP-based tools. The tools for building applications using CAF GP, VC, and PCS are Java- and SAP Portal-based.

The strategy behind SAP's decision to support the same tools on multiple language platforms is twofold:

- Provide a means for ABAP developers to work with newer technologies using a familiar language/platform
- Gain a wider acceptance of SAP NetWeaver technology by making it easy for Java and .NET developers to start developing NetWeaver applications

As shown in Figure 10-4, different tools are targeted toward users with different roles in the IT department. Content Administrators can build simple display-only portal content using the Portal Content Studio (PCS). Business experts can develop interactive portal content using VC. Business application developers can develop portal content with sophisticated user interfaces that utilize a variety of back-end data sources using Web Dynpro. Finally, developers who have the Java and .NET skills can build the most flexible portal content.

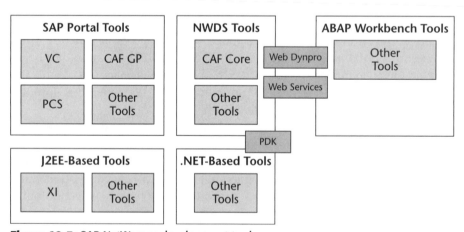

Figure 10-3: SAP NetWeaver development tools

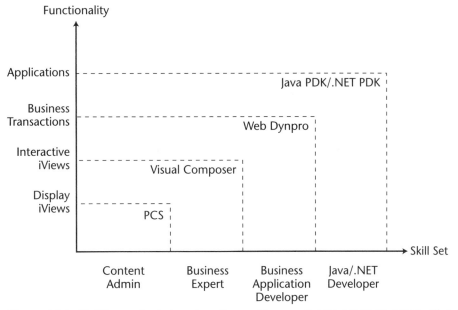

Figure 10-4: NetWeaver tools target audience (Source: © SAP AG 2005–2006. All rights reserved.)

NetWeaver Developer Studio

SAP NetWeaver Developer Studio (NWDS) is an IDE for developing applications for a variety of SAP technologies that run on the NetWeaver platform. NWDS is built on Eclipse, an IDE platform that is familiar to most in the Java developer community. Eclipse is open source software, and a variety of vendors that have Java-based IDEs have converged on using this platform. This section discusses the Eclipse platform to familiarize you with the core concepts underlying NWDS. The various tools that NWDS provides are discussed in later sections.

Eclipse Platform

The Eclipse platform is an IDE that "could be an IDE for anything." This is somewhat synonymous with any framework. *Frameworks* are software components or APIs that can be used by a variety of applications. Similarly, the Eclipse Platform can be used by a variety of IDEs. The platform, in itself, doesn't provide any compelling functionality. The front-end looks like any other

IDE (Microsoft Visual Studio or Borland's JBuilder, for example) that developers might be familiar with (see Figure 10-5). What makes the platform compelling is the way in which new functionality can be built and plugged into the platform, and then work seamlessly as an IDE.

Apart from the menus, the Eclipse Platform IDE has the following generic components. The Navigator pane in the top-left area of Figure 10-5 displays the projects in the workspace and their contents. The top-right area in Figure 10-5 holds the Editor pane. The bottom-right holds the Tasks pane, which shows a list of outstanding tasks. Finally, the bottom-left holds the Outline pane that displays an outline of the content in the Editor pane.

Workspace

When the IDE is opened, it is associated with a default *workspace*. A workspace is a location on the file system that consists of *projects*. While a workspace at a given location could hold projects that are located elsewhere on the file system, a good practice is to create a directory that maps to the workspace, and create all projects under the workspace directory.

NOTE If you are new to Eclipse or the NWDS, a good practice is to create directories that map to the workspace.

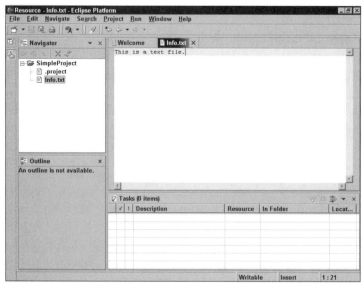

Figure 10-5: The Eclipse platform

Project

Projects are the top-level components in the development environment. They map to a directory on the file system. A development team working on an enterprise Java application would, for example, use one or more Web projects, at least one EAR project, and zero or more Java-based projects. The project knows its personality by its *project nature*. This metadata is stored in a specific file within the project directory, and is created when a new project is created in the Eclipse IDE. Projects are created using a wizard in the IDE.

Perspective

A *perspective* is a selection and arrangement of editors and views that are displayable in the IDE. While the layout of the views can be customized by the user, the set of editors and views that are available for a perspective are predefined. The artifacts in a project can be viewed in various forms in the different perspectives. Different perspectives are suitable for different tasks. Changing from one perspective to another changes the context-sensitive menus and views that are displayed. For example, the Web Services perspective would make available the option to access the Web Service Creation Wizard.

NOTE Changing perspectives changes context-sensitive menus.

View

All panels in the workbench that are not editors are *views*. Views give the user additional information on the environment, or the object that the user is currently working on. For example, the Outline view shows the user the outline of the currently opened file in the editor.

NetWeaver Developer Studio Plug-ins

NWDS provides a comprehensive set of tools to design, develop, and maintain applications in Java and J2EE. As suggested previously, new functionality can be added to the Eclipse workbench using plug-ins. Multiple plug-ins can work in a coordinated manner to provide a certain desired tool/functionality. SAP has built a number of Eclipse plug-ins as part of NWDS that manifest themselves as tools and help in building applications for WAS, including the following (see Figure 10-6):

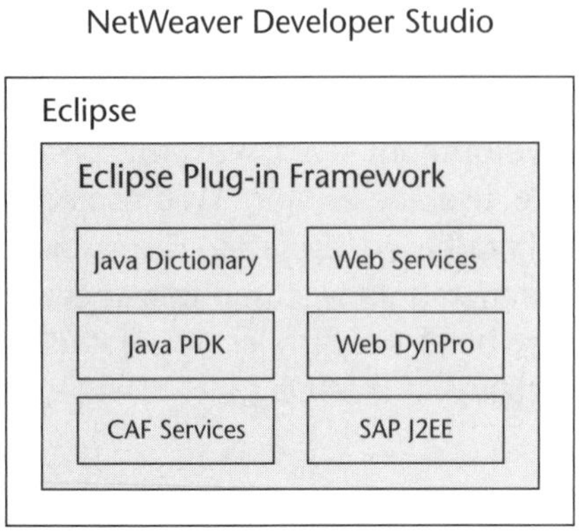

NetWeaver Developer Studio

```
┌─────────────────────────────────────────┐
│ Eclipse                                   │
│  ┌──────────────────────────────────────┐ │
│  │ Eclipse Plug-in Framework            │ │
│  │  ┌─────────────┐   ┌─────────────┐   │ │
│  │  │Java Dictionary│   │Web Services │   │ │
│  │  └─────────────┘   └─────────────┘   │ │
│  │  ┌─────────────┐   ┌─────────────┐   │ │
│  │  │  Java PDK   │   │ Web DynPro  │   │ │
│  │  └─────────────┘   └─────────────┘   │ │
│  │  ┌─────────────┐   ┌─────────────┐   │ │
│  │  │ CAF Services│   │  SAP J2EE   │   │ │
│  │  └─────────────┘   └─────────────┘   │ │
│  └──────────────────────────────────────┘ │
└─────────────────────────────────────────┘
```

Figure 10-6: NetWeaver Developer Studio plug-ins

- *Java Dictionary* — For centralized data type and data structure management
- *Web Services* — For creating Web Services
- *Web Dynpro applications* — For a model-driven approach to building Web applications
- *Portal Components* — For building Java iViews for the SAP Portal
- *Composite Application Services* — For building services for composite applications

Upcoming sections describe these tools. Note that the ABAP Workbench, which provides similar functionality as NWDS and is geared toward ABAP-based development, uses a different platform and is not discussed in this book.

Java Dictionary

The Java Dictionary is a means by which database metadata can be created and managed, independent of the deployment database. Developers can use a single tool for creating and managing database artifacts without having to worry about specific vendor database intricacies. Underlying databases can be swapped with minimal development effort. Java Dictionary has features such as associating text with column names that are leveraged by other NetWeaver technologies such as Web Dynpro. Hence, it is a natural fit for developing NetWeaver applications.

Data types can be created and stored centrally, independent of program code. The data types can then be used by multiple applications and databases. This allows an organization to develop a global repository that can be reused across organizational units. Data types are cross-platform because they are based on XML data types. SAP's Open SQL for Java is a persistence framework that facilitates application portability across various databases. Data access is done using Open SQL with JDBC or SQLJ. Run-time–type checks are done against the Java Dictionary.

The "Java Dictionary" perspective in NWDS (see Figure 10-7) is used to build Java Dictionaries. It provides tools to create data types, structures, tables, and a means to transfer this metadata into a database. Advanced features such as creating indexes on tables and table buffering are also provided. Figure 10-7 shows a table called SIMPLE_TABLE that was created in the Dictionary. The table has been opened so that it can be edited (columns with different characteristics can be added to the table). As of this writing, there is no mechanism to import existing database metadata into a Java Dictionary.

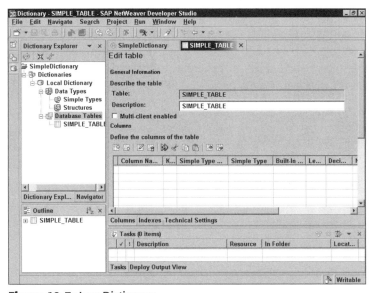

Figure 10-7: Java Dictionary

Web Services

NWDS has a Web Service Creation Wizard you can use to expose a simple Java class as a Web Service (see Figure 10-8). All deployable Web Service artifacts can be generated without writing a single line of code.

Client proxies for the Web Service (both deployable and standalone) can be created. Proxies provide a client API that consumers of the Web Service can use to make Web Service calls. Furthermore, some configuration parameters of the proxy can be modified using WAS administration tools. This feature is helpful in situations where the proxy is generated when the Web Service is hosted in one environment (the developer environment, for example) and then the Web Service and the proxy are moved to a production environment. The Client Proxy Wizard lets the developer choose the Web Services Description Language (WSDL) for the Web Service from a file on the file system, a URL on the Internet, a Web Service on the specified WAS instance, or from the UDDI.

With the Web Service Creation Wizard, either Web Services or virtual interfaces can be created. *Virtual interfaces* are a proprietary SAP mechanism used to expose parts of a Web Service as a separate Web Service. So, multiple views of a single Web Service can be created for consumption by different clients. Apart from hiding some of the Web Service operations, Virtual Interfaces are also useful for renaming operations and parameters, setting default values for parameters, and changing parameter types.

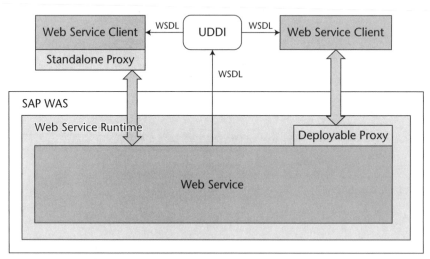

Figure 10-8: Web Services architecture

XI

SAP eXchange Infrastructure (XI) is a cross-system process-integration platform. It follows the well-known hub-and-spoke architecture, sometimes referred to as an *integration broker*. It provides capabilities such as connectivity between systems built on various platforms, message transformation, routing, and asynchronous message delivery. The platform is built using standards such as XML and Web Services. It also provides tools for message and component monitoring, and for modeling cross-component business processes.

The Integration Builder of XI encompasses a set of tools for design and configuration. The Integration Repository is used to store design-time artifacts. The Integration Directory is used to store artifacts related to configuration of design-time elements for a specific deployment. The System Landscape Directory (SLD) is a repository of all software components and their versions in the system landscape of a business. The SLD is used both by the design-time and run-time elements of XI.

Integration Repository

The Integration Repository is a repository for XI design-time artifacts. The artifacts are associated with Software Component Versions from the SLD (see Figure 10-9). Editors and wizards are provided for creation and maintenance for each of the artifacts.

Following are some of the components of the Integration Repository:

- *Message Interfaces* — Represent executable function calls that can be invoked for the purpose of message exchange.

- *Mappings* — Represent the mapping of messages of one format to messages of another format, and built with the Mapping Editor.

- *Integration Processes* — Used for stateful business processes and built using the Process Editor.

- *Integration Scenarios* — Represents the overview for a cross-component process and contains references to the relevant integration processes, message interfaces, and mappings. The Scenario Editor is used to build them.

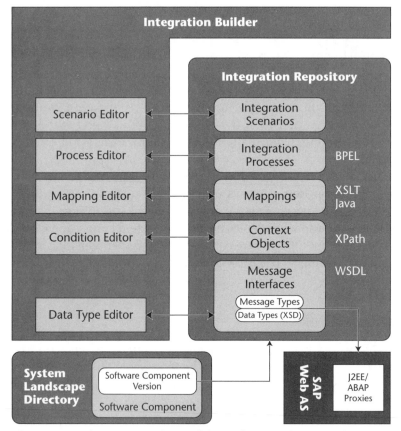

Figure 10-9: the XI Integration Builder and Integration Repository (Source: © SAP AG 2005–2006. All rights reserved.)

Integration Directory

The Integration Directory is a repository for XI configuration artifacts that are configured for a specific system landscape. Configuration artifacts are defined under three categories: Collaboration Profile, Logical Routing, and Collaboration Agreement (see Figure 10-10).

Collaboration Profile models are the units involved in the business process. They also specify the communication channels:

- *Communication Party* — Generally represents a real-world company.

- *Service* — Represents the sender or receiver system of a message. The service can be an actual business system in the landscape, a business service representing an abstract business entity, or an integration process running in the Integration Engine.

- *Communication Channel* — Contains the configuration for sender and receiver adapters.

Logical Routing defines how messages are routed from a sender system to a receiver system:

- *Receiver Determination* — Describes the sender and outbound interface for a receiver.
- *Interface Determination* — For a given sender or receiver or outbound interface, this defines the inbound interface used for receiving the message at the receiver.

Collaboration Agreement specifies which particular Communication channels defined in the Collaboration Profile should be used for a given sender and receiver of a message.

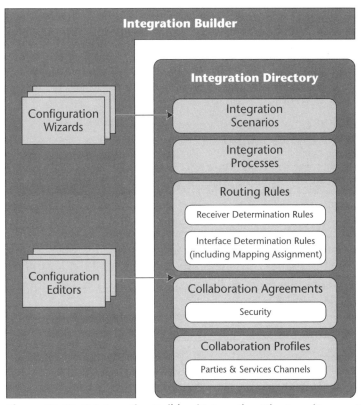

Figure 10-10: XI Integration Builder / Integration Directory (Source: © SAP AG 2005–2006. All rights reserved.)

XI Run-Time

As shown in Figure 10-11, XI Run-time consists of the following three engines:

- Adapter Engine
- Integration Engine
- Business Process Engine

The Adapter Engine is used for integrating heterogeneous system components. While it is a component of the Integration Server, it can also be installed standalone. It can continue to function when the Integration Server is down temporarily. This is because it is equipped with its own queuing and logging services. It provides adapters by which various systems can be connected to the XI Run-time. Following are available adapters and the type of systems with which they are used for connectivity:

- *RFC Adapter* — SAP systems
- *JDBC Adapter* — Relational databases
- *SOAP Adapter* — Web Services
- *Mail Adapter* — E-mail servers
- *FTP Adapter* — FTP servers
- *File Adapter* — Files
- *Marketplace Adapter* — Marketplaces
- *RNIF Adapter* — RosettaNet-based systems
- *CIDX Adapter* — Systems based on the Chemical Industry Data Exchange (CIDX)

The Integration Engine is responsible for receiving and processing XML messages, and then forwarding them to the receiver systems. Specifically, incoming messages are evaluated for collaboration agreements, the receiver system is determined, and mapping of the incoming messages to a format acceptable to the receiver system is done.

While messages must pass through the Adapter Engine before they are sent or received by the Integration Engine, there is an exception to this rule. Using the Proxy Run-time, senders and receivers can bypass the Adapter Engine. In this case, the XI protocol (the native protocol of the Integration Engine) is used for communication. SAP WAS has a built-in Proxy Run-time in which proxies can be executed. Proxies are a mechanism by which you can build applications using a native language API without having to worry about the task of conversion of native language objects to XML, and vice versa, and the destination for messages.

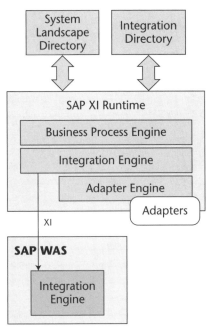

Figure 10-11: XI Run-time architecture

The Business Process Engine is the run-time environment for executing integration processes. An *integration process* is a cross-component process that spans across application and enterprise boundaries. Integration processes are created using a Graphical Editor, which is part of the Integration Builder, and are stored in the Integration Repository.

SAP NetWeaver Portal

The SAP NetWeaver Portal (SAP Portal) is being positioned by SAP as the platform by which all SAP applications can be accessed using a Web browser. SAP Portal runs on top of SAP WAS (see Figure 10-12).

In recent years, businesses have embraced portal technology for some obvious reasons. Portals allow interfaces for various applications and back-end systems to be componentized and made available for users over the Internet. Componentization of application features facilitates re-usability of IT assets. Portals allow these components to be exposed to users based upon their roles or relationships with the organization. Hence, users are able to access multiple applications and data from multiple back-end systems using a Single Sign-On (SSO). Portals also allow end user personalization.

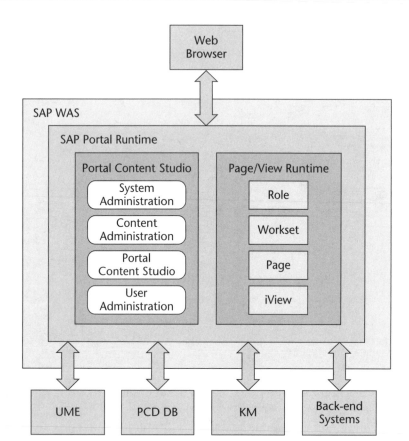

Figure 10-12: Enterprise portal architecture

The core component used for building content in SAP Portal is the *iView*, which is similar to a portlet, for those who are familiar with Java-based portal technologies. Apart from iView, other significant objects in the portal are pages, layouts, roles, worksets, business objects, and business object operations. Following is a brief description of some of the key components:

- *iView* — Smallest unit of UI-based information
- *Page* — A set of coherent iViews
- *Workset* — A set of pages of related tasks
- *Role* — A person's responsibilities in an organization

The two main tools that are used for building content are the PCS and the PDK.

Portal Content Studio

The Portal Content Studio (PCS) is a tool to create and manage all portal content. It is accessed using a Web browser, and is available when SAP Portal is installed. It consists of a set of templates, wizards, and editors by which content can be created and organized (see Figure 10-13). Users are allowed access to only the content that they are authorized to view.

Portal content is stored in the Portal Content Directory (PCD). The contents of PCD are represented by the *Portal Catalog*, a hierarchical tree structure in the PCS interface. The Browse and Search tabs of the Portal Catalog area facilitate browsing and searching of portal objects. The Navigation area displays tabs that correspond to areas of functionality in the portal for which the user is authorized. For example, a user with the Administrator role would, at a minimum, see the Content Administration, User Administration, and System Administration tabs.

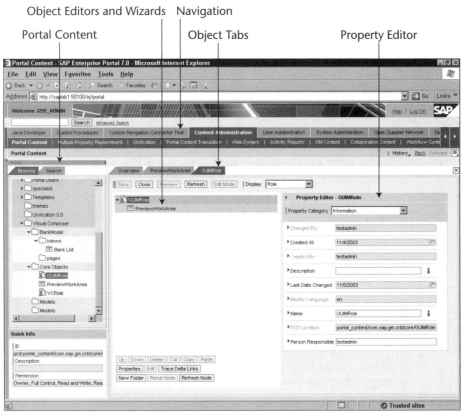

Figure 10-13: Portal Content Studio (PCS)

Objects in the catalog, when selected, have context menus for opening and editing the object and for editing the object's permissions. When an object is opened, a tab corresponding to the object is opened in the Objects Tabs area. Multiple objects can be edited simultaneously by switching between their tabs. Wizards for creating content and editors for managing content are displayed in the Object Editors and Wizards area. Properties and attributes for some of the objects can be edited using the editor that is displayed in the Property Editor area.

Portal Development Kit

There will be numerous occasions when the iViews created using wizards and templates provided in the PCS are inadequate for a certain business requirement. Here's where the Portal Development Kit (PDK) is useful. PDK is a business package that incorporates a set of tools, samples, and tutorials that can be deployed on the SAP Portal and viewed in a Web browser.

A second element of the PDK is tools in an IDE that facilitate development of custom iViews. The Java PDK comprises an Eclipse Plug-In that can be used to develop Java-based iViews. The .NET PDK consists of similar tools for the Microsoft Visual Studio .NET. This book presents only material relevant to the Java PDK.

Java PDK

The Java PDK tool can be accessed from the "Enterprise Portal" perspective of NWDS (see Figure 10-14). It provides a means to create Portal Application projects. When the portal application project is created, a number of directories and files are created in the project directory. The structure and naming conventions used in the directory layout provide for standardized locations where development artifacts can be stored. Also, this layout facilitates packaging of a built portal application. `portalapp.xml` is the Deployment Descriptor for the portal application.

Portal Components have a lifecycle that is similar to that of servlets. PDK provides wizards to create various portal components. The wizard creates the appropriate shell for the class, which can then be modified to add functionality. In addition, the newly created component is added to `portalapp.xml`. The PDK also provides the mechanisms to build the portal project, as well as to package and deploy the portal application. Portal applications are packaged as files with a `.par` extension.

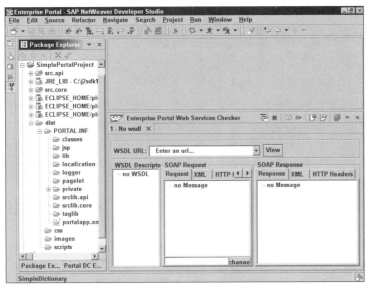

Figure 10-14: A look at the perspective in NWDS

Portal components are developed using Java, JSPs, cascading style sheets (CSSs), and so on — technologies familiar to Java developers. However, portal components are built on a framework that is built on top of Java servlet technology — similar to building a servlet application using the Struts framework. Views and view layouts are created using JSPs. UI controls in JSPs can be created using HTML-Business (HTML-B) for Java. HTML-B is implemented as a custom tag library by SAP, and the custom tags can be used in JSPs. Alternately, they can be created using HTML-B Java APIs. *Lifecycle methods* are those that are used for initializing data on a page, processing user data, or determining navigation logic, and are implemented in an `AbstractPortalComponent`, `DynPage`, or `JSPDynPage`. Once a portal application is deployed to a portal, its components then become available for use in the PCS.

Composite Application Framework

According to SAP, "Composite Applications are user-centric applications supporting highly collaborative and dynamic business processes which span several functional areas across and beyond organizations." The SAP Composite Application Framework (CAF) is the framework by which SAP supports its notion of building composite applications. CAF is a methodology and a set of tools used to build and manage composite applications in a standardized way. The key elements of CAF are Processes, UIs, and Services (see Figure 10-15).

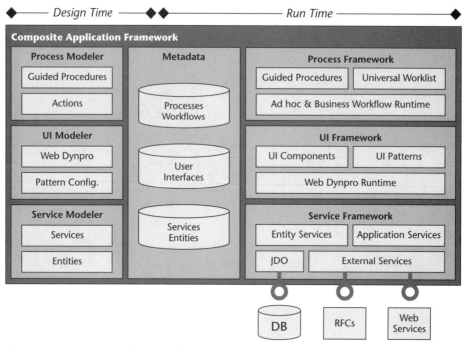

Figure 10-15: Composite Application Framework architecture (Source: © SAP AG 2005–2006. All rights reserved.

From a user's perspective, CAF provides all the advantages that a portal provides — supporting new roles, presenting data from multiple sources, and providing for a familiar and consistent user experience. Also, it provides for user-driven, workflow-like, collaborative business processes. Users who have the required authorization can monitor and adapt processes with relatively little effort because the features are built into the framework.

From a technical perspective, CAF applications are built using services provided by different applications and components. Services are composed and complemented with new application logic and user interfaces. CAF applications are loosely coupled with the services that they consume. They support user-driven business processes, and have a lifecycle independent of the backend systems.

Concepts

CAF, like many of the newer SAP technologies, is model-driven. The Guided Procedure (GP), which defines the steps in a business process using GP objects, is first modeled. GP objects are re-usable, pluggable objects, and are the key components that enable the flexibility and adaptability of CAF. A data model is then created in support of the business process. Finally, the portal UI navigation for end-users is modeled. All of the modeling artifacts are created during design time and are used by the run-time during execution of the process.

CAF provides the following tools to help in building the aforementioned models:

- *Guided procedure modeling* — Guided Procedures (GP)
- *Data/service modeling* — Service Modeler
- *Portal work center navigation modeling* — Web Dynpro and UI Patterns

The Service Modelers and Web Dynpro are plug-ins to SAP NetWeaver Developer Studio. GPs and UI Patterns are accessible using a Web browser for design-time development. All Web Dynpro components run in the Web Dynpro Run-time. GPs run in the GP Run-time. Services run in the CAF Run-time. All run-times are components of SAP WAS.

Guided Procedures

Guided Procedures (GPs) are a set of tools for modeling and executing user-centric workflows. GPs provide tools for business specialists to implement business processes. End users of the processes are guided through the navigation and execution of a collaborative process and, hence, are able to understand the context of the process better.

Each process in which a user is involved is defined by a *work package*. Outstanding work packages (where a user must take some action) are displayed in the user's GP inbox. This provides an entry point for a user to access the work item UI for the process, and to finish outstanding actions. Once the user finishes the process step, the work package is no longer displayed, unless a subsequent action is required by the user.

The three main elements of a GP process are Callable Objects, Actions, and Blocks A *Callable Object* is the implementation of an Action. An *Action* is somewhat similar to a Java interface. While business experts work with Actions to build their business processes, Callable Objects are implemented by developers and are then used by Actions. Figure 10-16 shows the start page of GP Designer, where you use all these objects and store them in a repository that has a file system–like structure.

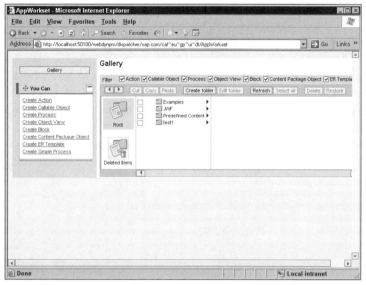

Figure 10-16: GP example

Composite Application Services

The Services Modeler (see Figure 10-17) is used for developing services for use by CAF applications. It is available under the "Composite Application Services" perspective of NWDS. Three types of services can be built using this tool: entity services, application services, and external services. The External Services Modeler provides a means to access external services such as RFC calls and Web Services. RFCs and Web Services can be imported, and then made available for CAF front-ends as CAF services.

Entity Services represent basic CRUD (Create, Read, Update, Delete) operations that can be done on entities in a database. The Entity Services Modeler is a tool for creating Entity Services and their relationships to one another. The tool captures metadata that is then used to create tables and their relationships. Metadata is also used for automated code generation. Table data can be stored in multiple locations. Infrastructure features such as collaboration, authorization, and logging and tracing are built into the framework.

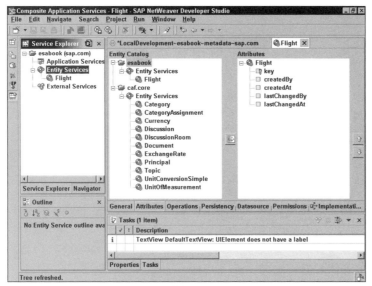

Figure 10-17: CAF Services Modeler

The Application Service Modeler is used to create Application Services. In CAF, Application Services represent the services through with the user interface elements can access Entity Services. They contain business logic and can be exposed as Web Services. Infrastructure features such as collaboration, authorization, logging, and tracing are built into the framework. A detailed explanation of the Services Modeler and how to use it are provided in Chapter 13.

User-Interface Patterns and Web Dynpro

User Interface Patterns are templates that encapsulate commonly used UI elements and, hence, can be used for rapid implementation of UIs. In CAF, the UI patterns are provided as part of the Web browser–accessible development environment. Where available, patterns are not adequate for an application; Web Dynpro can be used to develop custom UIs. Figure 10-18 shows an example of one of the patterns, Object Selector, a pattern that has a search control and a list control. Also, shown on the left part of the figure are other patterns that are available.

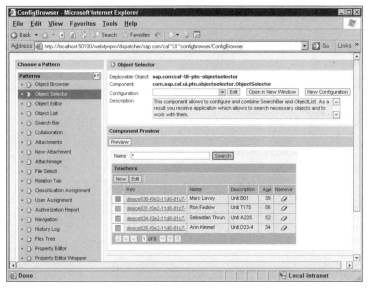

Figure 10-18: UI Patterns example

Web Dynpro

Web Dynpro is a framework for building Web-based UIs in SAP NetWeaver. For readers who are from a Java background, it is similar to Struts, a framework for building Web applications using the JSP/servlet technology of J2EE. While Web Dynpro and Struts both provide the means to create Web applications, they are different in many ways. Web Dynpro does not use servlet/JSP technology.

Web Dynpro provides declarative and graphical tools (discussed later in this section) for most of the development work (see Figure 10-19). It follows the Model-View-Controller (MVC) paradigm, which provides a clear separation between the user interface, the controller logic, and the model representing data. The declarative nature of development artifacts facilitates a client-independent programming model. Once a UI screen is developed, it can be delivered to various clients such as desktop browsers or PDA browsers through configuration rather than mere development. The notion of Developments Components (DC) that is built into the framework helps developers build reusable components that can be used by various applications.

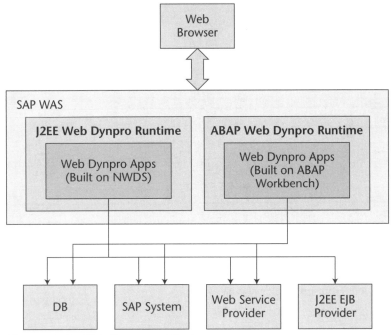

Figure 10-19: Web Dynpro architecture

Web Dynpro provides tools for "what you see is what you get" (WYSIWYG) development for UI and for navigation. This makes it easy to modify current behavior. Code is generated from design-time artifacts. Event-handling is the only area where code might need to be written. Features such as on-the-fly internationalization and client-side input data validation are built into the framework.

The Web Dynpro Run-time is a component of SAP WAS. All Web Dynpro-deployable objects and DCs run within the Web Dynpro Run-time. The run-time provides a series of hooks in which the components run. The hooks are called by the run-time a number of times during the request-response cycle, as defined by the Phase Model.

Web Dynpro Plug-in

The Web Dynpro tools of NWDS support the development of all aspects of a Web Dynpro application, starting with development of components through deployment and testing. Web Dynpro relies heavily on a model-based approach to Web application development through the use of wizards for creating Web Dynpro objects and capturing artifacts as metadata. Because Web Dynpro is based on the MVC concept, all tools are geared toward building components that constitute the model, the view, and the controller. Web Dynpro tools are accessed in the Web Dynpro perspective of NWDS (see Figure 10-20).

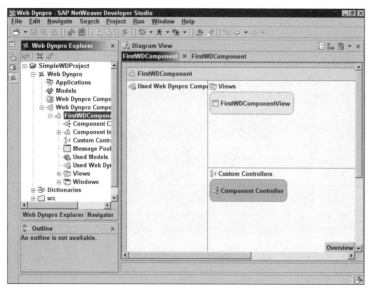

Figure 10-20: The Web Dynpro plug-in in the NWDS

Web Dynpro Explorer displays the logical structure of a Web Dynpro project. The project can be either standalone or a DC project. The intent of the DC is to be able to package the Web Dynpro artifacts as components and, hence, make them available for reuse by multiple applications. The significant elements of a Web Dynpro project are Application, Component, Component Controller, Model, View, and Window. All these elements can be created using wizards that can be triggered from the Web Dynpro Explorer (see Figure 10-20). Also, the elements can be opened for editing or deleted. The Java Dictionary is available through the Web Dynpro Explorer and can be used for manipulating the dictionary. For more details on using the tools, see Chapter 14.

The View Designer is used for creating screen layouts using a WYSIWYG editor. Many categories of interface elements are provided. For example, simple UI elements such as `InputField` and `Label` are provided in the Standard Simple category, whereas sophisticated UI elements such as charts are provided in the Business Graphics category. The Navigation Modeler is used to define logical views and to define the navigation logic between views.

All View Controllers, Component Controllers, and the Model have a *context*. The Context Editor is used to create the structure of the tree in a context, and also to define the data binding between various contexts and models.

The Data Modeler tool provides an overview of all elements of a Web Dynpro component. It also provides support for other development tasks, some of which are available in other Web Dynpro tools (such as Web Dynpro Explorer and View Designer). The Data Modeler can be used to create views, custom controllers, and models; add an existing model; embed an existing component; and to create data links between various elements.

Visual Composer

The Visual Composer (VC) is a browser-based, lightweight modeling tool that enables code-free development of portal components (see Figure 10-21). It is intended for use by business experts. Users can customize and reconfigure applications rapidly in this environment.

Design-time metadata is stored in a relational database. The design-time environment requires the Microsoft XML parser and Adobe's SVG plug-in for Internet Explorer. Metadata is used to generate code for various compilers/run-times. Examples of compilers are HTMLB and Flex. The generated artifacts can then be packaged and deployed to SAP Portal. To access data, whether from SAP or non-SAP systems, VC uses the Connector Framework of the SAP Portal during design-time. iViews that are built in VC use the same framework to access data during run-time.

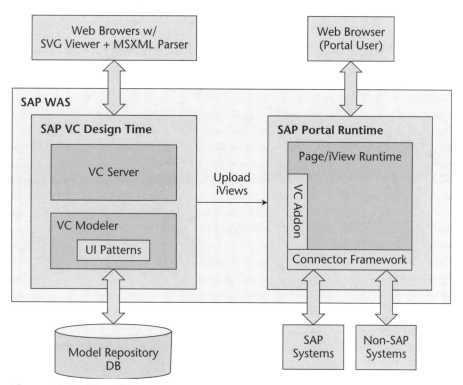

Figure 10-21: VC architecture

Visual Composer Modeler

Following are the four main areas in the VC Modeler (see Figure 10-22):

- *Main menu and Toolbar pane* — Where typical IDE features such as creating, opening, building, and deploying models are available
- *Workspace* — Where models and screen layouts are created and edited
- *Task Panel toolbar* — Where tools for finding data, deployment, configuration of elements, and so on are available
- *Toolset* — Where tools corresponding to the selection in the Task Panel toolbar are displayed

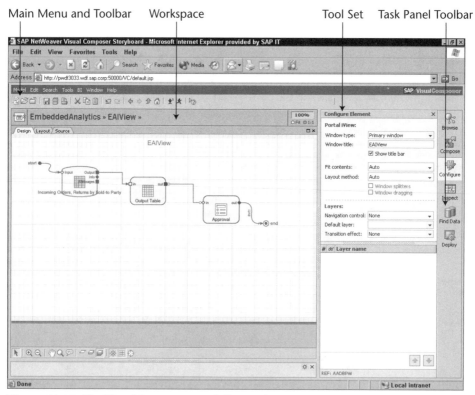

Figure 10-22: The Visual Composer modeling environment

VC *packages* are a placeholder for all elements that are needed to build an *iView*. Packages consist of *pages,* which in turn consist of one or more iViews. All these elements can be created in the VC Modeler (see Figure 10-22). The iView here holds all the metadata for the layout, UI elements, and data source. The modeler leverages the back-end systems and the related infrastructure in the portal to model data sources. The interface provides a mechanism to connect to the portal, and then access specific back-end services. Wizards are provided to create UI elements directly from the back-end service interfaces. The created UI elements can also be further tweaked. For detailed explanation of using the VC modeler, see Chapter 14.

Summary

SAP provides a variety of tools that can be used to build enterprise services and applications that leverage these services. Custom back-end services can be built using the NetWeaver Developer Studio or ABAP workbench. Existing assets built on legacy systems can be exposed as services using the SAP eXchange Infrastructure. Business process models built using these services can then be stored in the Enterprise Services Repository and used by applications supporting various business units across the enterprise.

Data can be exposed to users through the SAP NetWeaver Portal. You have a choice of tools that can be used to create content for the portal. The various tools and frameworks are geared toward users with varying technical skills. Content can be developed through templates and wizards using the Portal Content Studio. User interfaces that are more complex and sophisticated can be developed using the Portal Development Kit or Web Dynpro. Business Analysts can also develop applications through modeling using Visual Composer, the code-free modeling tool. Finally, user-centric business processes can be developed using the Composite Application Framework.

The remainder of Part III will take a closer look at many of these tools and how to use them, beginning with the discussion in Chapter 11 on creating enterprise services.

References

The following were used as general references and are good sources for additional information on SAP NetWeaver development tools and technologies:

J. Weilbach and M. Herger, "SAP xApps — and the Composite Application Framework," Galileo Press, 2005.

A. Goebel and D. Ritthaler, "SAP Enterprise Portal — Technology and Programming," Galileo Press, 2005.

J. Stumpe and J. Orb, "SAP Exchange Infrastructure," Galileo Press, 2005.

CHAPTER 11

Developing Enterprise Services

To move toward an ESA-based landscape and architecture, one of the important steps is to figure out how to service-enable existing applications and build new applications or components that are service-enabled. Existing assets include any application that currently solves a business problem. A typical system landscape consists of SAP, third-party ISV packages, and custom-developed systems. This chapter provides details on service-enablement of both SAP and non-SAP systems. Once service-enabled, the services can become enterprise services by adding the artifacts to the Enterprise Services Repository (ESR). Concepts surrounding SAP's Enterprise Services Infrastructure are also explained in this chapter.

SAP promotes two approaches to the development of Web Services–enabled interfaces: *inside-out* and *outside-in*. In the inside-out approach, you start with existing application functionality and then expose it as services. This is fairly easy to do when you have current interfaces, APIs, objects with public methods, integration schemas, and so forth. In fact, many IDEs offer tools and wizards to create Web Service interfaces based on this content. You will see how the SAP development environments support these capabilities for ABAP and Java developers later in the chapter.

Basically, current system implementations drive the details of how services are defined and created with the inside-out approach. This can limit your flexibility in terms of leveraging these services to compose other enterprise services, support business process models, or meet the needs of multiple service consumers.

In the outside-in approach, high-level business processes and enterprise services are first defined independently of any implementation details. This is followed by the implementation of the functionality and/or lower-level services needed to support the newly defined enterprise service model. This approach means that your service model is defined for ideal flexibility and use in multiple service-consumption scenarios. Note that your new service models can still be implemented based upon existing application functionality and services, or by developing new implementations.

NOTE The inside-out approach starts with existing IT assets and defines services based upon their details. The outside-in approach defines services independently of any implementation. The implementation can then be created in parallel using existing assets, or through new development.

The Enterprise Services Infrastructure

The SAP Enterprise Services Infrastructure defines the capabilities that NetWeaver offers to build, maintain, run, and manage enterprise services. It provides a single service-based infrastructure and has the following features:

- Provides a uniform mechanism to define and use services — all services are denoted by message interfaces that can be invoked by client applications in a similar way
- Uses Web Services standards to ensure interoperability with various systems within and outside the enterprise
- Provides services for use by UIs and in application-to-application (A2A) and business-to-business (B2B) models
- Provides synchronous and asynchronous modes
- Clearly separates service interface definitions from their underlying implementation
- Facilitates reuse of existing business application assets
- Provides a Global Data Type model
- Provides a Business Object model

The high-level Enterprise Services Infrastructure and the environment that it operates in are shown in Figure 11-1. The ESR was introduced in Chapter 5. It is the centralized repository that holds all enterprise services and related models offered by SAP, and can be extended by customers and partners for their own use. Included in the ESR are *Global Data Types* (*GDTs*) that define the integration standards used across different applications, integration points, business objects, and services. Ideally, these adhere first to international standards and are then extended as needed.

The ESR also contains a new *Business Object Model* that represents the new application structure for assembling SAP solutions based on real-world business entities. Like any objects, they provide functionality through methods and interfaces. These business objects are hosted as part of the future SAP application platform and can be leveraged by multiple services and applications. *Operations and Interfaces* are the standardized interfaces used to interact with enterprise services.

The ES Builder is an extension of the XI Integration Builder, and the ES Configuration is an extension of XI Configuration capabilities. These tools help in defining enterprise services and configurations. The Enterprise Services Runtime is hosted on the XI Integration Server. It relies on information from the Integration Directory to make execution-time decisions. Notice in Figure 11-1 that new service implementation can be created using either the ABAP Workbench for ABAP development or NWDS for Java development. This chapter discusses only the tools for the Java-based platform in detail. Also, service implementation could done on both SAP and non-SAP systems.

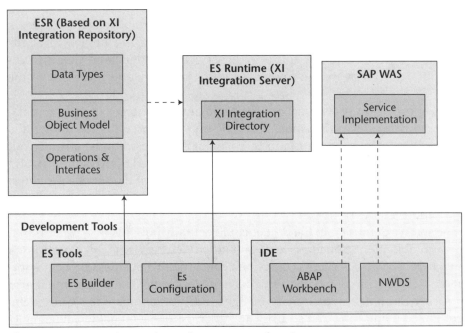

Figure 11-1: Enterprise Services Infrastructure and environment

It is important to note that SAP is in the process of defining and developing many new tools and capabilities for the Enterprise Services Infrastructure. Examples include a new enterprise services browser and business object builder. Because these tools will be built on top of the XI platform, developers who are comfortable working with enterprise service concepts through the use of XI Builder tools will find it easy to make the transition.

NOTE SAP will be evolving the features of the ESR and many of the model management and development tools upon the current foundation provided by XI.

Enterprise Services as Mediated Web Services

In the Web Services paradigm, a Web Service consumer can communicate directly with the Web Service. As explained in Chapter 5, this is not an ideal model. Even though Web Services offer platform and language neutrality, this type of interaction pattern still creates a form of tight coupling similar to what exists in today's client/server environment.

SAP's enterprise services are "mediated" or "brokered" Web Services (see Figure 11-2). Instead of communicating directly with the service provider, clients communicate with the SAP XI Integration Server, which provides a level of intermediation. Based on the configuration, the broker forwards requests from clients to the appropriate service providers, and then (if synchronous) gets the response from the service provider and returns it to the client.

This approach to providing services has many advantages including scalability, robustness, security, manageability, and supportability. It allows the intermediary to handle translations, coordinate orchestrations, abstract out limitations on the client or provider side (such as limited SOAP support), and so forth. The service provider (or the implementation of the service provider) can easily be changed or modified, as long as it adheres to the interface definition supported by the broker.

The service definition in the broker could actually be a business process that uses a combination of business logic and other Web Services. This clearly adds value because various clients could then consume this business process without each of them having to implement the process logic. The broker could also form a synchronous-asynchronous bridge for disparate consumers/providers. Centralized monitoring and security are other features you get when using XI as an intermediary for your enterprise services.

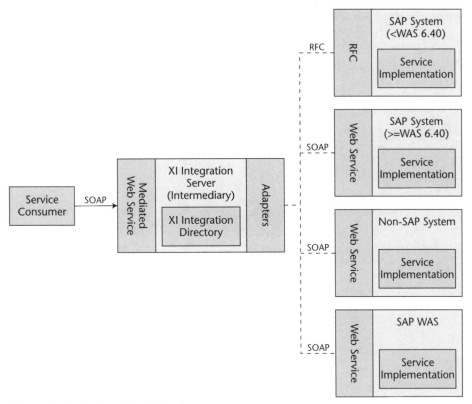

Figure 11-2: Mediated Web Services

Creating a Service Using the Inside-Out Approach

In this section, a Web Service is created for one of the pieces of functionality in the WaveCross supplier network scenario introduced in Chapter 9. The skeletal business functionality for processing purchase orders is first implemented and then exposed as a Web Service. The Web Service is then exposed through its addition into the repository, where it can be invoked through the XI intermediary. Figure 11-3 shows the inside-out development flow for implementing this service.

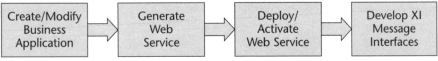

Figure 11-3: Creating a new enterprise service using the inside-out approach

Developing the Web Service

Different platforms offer different ways of developing Web Services. Business functionality that is written in Java is typically encapsulated in Plain Old Java Objects (POJOs) or in Enterprise Java Beans (EJBs). Apache AXIS and ActiveSOAP are examples of open source frameworks that can be used in Web-Service–enabling Java applications. This section details the development and deployment of a Web Service on the NetWeaver platform for a POJO that encapsulates some business functionality.

As shown in Figure 11-4, the steps for creating the Web Service are as follows:

1. *Implement the business application.* This also encompasses scenarios in which an existing business application is implemented in Java.

2. *Generate Web Service.* Use the NWDS Web Service Wizard to generate the Web Service.

3. *Activate/deploy Web Service.* Includes NetWeaver capabilities to view a listing of Web Services along with a simple client to test them.

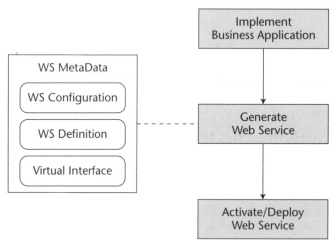

Figure 11-4: Developing a Web Service

Implementing the Business Application

This section explains how to build a sample business application in Java. The `POService.java` class has the implementation for handling purchase order requests. In this scenario, purchase orders that are created in mySAP SRM could be sent to the Wavecross Supplier Network by invoking this service. This example does not go into the details of the existing functionality in mySAP SRM that supports the purchase order process. Stubs and placeholders for the implementation of the actual functionality are demonstrated. This information is seen as sufficient to demonstrate the technical concepts of building some business application functionality, and then exposing it as a service. In fact, the idea is to create a service that could also be invoked by mySAP ERP or any other system you might use to generate a purchase order for a supplier network.

The service uses two Java bean classes that represent a purchase order and a purchase order line item. The corresponding java classes are `Purchase Order.java` and `PurchaseOrderLineItem.java`. If you are not familiar with the Eclipse IDE or NWDS, refer to Chapter 10 for an introduction.

A new Eclipse workspace is first created in `C:\projects\ESABook\ chapter11`. To create a workspace, create the directory structure using Windows Explorer or UNIX commands. To create and open NWDS in the new workspace, append `-data C:\projects\ESABook\chapter11` to the command that opens NWDS. For example, in Windows, create a copy of the NWDS launcher on the Desktop, and then right-click on the new icon to view a *context menu,* and append the string to the Target text field.

Create a Java project called `InsideOut` in the IDE. To create the Java project, in the Resource perspective of the IDE (in the context menu of the Navigator view), select New → Project → Java → Java Project. When prompted to change to the Java Perspective, select the Yes button. All Java classes for this exercise are created in a Java package. Packages are a good mechanism to compartmentalize the several classes that make up a Java application. Create the `com.wavecross.sn.bl` package in the `InsideOut` project (see Figure 11-5). To get to the New Java Package dialog box, in the context menu of the project, select New → Package.

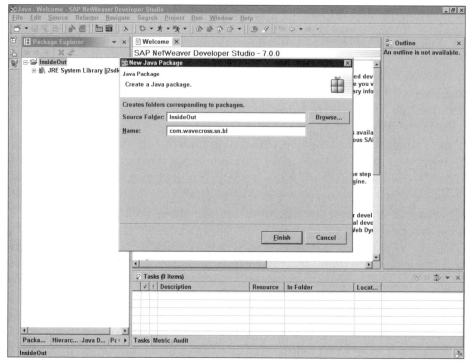

Figure 11-5: Creating a Java package

Create a new Java class called POService.java in the newly created package. The content of the class is as follows:

```
package com.wavecross.sn.bl;

public class POService {
  public POService() {
  }

  public void handlePORequest(PurchaseOrder po) {
    // process purchase data
    // ..
  }
}
```

This class will not compile yet because it has a reference to the Purchase Order class. Now, create the class PurchaseOrderLineItem.java as follows:

```
package com.wavecross.sn.bl;

public class PurchaseOrder implements java.io.Serializable {
  private String id;
  private PurchaseOrderLineItem [] items;
```

```
  private String buyer;
  private String seller;
}
```

Create the class `PurchaseOrder.java` as follows:

```
package com.wavecross.sn.bl;

public class PurchaseOrderLineItem implements java.io.Serializable {
  private String id;
  private String product;
  private String amount;
}
```

Both classes implement the `java.io.Serializable` interface. This is important because `POService` is intended to be exposed as a Web Service. This means classes that represent data and are part of the interface should be able to be sent over the wire. Implementing the `java.io.Serializable` interface is the Java platform mechanism for this.

The getter and setter methods for the member variables in `PurchaseOrder-LineItem.java` and `PurchaseOrder.java` can be generated using the context menu, as shown in Figure 11-6. After writing the code for all the files, save all the files and select Project → Rebuild All to compile all files in the project.

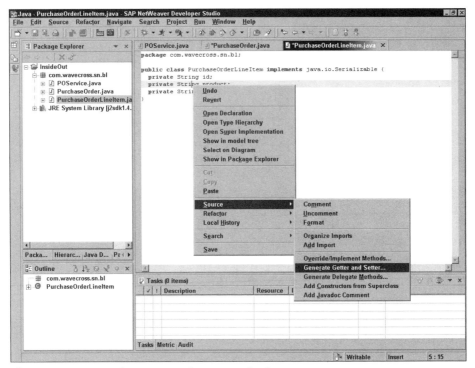

Figure 11-6: Generating getter and setter methods

> **NOTE** Java classes that you intend to expose as part of a Web Service interface should support the java.io.Serializable interface which is the platform mechanism to send objects over the wire.

Generating the Web Service

The Web Service Wizard in NWDS can now be used to create a Web Service from POService as follows:

1. Change to the Web Services Perspective by choosing Window → Open Perspective. Change to the Java Explorer tab of the Java Explorer view.

2. To start the wizard, in the context menu of POService.java, select New → Web Service (see Figure 11-7).

3. Enter the Web Service name and modify the configuration name as shown in the figure. The choices for Default Configuration Type can be used to specify various levels of security for the Web service. For the sake of simplicity, Simple SOAP (which is the default, and provides no security mechanism) is chosen here.

4. The Web Service is created when the Finish button is clicked.

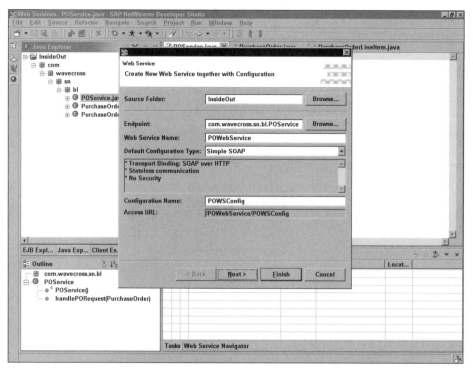

Figure 11-7: Using the Web Service Wizard

All the necessary classes and metadata that are needed to expose `POSer-vice` as a Web Service are created by the wizard at the completion of the previous step. The files that are created can be seen by switching to the Resource perspective. Following are the three significant artifacts that are generated:

- *Virtual Interface (VI)* — A NetWeaver-specific feature that can be used to replace method and parameter names, set standard values for hidden parameters, and make data type conversions. They can be useful to present various views of a single Web Service.

- *Web Service Configuration (WSC)* — These specify features such as communication type and authentication level.

- *Web Service Definition (WSD)* — These specify actual attributes to features specified in the WSD.

Activating and Deploying the Web Service

The Web Service application should now be packaged for deployment to the application server. Java applications that are to run on an application server are typically packaged as either Web Archive (WAR) or Enterprise Archive (EAR) files. In this example, the EAR format is used. To package the application, select Build EAR from the project's context menu. This builds the EAR file, `InsideOut.ear`, and places it in the project directory.

To deploy the Web Service application to SAP WAS, first ensure that connectivity information for the J2EE engine is correctly set up. This configuration can be found at the Window → Preferences → SAP J2EE Engine menu (see Figure 11-8). The application can now be deployed using the Deploy option in the context menu of `InsideOut.ear`.

Developing the Mediated Web Service

This section provides details on how to enhance the Web Service that was developed in the previous section into a mediated Web Service. The key to this process is to capture the Web Service metadata into SAP XI and then expose the metadata as a mediated Web Service. Note that according to SAP's road map and vision, SAP XI forms the basis of the ESR. The Enterprise Services Infrastructure is still being defined and developed by SAP. Hence the concepts demonstrated here are useful in an XI setting today, and you will simply need to evolve to whatever new methods come along for exposing your services for mediation.

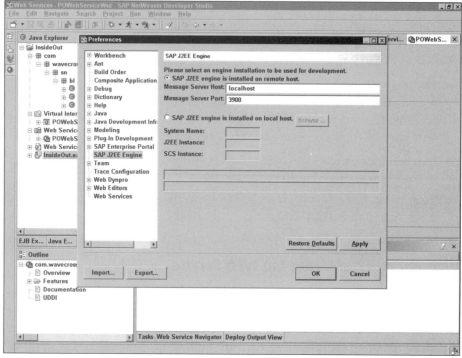

Figure 11-8: SAP J2EE engine settings

NOTE Remember that enterprise services are technically Web Services. The distinction is that enterprise services perform a function that is meaningful at a business level (in this case, processing a purchase order might be an enterprise service you need). By adding them to the ESR through your internal governance process, you can ensure a cohesive model of enterprise services is established in your organization. In addition, all Web Services and enterprise services can be mediated.

Download WSDL Using WebServices Navigator

Web Services Navigator is a tool that can be used to view a listing of deployed Web Services in SAP WAS. It also allows users to download various forms of WSDL for a given Web Service. Both SAP and non-SAP Web services can be tested with sample data without the need to implement a client. Web Services Navigator is a Web-based application that runs on SAP WAS. The home page for Web Services Navigator is shown in Figure 11-9. To open Web Services Navigator, use the URL `http://<hostname>:<port>wsnavigator/enterwsdl.html`.

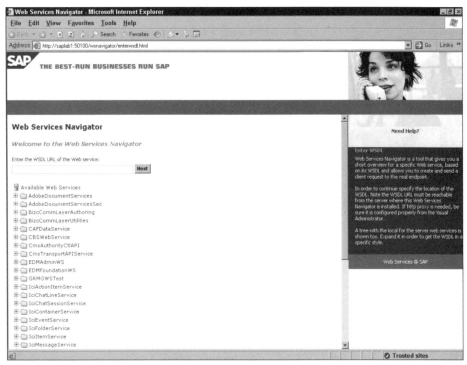

Figure 11-9: Web Services Navigator

POWebService (which was previously deployed to SAP WAS) is displayed as one of the items in the list of available Web Services. Click POWebService to see an overview of the Web Service. Click on the WSDLs menu to open the page from which various forms of the WSDL for the Web Service can be downloaded (see Figure 11-10). *Standard WSDL* refers to WSDL that can be recognized by all Web Service frameworks. *SAP WSDL* refers to WSDL that has additional features that can be interpreted only by SAP WAS. The other significant choices in the WSDL are *RPC* and *Document*. The default is the same as Document. RPC Encoded is an outdated format, and hence will not be discussed.

The WSDL for each of the available options (or at least a part of it) can be seen by clicking the appropriate link. The difference between the RPC-style WSDL and the Document-style WSDL is that, in the former case, the contents of <soap:Body> of messages is constrained by the SOAP specification rules. In the latter case, the contents of <soap:Body> of messages is specified by an XML schema. The Document style is considered more flexible and is predominantly used in most of the Web Services–related specifications.

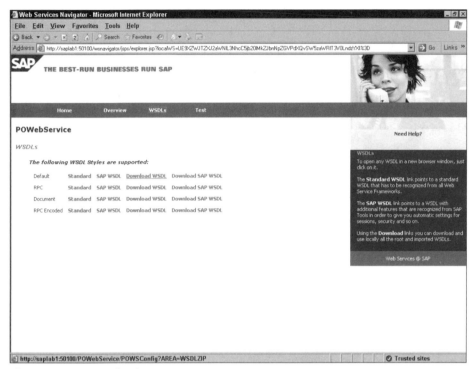

Figure 11-10: Download WSDL

To download the WSDL, click the Download WSDL link for the Default. The download, in fact, is a zip file that consists of multiple WSDL documents — `main.wsdl`, `porttypes/POWSConfig_POWebServiceVi_document.wsdl`, and `bindings/POWSConfig_document.wsdl`. `main.wsdl` includes the other two documents through the use of `<wsdl:import>` tags. `porttypes` refers to the interface/operations of the Web Service and `bindings` refers to how the interfaces can be called.

Create Namespace in XI

Design objects are built in Integration Builder: Design tool. This tool is a Java Web Start application. This tool can be accessed through a Web browser using the URL `http://<hostname>:<port>/rep/start/index.jsp` at the Integration Repository link.

XI uses the concept of namespaces to avoid naming conflicts for objects in the repository. Multiple similarly named objects can exist in the repository. Also, all design objects have to be part of a Software Component Version (SCV). This is the only way by which the XI design objects can be shipped or moved from a development system to a test system. The SAP SRM SERVER 5.5 SCV is used for this example.

A new namespace, http://wavecross.com/xi/XI/InsideOut, is used here. To create the new namespace, open the SAP SRM SERVER 5.5 (or some other modifiable SCV) by selecting Open in the context menu for the SCV. Make the SCV editable by clicking the toolbar button with the tooltip Switch Between Display and Edit Modes. Make the new entry in the Namespaces area and click the Save icon.

NOTE Understanding and using namespaces are key to avoiding naming conflicts in XI today, as well as future implementations of the ESR.

Create External Definition in XI

WSDL, XSD, and DTD are the three mechanisms by which message structures can be defined in XML. These message structures, when defined in the repository, can then be used as the input or output of message interfaces. They can also be used as the source or target structures of message mappings. While there are mechanisms by which the message structures can be defined from scratch, XI also provides a way by which the standard message structures such as WSDL can be imported into the repository. Because the WSDL for the POWebService is available, it can be defined in the repository as an External Definition. External Definitions are one of the many different kinds of design objects that can be built in XI.

To create the External Definition for POWebService (see Figure 11-11), perform the following steps:

1. Navigate to SAP SRM SERVER → http://wavecross.com/xi/XI/ InsideOut → Interface Objects → External Definitions.

2. From the context menu, select New. Enter **SRM2SN_POService** for the name of the External Definition.

3. Because a WSDL is being imported, select wsdl for Category.

4. Now select the porttypes/POWSConfig_POWebServiceVi_ document.wsdl file, which was downloaded in previous sections.

5. Save the object using the Save icon from the toolbar. Make a note of the messages, handlePORequestIn_doc and handlePORequestOut_doc, that are shown in the Messages tab. These represent the input and output messages for the Web Service.

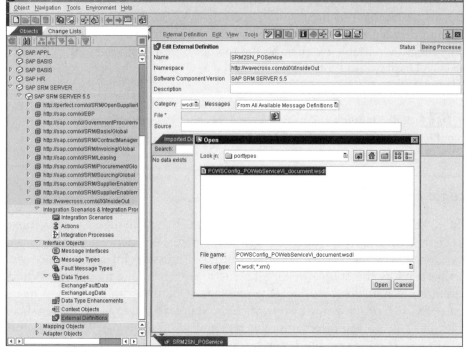

Figure 11-11: Importing WSDL for External Definition

Objects that are simply edited or saved are not available for use by the XI Integration Directory. When new objects are created or existing objects are modified, the changes must be activated (see Figure 11-12). Changed objects are organized by SCV in the Change Lists tab of the tool. Each object can be activated from its context menu. Also, it can be activated alone, or along with other changed objects in the SCV from the Change Lists tab.

Create Message Interfaces in XI

Message interfaces are the standard and platform-independent format for representing interfaces in XI. Interfaces for various formats such as IDoc, RFC, BAPI, and Web Services are represented in the same format in the Integration Repository of XI.

This feature is essential for various reasons. For example, the Business Process Engine (which is a run-time for cross-component business processes) can call into various systems by invoking similar interfaces. The interface for the back-end functionality is separated from the implementation and other layers of the platform can be used to do the integration with the systems that provide the implementation. Developers of front-end applications, as well as business analysts themselves, can use a single interface and repository to explore the capabilities of the IT organization and systems.

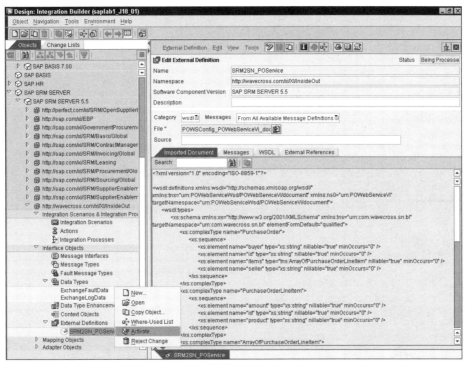

Figure 11-12: Activating an External Definition

Because XI is the broker and never the end point of any message, it needs two interfaces to handle any message that it sees — the inbound and the outbound interfaces. Interfaces can be designated with modes Synchronous or Asynchronous. Interfaces can also be of types Inbound, Outbound, or Abstract. The interface that corresponds to the request is always designated as the Outbound interface. The interface that receives the request is always designated as the Inbound interface. In this exercise, only the Outbound interface for the Web Service is demonstrated. To create the message interface for `POWebService` (see Figure 11-13), navigate to SAP SRM SERVER → `http://wavecross.com/xi/XI/InsideOut` → Interface Objects → Message Interfaces. From the context menu, select New and enter the name as shown in Figure 11-13. Also, select the Category and Mode as indicated. The Input and Output Messages for the interface should now be specified. At the far right of the Output Message row, click the Display Input Help icon. In the pop-up dialog box, select `handlePORequestOut`, as shown in Figure 11-14. Follow a similar procedure for setting the Input Message. Save and activate the object.

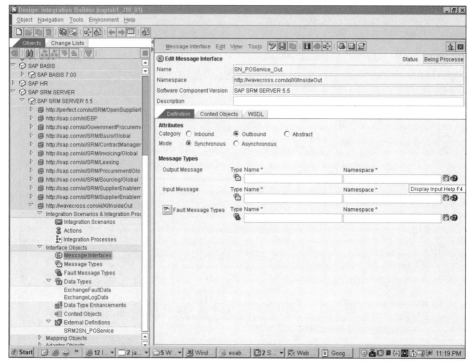

Figure 11-13: Creating a message interface

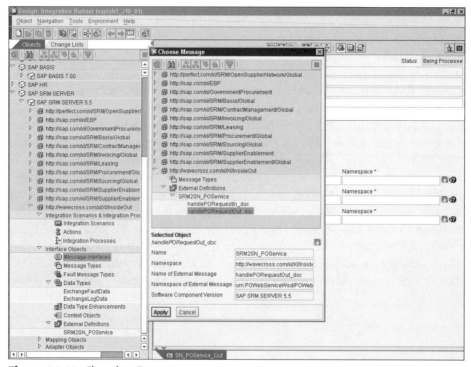

Figure 11-14: Choosing Output message type

Generate WSDL for Mediated Web Service

All message interfaces can be exposed as mediated Web Services. This section demonstrates how to generate the WSDL for the mediated Web Service. The WSDL can then be used by clients to consume the Web Service. Configuration objects are built in XI's Integration Builder: Configuration tool. This tool is a Java Web Start application that can be accessed through a Web browser using the URL `http://<hostname>:<port>/rep/start/index.jsp` at the Integration Directory link.

A number of configuration objects that use the message interface must be built in Integration Directory. These include the sender and receiver Communication Channels, Receiver Determination, Interface Determination, and Receiver Agreement. After this, the Web Service Wizard can be used to generate the WSDL for the mediated Web Service. Select the Tools → Define Web Service menu (see Figure 11-15).

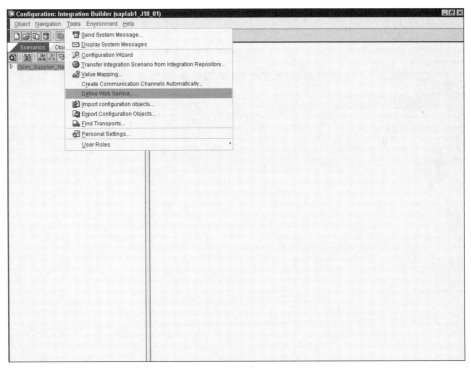

Figure 11-15: Opening the Web Service Wizard

For Step 2, "Specify the URL of the Web Service" (see Figure 11-16), enter the following:

```
http://<hostname>:<port>/XISOAPAdapter/MessageServlet/channel=<party>:
<ServiceName>:<ChannelName>
```

NOTE While going through this process, refer to the "steps" shown on the upper-left of Figure 11-16.

In this entry, `ServiceName` and `ChannelName` refer to the attributes for the sender. For Step 3, use the display input help feature and make the selection as shown in Figure 11-17. For Step 4, enter the following information:

- *Service* — `POService`
- *Interface Name* — `SN_POService_Out`
- *Interface Namespace* — `http://wavecross.com/xi/XI/InsideOut`

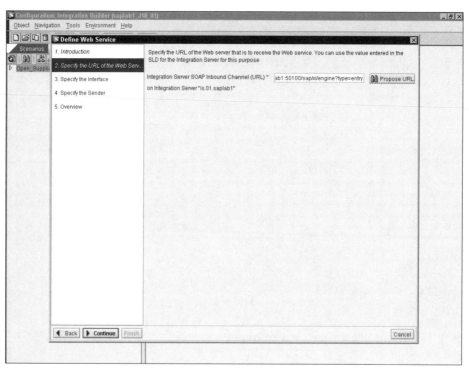

Figure 11-16: Web Service Wizard

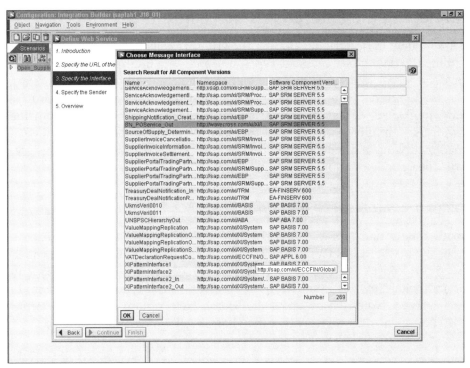

Figure 11-17: Selecting Message Interface

At the end of the final step of wizard, the WSDL is produced.

Creating a Service Using the Outside-In Approach

With the outside-in approach, the message interfaces and related XI artifacts are first developed, followed by the implementation of application functionality. Business analysts and architects can define a business process and the enterprise service interfaces needed to support it from the business point of view. Brand new implementations for the interfaces could then be developed on an appropriate platform, or glue code could be written to hook up the implementation to existing back-end functionality. Figure 11-18 shows the development flow for the outside-in development of services.

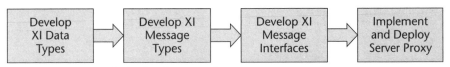

Figure 11-18: Outside-in development for ABAP

Developing the Enterprise Service Interface

As previously indicated, developing the enterprise service interface involves defining the data types, message types, and message interfaces. In the inside-out scenario, the data types and message types were used from a pre-existing external definition. Here, the data types are created from scratch. In our case study, mySAP SRM has to handle an invoice processing request from the WaveCross supplier network. For the sake of demonstration, assume that functionality beyond what is provided by mySAP SRM is needed. In this scenario, the outside-in approach is appropriate.

Create the Namespace and Data Type

Create a new namespace, `http://wavecross.com.xi/XI/OutsideIn`, under the SAP SRM SERVER 5.5 SCV. Now, create the new data type called `InvoiceRequest` (see Figure 11-19) by selecting New from the context menu of data types. Now, add the following elements, all of type `xsd:string`, to the data type. Note that by using the Search Help option of the Type drop-down box, elements of types other than basic XML types can be selected.

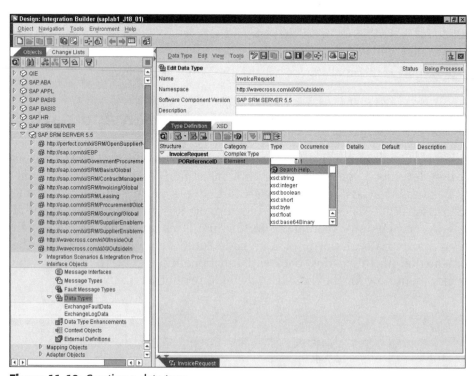

Figure 11-19: Creating a data type

- *ID* — Represents the invoice ID
- *Price* — Represents the invoice price
- *POReferenceID* — Represents the relevant purchase order

Create the Message Type

A message type, also called `InvoiceRequest`, is now created (see Figure 11-20). Use the Display Input Help icon to specify the used data type. Only a single message type is defined here because the intent here is to build an asynchronous interface, and so only an input message type is required. For a synchronous interface, a second message type representing the response is also needed.

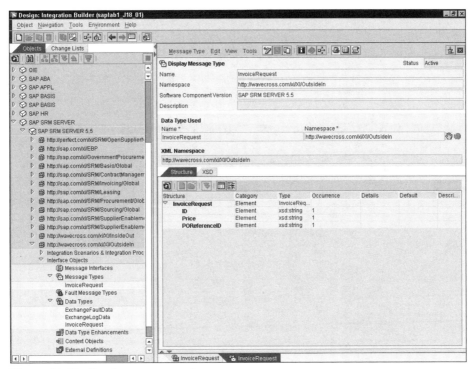

Figure 11-20: Creating a message type

Create the Message Interface and Generate the Proxy

The message interface called `CreateInvoice` is now created (see Figure 11-21). Use the Display Input Help feature to specify the message type. Because this interface is being built as a provider interface, it should be specified with the Inbound category. After the interface is saved and activated, the server proxy can be generated.

The wizard for the proxy generation can be started using the Java Proxy Generation option in the message interface's context menu (see Figure 11-21). The wizard generates a set of files that can be used to do the implementation of application functionality in a JAR/ZIP format. Use the option to create a new archive and specify a name for the archive, `CreateInvoice.zip`. Use the default selections for the SCV and message interface. The following files are created:

- `CreateInvoice_PortType.java` (server proxy interface class)

- `CreateInvoice_PortTypeBean.java`

- `CreateInvoice_PortTypeImpl.template`

- `InvoiceRequest_Type.java` (class representing the message type)

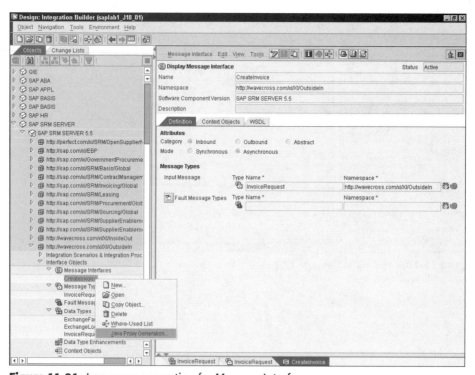

Figure 11-21: Java proxy generation for Message Interface

Developing the Server Proxy

The server proxy is the mechanism by which the implementation for a message interface can be provided. While the service is exposed and mediated by XI, the implementation can be done on a J2EE or ABAP Server. When the XI Run-time receives a request for this service, it forwards the request to the relevant J2EE or ABAP back-end system based upon routing rules. In the case of the J2EE Server (see Figure 11-22), the request passes through the message server and the proxy server to the Java Proxy Run-time (JPR)[1]. The JPR does a lookup in the JPR Registry and forwards the request to the appropriate server proxy application.

The files generated by the proxy generation wizard in the previous section must be packaged along the implementation class, and then deployed to the application server. In this case, the implementation class must implement `CreateInvoice_PortType.java`. The implementation class must be named by appending the string `Impl` to the name of the interface — `CreateInvoice_PortTypeImpl.java`. The application can be deployed using the deploy feature in NWDS, SDM, DeployTool, or Visual Administrator.

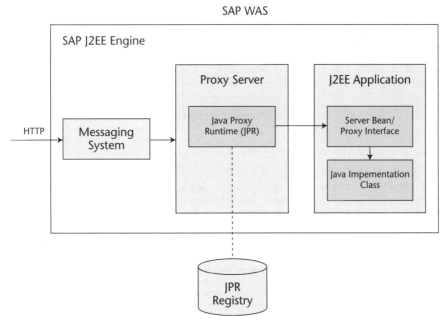

Figure 11-22: Java Proxy Run-time (JPR) environment

After the application is deployed to the J2EE server, the proxy server must be made aware of the implemented interface. This is done using the proxy server servlet. The proxy server servlet and the command that can be done using the servlet can be accessed at `http://<hostname>:<port>/Proxy Server`. Accessing this URL in a browser displays the list of available commands. Use the following command to register:

```
http://<hostname>:<port>/ProxyServer/register?ns=http://com.sap.aii&
interface=CreateInvoice&bean=sap.com/CreateInvoiceProject/CreateInvoice_
PortTypeBean &method=createInvoice
```

You have now successfully created a service interface independently of the underlying implementation. In this way, you could create different implementations for the same service. For example, if different business units require entirely different rules or workflows for handling the purchase order, you could support them both using your same loosely coupled interface definition.

Summary

The Enterprise Services Infrastructure comprises various tools and run-time components that facilitate the development and execution of enterprise services. The declaration of services in a system-independent format in a centralized repository makes it easy for an organization to locate and maintain all its existing business application assets provided a strong governance model is in place. Mediated Web Services provide many advantages over direct client invocations, including centralized monitoring and security, scalability, robustness, manageability, and supportability.

Outside-in and inside-out are two approaches to systematically create enterprise services. In the outside-in approach, platform-independent message interfaces are first defined and application functionality is either built in or invoked through the use of a server proxy. In the inside-out approach, existing application interfaces are imported into the repository and exposed as mediated Web Services.

This chapter explained how to use features in SAP NetWeaver to implement services using both the outside-in and inside-out approaches. Chapter 12 explains how to leverage these services and orchestrate them to create executable business processes.

References

The following were used as references, and are good sources for additional information:

R. Chu, "Service Enable Your SAP Application Components," 2005. Available at `https://www.sdn.sap.com/irj/sdn/weblogs?blog=/pub/wlg/2931`.

1. SAP, "Java Proxies as Receiver," 2005. Available at `http://help.sap.com/saphelp_nw04/helpdata/en/ce/81a797cc9642c8bbef249bfd84dd45/content.htm`.

CHAPTER 12

Orchestrating Business Processes

Applications and services that span the various business systems within a company's IT infrastructure and business partners' IT infrastructures must work together to automate business processes. Process automation is facilitated when the modeling of the business processes is supported by a mechanism to then execute the models. Service orchestration is one technique to enable this to happen. As discussed in Chapter 6, orchestration is a standards-based method to chain together multiple services into a coordinated, executable model. This is really a form of service composition that allows you to expose subsets of business processes as services.

SAP provides various tools and engines for this purpose. SAP Solution Manager provides process content and configuration capabilities that can be customized for a specific company's needs. ARIS for SAP NetWeaver is a third-party product from IDS Scheer that can be used to customize and enrich the SAP process content. SAP XI provides tools to build and configure business process orchestration models and the run-time engine to execute, manage, and monitor them across their lifecycle.

This chapter discusses some of the XI capabilities and related standards that enable service orchestration within SAP NetWeaver. You will see procedures for creating business process models, Integration Scenarios, and Integration Processes using XI. All of these are based around the WaveCross supplier network scenario for creating purchase orders.

Business Level Modeling

One pervasive theme for ESA is to close the gap between business and technology experts through the use of rich, model-driven design and development. As explained in Chapter 6, SAP NetWeaver offers Business Process Experts a set of tools to define business process models that can be bridged into executable definitions by solution architects and development teams. In other words, process definitions that are executed and maintained by IT are based off the same models as seen and understood by the business experts.

A business process architecture is represented in the Process Architecture model. Process Architecture models are based off of base models that are shipped as part of SAP Solution Manager (see Figure 12-1). They are modified and enhanced in ARIS, which is tightly integrated with SAP Solution Manager and with SAP XI. This means that solution models built or updated in ARIS can be synchronized with SAP Solution Manager, and executable models developed in ARIS can be synchronized with SAP XI.

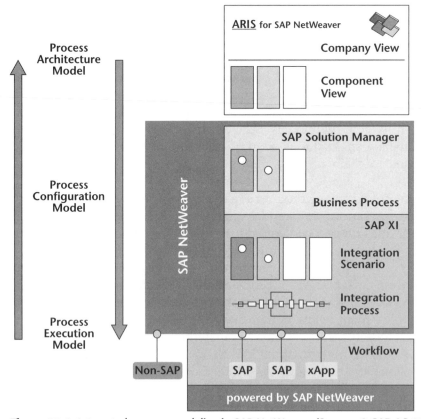

Figure 12-1: Integrated process modeling in SAP NetWeaver (Source: © SAP AG 2005–2006. All rights reserved.)

NOTE As described in Chapter 6, the integration between ARIS and SAP NetWeaver is currently done through synchronization. The companies have announced plans to implement a fully integrated modeling environment for the ESR within SAP NetWeaver that will have ARIS capabilities embedded within it.

SAP Solution Manager not only has predefined business scenarios, but also has the configuration for the entire enterprise system landscape. All available products and systems in the landscape and their capabilities are captured here. Hence, it is an ideal place to store the Process Configuration model. Business scenarios and business processes are represented as Integration Scenarios and Integration Process objects within SAP XI. Business Scenarios and Business Processes that are either built or enhanced in ARIS can be moved to SAP XI. Here, technology teams can then enhance, configure, and test the scenarios and processes, as well as monitor their execution in the SAP XI Run-time environment.

The notion of pre-defined content is a critical SAP NetWeaver differentiator relative to other technologies. *Predefined* content represents business scenarios and business processes that SAP has developed from working with businesses in a diverse array of vertical markets. It also captures the capabilities and built-in functionality in various SAP products. Hence, it gives a jump-start to process implementations. Figure 12-2 shows an example of the predefined content for the Processing Purchase Order business scenario in SAP Solution Manager.

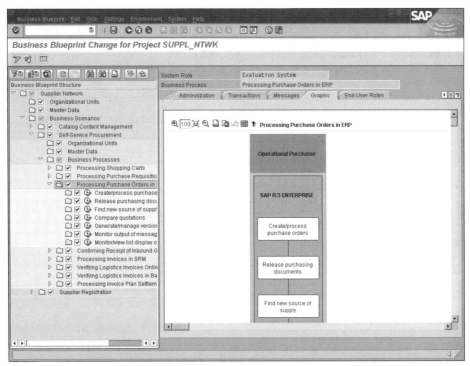

Figure 12-2: Example of business process content in SAP Solution Manager

Prerequisites to Effective Business Process Orchestration

There are two key requirements to effectively developing executable process models. First is establishing a governance program to manage all the underlying assets that you will build upon. Second, there is a need for technology standards that allow executable models to be developed in a platform-neutral way. These are discussed in the following sections.

Governance of IT Assets for Business Process Modeling

Earlier chapters have discussed the governance imperative for successful ESA adoption. It bears repeating that technical capabilities for modeling executable processes are diminished if the raw materials you have available to create your models are not reliable, coherent, consistent, or discoverable. An effective governance program ensures that the underlying models and assets used to build process orchestrations are well thought-out, managed, versioned, and documented; adhere to corporate policies; and are communicated across the enterprise.

SAP has been effective in creating an initial set of models in the ESR that you can use as a baseline for launching your own governance program. Recognize that the key to SAP's approach was creating the models in a top-down fashion, based on real business process definitions and the needs of applications such as the mySAP Business Suite. You can revisit the criteria SAP had for developing ESR content in Chapter 5. The key areas to be covered by the governance program would include the following:

- Global data types that are shared across all models and implementations
- Standardized enterprise service design and interaction patterns
- Business rules
- Coherent and trustworthy master data models
- Policy modeling and management for nonfunctional requirements such as security, high availability, and other ways of capturing the SLAs that are part of the business process
- Consistent human workflow interaction patterns
- Process models and portfolios from the value chain through the executable scenarios

Your enterprise architecture initiatives will be key to helping define, track, and enforce these standards so that all solution teams can rely on your official enterprise models for orchestrating business processes. Part of most good governance programs is encouraging the use of industry standards. There are many core technology standards that enable process orchestration, as discussed in the next section.

NOTE One of the big advantages of the ESA-based capabilities in SAP NetWeaver is the rich set of tools and embedded processes that allow you to automate and manage your SOA and BPM governance programs. SAP was able to capture some of its own internal best practices for managing content models, and then productize them for customers in a way you can leverage.

Key Standards for Enabling BPM

What enables true cross-component and cross-enterprise process orchestration is a set of widely adopted standards. Component-based integration technologies such as OMG's CORBA, Microsoft's COM, and Sun Microsystems' Java EJB and RMI were never universally accepted by technology vendors. Electronic Data Interchange (EDI), although widely recognized by standards bodies, had its limitations. The contents of EDI documents had to be agreed upon by the involved parties. This made it difficult to bring new partners on board. Also, the fixed-length definition of fields in an EDI document made each EDI document difficult for the involved parties to modify.

The standards that are part of the Web Services stack (see Figure 12-3) have played a huge role in the feasibility of current-day BPM Systems. This section discusses the key standards in the Web Services stack.

Web Services

The W3C offers the following definition of a Web Service:

A Web service is a software system designed to support interoperable machine-to-machine interaction over a network. It has an interface described in a machine-processable format (specifically WSDL). Other systems interact with the Web service in a manner prescribed by its description using SOAP messages, typically conveyed using HTTP with an XML serialization in conjunction with other Web-related standards.[1]

The machine-processable format of a Web Service's interface is important because it facilitates dynamic discovery and invocation of the Web Service.

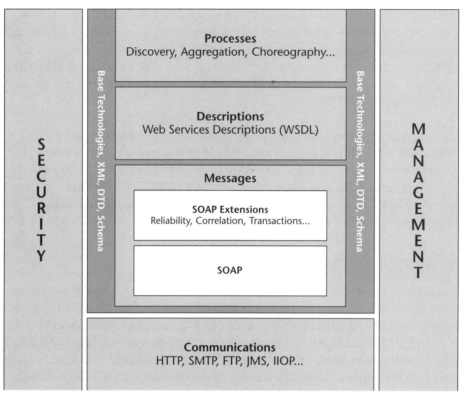

Figure 12-3: Web Services stack (Source: Copyright © 2004 World Wide Web Consortium [Massachusetts Institute of Technology, European Research Consortium for Informatics and Mathematics, Keio University]. All Rights Reserved. www.w3.org/Consortium/Legal/2002/copyright-documents-20021231)

Web Service interfaces can be stored in a Universal Description, Discovery, and Integration (UDDI) directory (see Figure 12-4). Generally, Web Service interfaces are published to and retrieved from the UDDI using SOAP calls. It is not a requirement for the interfaces to be published in the UDDI. They could be published over the Web, or the interface file could be sent through some other means. Clients use information in the interface file to create appropriate calls to the Web Service. Generally, automated tools are used to generate proxies, and applications that need data from the Web Service use the proxy API to communicate with the Web Service.

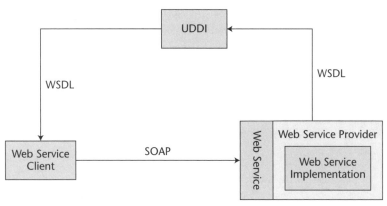

Figure 12-4: Web Services interaction paradigm

XML

A key revolution in the interoperability of disparate software systems is the advent of the Extensible Markup Language (XML). Prior to XML, different vendors used proprietary data formats to exchange data. The need to exchange data (with proprietary formats) between various systems contributed to the proliferation of point-point connectivity solutions. But with the wide acceptance of XML, interoperability has become less of an issue. As long as a system understands XML (either by itself or through an adapter), it can communicate with any other system that supports XML.

An XML document contains data and the definition of the data itself. Like Hypertext Markup Language (HTML), XML is a markup language that is characterized by tags. The tag for a data element describes the data that it contains. Because the content is in text format, it is human-readable. Also, XML parsers can parse any XML document in a generic manner. The structure of an XML document is defined using a Data Type Definition (DTD) or using an XML Schema Definition (XSD), like the Data Definition Language (DDL) used by relational databases. Currently, XSDs are almost universally used. XSDs define the following:

- Elements (tags) and attributes
- Data types and default values
- Containership and cardinality
- Element inheritance, attribute groups, and type restrictions

Following is an example of an XSD and an XML document that complies with the XSD:

```
The email.xsd XML schema definition.
<?xml version="1.0"?>
<xs:schema xmlns:xs="http://www.w3.org/2001/XMLSchema"
targetNamespace="http://www.esabook.com"
xmlns="http://www. esabook.com">
    <xs:element name="email">
        <xs:complexType>
          <xs:sequence>
              <xs:element name="to" type="xs:string"/>
              <xs:element name="from" type="xs:string"/>
              <xs:element name="heading" type="xs:string"/>
              <xs:element name="body" type="xs:string"/>
          </xs:sequence>
        </xs:complexType>
    </xs:element>
</xs:schema>

A XML document that complies with email.xsd.
<?xml version="1.0"?>
<note
xmlns="http://www.esabook.com"
xmlns:xsi="http://www.w3.org/2001/XMLSchema-instance"
xsi:schemaLocation="http://www.esabook.com/email.xsd">
    <to>Someone</to>
    <from>Someone Else</from>
    <heading>Hi</heading>
    <body>Call me!</body>
</note>
```

SOAP

Simple Object Access Protocol (SOAP) is a specification that "can be used for exchanging structured and typed information between peers in a decentralized, distributed environment."[2] SOAP is transport-independent. It can be used with multiple protocols such as HTTP or the Java Message Service (JMS). Also, SOAP is defined in XML, and hence is extensible. This means that while the core structure of a SOAP message is well-defined, there can be application-specific content in some specific areas of the message.

A SOAP message is made up of three parts (see Figure 12-5): Envelope, Body, and Header. The SOAP *Envelope* is a container for an XML message. It encapsulates the SOAP *Header* and the SOAP *Body*. The Envelope contains information on the kind of data inside the envelope, on how the data should be processed, and on the Sender and Receiver of the message. A SOAP message can be transported using various transport protocols. SOAP is a one-way message-exchange mechanism. Patterns such as request/response can be implemented based upon the underlying transport protocol that is used, as shown here:

```
A SOAP message as a HTTP request.
POST /webapp/servlet/rpcrouter HTTP/1.1
Host: www.esabook.com
Content-Type: text/xml; charset="utf-6"
Content-Length: nnnn
SOAPAction: ""

<SOAP-ENV:Envelope>
  xmlns:SOAP-ENV="http://schemas.xmlsoap.org/soap/envelope/"
  <SOAP-ENV:Body>
    <ns1:getMessage xmlns:ns1="urn:NextMessage"
      SOAP-
ENV:encodingStyle="http://schemas.xmlsoap.org/soap/encoding/">
      <UserID xsi:type="xsd:string">jsmith</UserID>
      <Password xsi:type="xsd:string">jspass</Password>
    </ns1:getMessage>
  </SOAP-ENV:Body>
</SOAP-ENV:Envelope>
```

WSDL

Web Service Description Language (WSDL) is "an XML format for describing network services as a set of endpoints operating on messages containing either document-oriented or procedure-oriented information."[3] So, a WSDL defines the location of a Web Service, the method in which the Web Service can be called, the operations that the Web Service supports, and the data types that are used by those operations. There are five parts in a WSDL document. Figure 12-6 shows the structure of a WSDL document and the definition of the types.[4]

Figure 12-5: SOAP structure

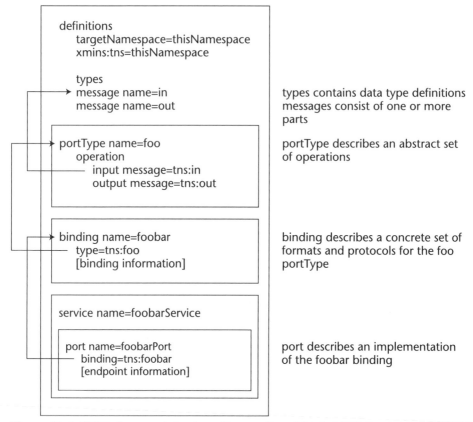

Figure 12-6: WSDL document structure (Source: Copyright © OASIS Open 2005. All rights reserved.)

The *definitions* section defines the namespaces for the document itself and the various elements/tags in the document. The *types* section defines data types and the various input and output message types that are used by the Web Service. The message types are based upon the data types. The *portType* section defines the operations/interfaces of the Web Service. The *binding* section defines the protocols that are associated with the port types. Finally, the *port* section provides end point information (that is, where exactly the Web Service is available).

The WSDL definition of Google's publicly consumable search Web Service is a good example and can be found at `http://api.google.com/GoogleSearch.wsdl`.

BPEL

Different standards organizations have come up with different languages for documenting and executing business processes. WfMC's XML Process Definition Language, BPMI's Business Process Modeling Language (BPML), and OASIS's Business Process Execution Language (BPEL) are examples. SAP NetWeaver uses BPEL to orchestrate Business Processes in its Business Process Engine. This is the prime reason why only BPEL is explained in this book.

BPEL, also known as WS-BPEL and BPEL4WS, is a notation for specifying business process behavior based on Web Services.[5] BPEL is an offshoot of the combination of IBM's Web Services Flow Language (WSFL) and Microsoft's XLANG. The support of BPEL by IBM, Microsoft, SAP, and others is a critical factor in the seeming popularity and acceptance of this standard.

BPEL process patterns describe best practices for message-based service orchestration using standard Web Service interfaces, adapters for third-party and legacy integration, as well as process-to-process communication.

Process Execution in XI

As explained in the previous section, business processes are represented in BPEL and are executed in the Business Process Engine (BPE) of SAP XI. BPEL bridges the impedance between business systems that need to communicate with one another. For example, a business system might be set up to make a synchronous call to access some data while the provider is able to support only asynchronous calls. In this case, a business process can bridge this communication mechanism gap.

Another example is a purchase order that is sent to a supplier network (see Figure 12-7). The WaveCross supplier network could implement the functionality of sending different purchase order line items to different suppliers, wait for the responses from each of the suppliers, combine the responses into a single response, and then send it to the requestor.

The actual interaction of the business process with the business systems is modeled as message interfaces in XI — an *abstract process*. The business process itself represents the enhanced behavior of a participant in a process and is modeled in BPEL — an *executable process*. The combination of the abstract and executable processes fully defines BPEL.

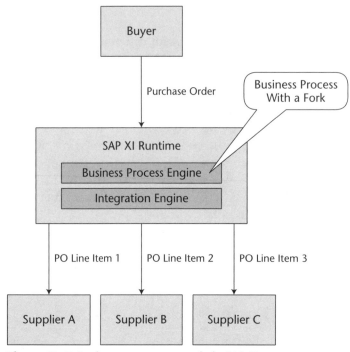

Figure 12-7: Business process scenario in SAP XI

In SAP XI, business processes are defined using a process editor (see Figure 12-8). As indicated previously, they are based on Abstract Message Interfaces. They are configured for a particular deployment in the Integration Directory. BPE works with XI's Integration Engine to communicate with business systems. The Integration Engine is responsible for receiving all incoming messages, transforming the messages to the receiver's format, figuring out the channel on which to send the message to the receiver business system, and then sending the message to the receiver. When an integration process is made a part of an Integration Scenario, the Integration Engine determines the BPE to be the receiver of a particular message and, hence, sends the message to the BPE.

Correlation is the mechanism by which the BPE determines the relationship between a message and a process instance. A specified set of fields in the content of a message is used for correlation. All messages that satisfy a given correlation condition are sent to the same process instance. The process is then executed based upon its definition. Once the process reaches a stage where it is ready to send out a message, the message is sent to the Integration Engine, which then follows its normal rules to process the message.

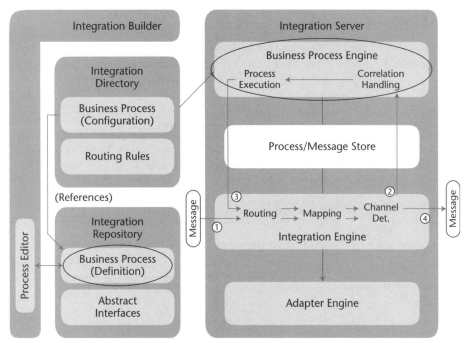

Figure 12-8: Business process orchestration is part of the XI design and run-time architecture. (Source: © SAP AG 2005–2006. All rights reserved.)

> **NOTE** The correlation capabilities are a critical enabler of process orchestration and process monitoring within XI.

Integration Processes

The SAP XI Integration Builder incorporates a tool to create business processes based on BPEL. In the Integration Builder, these business processes are called *Integration Processes*. The tool provides a graphical editor to build Integration Processes. Integration Processes are one of the many XI design objects that are stored in a Software Component Version (SCV) in the XI Integration Repository. They are made up of interconnected step types and can be exported as a BPEL file(s), which can then be used for execution on non-SAP BPEL engines.

Step Types

A *step type* is a processing step in a BPEL process and corresponds to XML tags in a BPEL file. Following are the main step types that can be used in an integration process (see Figure 12-9):

- *Receive* — Start an integration process, receive messages in integration processes, and define synchronous/asynchronous bridging.

- *Send* — Send messages from integration processes synchronously or asynchronously, send acknowledgments, and define synchronous/asynchronous bridging.

- *Receiver determination* — Determine the list of receivers for a subsequent Send step.

- *Transformation* — Transform a message of one type to a different type. Also, transformations are used to combine multiple messages into a single message, or to create multiple messages from a single message.

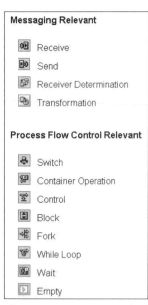

Figure 12-9: Step types in the Process Editor

Following are the main process flow control–relevant elements that can be used in an integration process:

- *Switch* — This is used to execute one of the branches in the switch based upon a condition for each branch. The `otherwise` branch is executed if the condition for none of the other branches is satisfied.

- *Container operation* — This is used to set values of variables in the process.

- *Control (deadlines, exceptions, alerts)* — This is used to terminate a process, trigger an exception, or to trigger an alert.

- *Block* — This is used to process a sequence of steps that must access some local variables within the block, that have the same deadline or exception handler, or that use a local correlation.

- *Fork* — This is used to continue execution of a process in two or more branches, independent of each other. A *union operator* is used to join the branches of a fork as soon as an end condition is reached. When a branch reaches a union operator, the condition is checked and must be satisfied before the process is executed beyond the fork.

- *While loop* — This is used to repeat the sequence of steps within the loop until the condition is not satisfied anymore. Conditions are specified using a condition editor.

- *Wait* — This is used to suspend the process flow for a specified period of time or for a certain point in time. Process flow resumes after the wait end condition is reached.

- *Empty* — This is used either for testing purposes, or as a placeholder for some other step. It does not affect process flow.

Graphical Process Editor

Integration processes are created under any namespace of an SCV. Creating a new integration process from this context menu, or opening an integration process, opens a graphical editor (see Figure 12-10) for processes.

The Header Area of the editor displays the name, the namespace, and SCV of the process.

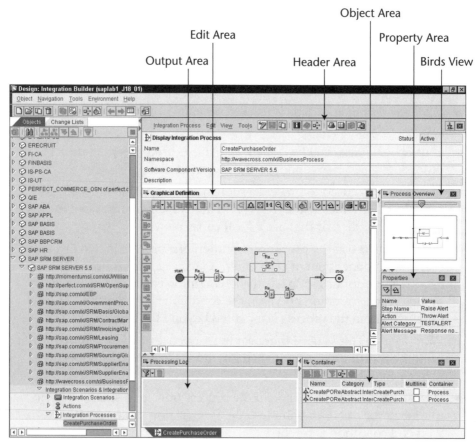

Figure 12-10: Graphical Process Editor

The Edit Area is where the process is graphically represented. It has two toolbars. The horizontal toolbar has a lot of elements that are found in a typical drawing tool (zooming in or copying, for example). The vertical toolbar has step types that can be dragged and dropped onto the diagram. The BPEL that corresponds to the graphical representation of the process can be viewed by switching to the BPEL4WS Display view. The view can be switched by selecting the drop-down arrow, which is to the left of the title of the Edit Area. The Correlation Editor view is also displayed in the Edit Area.

The Birds View area provides an overview of the process. The Process Overview view shows a bird's-eye view of the whole process. It is very useful when creating or editing very complex processes. The Process Outline view displays all the steps of the process as a hierarchy.

The Property Area shows the properties of the currently selected step type. Only the relevant properties for the selected step type are displayed.

Properties that are mandatory have a question mark in the value of the property. Properties that can have multiple values are represented in bold font.

The Output Area has the Tasks, Processing Log, Search Result and (optionally) the WSDL Display views. The Tasks view displays the results of checking an integration process. The Processing Log view displays editor messages. The Search Result view displays results of a step search. The WSDL Display view is available only when the BPEL4WS Display is displayed in the Edit Area. It shows data types and message types that are used in the integration process.

The Object Area has three views. Steps of type Container Element are created and edited in the Container view. Correlations are created in the Correlation List view. The Process Signature view is used to indicate whether a given abstract interface is inbound or outbound.

Creating an Integration Process

This section provides a step-by-step procedure to create an integration process. This integration process deals with receiving a "create purchase order" request from a sender system and forwarding the request to a receiver system. The business need for an integration process in this case is to be able to monitor the response for the "create purchase order" request.

If the response is not received within a specified time period, an alert is thrown to the Alert Management facility in SAP NetWeaver. The process continues to wait for a response and processes the response when it finally arrives. The alert, here, makes relevant users aware of the fact that a response for a particular purchase order was not received within the specified time period.

In this example, the Integration Process and all of its dependent objects are created in the `http://wavecross.com/xi/BusinessProcess` namespace.

Creating Data Types, Message Types, and Message Interfaces

Chapter 11 illustrated the detailed steps to create data types, message types, and message interfaces. You will want to mimic those procedures using the following specifications for the objects needed in this scenario. The data types that are used in this exercise are `PurchaseOrderLineItem` (see Table 12-1), `PurchaseOrder` (see Table 12-2), and `PurchaseOrderConfirmation` (see Table 12-3).

NOTE Refer to Chapter 11 to see the detailed steps you must follow to create data types, message types, and message interfaces.

Table 12-1: PurchaseOrderLineItem (Complex Type)

ELEMENT	CATEGORY	TYPE	OCCURRENCE
Id	Element	xsd:string	1
Product	Element	xsd:string	1
Amount	Element	xsd:string	1

Table 12-2: PurchaseOrder (Complex Type)

ELEMENT	CATEGORY	TYPE	OCCURRENCE
Id	Element	xsd:string	1
Seller	Element	xsd:string	1
Buyer	Element	xsd:string	1
Items	Element	PurchaseOrder LineItem	0 . . . unbounded

Table 12-3: PurchaseOrderConfirmation (Complex Type)

ELEMENT	CATEGORY	TYPE	OCCURRENCE
confNumber	Element	xsd:string	1
purchaseOrder	Element	PurchaseOrder	1

The message types used are `CreatePurchaseOrderRequest` and `Create PurchaseOrderResponse`. `CreatePurchaseOrderRequest` is of data type `PurchaseOrder` and `CreatePurchaseOrderResponse` is of data type `PurchaseOrderConfirmation`.

Message interfaces used in an Integration Process are always abstract. Abstract message interfaces don't have an implementation in an application system and, hence, a proxy cannot be generated for them. They are used to send messages to and receive messages from business systems. The same abstract interface can be used to send or receive messages. `Create PurchaseOrderRequest_Abstract`, which uses the message type `Create PurchaseOrderRequest`, and `CreatePurchaseOrderResponse_ Abstract` (see Figure 12-11), which uses the message type `Create PurchaseOrderResponse`, are the two message interfaces that are used here.

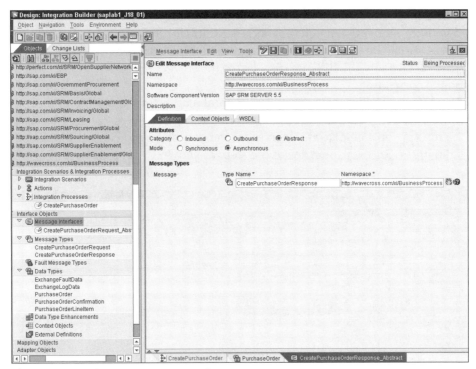

Figure 12-11: Abstract Message Interface

Creating the Integration Process

The Integration Process is created by selecting New from the context menu of Integration Scenarios and Integration Processes → Integration Processes in the relevant namespace. A dialog box appears where you enter the name of the Integration Process, CreatePurchaseOrder. When you click the Create button of the dialog box, the Process Editor is displayed. Initially, the connected Start and Stop markers are displayed. These markers signify the beginning and the end of the process.

Creating the ReceiveCreatePO Step

A Receive step is always required at the beginning of an Integration Process. This starts an instance of the process. The engine picks the right process for instantiation based upon the message interface that is associated with the step. A message interface is associated with the Receive Step using a Container Element. A Receive step can operate in two modes — Asynchronous and Opens

S/A Bridge (Sync/Async). The mode of the message interface that is associated with the step must match the mode selection for the step. Also, the incoming message can be correlated to the process in this step. Subsequent messages that are received by the BPE are directed to the correct process instance, based upon the correlation.

To create the Receive step, drag the relevant icon from the toolbar and drop it in the area between the Start and Stop markers (see Figure 12-12). It is easy to see the appropriate place to drop the icon because an indicator is displayed in valid areas. Set the properties of the step, as shown in Table 12-4.

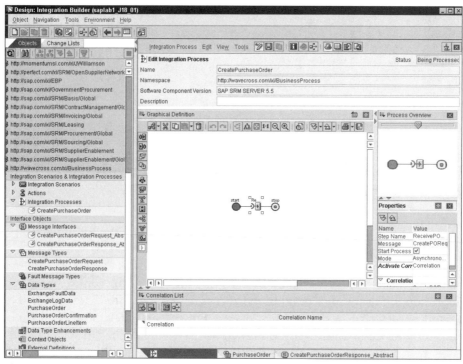

Figure 12-12: Receive step in Integration Process

Table 12-4: ReceiveCreatePO Step

NAME	VALUE
Step Name	ReceiveCreatePO
Start Process	(checked)
Mode	Asynchronous

The Receive step is associated with a message interface through the use of the `Message` property. When the text field associated with this property is clicked, the Input Help icon (icon with a question mark with a blue circular background) is displayed at the end of the text field. Clicking the Input Help icon for this field displays Container Elements. To create the Container Element for the `CreatePurchaseOrderRequest_Abstract` interface, switch to the Container view of the Object Area. Here, specify the Name as `CreatePOReq`. The Category is a drop-down list with three entries:

- *Simple Type* — This means that the value for the Type field is one of the primitive XSD types.

- *Abstract Interface* — This means that the value for the Type field is an abstract message interface.

- *Receiver* — This means that when a message is received by the process, it is temporarily stored until the process executes through a Receive step that has a correlation satisfying the contents of the message. Here, select Abstract Interface.

The value for the Type field can now be selected using the Input Help feature. Use the same process to create the `CreatePOResp` Container Element used later in the process.

Following the creation of the `CreatePOReq` Container Element, the Input Help feature of the Message field of the Receive step can be used to enter the value. The Receive step should now correlate certain fields of the message with the process. This is so that when the response message is received by the engine, the corresponding fields in that message can then be used by BPE to send the message to the correct process instance. Correlation values are stored in the Correlation Container as variables. The Receive step sets the value of these variables. Values from correlated fields in subsequent messages are compared with the Correlation Container variables to figure out which process the message is destined for.

To create a correlation, switch to the Correlation Editor view (see Figure 12-13) of the Edit area. Specify the Correlation Name, and the Name and Type fields of the Correlation Container as shown in the figure. Using Input Help, enter the two involved messages: `CreatePurchaseOrderRequest_Abstract` and `CreatePurchaseOrderResponse_Abstract`.

Now, the correlation fields for all the messages must be defined. Here, the ID field is a good candidate. Create Purchase Order requests sent to the receiver system and Create Purchase Order responses received from the receiver system belong to the same process when their purchase order ID is the same. The definition of these correlation fields is done using the Expression Editor (see Figure 12-14). The Expression Editor is invoked using the Input Help in the Value field of the Properties area of the Correlation Editor (see Figure 12-13).

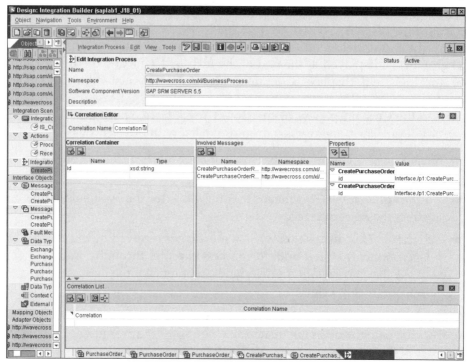

Figure 12-13: Correlation Send step in Integration Process

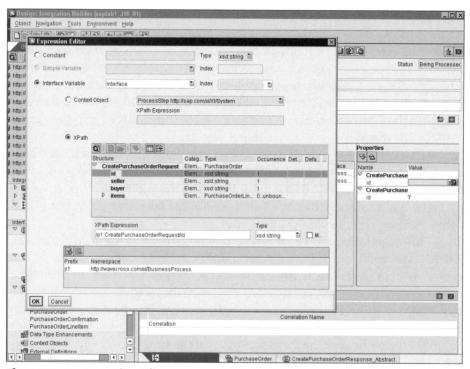

Figure 12-14: Expression Editor

The correlation fields can be one of the following:

- *Constant* — The value of the correlation variable is declared as a constant.

- *Simple Variable* — The value of the correlation variable is declared as a Container Element that is represented as a variable.

- *Interface Variable* — A specific element of the interface is used to determine the value of the correlation variable. The field can be specified as an XPath Expression. Alternately, the XPath Expression can be generated by the editor when the user chooses the appropriate element from the hierarchical message interface structure.

Select the correlation fields as shown in Figure 12-14 and click OK. The Activate Correlation field of the `ReceiveCreatePO` step can now be set using the drop-down list, which now shows the newly created Correlation.

Creating the SendCreatePO Step

Having started the Integration Process and then creating the correlation in the `ReceiveCreatePO` step, the process is now ready to send the purchase order to the receiving business system. This is accomplished using the Send step — `SendCreatePO`. To add the Send step to the process, drag and drop the step from the toolbar into the process after the `ReceiveCreatePO` step. Set the properties of the step, as shown in Table 12-5.

Creating the Control Step

The intent of the process is to throw an alert when a deadline (namely, receiving a response within a specified period of time) is not met. A deadline can be monitored by using a Control step in a branch.

Table 12-5: SendCreatePO Step

NAME	VALUE
Step Name	`SendCreatePO`
Mode	Asynchronous
Message	`CreatePOReq`
Acknowledgment	None
Receiver From	Send Context

The branch that holds the Control step should be able to monitor the Receive step for the Create Purchase Order response from the receiver system. One way to achieve this is encapsulate the branch with the Receive step and the branch with the Control step in a Block step. So, create a Block step with a Step Name of Block and a Mode of Default. The Block step should be placed after the `SendCreatePO` step. To create the Deadline branch (see Figure 12-15), click the drop-down list on the Other Insert Options of the top toolbar and select Deadline Branch. Set the properties as shown in Table 12-6. Now, create the Control step, as shown in Figure 12-16.

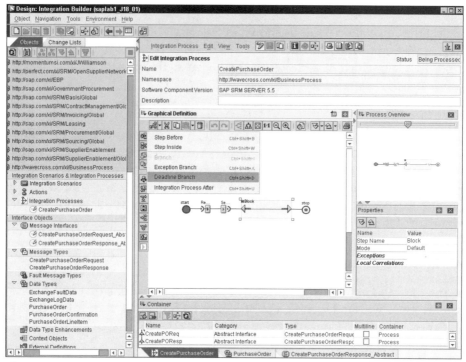

Figure 12-15: Creating a Deadline branch

Table 12-6: Deadline Branch

NAME	VALUE
Reference Date/Time	Creating the Step
Duration	60
Unit	Minutes

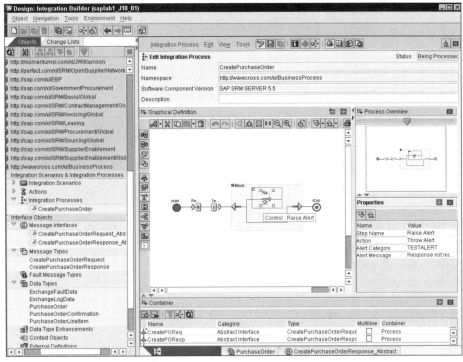

Figure 12-16: Creating an alert

Creating the ReceiveCreatePOResp and SendCreatePOResp Steps

To complete the process, you must incorporate the Receive and Send steps (see Figure 12-17) for the Create Purchase Order response from the receiver business system. Use the data shown in Table 12-7 and Table 12-8 to incorporate these steps. Note the correlation setting on the `ReceiveCreatePOResp` step.

Table 12-7: ReceiveCreatePOResp Step

NAME	VALUE
Step Name	`ReceiveCreatePOResp`
Message	`CreatePOReq`
Use Correlations	Correlation

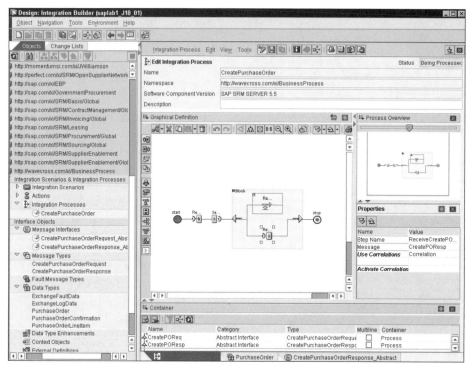

Figure 12-17: Creating Receive step for the response

Table 12-8: SendCreatePOResp Step

NAME	VALUE
Step Name	SendCreatePOResp
Mode	Asynchronous
Message	CreatePOResp
Acknowledgment	None
Receiver From	Send Context

Business Process Patterns

Some sequences of steps in business processes occur frequently in a variety of business processes. The Integration Process that was created in the previous section is a good example. These sequences are captured in XI as *business process patterns*, which are shipped as XI Content by SAP and are available in the `http://sap.com/xi/XI/system/patterns` namespace of SAP BASIS SCV. The obvious advantage of business process patterns is that they can be re-used in the implementation of business processes and can help in reducing the time for implementation.

> **NOTE** SAP includes business processes patterns that are shipped as XI Content and are available in the `http://sap.com/xi/XI/system/patterns` **namespace.**

Business process patterns can be broadly categorized under four categories: Serialization, Transformations/Merge/Split, Collect, and Multicast. Following are the patterns under the Serialization category:

- `BpmPatternSerializeOneTrigger` — Defines a process where multiple messages must be received in a particular sequence, and the messages must be sent out serially in a different sequence.

- `BpmPatternSerializeMultipleTrigger` — Defines a process where multiple messages must be received in any sequence, and the messages must be sent out serially in a specific sequence.

The patterns under the Transformations/Merge/Split category are as follows:

- `BpmPatternReqRespAlert` — Defines a process where a request message is sent to a system, and an alert is raised if a response message is not received in a given time period.

- `BpmPatternReqRespTimeOut` — Defines a process where a request message is sent to a system. An exception is thrown and the process terminated if a response message is not received in a given time period.

Following are the patterns under the Collect category:

- `BpmPatternCollectMessage` — Defines a process where of all the messages received by the process, only one specific message triggers an end to a certain stage of the process.

- `BpmPatternCollectTime` — Defines a process where all received messages are collected until a certain deadline is reached. Further process execution is continued after the condition is satisfied.

- `BpmPatternCollectPayload` — Defines a process where the number of messages received by the process must reach a certain number before proceeding with the rest of the process.

- `BpmPatternCollectMultiIf` — Defines a process that can be started with multiple interfaces. However, all represented interfaces should be received before the process can proceed.

- `BpmPatternCollectMultiIfCondition` — Same as `BpmPatternCollectMultiIf`, except some conditions may be specified for the process to proceed.

Following are the patterns under the Multicast category:

- `BpmPatternMulticastSequential` — Defines a process where a message is sent to multiple receivers in sequence. A Send to the next receiver is initiated only after the response from the previous Send is received.

- `BpmPatternMulticastParallel` — Defines a process where a message is sent to multiple receivers simultaneously. The process proceeds only after a response is received from each of the receivers.

- `BpmPatternSyncAsyncBridge` — This pattern is used to bridge a synchronous call to an asynchronous implementation of a function.

Integration Scenarios

Integration Scenarios define the flow of messages between various business systems for a particular business scenario. They provide a centralized location where all technical objects of a given scenario can be accessed. The key elements of an Integration Scenario include Application Components, as well as Actions and Connections. Each of these has an editor. Application Components roughly map to business components. But, they capture more intricate information such as application versions. Actions are the smallest business functions of an Application Component. An Integration Process can be represented as an Action. Each of the key elements has its own editor.

Creating an Integration Scenario

This section provides a step-by-step procedure to create an Integration Scenario. This Integration Scenario deals with a business system that sends a Create Purchase Order request to another business system that represents a supplier network. The Integration Process that was created in previous sections acts as a coordinator for this message exchange. The Integration Scenario and all of its dependent objects (with some exceptions, as explained later) are created in the `http://wavecross.com/xi/BusinessProcess` namespace.

The Integration Scenario is created by selecting New from the context menu of Integration Scenarios and Integration Processes → Integration Scenarios in the relevant namespace. A dialog box appears with the name of the Integration Scenario, `IS_CreatePurchaseOrder`, entered. When the Create button of the dialog window is clicked, the Integration Scenario Editor is displayed.

Creating Application Components

Each of the Application Components that participate in the scenario should be added in the swim lanes of the Integration Scenario. To create an Application Component, select Insert Application Component from the context menu of a swim lane. The Insert Application Component dialog box is displayed. One of three Application Component Types must be specified. The Product Version type represents a product from the System Landscape Directory (SLD). The Main Instance type represents a group of SCVs that are interdependent. The Template type represents a known software component that is not yet defined in the SLD.

In this scenario, create three Application Components (see Figure 12-18) with data, as shown in Tables 12-9, 12-10, and 12-11. The Title field for both the Product Version Type and Main Instance Type should be specified using Input Help.

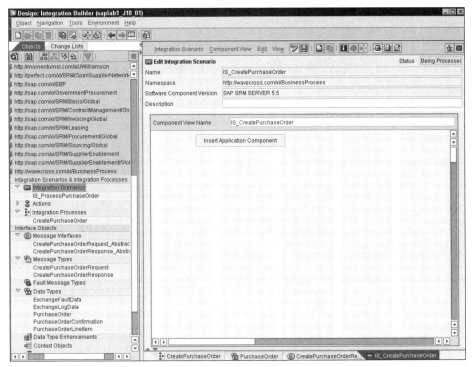

Figure 12-18: Application Component details

Table 12-9: Application Component for Sending System

NAME	VALUE
Application Component Type	Product Version
Application Component Type Title	SAP SRM (WITH SAP EBP) 5.0
Communication Type	Unchecked
Further Attributes — Extended Name	SRM50
Further Attributes — WSCI Name	SRM50

Table 12-10: Application Component for Coordinator

NAME	VALUE
Application Component Type	Product Version
Application Component Type Title	SAP EXCHANGE INFRASTRUCT. 3.0
Communication Type	Unchecked
Further Attributes — Extended Name	Coordinator
Further Attributes — WSCI Name	Coordinator

Table 12-11: Application Component for Receiving System

NAME	VALUE
Application Component Type	Template
Application Component Type Title	N/A
Communication Type	Checked
Further Attributes — Extended Name	WaveCross Supplier Network
Further Attributes — WSCI Name	WSN

Creating Actions

An Action represents the smallest application functionality that can be represented in an Integration Scenario. A new Action can be created from the Create Action context menu (see Figure 12-19) in the swim lane of an Application Component.

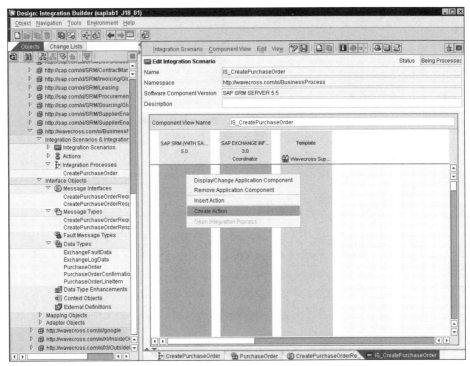

Figure 12-19: Creating an action

The menu selection displays the Action Wizard (see Figure 12-20). Create one Action for each of the Application Components with data, as shown in Tables 12-12, 12-13, and 12-14. Internal Actions generally represent existing application functionality with an Application Component. External Actions represent functionality that is available in a different Application Component than the one where the Action resides. External Actions could also represent non-existing application functionality. The inbound and outbound interfaces for Actions are set outside of the wizard (see Figure 12-21).

Table 12-12: Action for Sending System

NAME	VALUE
Type of usage	Internal
Name	`CreatePurchaseOrder`
Description	Create Purchase Order
Outbound Interface	`CreatePurchaseOrderRequest_Abstract`

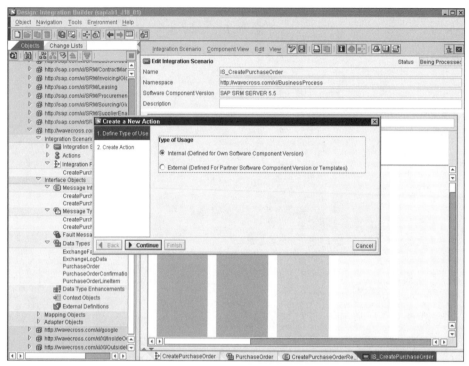

Figure 12-20: Create Action Wizard

Table 12-13: Action for Coordinator

NAME	VALUE
Type of usage	External
Name	ProcessPurchaseOrder
Description	Process Purchase Order
Outbound Interface	CreatePurchaseOrderRequest_Abstract
Inbound Interface	CreatePurchaseOrderResponse_Abstract

Table 12-14: Action for Receiving System

NAME	VALUE
Type of usage	External
Name	ReceiveCreatePO
Description	Receive Create PO

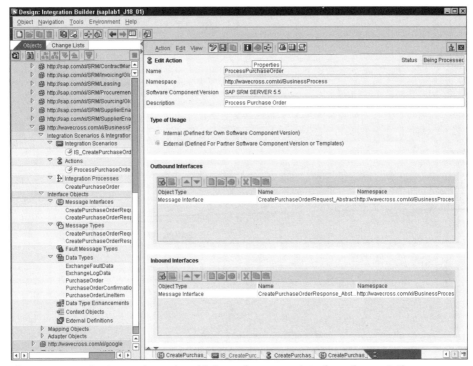

Figure 12-21: Setting outbound and inbound message interfaces for an Action

Creating Connections

Connections represent message exchange between two actions. There are two categories of Connections:

- Connections between Actions from different Application Components
- Connections between Actions from the same Application Component

In the latter case, the Connection is defined as a *sequence*. In the former case, the Connection can be either synchronous or asynchronous. When two Actions are on the same level in the Integration Scenario, the message exchange is synchronous. When the Actions are on different levels, the message exchange is asynchronous.

To create a Connection between two Actions, select the sending Action first and then select the receiving Action next by pressing the Shift key. When both Actions are selected, the context menu (see Figure 12-22) provides the option to create a new Connection between the selected Actions. The Connection Editor is displayed (see Figure 12-23). This editor can be used to assign interfaces and mappings to the Connection.

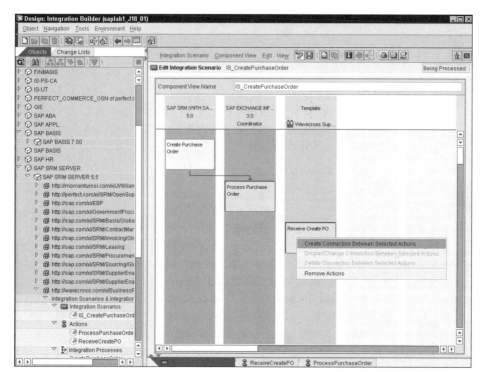

Figure 12-22: Creating a Connection between two Actions

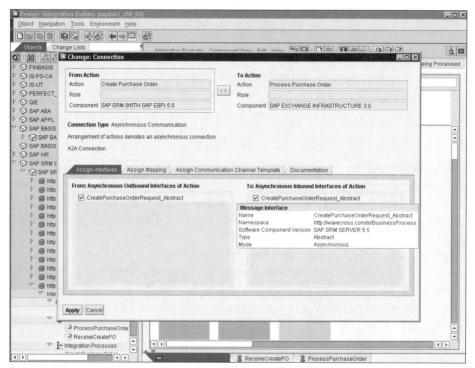

Figure 12-23: Setting Connection parameters

Summary

Business Process orchestration is key to integrating disparate Application Components within and outside a company's IT infrastructure. Process Architecture models, Process Configuration models, and Process Execution models all work in conjunction with one another and represent the business level models of business processes. The SAP NetWeaver platform provides a suite of tools to capture the various models. The key advantage of the platform is its ability to bridge the gap between business and technology experts.

SAP Solution Manager provides the means to configure process models over a productive system landscape. Pre-defined business scenarios in Solution Manager provide a path to capturing process models through customization. Integration Processes are executable business processes that can communicate with business systems through the use of platform-neutral message interfaces. Integration Scenarios provide a centralized location for accessing all design objects for a business scenario. Integration Processes denote message flow between various Application Components that are involved in a business scenario.

Chapter 11 covered aspects of how to build new services and how to service-enable existing business functionality. This chapter explained how to leverage services in executable business processes. Chapter 13 explains how to build composite applications, and then use them in a user-driven business process.

References

Following are references and recommended sources of additional information.

1. W3C, "Web Services Architecture," 2004. Available at `www.w3.org/TR/ws-arch/`.
2. W3C, "SOAP Version 1.2," 2003. Available at `www.w3.org/TR/2003/REC-soap12-part0-20030624/`.
3. W3C, "Web Services Description Language (WSDL) 1.1," 2006. Available at `www.w3.org/TR/wsdl`.
4. OASIS, "Using WSDL in a UDDI Registry," 2005. Available at `www.oasis-open.org/committees/uddi-spec/doc/tn/uddi-spec-tc-tn-wsdl-v2.htm`.
5. BEA, IBM, Microsoft, SAP AG, Siebel, "Business Process Execution Language for Web Services," 2003. Available at `http://ifr.sap.com/bpel4ws/index.html`.

J. Chang, "Business Process Management Systems," Auerbach Publications, 2006.

SAP AG, "Business Process Execution Language for Web Services (BPEL4WS)," 2006. Available at `http://ifr.sap.com/bpel4ws/index.html`.

SAP AG, "SAP Library," 2006. Available at `http://help.sap.com/saphelp_nw2004s/helpdata/en/`.

CHAPTER 13

SAP's Composite Application Framework and Guided Procedures

Chapter 12 covered the BPEL-based process orchestration capabilities within SAP NetWeaver. You saw how executable models allow you to leverage services to handle the technical integration aspects and flow of control associated with automating processes. This could include integration points and flows existing within your organization, or be expanded to address B2B scenarios as well. ESA-based services and related industry technology standards provide the context and enable this level of interoperability to be achieved.

As explained in Chapter 6, delivering on the promise of end-to-end BPM also requires effective human interaction with IT systems. The coordination, tracking, and support for offline processes also needs to be addressed. In fact, human intervention is a critical component of most business processes.

For example, employees' requests for vacation must be approved by their managers. Purchase Order requests must be approved by purchasing managers. Suppliers who receive purchase orders from buyers must either approve or deny the request. Executives prefer dashboards that give them information on metrics that they can then use to make critical decisions. All of these processes involve tasks that require human intervention.

The way in which people interact with processes and applications changes dramatically in an SOA world. Business task management is an area encompassing the technologies that support end-user integration and coordination of business processes. Multiple SAP technologies help address this requirement. These range from mature workflow capabilities that control interactions inside a specific business application to a new breed of composite applications that are fast becoming the ideal way to create loosely coupled UIs in an ESA world.

As mentioned, composite applications represent a whole new way for users to interact with processes independently of the underlying back-end applications. They are designed from the perspective of the user in the context of the process and tasks they support. There are many tools and technologies that can be used to create ESA-based composites. Generally speaking, all rely on a set of underlying enterprise services that can be used as foundational building blocks. The focus of this chapter is to explore the technology of SAP's Composite Application Framework (CAF). CAF-Core and CAF-Guided Procedures (CAF-GP) are the two main components of CAF that will be demonstrated.

Business Task Management — Core Capabilities

Business task management is the means by which tasks can be generated and routed to the users that are responsible for their implementation. The tasks could be generated automatically as part of a business process that requires human intervention. For example, a Purchase Order business process might create a task to verify an invoice before the goods related to a purchase order are shipped. Tasks can also be generated on an ad-hoc basis by users. For example, a manager might require an employee to work on an unexpected delivery item. He or she could create, define, and then assign that task to the employee. Apart from task generation, business task management also involves the business context and the framework to execute and monitor tasks.

The list that follows shows the main SAP technologies that enable business task management and provides a brief overview of their features[1]:

- *Universal Work List (UWL)* — This is a single point of access for a user to manage his or her work. It can be personalized and provides role-based access to process views.

- *Alerts* — These are notifications based upon exceptions in processes. (They can be cross-system.)

- *Collaboration Tasks* — End users can create ad hoc collaborative processes. Delegated tasks can then be tracked by all interested users.

- *Guided Procedures* — These provide a framework to develop user-driven business processes with a minimal amount of coding. They are easily modifiable and provide process templates that can be customized. They provide user interface (UI) patterns and provide mechanisms to integrate with various back-end systems.

- *Interactive Forms* — These are used for extracting data from back-end systems in forms (static or dynamic, online or offline).

- *Business Workflow* — This is used to build a variety of business process steps for task monitoring within an application, as well as to enforce compliance of service agreements and regulations.

A Solutions Perspective

As explained in previous chapters, business process orchestrations and integration between heterogeneous business systems in A2A and B2B scenarios is enabled by SAP Exchange Infrastructure (XI), which is part of the Process Integration (PI) IT Scenario. Business task management is enabled through the concept of a composite application. A *composite application* means an application that is composed on top of the functionality of various other systems and is delivered in the context of the user, as opposed to organized around the structure that the underlying systems provide. The service enablement of various back-end systems provides a cost-effective means to build composite applications. Figure 13-1 illustrates the high-level approach to creating composites with CAF.

A composite application that is geared toward enabling user-driven business processes must have certain elements, including the following:

- Business objects that represent the back-end systems' business objects, along with enhancements needed for the composite

- Ability to leverage remote services to access functionality from various back-end systems

- Local persistency/services to store data that cannot be stored in back-end systems for various reasons

- A UI by which users can act on tasks associated with data

- A representation of the business process model and associated actions

All of these requirements could be satisfied through traditional means of building applications. You could create a schema on a relational database, build persistency using entity Enterprise Java Beans (EJBs), build services using sessions EJBs, build business logic to capture the workflow, and then build UIs for users using Java Server Pages (JSP) technology.

A similar path could be followed to build the application using .NET technology. In fact, your organization has probably been building composites using traditional coding techniques for years.

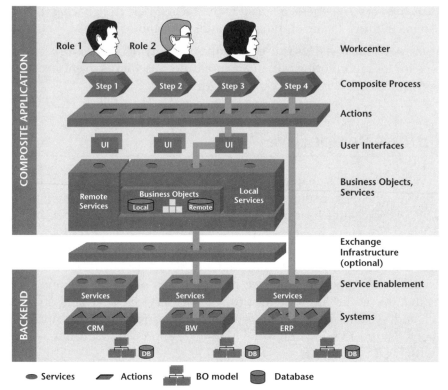

Figure 13-1: Anatomy of a composite application (Source: © SAP AG 2005–2006. All rights reserved.)

As part of the ESA road map, SAP has added additional mechanisms for creating composites. Visual composer is an ideal tool for creating analytics-based solutions or other "lightweight" composites. The company has also collaborated with Microsoft to develop a framework for creating Microsoft Office–based composites using Information Bridge Framework (IBF) technologies and SAP's Enterprise Services Inventory and Infrastructure. The Duet products (formerly Mendocino) use this technique, and you can leverage the same approach to create your own composites, as illustrated in Chapter 9.

Of course, the most important new framework from SAP for creating composites that take advantage of all the ESA features in SAP NetWeaver is CAF. The remainder of this chapter focuses on illustrating more details of CAF and how you can leverage its capabilities.

> **NOTE** You can create composite applications in several ways. Traditional coding (using ABAP, Java, and .NET) represents one way. Many specialized tools are also available from niche vendors. SAP has also developed new ways to leverage NetWeaver to create different types of composites. This includes Visual Composer for lightweight, analytics-based composites; Microsoft Office extensions to use Office productivity tools as front-ends to enterprise systems; and CAF for creating rich, full-featured ESA-based composites that leverage all of the SOA, embedded analytics and user-productivity features of SAP NetWeaver.

CAF makes it easy to build composite applications. This is accomplished through the use of a multitude of tools, wizards, and run-time engines that can accomplish a task in a fraction of the time versus traditional development. This is because models and code generators help reduce the coding effort significantly. A minimal amount of time is also spent on building frameworks that are typical of traditional Web-based applications. The model-driven nature of CAF lets developers build models for business objects, business logic, and user interfaces (UIs).

Code is generated based upon the developed models. This gives developers the opportunity to focus on the business problem. Because the framework leverages a lot of existing SAP technologies, the user experience is smooth. UI templates, for the most part, make it unnecessary to build time-consuming custom UIs.

Example Scenario

An example is used here to explore the CAF technology in more detail. A Purchase Order process involves users of type Seller and Buyer. The process is initiated when a user with the Buyer role creates a purchase order. A task is created for the user with the Seller role and it shows up in a work list when the user logs on to the system. The Seller can either approve or reject the purchase order request based upon a set of criteria.

If the Seller rejects the purchase order request, a task is created for the Buyer, who can then modify the data in the purchase order request. If the Seller approves the purchase order, the purchase order is persisted to local storage. The Create Invoice task is then created for the Seller. When the goods are ready to be shipped, the Seller can fill the data in the Create Invoice task. Tasks are then created for the Buyer to approve the invoice, after which the invoice is persisted to local storage.

Design

The design for developing the case study using CAF is shown in Figure 13-2. Data persistence is achieved through the use of services provided in the CAF-Core. Invoice and PO are the two entities that have to be persisted. The PO Entity Service, in turn, uses the PO Line Item Entity Service. The two main Entity Services, PO and Invoice, are wrapped in Application Services that are usable by CAF-GP.

User tasks and actions roughly map to CAF-GP Actions. Actions use Callable Objects to interact with services that are provided by CAF-Core. Actions are encapsulated in Blocks, which are, in turn, encapsulated in a Process. The Process maps to the Business Task in question. The CAF-specific terminology that is used here will be explained in more detail in the following sections.

CAF tools (which were previously discussed in Chapter 10) are used in the implementation of the solution. The CAF Core toolset is a plug-in of NetWeaver Developer Studio (NWDS) and is used to implement the CAF-Core–related development artifacts. CAF GPs and all related objects are built using Web-based tools and wizards. The upcoming sections discuss all of the tools in the context of the case study.

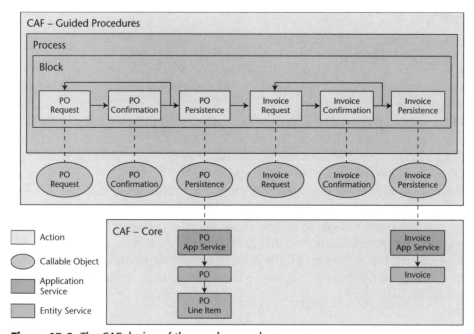

Figure 13-2: The CAF design of the purchase order process

CAF Core

The three kinds of services that can be built using the CAF Core technology are Entity Services, Application Services, and External Services. *Entity Services* represent the data layer while *Application Services* represent business logic. *External Services* can be Remote Function Calls (RFCs) or Web Service calls. Each of these services has a modeler in SAP NWDS.

External services can be used both by Entity and Application Services. When used as an Entity Service, they represent remote persistency. When used by an Application Service, they represent remote services. The methods by which both local and remote persistency are built are very similar, as are the methods by which local and remote services are built. Because of this, only the procedures for building Entity and Application Services are detailed in this section.

> **NOTE** External services can be used both by entity and Application Services. When used as an Entity Service, they represent remote persistency. When used by an Application Service, they represent remote services.

Creating the Project

To build all the services that are used in the case study begin with the following steps:

1. Open NWDS.

2. Create a new project in NWDS by changing to the Resources perspective. In the context menu of the Navigator view, select New → Project.

3. In the New Project dialog box, select Development Component → Development Component Project and click Next.

4. In the New Development Component project dialog box, select Local Development → My Components and click Next.

5. Enter the data as shown in Figure 13-3 and then click Finish.

The Service Explorer view of the Composite Application Services perspective displays the new project with three nodes under it — for each of the three service types.

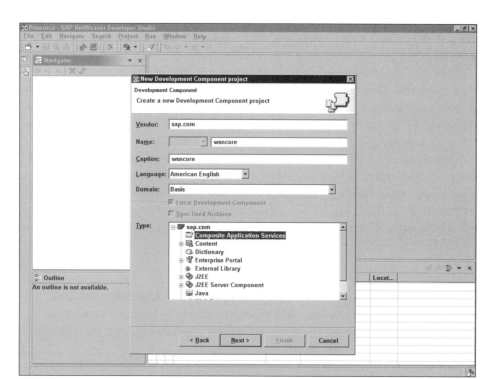

Figure 13-3: Creating the Composite Application Services project

Creating an Entity Service

Entity Services represent entity data in either local or remote storage. They can have references to other Entity Services. The Entity Services Modeler provides a code-free mechanism to build database tables, relationships between tables, and the methods to access the data.

In this section, three Entity Services — `POLineItem`, `PurchaseOrder`, and `Invoice` — are created. Select New from the wsncore → Entity Services context menu. Specify the Entity Service name, as shown in Figure 13-4.

Click Finish. This opens the Entity Service Modeler. By default, it has the `key`, `createdBy`, `createdAt`, `lastChangedBy`, and `lastChangedAt` attributes (see Figure 13-5). The attributes can be seen in the Attributes tab of the modeler.

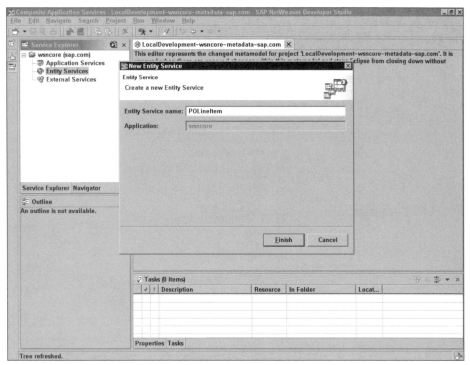

Figure 13-4: Creating a new Entity Service

To add attributes to the Entity Service, in the Attributes section, select Create Attribute from the POLineItem context menu. Enter the attribute name, description, and data type (see Figure 13-5). The Browse button should be used to specify the data type. Here, DtDictionary → com.sap.caf.core → short-Text is used. Using a similar process, specify the product and quantity attributes.

There are three types of attributes — Simple, Complex, and Entity Service. An attribute such as id (see Figure 13-5), which is of data type shortText, is an example of a Simple attribute. For the most part, this translates to a column in a database table. A Complex attribute is one that is represented by a foreign key relationship to another table. Entity Service attributes are attributes of an Entity Service, which themselves are Entity Services. The relationship between the tables corresponding to the two entities is established through a join table.

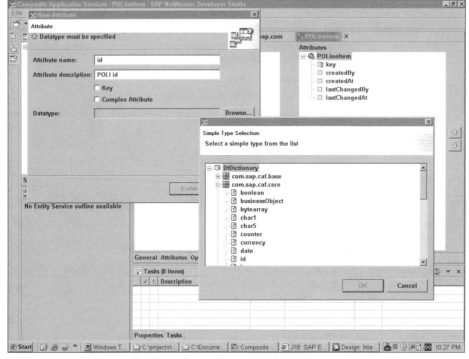

Figure 13-5: Adding attributes to the Entity Service

PurchaseOrder and Invoice are the other two entities that should also be created (see Tables 13-1 and 13-2).

Table 13-1: PurchaseOrder

ATTRIBUTE	DATATYPE
id	shortText
seller	shortText
buyer	shortText
items	com.sap.wsncore.besrv.purchaseorder.POLineItem

Table 13-2: Invoice

ATTRIBUTE	DATATYPE
id	shortText
amount	shortText
purchaseOrderRef	com.sap.wsncore.besrv.invoice.PurchaseOrder

The `items` attribute of `PurchaseOrder` and the `purchaseOrderRef` attribute of `Invoice` are Entity Service attributes. To add Entity Service attributes, the Entity Service should be dragged from the Entity Catalog frame to the Attributes frame. The Relationship Type of an Entity Service attribute can be of type *Composition* or *Association* (see Figure 13-6). *Composition* means that the data related to the entity data is also deleted when the entity data is deleted.

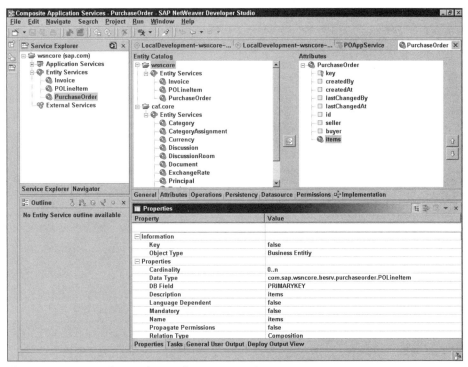

Figure 13-6: An Entity Service attribute

The Operations tab of the modeler reveals the default operations that are created for the service. By default, the `create`, `read`, `update`, `delete`, and `findByMultipleParameters` operations are created. These operations may not be sufficient for integration purposes, and new operations can be created as necessary. Here, for testing purposes, the `findById` operation is created, as shown in Figure 13-7. This operation takes `id` as a parameter and returns a Collection of `PurchaseOrders`. To create the new operation, use the Add button of the Operations frame in the Operations tab.

Entity Services can be protected by authorization rules. On the Permissions tab of the modeler is a means to enable this feature — the "Permission checks enabled" checkbox, which is checked by default. The purpose of this feature is to specify rules by which only a set of roles are authorized to call on the Entity Services. Because the CAF run-time runs in the context of a portal, the framework is able to check if the current user has the authorization to call on this service. In this case, this checkbox is disabled for all the Entity Services.

> **NOTE** Entity services can be protected by authorization rules. You enable this feature by clicking the checkbox on the Permissions tab.

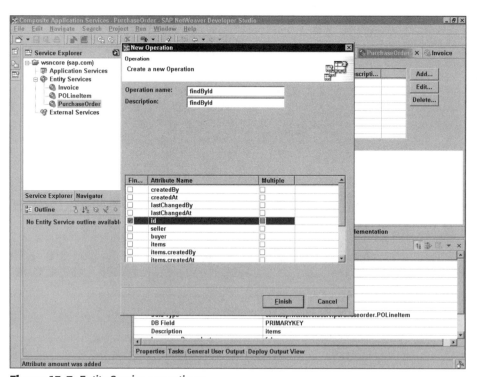

Figure 13-7: Entity Service operations

All changes made in the modeler can be saved by clicking the Save All Metadata icon (the one with an "M" and image of a floppy) in the toolbar. After saving all the metadata, the code generation must be done using Generate All Project Code from the project context menu (see Figure 13-8). This is because metadata created by the modeler must be converted to executable Java code. Following this, the application has to be built to make it feasible for deployment — Development Component → Build. If the build is successful, the project can be deployed to SAP WAS (use "Deploy to J2EE engine" from the context menu).

Entity Services can be tested from NWDS. To test the `PurchaseOrder` Entity Service, select the service in NWDS and select Test from the context menu. This opens the ServiceBrowser window (see Figure 13-9). On the initial screen of this window, data can be inserted into the database using the Add button. The default fields should be left empty before the Save button is clicked. After the data is successfully saved, you can navigate to the `findById` operation of the `PurchaseOrder` Entity Service (see Figure 13-9) to check if the data was actually saved, and also to see the values that were assigned to the default attributes.

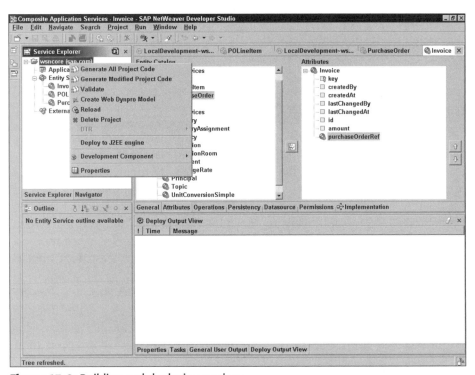

Figure 13-8: Building and deploying services

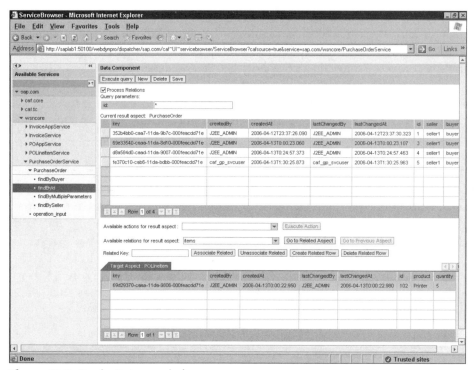

Figure 13-9: ServiceBrowser window

Creating an Application Service

While Entity Services are entirely code-free development, Application Services provide the flexibility by which code (that can add value) can be written. Primarily, the type of the transaction for methods and the means to specify input parameters, output parameters, and exceptions for custom methods (which, in turn, operate on Entity Services and/or External Services) are available. Custom methods are a crucial means to adapt the disconnect that occurs between what CAF GP can work with and what Entity and External Service method calls provide. Application Services are the only type of services that CAF GP objects can interact with.

The Purchase Order process involves steps that must persist a `PurchaseOrder` and an `Invoice`. This means Application Services must be created for the corresponding Entity Services. To create the Application Service for `PurchaseOrder` and `POAppService`, use the context menu for Application

Services to select the New option. In the New Application Service dialog box, enter **POAppService** for the Application Service name. In the Dependencies tab of the modeler, select the `PurchaseOrder` and `POLineItem` Entity Services from the Service Catalog and click the right-arrow button (see Figure 13-10) to add them to the list of Available Services. This enables the Application Service to use the added services.

In the Purchase Order process, the attributes of `PurchaseOrder` must be passed to the Entity Service when the purchase order is to be persisted. To facilitate this, a custom operation must be created. To create a custom operation, click the Operations tab and then click the Add button. Notice that in the displayed dialog box, there is an Access option, too. With this option, methods that directly map to the CRUD operations of an Entity Service can be automatically generated.

Select the Custom option and click Next. In the following screen, specify `createPO` for both the Name and Description fields. Leave the other fields as defaults.

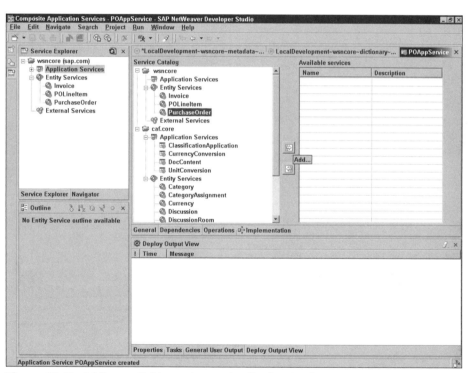

Figure 13-10: Adding available services to Application Service

Now, the input, output, and fault parameters for the custom operation must be specified (see Figure 13-11). In this case, the input parameters are `id`, `seller`, and `buyer`. First, select the custom operation from the Operations panel. To add the attributes, for each of them, select Catalog → Simple Types → com.sap.caf.core → shortText from the Attribute / Type Repository panel and click the Input button. This adds an `arg0` attribute in the Input, Output Parameters, and Exceptions panel. Select the `arg0` attribute and then switch to the Properties view. Here, type in the attribute name. For Output, use the `longText` data type and leave the default attribute name at Response. Finally, set the Fault to Catalog → Faults → caf.core → ServiceException.

A decent chunk of code is generated from the steps that have been done. To view the code, switch to the Implementation tab toward the bottom of the screen. Areas of the file that the user can modify are demarcated with the following:

```
//@@custom code start — xxxxx

//@@custom code end — xxxxx
```

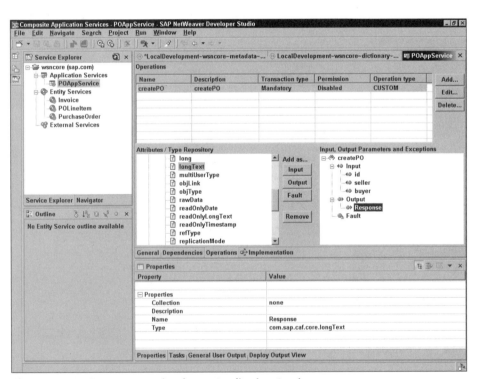

Figure 13-11: Custom operation for an Application Service

These areas of the file are not overwritten when the modifications are made to the metadata using the modeler. While the signature and parts of the implementation are code-generated, it is the responsibility of the developer to add the implementation for custom operations. The code for the `imports` section of `PurchaseOrder` class must be changed as follows.

```
//@@custom code start - [imports]

import com.sap.wsncore.besrv.purchaseorder.*;

//@@custom code end - [imports]
```

Further, the `createPO` method must be changed as shown in Figure 13-12. The added piece of code creates a `PurchaseOrder` object using the method from the Entity Service, gathers the input parameters, sets them in the newly created object, updates the object through the service call, and sets the return value of the method to the `key` field that was generated during the update.

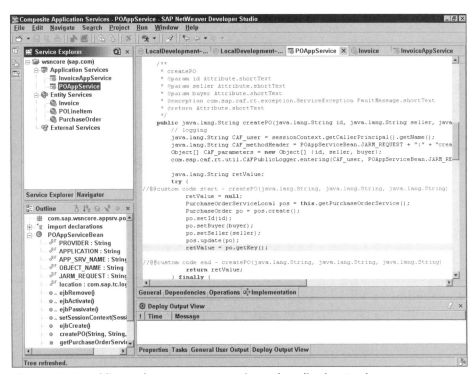

Figure 13-12: Adding code to custom operations of Application Service

Now, all the metadata must be saved, the application code generated, the development component built, and then the application deployed to SAP WAS. This concludes the CAF Core portion of the development.

Creating Guided Procedures

This section explains the procedures for creating all the GP objects for the Purchase Order process. A bottom-up approach to development is used. *Callable Objects* (*COs*) and corresponding *Actions* for each of the steps in the process are first created. The series of steps (Actions) are then added to a *Block*. The Block is then added to a *Process*. While the Purchase Order process has five steps, only the first three steps are considered in this exercise. These steps capture all the technicalities involved in the process. As alluded to in Chapter 10, COs represent the implementation of Actions.

The URLs for the various GP tools are as follows:

- *GP Design Time* — `http://<host>:<port>/webdynpro/ dispatcher/sap.com/caf~eu~gp~ui~dt/AppWorkset`

- *GP Runtime* — `http://<host>:<port>/webdynpro/ dispatcher/sap.com/caf~eu~gp~ui~rt/WorkCenterRT`

- *GP Endpoint Alias* — `http://<host>:<port>/webdynpro/ dispatcher/sap.com/caf~eu~gp~ui~admin/EptAliasApp`

- *GP Administrator* — `http://<host>:<port>/webdynpro/ dispatcher/sap.com/caf~eu~gp~ui~admin/AdminWorkset`

- *UI ConfigBrowser* — `http://<host>:<port>/webdynpro/ dispatcher/sap.com/caf~UI~configbrowser/ConfigBrowser`

Setting the Endpoint Alias

For COs to be able to use Application Services, the Endpoint Alias has to be set up. Endpoint Alias refers to the system that hosts the Application Services. To check whether the alias is set up, open the GP Endpoint Alias URL in a Web browser. For Endpoint Alias Type, select "Endpoint Alias for EJB Remote call" and click the Go button. If no results show up, click Add. This brings up the Add Endpoint Alias screen. Specify the values for fields, as shown in Figure 13-13. The Remote Provider URL field must specify the host where the Application Services were deployed and its P4 port number. P4 refers to the implementation of the Remote Method Invocation (RMI) protocol on the SAP WAS. For technical reasons, the Test button always displays an error. Ignore the error and click Save.

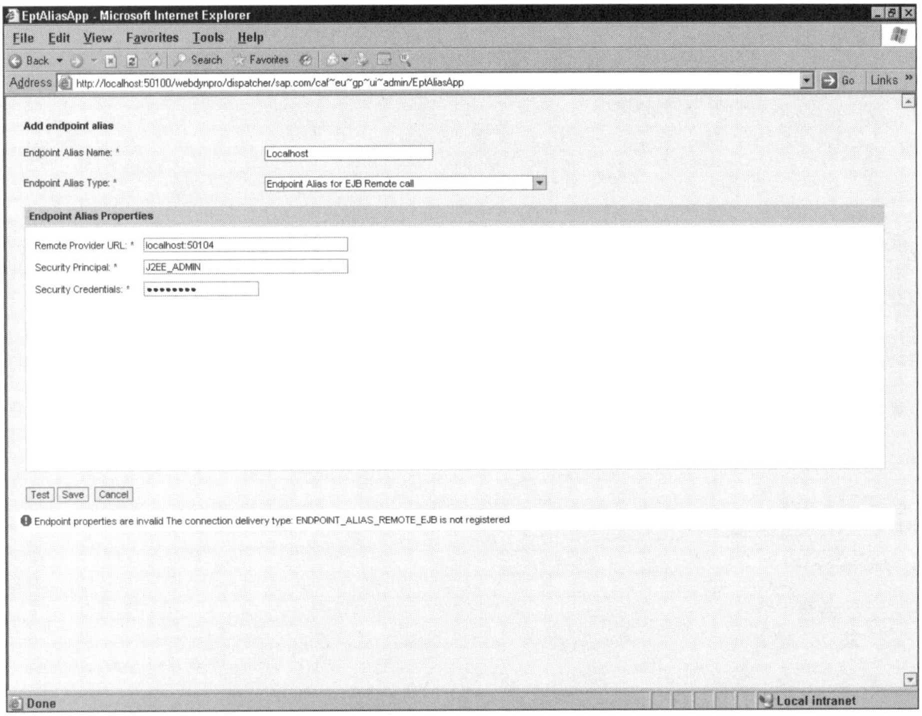

Figure 13-13: Setting the Endpoint Alias

Creating a Callable Object

To start creating the Purchase Order Persistence CO, open the GP Design Time using the URL specified previously. The first screen of GP Design Time is the gallery — a view of the folder structure of the GP repository. Folders can be created in a hierarchy with the root folder being the ancestor of all folders. Create the Wavecross folder under the root folder using the Create Folder button. Enter **Wavecross** for both the Name and Description fields in the Create Folder screen. Using a similar procedure, create the following folders under the Wavecross folder: Actions, Blocks, Callable Objects, and Processes. Now, select the Callable Objects folder and click the Create Callable Object link. In the following screen (see Figure 13-14), make the entries shown in Table 13-3 and click Next.

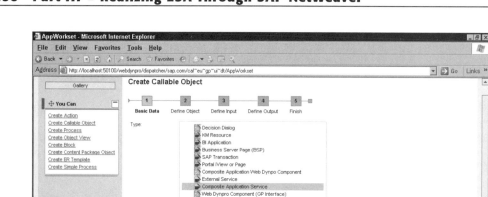

Figure 13-14: Creating the Purchase Order Persistence CO

Table 13-3: Purchase Order Persistence CO Basic Data

NAME	VALUE
Type	Composite Application Service
Name	Purchase Order Persistence
Description	Purchase Order Persistence
Original Language	English

In the Define Object step, the Application Service for the CO should be specified. Click the Choose button to navigate to the Endpoint selection screen. In the selection screen (see Figure 13-15) for the Endpoint Alias, select "Endpoint Alias for EJB Remote Call" for the Endpoint Alias Type field and click Go. Select the alias that was specified in the previous section and click the Choose button. The list of available Application Services for the Endpoint is displayed (see Figure 13-16). Navigate to and select wsncore → POAppService → createPO and click Next.

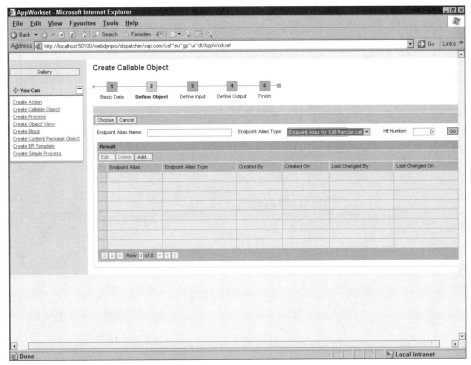

Figure 13-15: Selecting Endpoint Alias

Input and Output parameters are the mechanism by which data flows into and out of a CO. The output parameters become available to the next step in the process if they are part of the step's input parameters. Thus data flows through the whole process. The default input and output parameters that are displayed on the following two screens directly map to the method parameters and the return value of the `createPO` method of `POApService`.

Accept the defaults for both by clicking the Next button in each case. On the Finish screen, click the Finish and Open button. This opens the Callable Object Overview screen (see Figure 13-17).

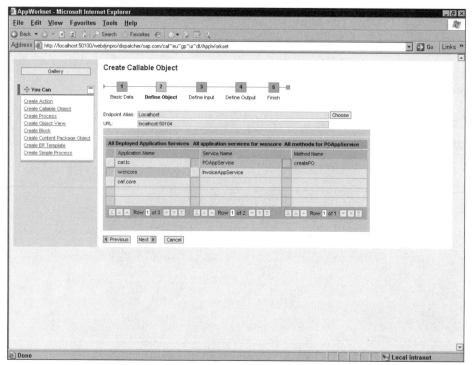

Figure 13-16: Available Application Services

Here, the object can be tested. Also, the object must be activated to make it available for subsequent steps. The Active/Inactive status is displayed at the top left of the Overview screen.

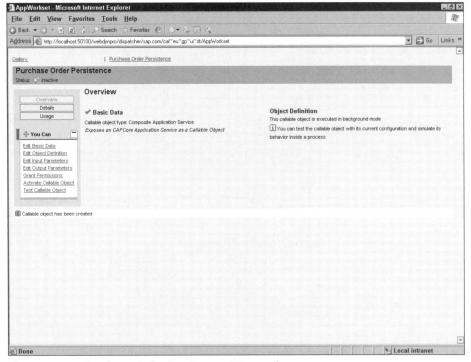

Figure 13-17: Purchase Order Persistence CO overview

GP provides a host of predefined COs that are exposed as templates. These templates can be customized and reused in other COs for a specific process. In the case study, the PORequest CO represents the first step in the Purchase Order process. This is where a Buyer would enter initial purchase order information. The Data Forms → Input template CO is a Web Dynpro–based form that can be used for general user input, and can be used for data transfer between two data steps. This is a good choice for the PORequest CO. With this information, the PORequest CO is now created. Use the information in Table 13-4 for Basic Data (see Figure 13-18).

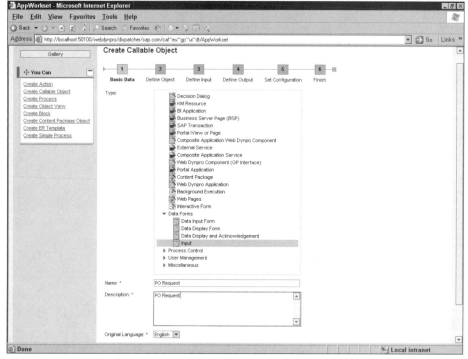

Figure 13-18: Basic data for PO Request CO

Table 13-4: PORequest CO Basic Data

NAME	VALUE
Type	Input
Name	PO Request
Description	PO Request
Original Language	English

The default selection in the Define Object screen can be used because it corresponds to the template CO that was previously selected. In the Define Input screen, the input parameters that map to the text fields in the form are defined. Click the Insert button to define an input parameter. Use the information given in Table 13-5. Use the same method to add the output parameters. Activate the object at the end of the Finish screen.

Table 13-5: PO Request CO Input and Output Parameters

PARAMETER	TECHNICAL NAME	NAME	TYPE
id	Id	id	String
seller	Seller	seller	String
buyer	Buyer	buyer	String

POConfirmation CO is the last CO that is created here (see Table 13-6). After a Buyer creates a purchase order, the PO Confirmation task is made visible to the Seller. The Seller has the option to either approve or reject the purchase order. Another Web Dynpro–based form template, Process Control → Visual Approval (see Figure 13-19), is used here.

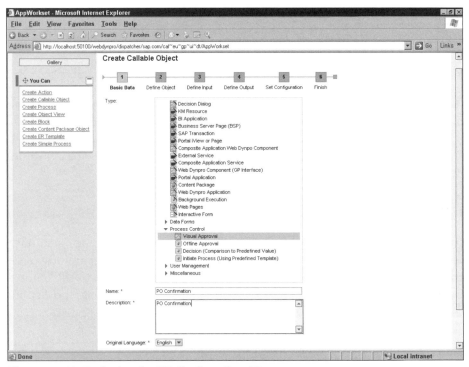

Figure 13-19: Basic data for PO Confirmation CO

Table 13-6: POConfirmation CO Basic Data

NAME	VALUE
Type	Visual Approval
Name	PO Confirmation
Description	PO Confirmation
Original Language	English

The input parameters are shown in Table 13-7.

Table 13-7: PO Request CO Input and Output Parameters

PARAMETER	TECHNICAL NAME	NAME	TYPE
id	Id	id	String
seller	Seller	seller	String
buyer	Buyer	buyer	String

The default output parameters — `Processor`, `Date`, and `Comment` (all of which are Strings — are retained. The usefulness of `Date` and `Comment` is obvious. The `Processor` field specified the processor of the request. The Set Configuration screen provides an optional means to send e-mails based upon whether the step was approved or rejected.

Creating an Action

Actions are the means by which GP processes interact with other applications. The other applications are in turn encapsulated in COs. Actions are now created for the three COs that were defined in the previous section. All Actions are created in the Wavecross → Actions folder of the gallery. Create the Action using the information shown in Table 13-8.

Table 13-8: Actions

ACTION/NAME/DESCRIPTION	CO
Purchase Order Persistence	Purchase Order Persistence
PO Request	PO Request
PO Confirmation	PO Confirmation

For each Action, the Basic Data in the Create Action screen must be filled and the object opened. The Action cannot be activated until the CO is attached to it (see Figure 13-20). Clicking on the "Callable objects have not been attached" link allows the user to browse through the gallery of COs (see Figure 13-21) and then make a selection.

Creating a Block

A Block represents a grouping of Actions, other Blocks, or processes, and is used to build a process in GP. The Type field of a Block defines how the units in the grouping are executed. The various types are shown in Table 13-9.[2]

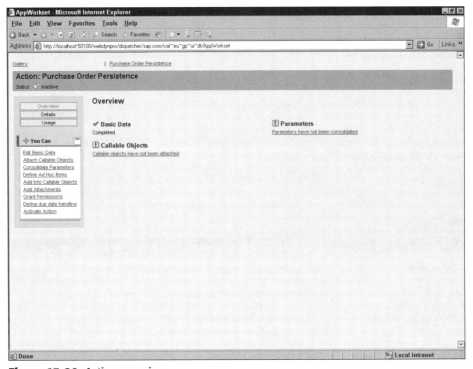

Figure 13-20: Action overview

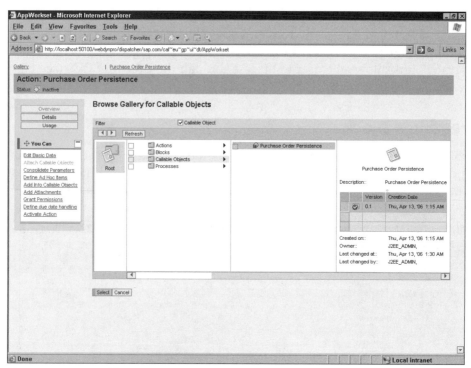

Figure 13-21: Attaching a CO to an Action

Table 13-9: Block Types

TYPE	DESCRIPTION
Sequential	The units are executed sequentially.
Parallel	The units are executed in parallel.
Precondition Loop	The units are executed in a loop — loop criteria is checked before every iteration.
Postconditional Loop	The units are executed in a loop — loop criteria is checked after every iteration.
Alternatives	The units are executed according to user's choice at run-time.
Parallel Dynamic	The Block has a subordinate Block. The number of subordinate Blocks is defined by the number of entries in the input table.

Block design follows the flow shown in Figure 13-22. The Block is created with some basic data. The units that form the Block are inserted into the Block during the Edit Block Flow step. The roles and the parameters are then consolidated. Finally, the Block is activated.

A single sequential Block is used in the Purchase Order process. Create a Block with the Basic Data, as shown in Table 13-10.

The Block Flow can be edited using the "Block flow has not yet been completed" link (see Figure 13-23). The following link allows you to insert Actions into the Block with the Insert button. Because all the required Actions have already been created, in the Insert Item screen, choose the "Use existing template(s)" option and then click the Select button. In the Select Item screen, navigate through the gallery and select Wavecross → Actions → PO Request Action. Follow the same procedure and insert the PO Confirmation and Purchase Order Persistence Actions in order.

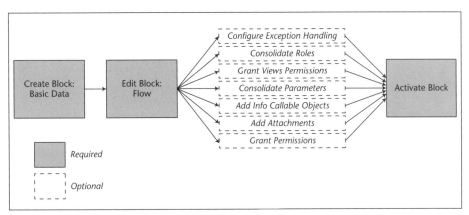

Figure 13-22: Block design (Source: © SAP AG 2005–2006. All rights reserved.)

Table 13-10: PO Process Block – Basic Data

NAME	VALUE
Name	PO Process
Description	PO Process
Original Language	English
Type	Sequential
Folder	Wavecross → Blocks

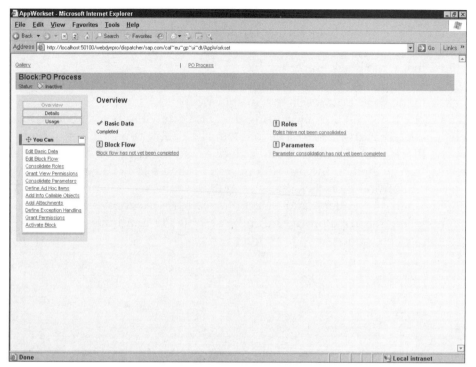

Figure 13-23: PO Process Block overview

For the PO Confirmation Action, the alternate path must be defined when the PO is rejected. To accomplish this, select PO Confirmation → Input data is rejected, and click the Define Target tab (see Figure 13-24). Choose the PO Request Action as the target. This means that the PO Request task is created for the Buyer when a Seller rejects the PO.

Each unit in the Block must be consolidated into a role. Users from the User Management Engine (UME) are assigned the GP roles so that they can participate in the process. Different tasks must be created by the GP for users with different roles. So, when a particular step is reached in a given instance of a GP, a task is created for the user with the role that is responsible for handling the unit. To consolidate roles for the units, click the "Roles have not been consolidated" link in the PO Process Overview. This opens the "Consolidate block roles" screen. Select the Processor of PO Request line item (see Figure 13-25), enter **Buyer** in the Consolidate To text field, and click Go. Use a similar process to consolidate Processor of PO Confirmation and Processor of Purchase Order Persistence line items to the Seller role.

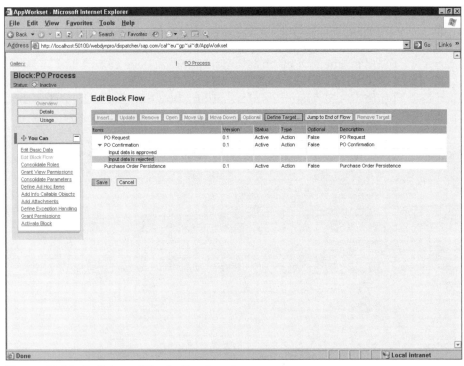

Figure 13-24: Defining a PO rejection target

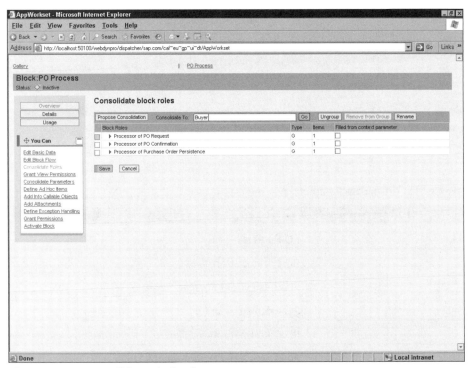

Figure 13-25: Consolidate Block roles

Finally, the context parameters must be consolidated. Context parameters are like global variables in a GP. The GP uses this information to store context data for an instance of the GP in a single location. To consolidate context parameters, click the "Parameter consolidation has not yet been completed" link in the PO Process Overview screen. This opens the Consolidate Parameters screen (see Figure 13-26). Use the information shown in Table 13-11 for this step. Click Save and then activate the Block.

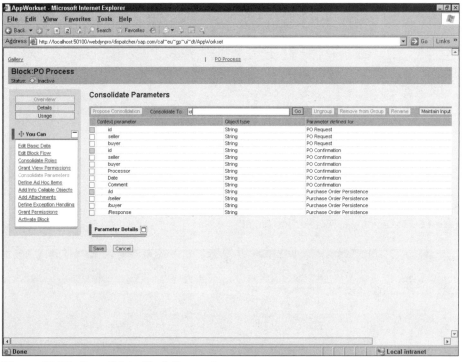

Figure 13-26: Consolidate Block Parameters.

Table 13-11: Consolidate Parameters

CONSOLIDATE TO	CONTEXT PARAMETER
Id	PO Request → id
	PO Confirmation → id
	Purchase Order Persistence → id
Seller	PO Request → seller
	PO Confirmation → seller
	Purchase Order Persistence → seller

Table 13-11 *(continued)*

CONSOLIDATE TO	CONTEXT PARAMETER
Buyer	PO Request → buyer
	PO Confirmation → buyer
	Purchase Order Persistence → buyer

Summary

Business task management is a subset of the end-to-end Business Process Management capabilities offered by SAP NetWeaver. It provides the advanced capabilities to enable user-driven processes, which complements the system-to-system executable process defined as orchestrations. In fact, an orchestration can hand off a step to a business task management feature and monitor for its completion. SAP provides a host of technologies that address various aspects of business task management.

The Composite Application Framework (CAF) comprising CAF-Core and CAF-Guided Procedures (GPs) is one of the newer SAP technologies that makes the task of building composite applications and user-driven business processes easier. These technologies minimize the amount of coding that must be done to build an application. Also, they promote re-usability of assets and flexibility of applications.

Entity, Application, and External Services are the building blocks with which GPs are built. They represent local persistency, remote persistency, local services, and remote services. They are built using NWDS. Application Services are the only form of services that can be used in GPs; GPs are built using browser-based tools without the need for writing any code.

This chapter covered Business Task Management and the use of CAF technology to implement it. The chapter also covered the issue of how CAF-GP provides user interfaces for users to interact with tasks. Chapter 14 examines the creation of additional user interfaces with SAP NetWeaver.

References

The following are sources for additional information on using CAF to create ESA-based composite applications.

1. SAP, "Creating Blocks," 2005. Available at `http://help.sap.com/saphelp_nw04s/helpdata/en/68/6182410349213ce10000000a1550b0/content.htm`.
2. J. Weilbach and M. Herger, "SAP xApps — and the Composite Application Framework," Galileo Press, 2005.

CHAPTER 14

Creating Additional User Interfaces Using Services

SAP NetWeaver Portal (Portal) provides secure, role-based, and Web-based access for users to a company's applications, information, and services. A company's employees can be provided with a customizable work area where they can perform all their activities, including the capability to act on the tasks in their work lists, report time sheets, access business data, or manage their tasks among others. Business partners can also be provided with a Portal work area where they can handle all of their interactions with the company. Using the Portal, end customers can be provided access to shopping cart–like applications as well. All of these require user interfaces (UIs) that interact with back-end systems.

The importance of using enterprise services to expose back-end system data and the technologies that can be used to create the enterprise services themselves has been established in previous chapters. It has also been mentioned that this allows the enterprise services to be consumed by many different types of clients, including mobile devices, Adobe Forms, Microsoft Office tools, and really any development environment capable of invoking Web Services and handling the related response.

This chapter discusses different ways to consume enterprise services and create UIs that display the data using the Portal. The chapter covers two of the newest SAP technologies (namely, Web Dynpro and Visual Composer). While Web Dynpro is used by application developers, Visual Composer is targeted for use by both developers and Business Process Experts.

Concepts

The task of creating a Web-based front-end can be performed by business experts or business application developers. When all the necessary services for working with back-end data and the UI templates for displaying the data are already available, Visual Composer is the preferred technology to use. This is because business experts who clearly understand the business requirements can use a model-based and completely code-free development environment to quickly develop the front-end.

On the other hand, if back-end services or required UI templates do not exist, or requirements require building more complex UIs, Web Dynpro should be the technology of choice because Web Dynpro provides the flexibility to accomplish these goals. However, that means developers with Web Dynpro technology expertise must also be available to work on these tasks.

Components for Web Dynpro for Java are built using NetWeaver Developer Studio, while components for Web Dynpro for ABAP are built using the ABAP Workbench (see Figure 14-1). Web Dynpro *patterns* are Web Dynpro components that can be used for building UIs. Web Dynpro *applications* can use patterns to build UIs quickly, without the need to build the templates for every single application UI. Visual Composer applications exclusively use patterns to build UIs.

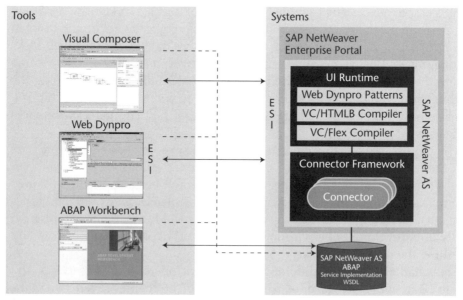

Figure 14-1: User interfaces for enterprise services (Source: © SAP AG 2005–2006. All rights reserved.)

As we outlined in Chapter 10, Visual Composer is a browser-based tool that runs on Microsoft Internet Explorer with an Adobe SVG Viewer. Models that are built in Visual Composer can be compiled using various compilers. The Visual Composer HTML for Business (HTMLB) compiler and the Visual Composer Flex Compiler are examples. The compilation mechanism that is used determines whether the code generated from the model is in HTMLB or in a Flash format. Both compilers are available in the Portal, and are used in the development process of Visual Composer applications.

All applications running on the Portal must access data using the Connector Framework. Generally, components built using Visual Composer and Web Dynpro are intended to be run on Portal and, hence, must use the Connector Framework to access data. Enterprise services (in the form of Web Services) are hosted on the SAP Web Application Server (WAS).

Creating a User Interface with Web Dynpro

This section describes the architecture of a Web Dynpro solution. It shows the process for creating a Web Dynpro component and a related Web Dynpro application that uses that component. The component that is built here is a simple UI that lets the user enter search criteria for Google Search in a form, submit the form data, and then view the search results.

Web Dynpro Component

Web Dynpro components rely heavily on the Model View Controller (MVC) architecture. Business logic and persistence are represented in the *model*. UI is represented by the *view*. Event handling, navigation logic, and interaction with the model is represented by the *controller*. This is a common software development pattern used to create more maintainable Web applications.

Context data is a set of nodes and attributes that captures the entities and relationships of *model data*. *Model binding* is the binding of model data to the context data of the Component Controller (see Figure 14-2) or a Custom Controller.

Each Web Dynpro component has a single Component Controller and zero (or many) Custom Controllers. The Component Controller can be viewed as the single default controller for every Web Dynpro component. The role of the Custom Controllers is to provide modularity (when needed) within a Web Dynpro component.

Model binding is the mechanism by which model data from the Model Interface is made available to the controllers. For data from the controller to be made available to the view, *context mapping* is done between the contexts of the Component Controller and the View Controller. Finally, UI elements from the view are bound to context data from the View Controller using the process called *data binding*.

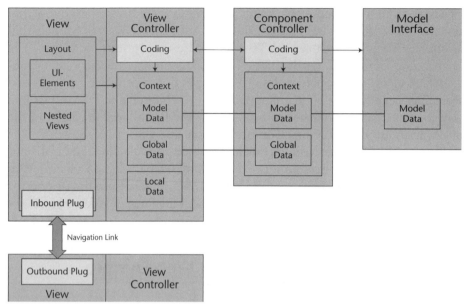

Figure 14-2: Web Dynpro component architecture (Source: © SAP AG 2005–2006. All rights reserved.)

A View represents a section or all of the area of a UI screen with a coherent set of UI elements. Views in Web Dynpro are entirely built using the "What You See Is What You Get" (WYSIWYG) approach with the View Modeler. Data binding between the UI elements and View Controller context elements is done using the Context Mapping tool. Inbound and Outbound Plugs are the mechanism by which navigation between views is defined.

To understand these concepts better, let's take a look at the process flow for the Web Dynpro component that is built in this section. The initial UI displays the UI form elements and a table with no data in them. This is because the context data is empty. After a user enters form data and clicks the Submit button, because of data binding, the form data is transferred to the context of the View Controller. The event-handling code of the View Controller invokes the event-handling code of the Component Controller. The form-related context data is transferred from the View Controller to the Component Controller. The event-handling code of the Component Controller invokes the business method of the Model Interface.

The Model Interface method returns with response data and is promptly placed in the context data of the Custom Controller. The context data is transferred to the context of the View Controller, and then the UI elements that are bound to context data are updated to display the context data.

Creating the Web Dynpro Component

Now, let's walk through an example of creating a Web Dynpro component. For this example, you will use the open source application Eclipse, which SAP has enhanced with a complete set of design, construction, and maintenance tools. The steps for this exercise are as follows:

1. Create a new Eclipse workspace in `C:\projects\ESABook\ chapter14`. Begin by creating a Web Dynpro Development Component (DC) project in the workspace.

2. To create the project, go to the Resource perspective of the IDE. In the context menu of the Navigator view, select New → Project → Development Component → Development Component Project.

3. When you click Next, you are prompted to assign the DC to a Software Component. Here, select Local Development → My Components.

4. Click Next and you are prompted to enter project data. Enter the project data, as shown in Figure 14-3.

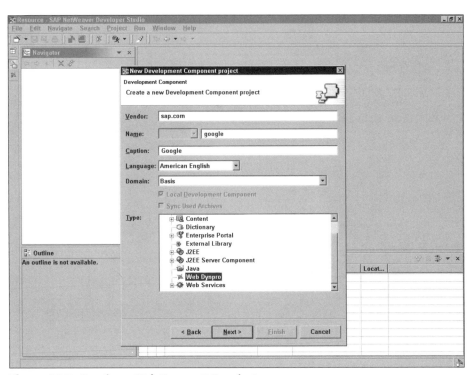

Figure 14-3: Creating a Web Dynpro DC project

5. The next window displays the project name and location. Enter the information as shown in Figure 14-4. The Window and View information should also be entered here. Window represents a displayable page in a browser. It consists of one or more Views. Each View is a collection of related UI elements.

6. Click the Finish button to create the Web Dynpro component project.

The Web Dynpro Explorer view of the Web Dynpro Perspective of NWDS (see Figure 14-5) displays all the objects that can be created in the project. All Web Dynpro development is done in this perspective and view.

The DC Metadata section contains the definition of the development component, as well as the definition for the Public Parts of the component. This is the information that other components use when integrating with this component. The Applications section contains Application objects, which are separately deployable objects that contain Web Dynpro components.

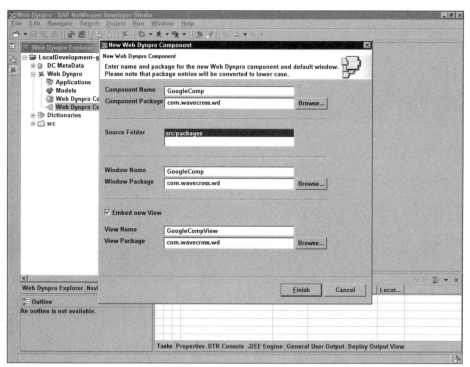

Figure 14-4: Web Dynpro DC properties

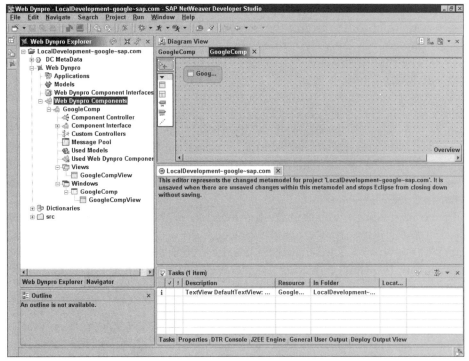

Figure 14-5: Web Dynpro Explorer

The Models section is the container for all models that are defined in this development component. The Component Interfaces section contains the interfaces for all the Web Dynpro components that are defined in this Development Component. The Web Dynpro Components section holds all the Web Dynpro components that are defined in this Development Component. The Dictionaries section has a listing of all the data types that can be used by the model and the context. The src section contains generated code for objects that are built in the Development Component.

The Web Dynpro component for the example presented here is created in the com.wavecross.wd package. The Window and View data are set as shown in Figure 14-4. The newly created component and all the types of objects that can be created in it are shown in Figure 14-5. All of the types of objects, except Message Pool, were explained previously. The Message Pool is the means by which string data for the UI can be externalized for easier maintenance purposes.

To create the model that is to be used in this example for `GoogleComp`, select Create Model from the context menu of LocalDevelopment~ google~sap.com → Web Dynpro → Models. The New Model wizard is displayed. The intent here is to consume a Web Service, so select the Import Web Service Model option.

The next screen allows you to enter the model name and package, as shown in Figure 14-6. The Web Services Definition Language (WSDL) for the GoogleSearch Web Service is obtained from `http://api.google.com/Google Search.wsdl` and saved locally. Hence, select the Local File System or URL option for this example. The other options allow the WSDL to be specified from the list of WSDLs that are available on a SAP WAS server, or from a UDDI or URL. Click Next.

In the next screen, you specify the location of the `GoogleSearch.wsdl` file. Finally, the model is created by selecting the Finish button of the final screen of the wizard. The wizard creates the Web Service proxy classes and the classes can be viewed under LocalDevelopment~google~sap.com → Web Dynpro → Models → Google Model.

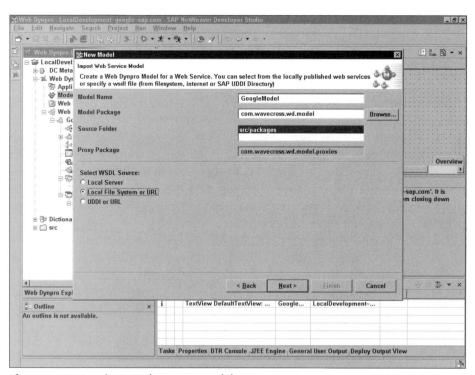

Figure 14-6: Creating a Web Dynpro model

As mentioned in Chapter 10, the Data Modeler can be used to create views, create custom controllers, create models, add an existing model, embed an existing component, and create data links between various elements. To open the Data Modeler, double-click on LocalDevelopment~google~sap.com → Web Dynpro → Web Dynpro Components → GoogleComp. The Diagram View on the edit area is the Data Modeler. When double-clicked, the title area of the Diagram View occupies the entire IDE, as shown in Figure 14-7.

Add the previously created Google Model to `GoogleComp` by selecting Add Existing Model from the context menu in the Used Models area. In the Selection Needed dialog box, choose Google Model from a list of available models.

The Custom Controller for the component should now be added. From the context menu in the Custom Controllers area (see Figure 14-8), you have options to add an existing controller (Select in Web Dynpro Explorer), create a new controller (Create Custom Controller), or apply an existing Template (Apply Template). Templates are the mechanism by which the most commonly used patterns are pre-built. Only a minor amount of customization must be done on a template for it to be used in a Web Dynpro component.

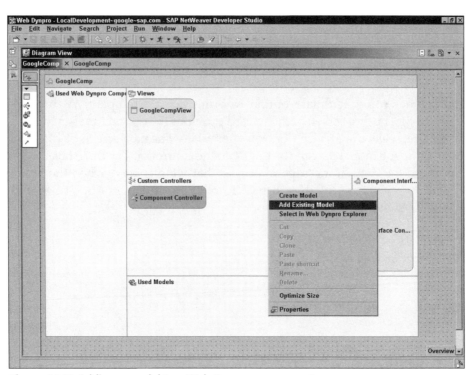

Figure 14-7: Adding a model to a Web Dynpro component

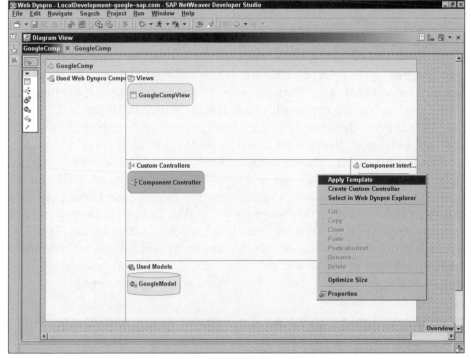

Figure 14-8: Adding a custom component controller

Select the Apply Template option to bring up the Template Wizard (see Figure 14-8). The first screen of the wizard provides the option to select the template. Here, select the Service Controller template. The next screen displays the objects from the model that can be bound to the controller. The three objects correspond to the request message interfaces that were created when the model was created. Here, select the class corresponding to the doGoogleSearch method, as shown in Figure 14-9.

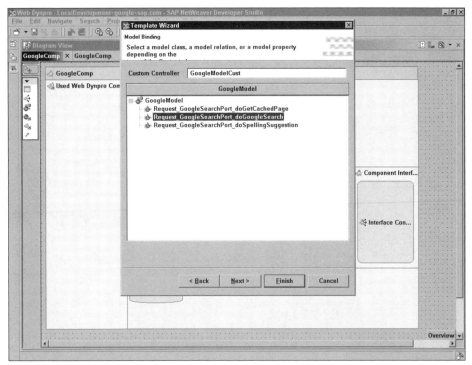

Figure 14-9: Selecting a model property

In the next screen of the wizard, the model elements must be bound to elements in the context of the controller. All context elements of the model are displayed in the left pane (see Figure 14-10). When selected in the left pane, an element is then displayed in the right pane. The name of the element, as displayed in the right pane, is the name that it assumes in the controller context. These names can be modified in this dialog box. Only elements whose checkbox is selected are added to the controller context.

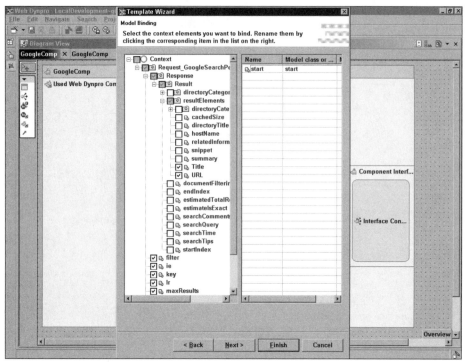

Figure 14-10: Model binding

In this example, select all simple attributes of the class (which are the `Request` parameters to the `doGoogleSearch` method). In other words, all the method parameters to the `doGoogleSearch` method must be selected. Also, in the `Response` attribute, select the `Title` and `URL` elements (as shown in Figure 14-10) because, in this example, the intent is to display only the title and URL of each of the search results.

The next screen of the wizard (which is also the final screen) enables you to specify the method name that should be used for the method that would make the Web Service call. In this example, use the suggested default, `execute` `Request_GoogleSearchPort_doGoogleSearch()`.

The generated code can be seen in the Implementation tab of LocalDevelopment~google~sap.com → Web Dynpro → Web Dynpro Components → GoogleComp → Custom Controllers → GoogleModelCust, as shown here:

```
//@@begin javadoc:executeRequest_GoogleSearchPort_doGoogleSearch()
/** Declared method. */
// d
public void executeRequest_GoogleSearchPort_doGoogleSearch( )
```

```
{
  //@@begin executeRequest_GoogleSearchPort_doGoogleSearch()
  //$$begin Service Controller(1895367545)
  IWDMessageManager manager = wdComponentAPI.getMessageManager();
  try
  {

wdContext.currentRequest_GoogleSearchPort_doGoogleSearchElement().modelO
bject().execute();
    wdContext.nodeResponse().invalidate();
    wdContext.nodeResult().invalidate();
    wdContext.nodeResultElements().invalidate();
  }
  catch(Exception e)
  {
    manager.reportException(e.getMessage(), false);
  }
  //$$end
  // d
}
```

When the Web Dynpro component `GoogleComp` was created (see Figure 14-4), the view called `GoogleCompView` was created and embedded in the component. A data link should now be created between this view and the custom controller, `GoogleModelCust`, which was created in the previous step. To create the data link, from the toolbar of the Data Modeler (which is in the upper-right corner of the Diagram View), click the arrow icon ("Create a data link" tooltip), click `GoogleCompView`, and then drag the mouse to, and release over, `GoogleModelCust`.

The elements of the view and associated context mappings and data bindings must now be created. The view should have a form where a user can enter all the fields required for the call to the Web Service. It should also have a Submit button that initiates the call to the Web Service. Finally, it should have a table that displays the search results. Templates are again used for each of these elements.

To create the form, select Apply Template from the context menu of the view. In the Template Wizard, select the Form template. In the next screen, bind the context attributes to form elements. All of the simple attributes of the request are bound, as shown in Figure 14-11. Follow a similar process for the table. Apply the Table template to `GoogleCompView`, and bind the `Title` and `URL` elements to the table. At run-time, the data from these elements shows up in the columns of the table.

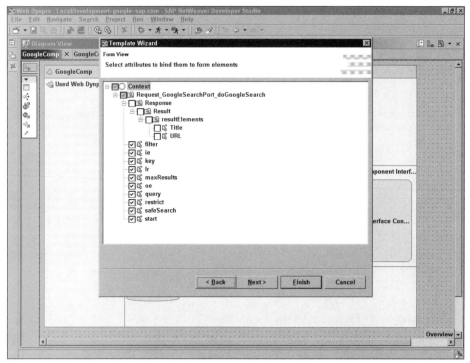

Figure 14-11: Binding for Form template

Finally, you must use the Action Button template to add the button element and associate an action with the button. The label of the button is set to Search, and the default entries for Action (Search) and Event (OnActionSearch) are retained. The event handler for the button is set as shown in Figure 14-12. When the Call Method checkbox is selected, only the allowable values for Controller and then Methods are displayed.

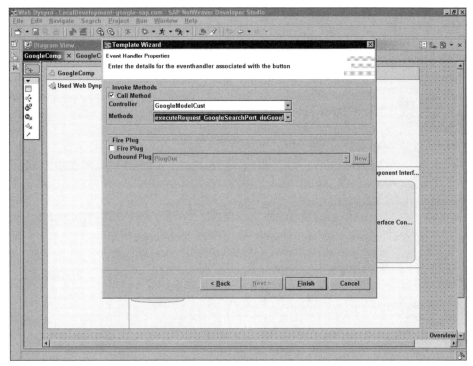

Figure 14-12: Action Button Wizard

Figure 14-13 shows the visual impact of applying the templates on the view. This is the `GoogleCompView`, which can be viewed by double-clicking LocalDevelopment~google~sap.com → Web Dynpro → Web Dynpro Components → GoogleComp → Views → GoogleCompView. The view is, in fact, opened in the View Modeler tool. The form, table, and the button are shown in order. Context elements that map to form and table elements are displayed.

If the template mechanism is not used, you can use the View Modeler to create the UIs by selecting UI elements from various categories such as Standard Simple, shown on the bottom-left of Figure 14-13.

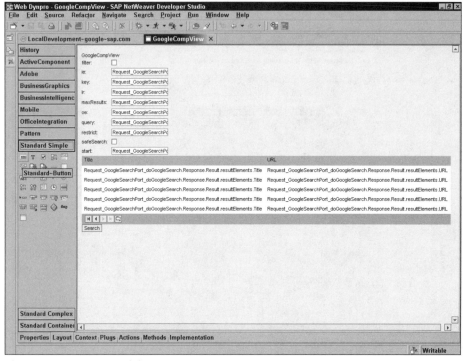

Figure 14-13: View Modeler

The generated code for the event handler can be seen by clicking the Implementation tab shown at the bottom of Figure 14-13. The relevant code is as follows:

```
//@@begin javadoc:onActionSearch(ServerEvent)
/** Declared validating event handler. */
// d
public void
onActionSearch(com.sap.tc.webdynpro.progmodel.api.IWDCustomEvent wdEvent
)
{
  //@@begin onActionSearch(ServerEvent)
  //$$begin ActionButton(-533115457)

wdThis.wdGetGoogleModelCustController().executeRequest_GoogleSearchPort_
doGoogleSearch();

  //$$end

  // d
}
```

A Web Dynpro component can be used as an iView in the Portal. To test the component without setting up the Portal business package, an Application object must be created in the Web Dynpro project.

NOTE Business packages are discussed in more detail later in this chapter.

To open the New Application Wizard, select Create Application from the context menu of LocalDevelopment~google~sap.com → Web Dynpro → Applications. Enter **GoogleComp** for the Name field and **com.wavecross.wd** for the Package field. In the following screen, select the Use existing Component option for Referenced Web Dynpro Component. Enter the Web Dynpro component and other fields on the next screen, as shown in Figure 14-14.

The project is built using the LocalDevelopment~google~sap.com → Development Component → Build context menu. The application is deployed and run by selecting Deploy New Archive and Run from the context menu of LocalDevelopment~google~sap.com → Web Dynpro → Application → GoogleApp.

A browser window is opened with the component UI (see Figure 14-15). The data for the "key" field must be obtained by registering with Google. For technical reasons, all of the text fields in the form must have at least the space character as a value.

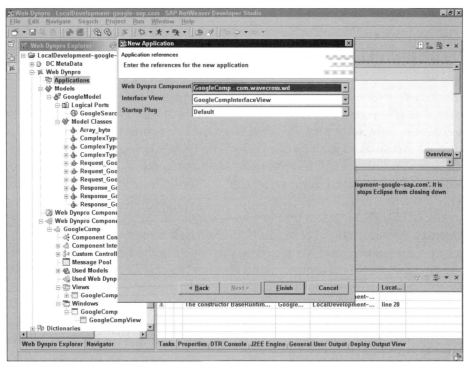

Figure 14-14: Creating a Web Dynpro application

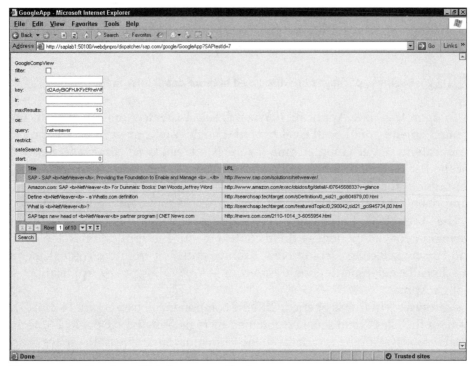

Figure 14-15: Running a Web Dynpro application

Creating a User Interface with Visual Composer

This section demonstrates the process for creating an iView using Visual Composer. A BAPI, exposed as a Web Service from SAP's ES Workplace (formerly the ESA Preview System), is invoked from the iView and the response that is returned is displayed in the same iView. The ES Workplace exposes functionality from an ERP system as enterprise services. In our example, the Control Recipes within a given time range for a Production Planning system are requested from the enterprise service and then displayed.

The exercise presented in this section is similar to the Web Dynpro exercise presented earlier in this chapter. In both exercises, a request is made to a service in some fashion, and the response displayed to the user. The user is provided with a form to enter input data. A button triggers a request to the service using data entered in the form, and then displays response data in a table.

Begin by opening Visual Composer in a browser window using a URL similar to `http://<host>:<port>/VC/default.jsp`. Create a new model by selecting the File → New Model menu. This brings up the Create New Model dialog box, as shown in Figure 14-16.

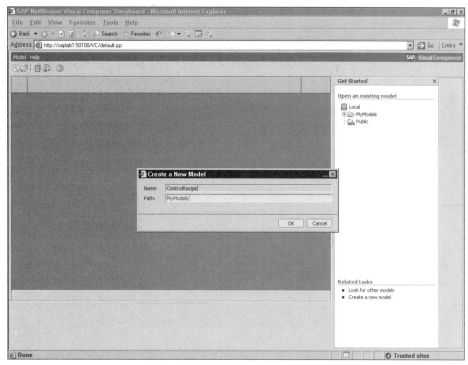

Figure 14-16: Creating a new model

As shown in Figure 14-17, the Visual Composer desktop consists of the main menu, main toolbar, the workspace, the task panel toolbar and the toolset. The main menu provides the functionality that is expected in any IDE — creating and working various objects, building and deployment of models. The main toolbar provides the same functionality in the form of icons. The Workspace is where the models and their contents are actually built. The Task Panel toolbar provides the means to work with various toolsets that are displayed in the Tool Set area. The content of the Tool Set area is dependent upon the selection made in the Task Panel toolbar area, as well as the model element that is currently displayed in the Workspace area.

The hierarchy of the model elements is as follows: Package → Page → iView. A package is a means by which other objects such as Page and iView can be organized in a model. A Page corresponds to a page or a single Web page in a portal. An iView corresponds to an iView in a portal. An iView represents a certain viewable area on a portal page.

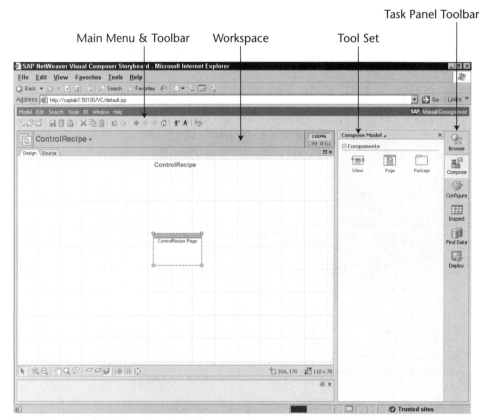

Figure 14-17: Creating a new module

As indicated previously, Visual Composer uses the Connection Framework in SAP Portal to connect to data sources. In the newer versions of Visual Composer, by default, the Connection Framework of the Portal that is hosting Visual Composer is available for use in Visual Composer. During the modeling process, the metadata for the service call for the back-end system must be imported into Visual Composer model. The back-end systems are defined in the Portal and are available for use in Visual Composer. The only exception is when the back-end system is a Web Service provider. To consume from a Web Service, the system that provides the Web Service must be defined in Visual Composer.

To add the System Definition for the back-end system to Visual Composer, start by selecting the Tools → Define Web Service System . . . menu. This brings up the System Definition dialog box. Enter data as shown in Figure 14-18. Here, the WSDL file is specified from the local file system. Click the Create button to finish creation of the system.

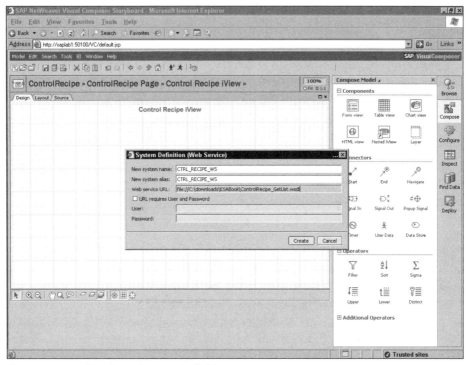

Figure 14-18: Creating a System Definition

Select the Find Data icon of the Task Panel toolbar to display the Find Data Services toolset. The System drop-down displays the list of available back-end systems (see Figure 14-19). Here, select the Web Service system that was previously defined. The list of available operations can be searched using search strings. In this example, there is only one operation, and this can be displayed by simply clicking the Search button. Here, you should select BAPI_CONTROL_RECIPE_GET_LIST, and then drag and drop the operation into the iView.

When the operation is dropped into the Workspace area, the Define Data Service dialog box is displayed. This dialog box allows the selection of input and output fields of the operation that can be bound to UI elements (see Figure 14-19). When the port in the left pane is selected, the selectable fields for the option are displayed in the right pane. In this example, the DATEFROM and DATETO fields are selected for the INPUT port, and BATCH, MATERIAL, PLANT, SCHEDULED_START_TIME, and SCHEDULED_END_TIME fields are selected for the CNTLRECHEADER port. No selections are made for the RETURN port.

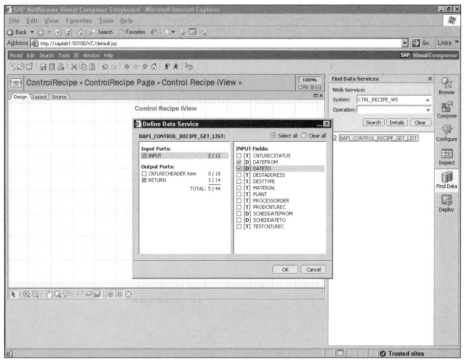

Figure 14-19: Searching and adding a service to iView

To add the Input Form for the iView, click the Input node, and drag the node before releasing the mouse. The menu shown in Figure 14-20 pops up, enabling you to select the Add Input Form item. Selecting the menu item adds a representation of the form to the iView. If desired, you can specify the name of the form.

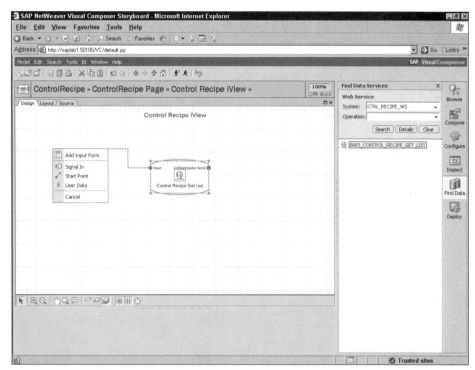

Figure 14-20: Adding the input form

You should use a similar process to specify a table view for the output. The other available options shown in Figure 14-21 for the output are Add Table View and Add Chart View. The second set of options may be used to do additional operations on output data before they are displayed. For example, the Sort Data option may be used to sort the list by certain criteria. Filter Data and Aggregate Data are the other options.

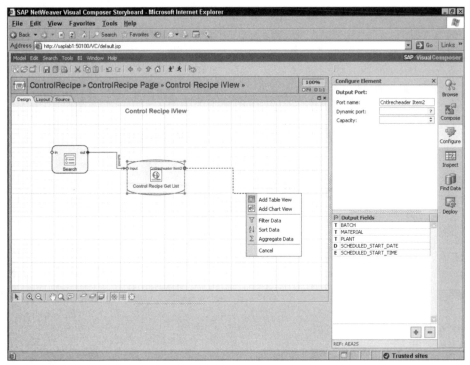

Figure 14-21: Adding the output table

Various UI customizations can be done by selecting the Configure icon in the Task Panel toolbar. Double-clicking Input Form or the output table elements in the workspace pre-selects the Configure option. The Task Panel area displays the customizations that can be done. The data elements from the model that are bound to the UI elements are displayed. Double-clicking a data element displays the Control Properties dialog box (see Figure 14-22). Here, you can specify display features and data formatting and validation, and you can tie the control to custom actions. In this example, the labels for both the input and output fields are changed for better readability.

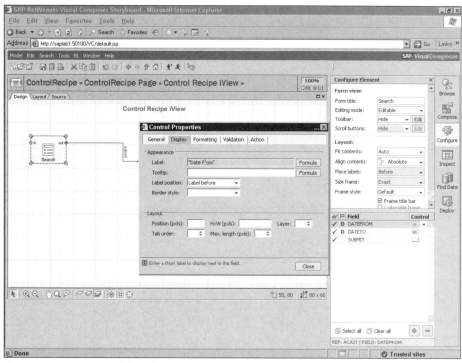

Figure 14-22: Customizing the UI

You can use the Deployer icon of the Task Panel toolbar to deploy the development artifacts to the portal (see Figure 14-23). Code is generated from metadata for the model. The generated code is compiled, packaged, and deployed to the portal. All of this is done by clicking the Deployer button in the Task Panel area. Deployment can also be initiated from the icon in the toolbar or the Tools → Deploy Model menu. Generated code is in HTMLB or in Flash, depending upon the option selected using the Tools → Options menu. The Flash option is available only when the Flex server is installed.

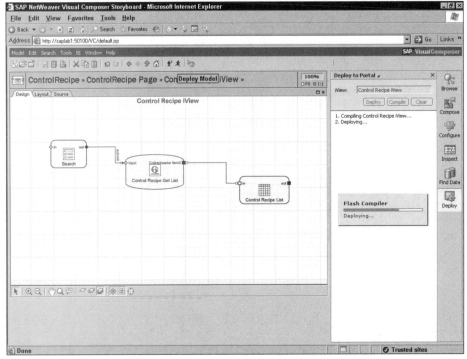

Figure 14-23: Deploying the model to SAP Enterprise Portal

The deployment process also runs the deployed iView. Figure 14-24 shows the screen that is initially displayed in the Portal.

Business Packages in Portal

During the deployment process in Visual Composer, a business package is also created in the Portal Content Studio of SAP Portal (see Figure 14-25). A *business package* is a set of portal content artifacts that are assembled to solve a particular problem. Specifically, when a particular piece of back-end functionality is intended to be exposed to users through the Portal, this involves two major development artifacts: UI content and business package. iViews are the mechanism by which UI content is built. The framework in which the iViews are displayed is defined by the business package.

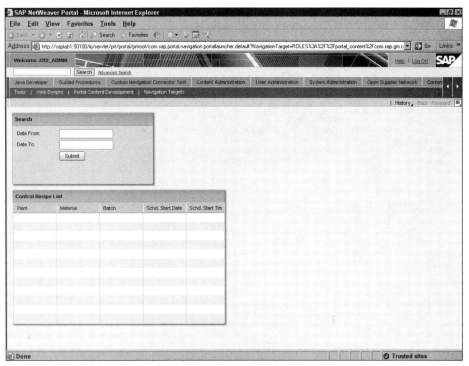

Figure 14-24: Running the VC application

NOTE A business package is a unique set of portal content artifacts that are assembled to provide a specific solution. They can contain roles, worksets, pages, and iViews.

Let's take the example of a Timesheet functionality that has to be exposed to employees. One way to elegantly expose this to users is to have a Timesheet tab in the portal for all employees. When users navigate to this tab, they can then be given the option to view old timesheets, create a new timesheet, and so on. While the tables and forms that let users view and modify data are a part of the functionality of the iView, the definition of the navigation tabs, the definition of the role that you would need to have to access the tab, and other similar aspects are captured in the concept of the business package.

The most relevant portal objects can be defined in a hierarchy — Role → Workset → Page → iView. A role from a business package is assigned to users. Users with the specified role then have access to the navigation tab, which is defined by the Workset. The Workset can have secondary navigation tabs in the portal, and these correspond to Pages. A Page can have one or more iViews in it.

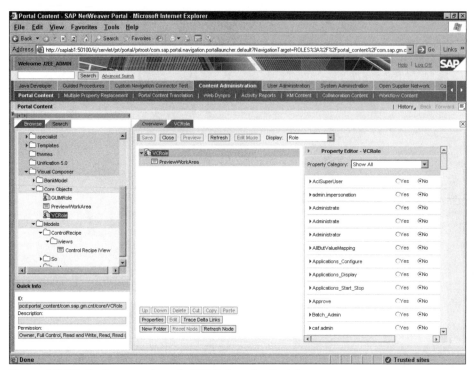

Figure 14-25: Business package in SAP Enterprise Portal

Summary

The SAP NetWeaver Portal is the prime mechanism by which a company's applications and services can be exposed to employees, business partners, and end customers. SAP Portal provides connectivity for portal applications to back-end system data through the Connection Framework. Enterprise services that are provided by SAP WAS are a subset of the services that can be provided to Portal applications through the Connection Framework.

UIs in Portal are built from portal components and are represented in Portal as Pages and iViews. Web Dynpro and Visual Composer are two of the newer SAP technologies that can be used for this purpose. Web Dynpro is intended for business application developers, and Visual Composer is intended for business experts. Simple examples for building portal components in Web Dynpro and Visual Composer and the underlying concepts have been described in this chapter.

Chapter 15 explains the concepts of embedded analytics and the mechanism to create applications with embedded analytics using Visual Composer.

Embedded Analytics

Decision-making is a key part of any business activity. When making a decision, you need relevant information presented to you in such a way that it is usable, and you need the ability to take action based on the decision you make. Thus, supporting decision-making means providing both information and the ability to take action based on that information.

This chapter explains how embedded analytics create very tangible business benefits by supporting people in making decisions. For the sake of argument, imagine that all business tasks that can be automated have been automated. What remains are those tasks that actually require human beings to make decisions. Humans have tremendous brain power, and they want to apply that to logical reasoning and decision-making, not to search for information, guess at things they do not know, or run around trying to find a way to implement their decisions. Embedded analytics, done right, allow you to put your powers to work where they create the most benefits.

This is, of course, not just a technical problem. On the one hand, you must understand a lot about the business to be able to choose the right data and actions for any particular task that involves decision making. On the other hand, you must also know a lot about your IT landscape to know where to find this data, and where to execute these actions. Designing embedded analytics brings these two skills together.

From this, it should be quite obvious how ESA and SAP NetWeaver support embedded analytics. Data and actions are made available in the form of enterprise services, and SAP NetWeaver provides a platform to bring them to the user. As a matter of fact, efficiently building good embedded analytics is virtually impossible without ESA.

As a result of reading this chapter, you will:

- Understand the nature of embedded analytics
- Understand how embedded analytics improve decision making
- Be able to design embedded analytics to address a specific business problem
- Know how to use SAP NetWeaver to incorporate embedded analytics into any application

Understanding Embedded Analytics

Embedded analytics span a wide range of the IT landscape. Let's follow the flow of data and start with the point in time when information about a business event is recorded in an online transaction processing (OLTP) system, such as mySAP ERP.

At this point, the information exists somewhat in isolation, but using the object model of the system, you can correlate it with other data in that system and with possible actions. Think of an order from a customer that gets recorded in the system. The order itself contains important information, such as who ordered what product, at what price, when they want it delivered, and so on. By using the object model, you can find important related information (such as stock levels for the product) and related actions (such as triggering delivery and invoicing).

Data is regularly transferred from one or more OLTP systems to data warehouses such as SAP NetWeaver Business Intelligence (BI) or other online analytical processing (OLAP) systems. Not only does this allow for more efficient reporting on the data itself, but transforming and integrating data from multiple systems and other sources into a single format allows you to also see trends and other big-picture information in many dimensions.

For example, data from a customer order can be correlated with lots of other data from internal and external sources to help understand such widely varying metrics as your risk exposure to this particular customer and the customer's ability to pay you. Other examples of information available from OLAP systems include seasonal sales statistics of products on the order, how those statistics are correlated with the weather, and the order processing times in a division of your company.

Data from OLTP and OLAP systems can again be brought together in dashboards used by business users to make decisions. The decision-making can be associated with specific events, or be part of generally managing your business. A specific event associated with your order may be that the customer wants to cancel it. To be able to decide whether to allow this, you need a lot of information, such as what the contract says, what status the order is in, whether the customer regularly cancels orders, how profitable this customer is to you, and so on.

An example of more general business management may be that you want to identify popular bundles of products that you see people buy together, so that you can promote the products together, use them as cross-selling opportunities, or price them together. To make these decisions, you must know what products are bought in what combinations, which customers buy them, what your profitability is for various products, and so on.

Once you have all this information, you can process it and make a decision. The decision usually results in one or more actions that go back to the underlying OLTP systems. In the case of the canceled order, you may decide to accept the cancellation, which triggers a transaction in the order processing system and perhaps other systems (for example, halting delivery if it has been triggered, or sending a credit note if an invoice has been sent). In the case of the product bundles, you may decide to promote a certain complementary product as a cross-selling opportunity on a Web site, which requires updating the cross-selling preferences behind the site.

In this chapter, all aspects of this data flow will be reviewed, but rather than viewing the concepts from the standpoint of data flow, the concepts are reviewed from the user's point of view. We will:

- Look more into how analytics are embedded into business processes
- Give some tips on how to design great embedded analytics
- Introduce the tools within SAP NetWeaver you can use to build embedded analytics
- Explain how you can get to the data you need
- Investigate different strategies to manage the underlying data and how that affects your ability to build embedded analytics
- Look into the future and speculate a little about how technological advances will affect embedded analytics

Closing the Loop

How are embedded analytics different from "ordinary" analytics? Are they? By using the term *embedded analytics*, the intent is to stress the fact that these analytics are embedded into business processes. Of course, all analytics are part of a business process one way or another. However, here the focus is to bring the analytics into the application that supports the process so that the user has access to analytical information and process control, including actions to be taken, at the same time, in the same place.

Therefore, a closed loop is provided in support of a business process, from a business event through analysis and decision making, to subsequent business events. The applications in question are usually composite in nature because they pick up events from multiple sources, draw upon information from multiple sources, and trigger events in multiple targets. The sources and targets all expose their data and functionality as services. Chapter 13 discussed the process of how to build composite applications, so here the focus will be more on the analytics part.

At some point in time, let's hope all analytics will be embedded analytics. At the moment, it is worth stressing the fact that you need to embed analytics into business processes to be able to run them better. Before explaining how to do that, two examples help demonstrate where this is important.

Example #1: Creating Context for a Vacation Request

Let's start with something really simple: a vacation request from an employee. You may think that such a trivial example does not belong in a serious book about how to address business challenges through a new IT architecture, but look at all the information needed by the manager who has to approve or reject the request. The actual value of a composite application for this will not be that big in many industries, but as soon as you deal with key individuals working on large projects, this is an issue.

The event that starts the process is the employee entering a vacation request — for example, through an employee self-service application. This gets recorded in a system, such as mySAP ERP and triggers a workflow task. The task is routed to the appropriate manager, who then needs to make a decision. When making the decision, the manager may want to know the following:

- How much vacation does the employee have left to take?
- What projects is the employee working on?
- What is the status of these projects now?
- What tasks and milestones lie between now and the end of the vacation?
- Who else is working on those projects?
- Are they planning to take vacation?
- Is there anyone available with similar skills?
- Who do we need to contact to get a substitute?

All of this information taken together is the context of the vacation request, and the manager should be given access to it through embedded analytics. To be able to do this, you must tap into various data sources:

- A human resources system to get vacation balances
- A human resources, project management, or portfolio management system to get the association to projects
- A project management system to get the status and plans
- A skills database to find potential substitutes
- A human resources system to find the manager of the substitute

All of this information is useless, of course if the user does not take action based on it. The actions the user can trigger also span a wide set of systems:

- Accept or reject the request in the human resources system
- Reschedule the project in the project management system
- Reassign resources from other projects in the human resources, project management, or portfolio management system
- Send an e-mail to another manager to request a substitute

Already in this simple example, you can see how embedding analytics into a business process can improve decision-making. If you are part of a team building a power plant, you don't suddenly want to notice that you have approved vacation requests from your employees in such a way that the project gets delayed.

Example #2: Creating Context for a Goods Return Request

Goods returns are a major cost factor in some industries, both consumer- and business-focused. There can be many reasons why customers want to return goods previously ordered. Customers may have ordered the wrong goods or the wrong quantity, may have received something they did not order, may have changed their minds, may not be able to pay for the goods, and so on.

How you respond to a request to return goods can greatly influence your relationship with a customer. If it is a profitable repeat customer, you want to respond differently than if it is a one-time customer, or perhaps even an unprofitable repeat customer who regularly returns goods or does not pay for them.

This process is started by a request from a customer to return goods. This request may be made in a number of ways, such as sending an e-mail, making a phone call, filling out a form on a Web site, or simply sending back the goods.

These events may or may not be formally recorded in a system, but they show up in the task list of the person who decides whether to approve or reject them.

When making the decision, this person may want to know:

- What is the contractual status? (That is, does the return have to be accepted?)
- What is the order value?
- What are the costs of accepting the return?
- How profitable is this customer?
- Can the goods be sold again?
- Are there a lot of returns of these goods?

This information makes up the context of the goods return request, and should be available to the person making the decision. Again, you must tap into various data sources:

- A contract management system to get contractual status
- An order management system to get the order value
- A cost database (perhaps including data from a shipping company) to get the cost of the return
- Customer relationship management analytics to get the profitability of the customer
- An ordering pipeline system to see what other orders are about to come in
- Product analytics to see return statistics

Once the user has made the decision to accept or reject the request, a number of actions follow. These actions again affect multiple systems. How many of these you must directly update depends on how integrated they are. One of the big benefits of tightly integrated systems such as mySAP ERP is that you usually have to call only one service to trigger all relevant actions. Following are some actions to consider:

- Accept or reject the request in the system where it originated
- Update the order status in the order processing system
- Update dependent systems (such as financial systems)
- Update customer and products statistics
- Send an e-mail to the customer to inform him or her of the decision

This example shows how embedding analytics in the decision-making process improves business decisions made. Directly linking the decision to necessary actions ensures efficient and consistent processing.

Designing Embedded Analytics

The focus of designing embedded analytics should be all about supporting the potential user's decision-making. A good mechanism to achieving this is to take the outside-in approach.

To begin with, the business process should be modeled from the user's perspective. The technology to achieve the business process and the means by which functionality is mapped to various back-end systems should come later. Desirability, viability, and feasibility of the solution must be carefully balanced.

Desirability is a metric that is associated with users. Interviews must be conducted with potential users to understand the kind of information that would help them do their jobs better. This translates to the quality of information that is presented to them. It is not about presenting some nice-looking charts that don't support the user's ability to make better decisions.

Viability is a metric that is associated with the business sponsors. While users are important part of the equation, they may not have an overall view of the business. The business sponsors would have a better understanding of this. The strategy for the solution must be defined in concert with this group to end up with a longer-lasting deliverable. The implementation must be carefully aligned with the strategy.

Feasibility is a metric that is associated with technology. The technology that is chosen must support the implementation of the design. What is technically challenging or elegant may not really support what the users want. The focus should always be on the users' abilities to use the system in ways that support their jobs.

An iterative approach must be taken in the design process. Use case and design models must be developed and refined iteratively while eliciting feedback from all stakeholders.

Data Strategy

Obviously, analytics has everything to do with data. Key questions that must be answered are whether data should be obtained from an OLTP or an OLAP, and when data is actually transferred from the OLTP system to the OLAP system. The performance of queries is typically not as good in OLTP systems as in

OLAP systems because data is in normalized form. The other consideration is that detailed data is sometimes not available in OLAP systems. What the business needs (and also is able to perform acceptably) should drive such decisions. You must also consider the lag of the extract/load/transfer (ETL) process, and the effect of this on rapidly changing data.

Case Study and Design

Let's use a case study to explore some of the technologies through which embedded analytics can be achieved. The case study here is really a compact version of the Goods Return process that we discussed earlier in the chapter.

To recap, personnel in the Returns department of a business receive goods return requests from multiple sources, such as phone calls, faxes, and e-mails. Some members of this team enter this data into a goods return system. Other personnel in a supervisory role make the decision as to whether to approve each goods return request. For this, they view the order data and the past behavior of the customer — whether the customer is a repeat customer, and the amount of orders and returns involving this customer. Based upon this information, the supervisor makes the decision to either approve or reject the request. Following this, the information is updated in the order management system, and an e-mail is sent to the customer.

The Composite Application Framework (CAF) discussed in Chapter 13 is a viable technology to solve the problem at hand. Figure 15-1 shows the design of this business process, with subtle references to the implementation in CAF. User tasks in the business process are captured as Actions. Actions use Callable Objects. Callable Objects use CAF-Core services. CAF-Core services actually invoke functionality in back-end systems. As shown in the figure, the business process makes use of both an OLTP and an OLAP system. The Goods Return Approval Action implies that the user needs to see data from both the Order Management (OLTP) and the SAP BI (OLAP) systems. Following the approval action, the order status is updated in the Order Management system, and an e-mail triggered through the E-mail System.

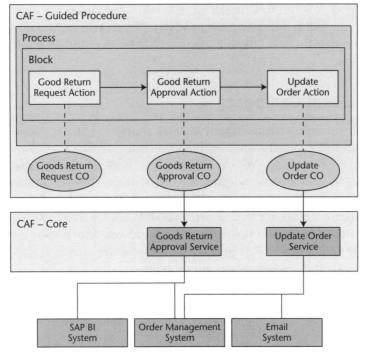

Figure 15-1: Business process with analytics

Building Embedded Analytics

This section examines how some technologies can be used to build embedded analytics applications. Also explained is the procedure for using one of the technologies to implement a relevant portion of the case study.

Using embedded analytics implies that the application must be able to access multiple back-end systems and present disparate data within a single view (screen) of the user interface. This means that there must be an ability to compose services from multiple back-end services. The composed services can then be presented to the user through a user interface.

The Universal Work List (UWL) and CAF-Guided Procedures (CAF-GP) are two technologies that can be used to implement user-driven business processes. Web Dynpro, Visual Composer (VC), Adobe Document Services, and, in some cases, even Microsoft Excel are tools by which user interfaces can be embedded in the business process.

Because CAF-GP was covered in Chapter 13, the following discussion will assume the usage of this technology. The use of VC in concert with CAF-GP is particularly compelling for business experts because it involves modeling and code-free development.

Analytics with Visual Composer

The design-time and run-time architecture of Visual Composer (VC) was covered in Chapters 10 and 14. Here, the architecture (see Figure 15-2) for the Analytics portion of VC is explained. VC development is done in an Internet Explorer browser with Adobe SVG, Viewer, and Microsoft MSXML Parser plug-ins. The VC Server provides the run-time environment for the modeling phase and VC models are stored in the J2EE DB of SAP WAS. Users access VC applications through the portal. The portal has a VC Add-on, which uses the VC Server to access the VC models. The portal provides the Connector Framework for portal applications to access back-end systems.

With respect to accessing analytical data, the portal provides various connectors for accessing SAP Enterprise systems, SAP BI systems, and non-SAP systems. Table 15-1 shows the available connectors and their brief descriptions.[1, 2]

Table 15-1: BI Connectors

TYPE	DESCRIPTION
XMLA Connector	This is used for connecting to OLAP data sources. Uses Microsoft's XML for Analysis (XMLA), which provides Web Services–based access.
ODBO Connector	This is used for connecting to OLAP data sources that are compliant with Microsoft's Object Linking and Embedding (OLE) DB for OLAP (ODBO). Uses the ODBO API.
JDBC Connector	This is used for connecting to JDBC-compliant relational data sources. Uses JDBC API.
SAP Query Connector	This is used for connecting to SAP systems. Provides access through SAP queries.
SAP BI Connector	This is used for connecting to SAP systems and uses the BW Web API.

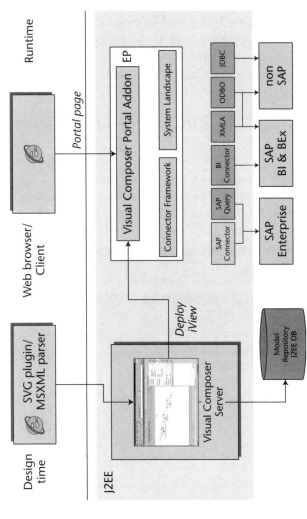

Figure 15-2: Analytics with Visual Composer (Source: © SAP AG 2005–2006. All rights reserved.)

Implementation

As discussed in Chapter 14, iViews for the portal can be built using VC. In Chapter 13, user interface screens were added to the CAF-GP using Web Dynpro templates. When suitable templates are not available, iViews that can be built either with Web Dynpro or VC can be used instead. Because all of these mechanisms were explained in detail in previous chapters, the only implementation that is demonstrated here is the procedure for building an iView using VC that uses a BI connector. The iView can then become part of a CAF-GP and, hence, become part of a business process. The details of the VC design tool were covered in Chapter 14. Here, only the high-level procedure is explained.

All of the modeling is in the EAIView iView, which is created in the Embedded Analytics model. The BI system called AB5 is created in the portal. Using the Look for a query filter (see Figure 15-3), you find the Incoming Orders, Returns by Sold-to Party query. This query returns all of the incoming orders and returns and the associated value of these for a given customer. This query is added to the iView by means of the drag-and-drop feature.

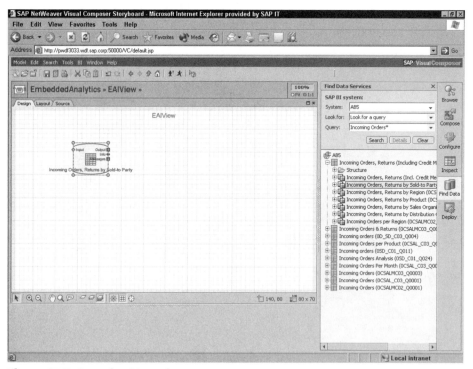

Figure 15-3: Accessing BI queries

The input node is specified as a Start Point. The Output node is tied to a form. Both of these operations are done by clicking the relevant node, and dragging and releasing the mouse button. That brings up the context menu where the selections are done. A field called Radio (see Figure 15-4) is added to the Approval form. Then, the properties of the new field are modified. One of the options is specified with the label Yes, and its value specified as True. A second option is specified with label No and value False. The idea is that the user should be able to view the historical data of the customer, make a decision, and then be able to approve or reject the Goods Return process on the same screen. Figure 15-5 shows the final VC model.

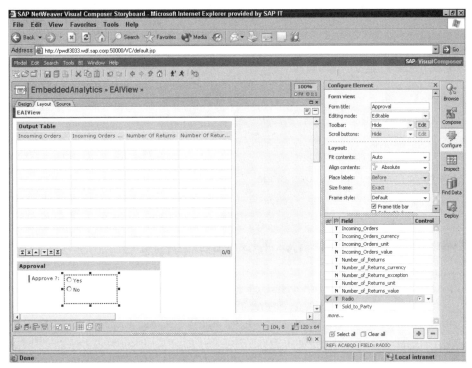

Figure 15-4: Creating the approval form

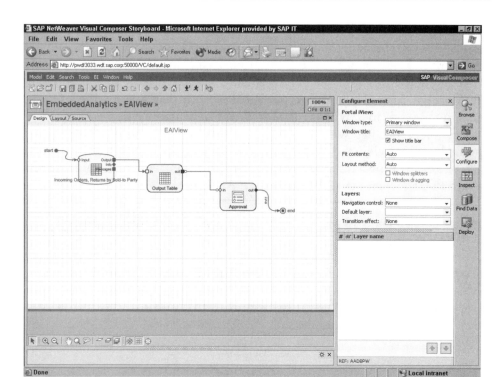

Figure 15-5: Final Visual Composer model

The Outlook for Embedded Analytics

Embedded analytics is somewhat of a new concept and, therefore, can be expected to evolve rapidly over the next few years. Not only will greater awareness about the value of embedded analytics and improved tooling to build embedded analytics lead to greater adoption, but also it is very likely that some large trends in the software industry will take embedded analytics to new levels. It will be worthwhile for you to watch for industry maturity in the following areas to occur and think about how they will affect embedded analytics in your business.

Business Event Networks and Event-Driven Architecture

Once SOA has become more widespread, a next logical step is to start using events to drive business processes. An event could occur that directly or indirectly is associated with a number of services called in an orchestrated fashion. The ultimate goal may be to automate most of this, and with tens of thousands of events occurring every hour, there will be no choice but to automate. Nevertheless, in many cases, people will be involved in this loop. When the event occurs, the context is created, and the event, the context, and the possible actions (service calls) can be presented to a human user. With the emergence of event networks and event-driven architectures, the number of events increases and this form of embedded analytics becomes more important.

High-Performance Analytics

New approaches to business intelligence not only make traditional analytics a whole lot faster and, therefore, accessible to new user groups, they also enable you to run new types of business intelligence that you could not previously imagine. This will both lead to more events being triggered that, in turn, will need embedded analytics to create the context and enable the created context in new ways.

As an example, the SAP BI Accelerator solution was developed in conjunction with HP, Intel, and other ecosystem partners. It leverages optimization of hardware, networking, and infrastructure, along with the data and OLAP world itself, to deliver vast performance improvements at a much cheaper cost than upgrading servers and database engines. It achieves this through mechanisms such as the following:

- Massive amounts of main memory
- Parallelism and other advanced computing techniques
- Multiple DBMS optimization features for analytics queries and specifically dealing with SAP BI schemas

The result is that, rather than having to pre-suppose the questions end users may ask of the analytics system, many new combinations of on-the-fly inquiries are possible that can be tackled with reasonable response time and little impact to the analytics engine.

> **NOTE** You can find out more about SAP's BI Accelerator solution by following the links available from `www.sdn.sap.com/irj/sdn/developerareas/bi`.

New Front-End Technologies

Currently, there is a rapid evolution of front-end technologies that can be used to bring enterprise applications to human users. SAP's collaboration with Microsoft around Duet, and with Adobe around interactive forms, Flex, and most recently Muse, are examples of this. Overall, this means that more tools will be available to bring embedded analytics to the right user groups in the right form on the right device. Add to that 64-bit client capability, advances in connectivity, as well as technologies for occasional connectivity, and you have many new ways in which people will access analytics.

Dynamic Service Composition

One of the challenges in building embedded analytics today is finding the services available to react to an event. With a relatively limited number of services (say, a few hundred available in a typical enterprise today), this is not such a big deal. However, it still takes knowledge about the back-end applications implementing the services to know which ones to call.

You can expect great advances in the metadata available about a service that will actually tell you what the service does (as opposed to just what its interface looks like), what other services it can be used with, what the pre and post conditions are, and so on. If this is all expressed in a machine-readable form, you can build tools that pick the services that are relevant in a particular case out of tens or hundreds of thousands of services, making the development of embedded analytics in a truly service-oriented world feasible.

All in all, it is very likely that embedded analytics will become so pervasive that you will stop talking about it as "embedded analytics." It will simply become the way most business users interact with enterprise systems and a common pattern for developers and architects to apply to their solution designs.

Summary

This chapter explained the concept of embedded analytics as part of any composite application. Also explained was how to bring analytics to the user as part of a business process.

When designing embedded analytics, the metrics of viability, desirability, and feasibility of the solution ultimately determine its value. When users are made the focus of the design process, it is easy to arrive at the right analytics for users.

SAP NetWeaver tools such as Visual Composer, when combined with a user-driven business process technology such as CAF-GP, can create a user experience that provides a lot of business value. What is very valuable in this effort is combining data from transactional as well as analytical systems to give the users the right information at the right time.

The embedded analytics space is rapidly evolving. Important concepts such as business-event networks and technological advances (such as high-performance analytics) can dramatically alter the way businesses look at analytics.

This chapter concludes the tour of SAP NetWeaver features that come together to enable you to create ESA-based solutions. You saw examples that included service-enablement and process orchestration to the development of composite applications using a variety of UI techniques that can be combined with embedded analytics into a rich process-driven experience for end users.

In Chapter 16, all the concepts of the book are brought together and summarized, along with a look at a few scenarios regarding what companies are doing with ESA today. It concludes with a description of additional resources for you to take the next step, as well as additional insights on what to expect as the SAP road map and SOA, BPM, EDA, and other industry capabilities continue to evolve.

References

1. E. Schemer, A. Graf, S. Cairncross, and S. Jiang, "IM254: Modeling SAP NetWeaver BI Data with SAP NetWeaver Visual Composer," SAP TechEd, 2005.
2. M. Herger, "Adventure of our times: Visual Composer & BI Kit," 2005. Available at `https://www.sdn.sap.com/irj/sdn/weblogs?blog=/pub/wlg/3628`.

CHAPTER 16

ESA Today and the Road Ahead

This book has provided an end-to-end perspective on SAP's strategy for ESA. Part I described the major business and technology changes motivating SAP. These have influenced the company's overall product direction, beginning with the integrated SAP NetWeaver platform, the latest mySAP Business Suite solutions, and the delivery of new composite business applications. The trend will continue as SAP unveils a fully ESA-enabled set of platform-based business solutions.

Part II described the major technology and architectural considerations supporting ESA. This included an understanding of SOA and BPM, along with the value of taking a strategic approach toward creating your unique adoption road map and the importance of enterprise architecture and governance in that process. Part III looked inside various SAP NetWeaver tools and technologies that help enable the user-centric, process-driven, analytics-based composition aspects of ESA.

SAP has laid out a clear road map for ESA and the foundations of the Business Process Platform (BPP) are in place and ready to use today. More important, you can predict how SAP-based solutions will continue to evolve based upon the ESA strategy and other industry developments well into the future.

The purpose of this chapter is to serve as a summary of the major elements of the ESA strategy, to review the usefulness of current SAP product releases, and to consider how things will evolve as the next wave in the overall IT industry unfolds. As a result of reading this chapter, you will be able to:

- Summarize the strategic principles and technology drivers for ESA as major takeaways from this book

- Evaluate scenarios of how organizations are realizing value from getting started with ESA today

- Consider areas of technology and market evolution that will allow you to "future-proof" your road map

- Identify additional sources of information for you to leverage in your next steps

Reviewing the Strategic Direction for ESA

This section recaps the overall vision for ESA and the major themes that serve as the foundation for the strategy.

Technology Direction for ESA

The IT industry is going through a major change as a number of distributed computing technologies converge. The goal is to make IT solution delivery more efficient by tackling some of the "pain points" of the past, while also improving effectiveness in aligning IT and the business through common models that bridge the two worlds.

SAP is essentially revamping its entire product suite around these new technologies, just as it did when the company moved from the mainframe-based R/2 application to the client/server-based R/3 edition. In fact, the change is probably much greater this time around because the power, flexibility, and distributed nature of SAP solutions expand significantly through SOA enablement.

Phase I involved creating a standards-based application and integration platform in SAP NetWeaver that embraces Java, XML, Web Services, and many other Web-based distributed computing technologies, in addition to the core ABAP stack. The result was the ability to use Web Services on top of existing RFC interfaces, with little change in semantics or interface definitions themselves.

Phase II involved the creation of an "applistructure." Recall that this is the marriage that takes place when business applications such as the mySAP ERP and the Business Suite leverage functionality of the SAP NetWeaver platform. The business solutions are now built using platform features such as personalized portal interfaces for user interfaces, A2A and B2B integration content, analytics, and composite application development techniques. In addition, the business applications become open "at the edges," making it much easier to customize them with standards-based interfaces and development techniques from other platforms. This allows SAP, customers, and partners to all employ the same development model for creating solutions. In effect, the products are greatly enhanced, but the semantic issue of using services is tackled only in a few A2A and B2B scenarios.

Phase III has resulted in a more complete merging between the business applications and the SAP NetWeaver platform. The semantic issue of service modeling is being tackled systematically by SAP. This is achieved through a combination of remodeling some of the existing business solutions, developing a new interface layer on top of others, and, in some cases, implementing new components from the ground up based upon converging technology trends such as the following:

- Service-oriented architecture (SOA) for creating loosely coupled software solutions based upon reusable building blocks of varying degrees of functionality and granularity

- Event-Driven Architecture (EDA) that enables real-time processing of complex events detectible in IT systems to improve response times, increase visibility, and enable more agile response to these events

- Model-driven design and development that leverages comprehensive metadata to model business solutions and architectural elements and, among other things, turn the models into implementations

- Composite application development that enables the rapid assembly of new business solutions by combining features and functions from multiple underlying applications in a loosely coupled manner

- Business Process Management (BPM) that focuses on transforming business process models that analysts define into executable solutions that control execution flows, monitor process activities, coordinate online and offline tasks, and facilitate management by exception

- User-centric computing that tailors applications according to a user's responsibilities and preferences, including whichever location, device, and front-end tool makes him or her the most productive

- Virtualization of infrastructure that takes advantage of the loosely coupled distributed nature of new applications and allows optimization of the supporting hardware and networking infrastructure

- Solution lifecycle management that enables the end-to-end definition of a business solution and monitors the operational aspects, facilitates versioning and changes, and ensures corporate policies and governance are supported at design and run-time

The overlap across these trends makes it fairly obvious as to why they are converging at an industry-wide level. SAP has designed its platform to support these capabilities based on standards where available, and obviously augmenting with proprietary features as necessary.

The Impact on SAP Solutions

As mentioned, the standard technology foundation underneath SAP business solutions is the integrated SAP NetWeaver platform. The platform itself will continue to evolve in line with the capabilities mentioned previously. As a result, each iteration of mySAP ERP, other Business Suite applications, and future product generations will increasingly leverage those capabilities. Some of the major changes in the platform and the business solutions are summarized in the following sections.

New Features of the SAP NetWeaver Platform

The latest editions of the SAP NetWeaver platform unveiled a new architectural model, along with capabilities that support the ESA strategy. These include the following:

- Further consolidation of the underlying technology platform away from discrete components into an integrated set of features organized by IT Practices and Scenarios, and deployed physically as usage types, clients, and engines

- The introduction of an Enterprise Services Repository (ESR) to house the common service, process, object, and data type models for interacting with all current and future SAP business solutions, and for designing and managing the models created by customers or offered by SAP partners

- Expanded business content for integration, analytics, and user interfaces, as well as a more efficient mechanism for implementing SAP updates to business packages and adding to the service, process, and other models within the ESR

- An enhanced suite of development tools and building blocks based on the platform metadata for modeling processes, coding application functionality, assembling composite applications, and modeling user interfaces by developers and, in some cases, business analysts

- An enhanced run-time infrastructure providing process lifecycle management and run-time governance capabilities

- Better integration with other major technology platforms such as Microsoft .NET and IBM WebSphere, as well as infrastructure solutions from strategic platform ecosystem partners such as Cisco, Intel, Hewlett-Packard, Mercury, and others

New Approach to Business Solutions

This technology transformation is affecting SAP's approach to delivering new business applications in three major ways.

First, as mentioned earlier, the mySAP Business Suite now leverages many of the features of SAP NetWeaver. Many user interfaces are implemented as role-based solutions within the portal, pre-built integration content supports common A2A and B2B scenarios, and so forth.

Second, many new features and functions are now being created by SAP as packaged composite applications (xApps). SAP is essentially using the platform models and capabilities to build on top of the older, monolithic Business Suite applications in more loosely coupled ways, as opposed to just continuing to expand the core functionality. A perfect example is the Duet products that use Microsoft Office UIs to enable traditionally non-SAP GUI users to interact with a number of SAP business processes. Another example is the demonstration of "Project Muse," which becomes a new composite front-end that provides rich role-based and process-driven access to SAP business content and functionality.

At the same time, expect to see the internal workings of mySAP ERP and other Business Suite applications continue to be refactored to provide greater support for ESR models as well as general improvements in SAP's own internal maintenance efficiency and reuse. This will allow new versions of both core applications and industry editions to come to market faster and enable easier upgrading by customers on a selective basis.

Finally (and perhaps most important) is the new way in which SAP is heavily relying on its customer and partner ecosystem to define and implement new business solutions on top of the SAP NetWeaver platform. This includes the following:

- The Industry Value Networks and the Enterprise Services Community for defining requirements and reviewing proposed solutions for different industries and business domains as a means of guiding future application capabilities

- Publishing of "white space" functionality within SAP solutions, which partners are encouraged to fill in with SAP-certified solutions

- Partner-developed xApps that offer high-value business functionality available directly from SAP, or strongly endorsed and co-marketed by the company as part of a strategic alliance

- A certification process for other third-party solutions that ensures the offerings come pre-integrated with SAP business functionality and support for the SAP NetWeaver platform

By cultivating the ecosystem, SAP is better defining and prioritizing common customer requirements and interfaces and expanding the content within the ESR. It is also speeding up the delivery of new business applications to customers by leveraging ISVs and system integrators that offer proven solutions on top of its platform. These partner xApps have become a whole new way of creating and distributing products outside the traditional SAP environment.

Customer Implications

There are many compelling reasons customers are pushing for SOA-based capabilities from their vendors. Tactically speaking, SOA offers the potential to make IT more efficient by reducing the cost of integration and maintenance, while increasing ROI through reuse. From a more strategic perspective, the model-based aspects and business alignment, as well as the modeling features inherent in SOA, make it an ideal enabler to transform the effectiveness of IT.

IT industry trends, in general, and SAP's ESA strategy, in particular, create a number of choices and potential options for SAP customers. It is clear that all major application and technology vendors are adopting support for SOA and that the value of highly integrated platforms and applications will enable a more business process–driven IT. One way or another, SOA, BPM, and the other capabilities will spread throughout your landscape.

The choice for customers is the degree to which they want to leverage SAP's ESA strategy and SAP NetWeaver to deliver these capabilities, or simply to take advantage of the more open and standards-based nature of SAP applications through another platform.

Some of the unique advantages SAP offers through ESA include the following:

- Consolidating infrastructure because SAP NetWeaver will already be implemented in environments that have recent editions of mySAP ERP or other Business Suite applications

- Leveraging a common platform for managing your process portfolio, including composing solutions to highly differentiated business process requirements, and more easily consolidating non-differentiated processes into packaged applications from SAP or ecosystem partners

- Eliminating integration "taxes" from third-party vendors by acquiring solutions from the ecosystem that have "productized" traditional custom solutions or the ISV touch points with SAP business applications

- Enabling user productivity by supporting and coordinating business processes through a variety of UI technologies, including SAP and non-SAP environments and the inclusion of embedded analytics within process flows

- Maximizing the use of out-of-the-box pre-configured and integrated business content offered by SAP and its partners, which can accelerate time-to-market and improve reusability of your solutions

This leaves SAP customers with three basic options:

- Make a commitment to an SAP first approach to SOA and maximize adoption of its ESA-based solutions and the SAP NetWeaver platform

- Focus on other platforms as your primary SOA environment, and simply leverage the openness and SOA and ESR features now available for mySAP ERP and other Business Suite applications

- Take a hybrid approach, consolidating to a few platforms with a reference architecture and guidance on which to use when

Some of the factors that weigh into decision-making are concerns over vendor lock-in by really embracing the SAP platform and the inevitable feature and function debates around best-of-breed products and other platforms. Unfortunately, the way IT consolidation continues and standards evolve makes these best-of-breed debates a moving target for most companies. That alone makes the major vendor platform strategies such as SAP's more compelling.

More than likely, customers in industries where SAP is the most established (such as manufacturing and oil and gas), or where SAP is the dominant part of the landscape, will move more aggressively toward ESA. Customers in industries where SAP's penetration is less or there is a history of complex, heterogeneous IT environments with lots of custom applications (such as in financial services) will tend toward the other extreme in adopting SOA and BPM capabilities. Those customers falling somewhere in between will likely consolidate around a hybrid infrastructure leveraging SAP NetWeaver in their SAP environment, and attempting to consolidate as much as possible around other platforms and vendors for the rest of the landscape.

Regardless, the move to SOA, BPM, and model-driven development has major implications in terms of enterprise architecture, governance, and how IT itself is organized. No two companies will have the same road map. This book described a number of these considerations and how they affect your adoption plans. Like any change, SOA adoption will be as successful as the people driving it and the business case that they can create.

Partner Implications

SAP ISV and system-integration partners now need to decide the degree to which they can (and wish to) participate in the ecosystem. This can be as simple as supporting new SAP interfaces and certifying solutions on SAP

NetWeaver all the way to industry leadership and participation in the product definition opportunities mentioned earlier. Obviously, these decisions will largely be driven by customer and market feedback, and the partner's overall strategy and relationship with SAP.

ISVs who want to form a more strategic sales and marketing relationship with SAP will need to clearly define the areas where they complement existing SAP business solutions, and fill in the white space that is important to one or more SAP solution groups. In addition, they will need to have a successful track record with common customers, and secure sponsorship from at least one SAP Industry Business Unit (IBU). This will trigger the process of defining joint composite application solutions that the partner can then develop, certify, and bring to market.

SIs have unique consideration as to whether they want to productize some of their expertise as composite applications. Entering the product business is not always easy for a services company, so there are alternatives to actually support SAP or work with another third-party ISV on a joint venture to create the new products.

Another alternative is for SIs to create composite applications that they use as building blocks to jumpstart engagements. This creates a new way to deliver company expertise in a much more consistent and valuable manner to customers. For those SIs with specific industry process and analytics expertise, there are a number of ways to design composite frameworks that leverage those capabilities. In addition, SIs have the most experience integrating SAP with non-SAP products, which creates another area to standardize around through composite frameworks and toolkits.

Scenarios Where Organizations Are Leveraging ESA Today

Many companies have begun to pilot ESA capabilities by using features of the SAP NetWeaver platform in conjunction with their R/3 landscapes to solve high ROI business opportunities. Those organizations that have upgraded to the latest mySAP ERP editions (which include the ESR models and more advanced ESA capabilities of SAP NetWeaver) are taking more aggressive approaches to ESA adoption. Following are some sample scenarios of ways organizations are currently working with the environment. The companion Web site for this book provides additional case studies and links to other adoption scenarios.

Consolidation and Process Optimization Scenario

A global manufacturer was struggling with a number of business process inefficiencies. In evaluating its IT environment, the organization discovered its complex landscape was a huge barrier to effectively addressing those opportunities. Saddled with a number of legacy systems and platforms from merger and acquisition activity, a complex SAP landscape, and distributed IT with no central enterprise architecture road map, the amount of dollars needed to maintain non-differentiated, poorly performing processes and IT systems was growing rapidly.

The company chose to tackle the consolidation problem and then use the savings to drive business process innovation. Led by a newly formed enterprise architecture group, the company tackled the following:

- Consolidating mySAP ERP and other Business Suite applications, including adopting xApps where appropriate

- Reducing the number of SAP instances supported globally

- Eliminating a best-of-breed integration platform, replacing it with SAP NetWeaver

- Standardizing on SAP NetWeaver and Microsoft .NET platforms for composition and user productivity, and building reference architectures and recommendations on which to use when

These activities led to savings that amounted to tens of millions of dollars per year simply in licensing, reductions in hardware, and maintenance alone. Additional tens of millions of dollars were also realized in productivity benefits from using the new SAP applications to resolve tactical process efficiencies. Most important, the new, simplified environment has paved the way for strategic business process improvement based on SOA and SAP's ESA capabilities.

While the consolidation efforts were underway, the organization formed a business process improvement initiative to evaluate opportunities across the supply chain, manufacturing, and order-to-cash processes. Opportunities were evaluated based on their strategic impact and the relative cost and time to implement to come up with a prioritized set of solutions. The company is now in the process of executing on these initiatives using the simplified infrastructure and its ESA-based reference architecture as the foundation.

Process Composition Scenario

A global manufacturer had an IT landscape that was largely based on SAP R/3 surrounded by a number of custom corporate and departmental applications. These non-SAP applications were built using a variety of mainframe, client/server, and Web application development tools.

The organization had a number of process improvement initiatives identified with clear ROI in place, but wanted to create new enterprise architecture standards for performing the application development and composition. After looking at a number of platforms and options, the organization decided to leverage SAP NetWeaver because it met all known needs and they would already be adopting the platform when they upgraded to mySAP ERP. The company did, however, keep its best-of-breed EAI solution as an internal standard, and leverages it along with the NetWeaver environment.

The initial set of projects centered around scenarios for optimized customer and supplier self-service. Many of these projects had an ROI based on reducing errors, increasing satisfaction, and lowering costs in its service centers. Others involved business process transformations, whereby a process used by a small number of partners was extended to a much larger distributor and consumer network. This required changes in many business rules and constraints.

The enterprise architecture group worked with the applications teams to develop a reference model for creating compositions across SAP and the other underlying applications. Time was also spent evaluating reuse opportunities from shared services across the project portfolio. These services were evolved from one project to the next. As a result, the organization was able to do the following:

- Use SAP NetWeaver to develop the initial composite application on time and within budget

- Implement multiple services that were reused in subsequent solutions

- Realize a 25 percent reduction in cost and time to delivery of solutions that reused services

- Standardize its reference architecture and design templates for future composite application solutions

As an interesting side note, the company was also able to realize significantly improved maintenance cycles from its outsourcing partner. This is because the maintenance partner had broader capabilities in a standard platform such as SAP NetWeaver, as opposed to the many legacy client/server environments that were being supported previously.

SOA Adoption Scenario

A major healthcare provider had a large and very heterogeneous IT landscape that included both R/3 and mySAP ERP instances, along with many other platforms, business applications, and infrastructure components spread across multiple business units. The CIO and enterprise architecture team were chartered with creating an SOA blueprint and road map for the organization to help simplify future development initiatives, create standards, and align IT investments with the business.

The organization took a dual approach of business process analysis and modeling to define the ideal services reference architecture for the enterprise, and for a number of key business units. This included both logical definitions and standard corporate WSDL interfaces for common functions that future solutions would be required to use. This approach was important because different business units had different products supporting various functions. For example, one might use mySAP CRM, another a homegrown CRM solution, while a third leveraged a different packaged CRM product.

The company then adopted a platform-neutral SOA infrastructure. This included best-of-breed intermediaries, ESBs, composition tooling, management, and an SOA governance suite to support their service models. The organization was able to leverage SAP NetWeaver to expose SAP service implementations on both R/3 and mySAP Business Suite applications, based on its company-defined WSDLs. This was important because composition scenarios designed to support multi-channel solutions for customers did not have to worry about the different back-end applications used by the various business units. The company was able to implement more than 100 services into production shared across multiple business units. As a result, they were able to buy time and extend their existing business unit application infrastructures' lifetimes, while getting many of the modeling and reuse benefits of SOA.

Ecosystem ISV Partner Scenario

An ISV that had a number of customers using SAP began to notice a pattern. The advanced analytic capabilities of its products produced information that could optimize a number of ERP processes. As the vendor delivered custom integration solutions, it began to evaluate which were the most common and offered the greatest ROI. The vendor also developed a road map for integrating its full product line with SAP NetWeaver for customers who had this need.

At the same time, the vendor entered into discussions with relevant SAP IBUs around options for productizing these capabilities as composite applications. Customers made it very clear that better out-of-the-box integration with SAP, and particularly SAP's certification and marketing endorsement of the solution, would have a significant influence on their decision to purchase from the ISV, as opposed to a competitor. In essence, the ecosystem participation would influence buying decisions.

This ISV worked with SAP to create specifications for a series of xApp solutions. Initial composite application iterations have focused on functional solutions to common process problems. The longer-term release plans include greater integration with SAP NetWeaver Portal and SAP Analytics.

Future Industry and Technology Trends That Will Affect SAP's Strategy and Solutions

These scenarios highlight only a few of the ways customers and ecosystem partners are beginning to leverage ESA to have an impact on their organizations. Some are pursuing very strategic road maps. Others are simply planning to use some of the new features and technology on current and future projects. Both approaches are working to add value. The point is that there are plenty of opportunities to get experience now, but keep in mind that it will take your organization time to make the type of deep transformation described in this book.

At the same time, the ESA strategy and SAP and partner solutions will continue to evolve along with the market. While the direction is clear, the strategy is tied to overall industry IT trends, standards, and ecosystem partnerships that will continue to unfold. As breakthroughs are made, they will guide SAP's evolution of NetWeaver and its business application solutions.

Following are some of the main areas that continue to have a lot of industry momentum behind them, as well as areas of focus for SAP.

Modeling of Business and IT

Modeling in IT has improved greatly in the last decade, especially in the areas of model-driven design and development. The "holy grail" of modeling is to achieve standardized models that align strategy, process value chains, detailed process execution models, application implementations, services, and infrastructure in a round trip manner. You will see more and more development tools, including those in SAP NetWeaver, adopt these multiple views.

Standards groups have been actively working on this challenge and different pieces of the puzzle continue to come into place. Meanwhile, vendors such as SAP and its partners develop proprietary extensions and links to support product needs today. Eventually, your organization will begin to consider what it means to move beyond simply using disparate modeling tools for efficiency to having a real strategy for modeling in the enterprise. Because modeling is at the heart of the ESA strategy, advances and standards in this space will influence SAP's direction. Of course, SAP also actively participates in a number of key standards tied to this space.

You should be closely tracking the details of how all of this will evolve. Modeling becomes a very tricky issue, especially when dealing with the more detailed implementation and execution models. At some point, models that become as complex as (or even more complex than) what they are intended to abstract defeat the purpose. Just moving complexity from developer IDEs to new modeling tools ends up being about the same as just enhancing the IDE to begin with. Again, SAP is investing heavily in determining the ideal ways to embrace models to support ESA within the NetWeaver platform.

Greater Unification Inside the SAP NetWeaver Platform

The consolidation of features away from components will continue to accelerate inside of SAP NetWeaver. While today's IT Scenarios and usage types still feel tied to the older components, it will become more natural to developers and administrators that the capabilities are merging into a unified platform. This will lead to simplification of the different IDEs associated with SAP NetWeaver development, as well as changing models, tools, and skill sets for deployment, administration, and support. This, in turn, will require technology professionals to adapt their skill sets if they have a largely component-oriented view of their work.

In the end, you will be able to have many of the same platform features and experiences working with NetWeaver, regardless of the design-time environment you use. You can pick from the Visual Composer, NWDS perspectives, PI and BI tools, and so forth, that are right for you, without having to sacrifice underlying features such as how you leverage alerting.

Improved Business Service Semantics

As anyone who worked with EDI and later Internet-based B2B solutions knows, ubiquitous technical-level integration standards are only a small part of the story. Knowing the elements of a service, versus what they actually mean, are two different things.

Many efforts are underway to improve how semantics of services are applied for auto discovery, searching, and supporting decision-making on where and how to use these services. Again, better metadata descriptions are useful, but the real value will come from agreeing on the actual business meaning and usage scenarios of services, along with how they can be modeled together across organizations. SAP has activities underway with its Industry Value Networks, and is actively working with broader standards organizations to help develop these semantic service definitions and models. In fact, this is probably the key differentiator between SAP's approach to ESA and the technology platforms offered by other vendors.

Technology Standards

A key to SOA is the assurance that enterprise-grade transaction management, reliability, security, and other non-functional concerns that you get with existing SAP applications will translate into the SOA world. Chapter 5 described many of the WS-* standards and other approaches the industry is taking to provide policy support in a common, effective manner. As these and other standards evolve, you can expect SAP NetWeaver to adopt them. And, as mentioned, in some cases, the capabilities may be commoditized into the network and hardware layers where platforms such as SAP NetWeaver can simply rely on vendors in those areas to provide appropriate support for policies and other non-functional requirements.

Evolving technology standards will also improve compatibility between SAP NetWeaver and other platform products and tools in your landscape. This should make ESA even easier to adopt and use across the ecosystem. For example, having the opportunity to share views between Microsoft SharePoint and SAP NetWeaver Portal users would simplify challenges many organizations are facing today. Turning design models into run-time execution models that span multiple platforms is another area of future focus. Finally, the relationship between IBM, SAP, Oracle, BEA, and others around Service Component Architecture (SCA) and Service Data Object (SDO) specifications will help improve composition and data exchange in mixed SOA-based landscapes.

Service-Oriented Analysis and Design Methods

Chapter 7 identified some of the characteristics that go into creating reusable services. Today, this is still more art than science because services exists at multiple levels of granularity and have differences between, process, domain, technology utility, and other types of services. As your organization begins to develop its own service models, advances in the practice of service-oriented analysis and service-oriented design methods will be quite valuable.

There are many differences between former approaches for object and component analysis and design because the scope and granularity of services is different. Service models sometimes must also account for back-end implementations if they are based on existing applications where flexibility is limited.

While SAP's Enterprise Services models serve as a useful blueprint on how to create these models, the company itself is doing a lot of learning in this area. A big part of the Enterprise Services Community is to bring customers and partners together to define specific requirements for service-oriented solution models. In addition, most tool vendors (including SAP) will provide improved service analysis and design capabilities to support SOA. That includes specific modeling of policies and other aspects of design and deployment time governance. Ultimately, customers, partners, and SAP itself cannot be effective with ESA technologies and the modeling and governance maturity is also established.

Enhanced Infrastructure Capabilities

Application integration and monitoring technologies are being standardized and commoditized into application server platforms today. It's likely that this trend will continue along with the trend to drop some of this capability into hardware and networking layers.

Basic virtualization is already in place to support more efficient utilization of the infrastructure. As networks and hardware become more aware of the business and data environments they are supporting, more granular and business-driven activity monitoring, compliance, real-time event management, lifecycle support, and control of quality-of-service characteristics can take place at a value level within them.

All of these are elements of sound run-time governance capabilities. This means the way in which services are partitioned between application servers, hardware, and networks will mature and evolve in a way that gives business considerations more control of all layers. SAP NetWeaver will need to evolve along with this trend. More and more definition can take place at an application level and then be enforced and implemented at run-time.

Advances in the Discipline of Enterprise Architecture

Chapters 7 and 8 focused on the importance of EA in enabling SOA and ESA adoption. The discipline of EA is starting to change in many organizations. The most important shift is the degree to which EA moves from a largely IT-focused and technology-oriented activity to becoming more business-driven. Although the many classical EA frameworks encouraged this, the business side has often been overlooked or minimized.

The shift away from static definitions to dynamic, integrated models will be one major enabler of better EA alignment. Another will be the degree to which both business and IT level governance can be defined and applied in a more automated manner. SAP (along with many other vendors and analyst firms) will be making a major push to better equip EA organizations for the changes SOA and ESA adoption will create. In addition, overall industry-wide efforts to transform the EA discipline will likely continue and should have an impact on SAP's strategy.

Maturity of the SAP Ecosystem

As mentioned in Part I, SAP's ability to attract ISVs and systems integrators to the NetWeaver platform and help make them successful will go a long way in determining the overall success of ESA. SAP has moved beyond working with a few strategic partners and opened the door for large numbers of ISVs and system integrators to get involved.

Many solution vendors are using the NetWeaver platform to integrate their applications with mySAP ERP or other Business Suite products. However, in all but a few cases, this looks to customers much like the data and API-level integrations of the past. The degree to which the ecosystem creates a portfolio of rich composites that fill in meaningful functional gaps is a trend to watch. The more these solutions take advantage of NetWeaver platform features (such as role-based interfaces, SAP Analytics, BPM, and Guided Procedures workflows), the more likely your acquisition decisions for these solutions may change. As also mentioned, you will want to closely monitor how this affects licensing and support. Some customers may help co-develop these solutions, and then allow them to be commercialized in exchange for significant licensing and support benefits.

Conclusion and Additional Resources

The previous section described a few of the trends that will affect the SAP ESA strategy for years to come. We hope you have seen in this book that ESA really is a significant change for SAP. It spans the full depth and breadth of the company's product lines, service offerings, and beyond.

The authors have tried to convey the full scope of ESA and SOA along with exposing you to some of the major SAP NetWeaver enabling technologies. Not everything applies to every role. The intent was to provide plenty of insights to help stimulate your thinking and determine which areas you or others in your organization should pursue further.

Table 16-1 provides a list of some resources recommended by the authors that can be valuable to you and your team in taking the next step with ESA. The companion Web site to this book will keep this list updated and include additional information useful for moving ahead. There is no shortage of opportunities for taking your next steps.

Table 16-1: Additional Resources Supporting ESA and SAP NetWeaver Adoption

RESOURCE	DESCRIPTION AND LINKS
SAP Developer Network (SDN)	The premier community for detailed information on ESA and SAP NetWeaver. The site includes articles, blogs, forums, documents, presentations, e-learning, and software downloads, and the authors strongly recommend you register. The homepage is available at `https://www.sdn.sap.com`.

Table 16-1 *(continued)*

RESOURCE	DESCRIPTION AND LINKS
ESA Resources from SAP, Including the ES-Workplace	SDN includes a number of resources specific to ESA. There is a hosted preview and exploration system for browsing and testing SAP Enterprise Services (ES Workplace), a launching point for members of the ES Community who are working together to help define and review SAP's Enterprise Services models, and information on SAP's ESA Adoption Program. The ESA homepage is available at `https://www.sdn.sap.com/irj/sdn/developerareas/esa`.
The Business Process Experts (BPX) Community	The newest SDN community that supports professionals who have the aptitude to balance all the business process and technology expertise to facilitate end-to-end BPM. There are many resources tied to understanding SAP NetWeaver, the business process analysis discipline, and specific business domains such as sales order management or supply chain expertise. You can access the BPX community at `https://www.sdn.sap.com/irj/sdn/developerareas/bpx`.
ASUG Enterprise Architecture Community and ESA SIG	ASUG community efforts that host regular "Webinars" and sponsor sessions at ASUG and SAP TechED events. More information is available at `www.asug.com/groups/group.cfm?group_pk=195`.
Magazines covering ESA and SAP NetWeaver	*SAP Info* at `www.sap.info/`. *SAP NetWeaver Magazine* at `http://sapnetweavermagazine.com/`. *SAP Professional Journal* at `www.sappro.com/`. *SAP Insider* at `www.sapinsideronline.com`.

(continued)

Table 16-1 *(continued)*

RESOURCE	DESCRIPTION AND LINKS
Selected Books on SOA, BPM, and SAP NetWeaver	*Dealing with Darwin: How Great Companies Innovate at Every Phase of Their Evolution* by Geoffrey Moore (New York: Penguin, 2005). *SAP NetWeaver For Dummies* by Dan Woods (Indianapolis: Wiley, 2004). *mySAP ERP For Dummies: ESA Edition* by Andreas Vodel and Ian Kimbell (Indianapolis: Wiley, 2005). *Mastering the SAP Business Information Warehouse, Second Edition* by Andreas Wilmsmeier, David Dixon, W. H. Inmon, and Kevin McDonald (Indianapolis: Wiley, 2006). *Business Process Management: Practical Guidelines to Successful Implementations* by John Jeston and Johan Nelis (Oxford, England: Butterworth-Heinemann, 2006). *Service-Oriented Architecture (SOA): Concepts, Technology and Design* by Thomas Erl (Upper Saddle River, N.J.: Prentice-Hall PTR, 2006). Multiple titles on Composite Applications and xAPPs from SAP Press available at `www.sap-press.com/`.
SAP and Microsoft Relationship	The joint strategy and direction communicated by Microsoft's SAP Global Alliance team covering technologies tied to portal, development, integration, business intelligence, and platform infrastructure interoperability between the companies is available at `www.microsoft-sap.com`. Information on the Duet applications that integrate SAP with Microsoft Office is available at `www.duet.com`.

Table 16-1 *(continued)*

RESOURCE	DESCRIPTION AND LINKS
SOA and BPM Reference Sites and Resources	InfoWorld's SOA Center including John Udell's blog at `www.infoworld.com/techindex/service-oriented_architecture_-_soa.html`.
	IBM developer information on SOA and Web Services including specifications like SCA and SDO developed with SAP are at `http://ibm.com/developerworks/webservices`.
	SOA Training topics and course outlines at `www.momentumsi.com/services/training.html`.
	ZDNet SOA blog available at `http://blogs.zdnet.com/service-oriented/`.
	BP Trends at `www.bptrends.com`.
Enterprise Architecture References and Resources	The Institute for Enterprise Architecture Developments at `www.enterprise-architecture.info/` including an excellent overlay between EA and SOA.
	The Zachman Institute for Framework Advancement with a 3D view of the EA framework at `www.zifa.com/`.
	The Open Group Architectural Framework at `www.togaf.com/`.

Summary

This chapter offered a summary of some of the major elements of SAP's ESA strategy and key takeaways for customers and partners. Some examples of how organizations are taking different paths to leveraging ESA with SAP NetWeaver, mySAP Business Suite applications, and packaged composites were provided to illustrate the many options.

Technology and business trends that will affect the future of ESA were described to help you track where and how things will evolve. The authors also provided a number of references for ESA, SAP NetWeaver, and the more general topics of SOA and BPM that can help you stay current on these topics. These references and more will be found on the book's companion Web site.

Abbreviations and Acronyms

ABAP: Advanced Business Application Programming

ACC: Adaptive Computing Controller

ADM: Architecture Development Method

AON: Application Oriented Networking

AS: SAP NetWeaver Application Server (AS-Java and AS-ABAP are two usage types in SAP NetWeaver to represent the Java and ABAP stacks, respectively)

B2MML: Business to Manufacturing Markup Language

BAM: Business Activity Monitoring

BAPI: Business Application Programming Interface

BI: business intelligence

BPE: business process engine

BPEL: Business Process Execution Language

BPM: business process management

BPML: Business Process Modeling Language

BPMN: Business Process Modeling Notation

BPMS: Business Process Management Systems

BPO: business process outsourcer

BPP: Business Process Platform

BPR: Business Process Re-engineering

BPX: Business Process Expert

BSPs: Business Server Pages

BW: Business Information Warehouse

CAF: Composite Application Framework

CAF-GP: CAF Guided Procedures

CEL: Customer Engagement Lifecycle

CIDX: Chemical Industry Data Exchange

CRM: customer relationship management

CSR: customer service representative

CSS: cascading style sheet

DC: Development Component

DDL: Data Definition Language

DTD: Data Type Delimiter

EA: enterprise architecture

EAI: enterprise application integration

ECC: ERP Central Component

EDA: event-driven architecture

EDI: Electronic Data Interchange

EI: enterprise inventory

EP: Enterprise Portal

ERP: enterprise resource planning

ESA: Enterprise SOA / Enterprise Service Architecture

ES: enterprise services

ESB: enterprise service bus

ES-Workplace: Enterprise Services Workplace

ES-Community: Enterprise Services Community

ESI: Enterprise Services Infrastructure

ESR: Enterprise Services Repository

ESS: employee self-service

ETL: extract/transfer/load

GDT: Global Data Type

GIS: geographical information system

GP: Guided Procedure

HTML: Hypertext Markup Language

HTML-B: HTML-Business

IBF: Information Bridge Framework from Microsoft

IBU: Industry Business Unit

IDE: Integrated development environment

ISV: independent software vendor

IT: Information Technology

ITS: Internet Transaction Server

IVN: Industry Value Network

J2EE: Java 2 Enterprise Edition

JCO: Java Connector

JMS: Java Message Service

JSR: Java Specifications Request

KM: Knowledge Management

KPI: key performance indicator

MDA: Model-Driven Architecture

MDM: Master Data Management

MI: Mobile Infrastructure

MOF: MetaObject Facility

MSS: manager self-service

MVC: Model View Controller

NWDS: NetWeaver Developer Studio

O2C: order to cash

ODBO: OLE DB for OLAP

OEM: original equipment manufacturer

OLAP: online analytical processing

OLE: Object Linking and Embedding

OLTP: online transaction processing

PCA: packaged composite application

PCD: Portal Content Directory

PCS: Portal Content Studio

PDK: Portal Development Kit

PI: Process Integration

PLM: product lifecycle management

RFID: Radio Frequency Identification

RPC: Remote Procedure Call

SAAS: software as a service

SCA: Service Component Architecture

SCM: supply chain management

SCV: Software Component Version

SDN: SAP Developer Network

SDO: Service Data Object

SEM: Strategic Enterprise Management

SI: Systems Integrator

SLAs: service level agreements

SLD: System Landscape Directory

SDLC: software development lifecycle

SOA: Service-Oriented Architecture

SOAP: Simple Object Access Protocol

SOBA: Service-Oriented Business Applications

SOI: Service-Oriented Infrastructure

SRM: supplier relationship management

SSO: Single Sign-On

TCO: total cost of ownership

TQM: Total Quality Management

UDDI: Universal Description, Discovery, and Integration

UI: user interface

UML: Unified Modeling Language

UWL: Universal Work List

VC: Visual Composer

W3C: World Wide Web Consortium

WAS: SAP NetWeaver Web Application Server

WSDL: Web Services Definition Language

WSFL: Web Services Flow Language

WS-I: Web Services Interoperability Organization

WSRP: Web Services for Remote Portlets

XI: Exchange Infrastructure

xMII: xApp Manufacturing Integration and Intelligence

XML: Extensible Markup Language

XMLA: XML for Analysis

XPDL: XML Process Definition Language

XSD: XML Schema Definition

XSLT: Extensible Stylesheet Language Transformation

Index

W